THE
END TIMES
AND
ARMAGEDDON

The End Times and Armageddon

Copyright 2023 by Time Worthy Books
P. O. Box 30000
Phoenix, AZ 85046

Hardcover: 978-1-62961-093-1
Paperback: 978-1-62961-092-4
eBook: 978-1-62961-094-8

THE
END TIMES
AND
ARMAGEDDON

#1 *NEW YORK TIMES* BESTSELLING AUTHOR
MIKE EVANS

TimeWorthy
BOOKS

P.O. Box 30000, Phoenix, AZ 85046

I want to dedicate this book to my beloved son,
Michael David Evans II,

Michael, the President of the Friends of Zion Museum, was named by my wife Carolyn, who told me that even before she became pregnant, God said she was going to have a son who would grow to be a mighty man of God. When the baby was born, God told her his name was Michael David Evans the Second, and that's what she named him. The problem was that my name was Mike Evans, so I had to go to a judge and get my name changed and be named after my son!

Michael has grown up to be everything Carolyn said. In Ukraine, he is the only US minister of the gospel who has gone to the frontlines to minister to suffering and hurting people. Since the war began, and at the time of this writing, his ministry in Ukraine has delivered over 10 million pounds of food to suffering souls including impoverished Holocaust survivors, Jewish orphans, and Christian refugees living in church buildings and Sunday school rooms. Michael, a mighty man of God indeed.

PROLOGUE

YESTERDAY:

LET ME TELL YOU A STORY. . .

On February 24, 2022, the Russian Army invaded Ukraine in a major escalation of the ongoing, undeclared war between the two countries that began in 2014. Assured of easy victory by his intelligence services, Russian President Vladimir Putin was so confident that he had his frontline troops pack dress uniforms to wear in the victory parade following the inevitable fall of Kyiv.

Volodymyr Zelensky, the recently elected president of Ukraine, was expected to flee the invading Russian forces moving at blitzkrieg speed toward Kyiv. Zelensky had assumed control of an entirely corrupt government torn apart by various internal factions, and he was woefully unprepared to lead a nation in war with his background as a former comedian and actor.

The invasion, however, did not go as planned for Putin's military. Ukrainians turned to guerilla warfare and bedeviled the advancing Russian columns. Massive internal inefficiencies and failures within the Russian forces bogged down the attack.

Zelensky also surprised Putin by refusing to flee. He used his media skills to mobilize the world through social media and video production to release a series of inspirational and effective statements to rally his own people and the Western world to Ukraine's support.

Days turned into weeks, and weeks turned into months. Military equipment and humanitarian aid flowed into Ukraine. The resources were enough to keep Ukraine standing, though not enough to make significant advances against Putin's invading forces.

Russian losses in soldiers and equipment mounted, and Putin began to face serious consequences as the weakness of his army was exposed before the world.

THE WEST RESPONDS

Finland and Sweden voted to join NATO soon after Russia's invasion of Ukraine. Zelensky pushed for his nation to join the European Union. Russia's military plans began to unravel as the West continued to pour money, machinery, technical advice, intelligence, and other resources to support Ukraine's military and offer humanitarian assistance.

Russia refused to fall back, instead sending huge infantry forces through the former Soviet republic's mud and snow while massive artillery bombardments struck from a distance.

Frustrated with his lack of progress, Putin mobilized 300,000 troops to bolster his ground forces in eastern Ukraine. Taken mostly from poor, isolated areas, his state security force's tactics in snatching young men randomly off the street and sending them off to war remained largely unreported in Russian media.

Putin gave orders to pulverize Ukraine from the air, throwing every artillery shell, missile, and drone he could scrape together. Many of his weapons missed their intended targets, leading to a number of civilian casualties.

RUSSIA'S HISTORY WITH UKRAINE

Few Americans cared that Russia annexed Crimea in 2014, and even fewer knew it was part of Ukraine. Almost no one can name the towns where the war is being fought or could spell the names of locations like Bakhmut, Slovyansk, Lyman, or Kramatorsk.

Ukraine was known as Soviet Ukraine, a republic of the Soviet Union from 1922 until 1991. The republic gained independence in 1991 as the Soviet Union dissolved and declared itself neutral.

Ukraine was the third-largest nuclear power in the world and held about one-third of the former Soviet Union's nuclear weapons, delivery systems, and significant means of its design, knowledge, and production. However, the Budapest Memorandum, signed on December 5, 1994, resulted in a multilateral agreement affirming Ukraine's security and sovereignty in exchange for giving up the nuclear stocks.

The United States, under President Clinton, took credit for achieving it. The warheads were shipped intact to Russia, a procedure the United States insisted upon.

A new constitution was adopted in 1996. A series of mass demonstrations, known as the Euromaidan, led to establishing a new government in 2014 after a revolution.

Russia then unilaterally annexed Ukraine's Crimean Peninsula.

Pro-Russian unrest culminated in a war in the Donbas between Russian-backed separatists and government forces in eastern Ukraine. This ongoing regional conflict was the background of Russia's full-scale invasion of Ukraine in February 2022.

IRAN JOINS THE FIGHT

Ukrainian officials watched nervously as Russia turned air-defense missiles into attack missiles and sent them into Ukraine *en masse*. Meanwhile, Iran mass-produced small, cheap, Shahed-136 attack drones that cost a mere $20,000 apiece and sent them to Russia by the thousands.

The Iranian drones were difficult to knock out of the sky. The only effective countermeasure was to fire expensive American air-defense missiles provided in limited quantities to Ukraine. The estimated cost of knocking down each Iranian drone ran between $140,000 and $500,000 apiece. In addition, Ukraine is estimated to have lost more than 60 aircraft, and Russia more than 70 aircraft.

Belarus, closely tied to Russia, was happy to let Putin fire artillery attacks from inside its country, which was even closer to Kyiv than most military bases inside Russia. Belarus also provided a convenient staging ground for resupply operations and medevac trains.

The scale of destruction on the ground in Ukraine was difficult to comprehend as artillery attacks, numbering in the hundreds of shells or drones at a time, rained down on Ukraine daily.

Zelensky begged the West for the weaponry he needed to counter the incoming missiles, drones, and artillery barrages that steadily destroyed villages, towns, schools, hospitals, the water supply, dams, and Ukraine's power grid. The West sent billions of dollars in supplies, but not enough for Ukraine to push Russia out of its territory.

It began to look like the West was content to fight a proxy war with Russia in Ukraine, using the Ukrainian army and its civilian population as cannon fodder. Russia appeared committed to fighting a long-term artillery battle in Ukraine despite Western opposition.

On March 14, 2023, the U.S. military confirmed that a Russian fighter jet collided with an American Reaper drone over the Black Sea, bringing the unmanned aerial vehicle (UAV) down. The military said one of two Russian fighters clipped the drone's propeller, forcing the U.S. to bring it down in the area of intense NATO military activity close to the Ukraine war frontlines amid Russia's ongoing invasion of the country.

"Our MQ-9 aircraft was conducting routine operations in international airspace when it was intercepted and hit by a Russian aircraft, resulting in a crash and complete loss of the MQ-9," U.S. Air Force General James Hecker, who oversees the U.S. Air Force in the region, said in a statement.

THE RUSSIA-IRAN PROBLEM FACING ISRAEL

Russia and Iran grew closer and strengthened their political and ideological ties. The common interest included a desire for the demise of a democratic West with its decadent lifestyle, corrupt political systems, and morally bankrupt societies.

What had been a relatively loose alliance in the past between Russia and Iran grew much more serious. Russia began offering

Iran support similar to its backing of Syria in the early 2000s. In return for the drones and artillery shells Iran provided for Russia, Iran asked for the final pieces to complete its nuclear weapons development program to become a nuclear nation. Russia didn't immediately agree to provide this assistance but soon offered the needed resources to help.

TODAY:

THE NUCLEAR QUESTION

Putin also considered using a nuclear weapon in Ukraine. As the war stalled, he needed a dramatic move to force the Ukrainian people to surrender and bolster his flagging image as an invincible strongman.

American intelligence sources began to warn that Iran had already made more enriched uranium than it needed for its nuclear energy program. According to the latest intelligence, Iran was only a matter of weeks away from being able to produce the materials it would need to make a nuclear weapon.

Israeli leadership frantically considered how to defend itself against a nuclear Iran. None of the options were good ones. It was left pondering the least terrible outcomes of various possible responses to this existential threat. Worse, its warnings to the United States of a nuclear arms race in the Middle East fell on mostly deaf ears.

The U.S. president and a majority of Congress were fully

THE END TIMES and ARMAGEDDON

convinced Putin was a leader who needed to be defeated at any cost. They completely ignored the larger international implications of humiliating a cornered dictator with half the nuclear weapons of the world at his disposal.

Putin was a demon-possessed madman whose delusion was that he was the savior of Orthodox Christianity and civilization. He believed that Russia's mortality and his own were one and the same. The head of the Orthodox Church in Russia anointed Putin as the "chief exorcist" to bring about the de-Satanifcation of Ukraine and America, the Great Satan.

PUTIN'S MOVE

As much as the Americans would've loved to see him go away—either from rumored illness or from a coup d'état inside the Russian government—neither happened. Putin was not on death's door as it was optimistically rumored, and furthermore, he was firmly in control of his government and his country. In fact, he held all of Russia in an iron fist.

Putin made it clear he was prepared to wait for recession and famine to settle in across the world. Going into the war in early 2023, grain reserves stored around the world were tapped to feed many nations as Ukraine missed most of its growing season that year and Russia chose to hoard grain at home.

In addition, the price of oil continued to be volatile. After the European Union imposed a price cap on what it was willing to pay for Russian oil (enough to pay for production but not enough to give any leftover profit to Putin to pay for his war), Putin cut off all oil shipments to Europe.

As Putin ran low on artillery shells, weapons, and ammunition, he increasingly turned to Iran to provide him with the equipment he needed to continue his relentless attack on Ukraine. Iran was happy to oblige. The larger the debt Putin owed them, the less able he would be to turn down the payment they asked for in return. Iran's Supreme leader, Ali Khamenei, another demon-possessed madman, and Putin were a marriage made in hell. Khamenei, a Twelver Shia believer, was convinced an apocalypse would usher in the Mahdi—the Islamic messiah.

As the one-year anniversary of the war approached, Zelensky was invited to speak to the United States Congress and made a press junket across Europe, rallying his allies to continue pouring aid into Ukraine. The United States and other Western nations proudly vowed to continue supporting Ukraine to the bitter end and never to abandon their ally. The U.S. has provided $113 billion so far.

The Russian Orthodox Church originated in Kyiv. The country had been considered Orthodox since 988 when the bishops of Constantinople baptized the land, which was then ruled by the Kievan Rus. In 2022, cathedrals and monasteries were searched by Ukrainian intelligence who reported that they eventually found evidence of collaboration between the bishops and priests and Russia's secret police.

In 2023, Ukraine's President Volodymyr Zelensky began stripping priests of the country of citizenship beginning in Kyiv. Ukrainians usually celebrate Christmas on January 7, as do the Russians, but the date was changed to celebrate it on December 25 in Ukraine to move Ukrainian churches away from their alliance with the Russian Orthodox Church in light of the Archbishop of the

Russian Orthodox Church Patriarch Kirill giving Vladimir Putin his blessing for the denazification of Ukraine and Putin proclaiming him the chief exorcist.

Russia has also increased its connections with China. President Xi Jinping of China met with Putin on March 20, 2023, to strengthen bilateral relations, regardless of the continued fighting in Ukraine. Xi made it clear that he remained committed to building a strong relationship with Russia as an invaluable partner in countering American global influence.

"Consolidating and developing Chinese-Russian relations is a strategic choice that China has made in the light of its own fundamental interests and the broad trends of global development," Xi said.

The meeting provided a giant morale boost and a chance to showcase the much-vaunted new world order that the Russian leader believes he is forging through his war on Ukraine in which the U.S. and NATO can no longer dictate anything to anyone. Xi's visit to Russia brought together two leaders who have positioned themselves for life, setting a scene for global confrontation. China is increasingly willing to use its partnership with Moscow to counter Washington, even if that means granting approval to Putin's brutal, destabilizing war.

ISRAEL'S RESPONSE

Notably absent from that group of nations flooding military aid into Ukraine was Israel. Not many people thought to ask why Israel was not uniting in potential World War III against Russia, particularly while Putin claimed to be de-Nazifying Ukraine, which was led by a

Jewish president. Israel gave massive humanitarian aid to Ukraine and also opened its nation to over 15,000 Ukrainian refugees, along with much more done covertly.

But Israel realized a pogrom could easily happen in Russia, making life a living hell for its Jewish population. Russia also controlled the airspace in Syria and could shut the skies down at any time, keeping Israel from flying missions to attack Iran's arms shipments going into Lebanon. Iran had already shipped 250,000 missiles into Lebanon. Most importantly, Israel feared that the Russia-Ukraine war going badly for Putin could force him to grant Iran its atomic ambitions in exchange for missiles and drones and to also open another front complicating the West's ability in Ukraine.

THE FUTURE:

THE WEST CONTINUES SUPPORTING UKRAINE

The West had a limited supply of high-tech, expensive air defense missiles to give to Ukraine. That disparity took its toll, and over time, the Ukrainians were unable to stop the ongoing barrage of artillery attacks. The Ukrainian people on the ground were left to hide in bomb shelters and carry on with life in an increasingly ruined landscape with little to no surviving infrastructure. Running water, flushing toilets, electricity, cell phone towers—they all became luxuries that few had access to.

Some 15 million Ukrainians were displaced by the end of 2023, and that number—and the flood of refugees into Europe—only continued to grow. The strain on European economies was immense and contributed to recessions and shortages across the Western world as 2024 advanced.

Meanwhile, the civilian death toll in Ukraine continued to climb alarmingly. Over 100,000 Ukrainian soldiers were either killed or wounded on the battlefield while many more civilians died as a result of the incessant shelling, war crimes by the Russian army, and the privations and lack of medical care available on the ground. The entire nation of Ukraine was suffering from post-traumatic stress after a nine-and-a-half-year war with no end in sight.

The West was forced to send massive military weapons to Ukraine to compensate for the exhaustion of its increasingly outnumbered and beleaguered Ukrainian army forces.

Although Russia's forces vastly outnumbered Ukraine's, the West still had weapons and technology superior enough to Russia's to keep Ukraine in the fight. As long as Ukraine continued to have warm bodies to operate the West's excellent military equipment, it could continue to fight on. Ukrainians were making astonishing sacrifices and were astonishingly brave. As long as they were willing to keep fighting, the West was willing to keep arming them.

Putin was able to sit back and continue to lob artillery shells without end at Ukraine, not putting much of his army at risk and managing to keep the Ukrainians pretty much on their heels as he finished, literally, leveling Ukraine. In his mind, time was his friend and the West's enemy. He was able to defeat the West in Syria by fighting a war in its twelfth year with the support of Iran, thanks to

General Qasem Soleimani, who forged an Iranian-Russian alliance in support of President Assad.

The pressure on the West began to build. They were going to have to send not only the best of their weapons, and a lot of them, but tanks and planes to prevent Ukraine from losing.

Europe had stockpiled enough heating oil to get through the winter of 2023, but it did not have sufficient reserves left to see it through the winter of 2024. Putin's long-game strategy of using food and oil and refugees as weapons finally began to bite. Recession, fuel and energy shortages, and famine struck on a global scale. More people in Africa died from famine because of food shortages in Ukraine than had died in the war with Russia.

WAR FATIGUE SETS IN

Fatigue for the war built in the West. There wasn't enough food to go around, prices were skyrocketing, fuel was scarce, and people began to ask if it was worth it just to keep a completely destroyed Ukraine drawn on the map. Plus, a U.S. presidential election was taking place, and the election became a referendum on Ukraine. America was disgusted over the last two wars in Iraq and Afghanistan. The humiliation of the U.S. withdrawal in Afghanistan, in addition to the outcry that we needed to protect our border, not Ukraine's, pressured candidates into promising to stop supporting Ukraine if elected. With over $100 billion of taxpayer dollars given to the most corrupt country in Europe, it was not sitting well with U.S. taxpayers.

Protecting Ukraine is not a "vital" national interest for the U.S. While the U.S. has many vital national interests—securing our borders, addressing the crisis of readiness within our military, achieving energy security and independence, and checking the economic, cultural, and military power of the Chinese Communist Party—becoming further entangled in a territorial dispute between Ukraine and Russia is not one of them, according to some conservatives.

Republicans said that the administration did not have a clear policy objective and a clear goal except to drag things out in Ukraine and that the U.S. was giving Ukraine just enough to survive but not to win. If we will not give Ukraine the weapons to win the war, why are we giving them the weapons to fight one?

Research done by a Washington think tank was being used by the anti-Ukraine faction of the Republican Party. It said the slow pace of U.S. production means it will take us as much as 15 years at peacetime production levels and more than eight years at wartime tempo to replace the stocks of major weapons systems such as guided missiles and drones if they were destroyed in battle or donated to Ukraine.

RUSSIA'S DESPERATION

Russia also paid a heavy price for continuing the war. The inefficiencies and corruption of its army meant that thousands of Russian soldiers died or were seriously injured. Hundreds of thousands more men fled Russia to avoid the draft, and as the war dragged on, those refugee men began to settle abroad and give up on ever returning home to Russia.

Russia considered the loss in Afghanistan a key reason for the collapse of the U.S.S.R. Tens of thousands of dead soldiers were never acknowledged—they were simply called black tulips—an omission that offended the Russian population and helped lead to the fall of the Soviet Union. The Soviet Army lost hundreds of aircraft, and two million Afghan men, women, and children died in the war.

Plus, Putin knew that the U.S.-funded Islamic Jihadists spent billions in arms to defeat the Russians in Afghanistan while at the same time, the U.S. was orchestrating a massive arms race along with pushing the price of oil down, which would ultimately bankrupt the Soviet Union. Ronald Regan did more than say, "Tear down this wall." He actually tore it down.

Putin believed his battle was a war between the West and Russia—World War III—and that America's goal was to wipe Russia off the map as it did the U.S.S.R.

The Russian economy reverted to the most basic production—food, fuel, and materials for war. Quality of life in Russia plummeted. Although there was deep discontent among the population, the complete control exerted by Putin through his massive State Security Force held, and he maintained an iron grip on everyone and everything.

However, Russian military generals and high-ranking government officials began to pressure Putin to stand up to America with its greatest weapons. They needed a decisive victory sooner rather than later if Russia was to emerge from the war with any capacity to rebuild itself into a global power. Frankly, all it had left that qualified it for that title were half the world's nuclear weapons. By every other measure, Russia had slipped out of world power status months ago.

IRAN'S NUCLEAR AMBITIONS FULFILLED

Meanwhile, Iran was feeling pressures of its own. Starting in the fall of 2022, widespread protests were taking place across Iran in response to excessive police brutality in the murder of a young woman, Mahsa Amini, arrested for the simple crime of showing too much hair.

The Russians sent security specialists to Iran to teach the Iranian government how to suppress dissent and control the population more effectively. As a result, sports figures, celebrities, and outspoken activists were arrested by the hundreds, and some of them were very publicly executed in an effective campaign to terrorize the population into settling down.

The majority of regular Iranian people did not support their religiously controlled government's extreme stance nor its fanatical belief in the coming of a Mahdi—a messianic figure who would come at the end times to usher in a golden age of Islam just before the end of the world. But there was nothing they could do about it since the Mullahs ran the country.

The Iranian regime, bolstered by support from Putin, refused to continue negotiating for any sort of return to the JCPOA, the Iran Nuclear Arms Deal of 2015, that prohibited it from developing nuclear weapons, and which the U.S. withdrew from in 2018, ultimately collapsing it.

Iran already had enough enriched uranium stockpiled to create at least a dozen nuclear bombs. It ordered its 4,000 accelerated advanced centrifuges—nearly double the number it had at the beginning of the Ukraine-Russia War—to spin up to maximum capacity. Working to produce enriched uranium in the shortest amount of time, it fed uranium enriched up to 60% U-235 into all the cascades at its fuel enrichment plant.

It took Iran less than one week to accomplish the necessary enrichment work for each bomb it planned to build. For each week Ukraine survived and the Russia-Ukraine war dragged on, propped up entirely by the West at this point, Iran made enough weapons-grade uranium for another nuclear weapon.

Israel waited and watched nervously as Russia began to discuss more openly the idea of providing Iran with the resources to not only build nuclear weapons but provide the missiles to deliver them. In the spring of 2023, a deal was reached between Russia and Iran to buy SU-35 and F-35 fighter jets.

U.S. intelligence leaked a secret deal between the Chinese and Saudi Arabia in which the Chinese negotiated a peace deal between Iran and Saudi Arabia in exchange for China guaranteeing Saudi Arabia a nuclear reactor if evidence proved Iran was going nuclear.

In recent years, China has helped Saudi Arabia build its own ballistic missiles, consulted on a nuclear program, and begun investing in Prince Mohammed's projects, such as Neom, a futuristic new city. China has also pitched to Saudi officials on setting up a local defense-manufacturing industry, while Russia has signed a nuclear cooperation deal with the kingdom. China also began to sell Russia its Mugin-5 drones, manufactured by Mugin Limited, a Chinese company based in Xiamen, on the east coast of China.

Why does China support Russia's war in Ukraine? Because it weakens America's military arsenal. If a nuclear war happened between Russia and the European Union with the U.S., China would be the only one standing and would rule the world.

THE POINT OF NO RETURN

The President called for a meeting with America's leading military contractors, dubbed "The Last Supper." The purpose of the meeting was to inform them of the massive weaponry that the U.S. would require, the looming threat of a Chinese invasion of Taiwan, and the need to prepare for a potential war with China.

During the meeting, The Last Supper group informed the president that in the event of a large-scale war with China, the United States would run out of long-range anti-ship missiles within a week. They explained that due to the depletion of resources during the Ukraine war, key components such as artillery shells, missiles, air defense systems, counter artillery radar, Javelin missiles, SM-6 missiles, unmanned aerial vehicles, cruise missiles, Stinger anti-aircraft missiles, and ball bearings were all exhausted.

As an example, the United States has given up over one-third of its Javelin missile inventory to Ukraine. Surprisingly, one arms package included 1,000 Javelin missiles despite the low inventory. The current production rate is about 1,000 per year.

The group further clarified that the U.S. had given 7,500 HIMAR launchers to Ukraine in the first year and 10,000 in the second year, leaving the U.S. in no position to provide Taiwan with the necessary weaponry or even defend the country adequately. The group concluded that under no circumstances would the U.S. be able to defeat China if a large-scale war broke out over the Taiwan crisis, due to the depletion of U.S. firearms and resources in Ukraine.

Then American intelligence sources confirmed a sighting made by the Mossad, that the crates of equipment and parts had been loaded on a cargo ship in the Russian port of Astrakhan, where the mighty Volga River empties into the Caspian Sea and the site of Russia's largest Caspian Sea port.

The ship set sail across the Caspian Sea bound for the port of Anzali, Iran's largest Caspian Sea port. The crossing would take four, maybe five, days. When that ship arrived, the time it would take for Iran to become a nuclear power would go from weeks to days. Russia possessed a total of 5,977 nuclear warheads, the largest stockpile in the world, along with the world's largest arsenal of ballistic missiles. All of Iran's dreams were about to come true.

And then Putin dropped a low-yield nuclear weapon on Zelensky's hometown, Kryvyi Rih, in south-central Ukraine. It was a warning shot across the bow to Zelensky and the West that Putin was prepared to do whatever it took to win the war. At all costs.

The world, while horrified, was not prepared to launch retaliatory nuclear strikes against Russia and risk provoking the end of the world with a free-for-all nuclear exchange between Russia and the West.

In light of the seriousness of the attack and thermal radiation winds, the nuclear attack provoked an instant response from NATO announcing that Article 5 had been invoked. Article 5 says that an attack on one is an attack on all NATO members.

The U.S. president was informed that a nuclear war between the United States and Russia would plunge the Earth into a nuclear winter within days due to the level of smoke and soot released into the atmosphere which would ultimately mean the death of one-third of humanity.

⁶ *Then the seven angels who had the seven trumpets prepared to sound them.*

⁷ *The first angel sounded his trumpet, and there came hail and fire mixed with blood, and it was hurled down on the earth. A third of the earth was burned up, a third of the trees were burned up, and all the green grass was burned up.*

⁸ *The second angel sounded his trumpet, and something like a huge mountain, all ablaze, was thrown into the sea. A third of the sea turned into blood, ⁹ a third of the living creatures in the sea died, and a third of the ships were destroyed.*

¹⁰ *The third angel sounded his trumpet, and a great star, blazing like a torch, fell from the sky on a third of the rivers and on the springs of water— ¹¹ the name of the star is Wormwood. A third of the waters turned bitter, and many people died from the waters that had become bitter.*

¹² *The fourth angel sounded his trumpet, and a third of the sun was struck, a third of the moon, and a third of the stars, so that a third of them turned dark. A third of the day was without light, and also a third of the night.*

¹³ *As I watched, I heard an eagle that was flying in midair call out in a loud voice: "Woe! Woe!*

Woe to the inhabitants of the earth, because of the trumpet blasts about to be sounded by the other three angels!" (Revelation 8:6-13).

15 And the four angels who had been kept ready for this very hour and day and month and year were released to kill a third of mankind. . . .

18 A third of mankind was killed by the three plagues of fire, smoke and sulfur that came out of their mouths (Revelation 9:15, 18).

China, calculating that a window of opportunity was available to invade Taiwan, launched a massive, conventional preemptive strike on the island nation and seized it almost overnight. The Chinese watched and waited until the U.S. weapon supply was dangerously low.

Iran announced that it was a nuclear state, and all the Sunni, oil-rich nations in the Gulf region announced an urgent nuclear arms race of their own. In just a few years, Saudi Arabia, Bahrain, Kuwait, Oman, Qatar, and the United Arab Emirates would obtain nuclear arsenals of their own as enemies of Iran. Only the Persian Gulf would separate them—a less than one-hour missile flight.

THE SAMSON OPTION

Israel realized that Russia had acquiesced to Iran's insistent requests for nuclear weaponization help. Russia decided to not only share information and technicians on how to build a miniaturized nuclear warhead that would fit on an IRBM—an intermediate-range ballistic missile—but it also shared information, tools, and technical instruction on how to build MRVs—multiple re-entry vehicles, where up to three warheads with three separate targets could be mounted on a single ballistic missile delivery system.

In the days before the 1967 Six-Day War, Israel planned to insert a team of paratroopers by helicopter into the Sinai. Their mission was to set up and remotely detonate a nuclear bomb on a mountaintop as a warning to belligerent surrounding states. The greatly outnumbered Jewish state in a surprising turn of events effectively eliminated the Egyptian Air Force and occupied the Sinai, winning the war before the test could even be set up. Retired Israeli brigadier General Itzhak Yaakov referred to this operation as the Israeli Samson Option.

In the 1973 Yom Kippur War, Arab forces were overwhelming Israeli forces and Prime Minister Golda Meir authorized a nuclear alert and ordered 13 atomic bombs be readied for use by missiles and aircraft. The Israeli Ambassador warned President Nixon of "very serious conclusions" if the United States did not airlift supplies. Nixon complied. This is seen by some commentators on the subject as the first threat of the use of the Samson Option.

Iran realized that with the introduction of missiles in silos on Iranian soil and the completion of its nuclear development program, it was opening itself up to a preemptive strike of some kind from Israel. It would not be enough for Iran simply to have nuclear weapons. It would also need some sort of umbrella of protection for itself. And Russia could also provide that protective umbrella over Iranian airspace.

Israel has for many years had one of the best-equipped and best-trained air forces in the world. Iran could never hope to match Israel in either quality or quantity of airplanes, top-notch pilots, or air defense systems. But with Russia's help, it didn't have to if it went atomic and had Russian planes controlling its airspace.

If Russia was willing to put its own airplanes in the skies over Iran, both Russia and Iran could dare Israel to shoot those planes down and risk massive retaliation. It wouldn't even have to be nuclear retaliation. Israel realized Iran would momentarily be protected by a nuclear umbrella, as it were. Possession of nuclear weapons would protect Iran from any future attacks against it.

IRAN'S OPERATION MAHDI

Iran, not satisfied to destroy the Little Satan, Israel, decided to position itself to attack the Great Satan, the United States, as well.

Iran launched Operation Mahdi, and hundreds of lead-lined containers were shipped, filled with chemical and biological weapons through LCL (less than container load). When cargo shipped by sea is not enough to fill a container, buyers often opt to share container space with other shippers, but for Iran, the plan was to ship in from 26 countries so the U.S. could not detect them. They were all lead-lined, being shipped to major U.S. cities to be detonated in simultaneous attacks.

One hundred jihadist suicide bombers carried backpacks weighing 80-100 pounds. In them were suitcase nuclear bombs. Each bomb had a charge of one kiloton equivalent to one thousand tons of TNT. One device in Washington, D.C., would destroy everything within a half-mile of the capital. Within hours the prevailing winds would carry the nuclear fallout throughout Washington. The Nuclear Threat Initiative (NTI) published a report in September 1997 that quoted the Russian national security advisor Alexander Lebed who claimed that the Russian military lost track of upwards of 100 nuclear suitcase bombs.

These sleeper cells, made up of kamikaze Iranian Revolutionary Guards, were given instructions to attack the government, culture, and unsuspecting citizens, cause mayhem, and destroy the United States from within.

For decades before and after the fall of Iraq, Iran funded and infiltrated Shiite assets all over the Middle East, ready and waiting for the order to attack America the great Satan and Israel the little Satan from inside and from without. Iran attacked Israel through its proxies: Hamas, Islamic Jihad, the Mahdi army, Hezbollah, and others.

Although Israel's air defense system, Iron Dome, was able to stop about 90% of incoming rockets or missiles, there came a point when sheer numbers of incoming projectiles would overwhelm the system. Israel urgently worked to upgrade its Iron Dome Defense system with Iron Beam, a directed energy fiber laser system to knock down airborne targets, but it would take time to operationally deploy the system.

Aware that quantity was the only way to overwhelm the quality of the Israeli air defense system, Hezbollah, an Iranian proxy in Lebanon, stocked up on as many as 300,000 Iranian rockets and small missiles which Iran was delighted to provide. Syria, another Iranian proxy, launched its planes with bombs with zero warning time toward Israel.

ISRAEL STARES AT AN APOCALYPSE

Israel was staring an apocalypse in the face—a nuclear Iran with its skies aggressively protected by Russia under a nuclear umbrella was on the horizon.

Israel, which had excellent intelligence assets throughout the Gulf region, caught wind of the Iranians' preparations for war. The 24 SU-35 Flanker fighter jets that Iran purchased from Russia when the U.S. blocked their sale to Egypt were delivered, along with the 60 fully operational Iranian pilots the Russians had trained. While the Israeli Air Force could make short work of the SU-35s and their inexperienced pilots, doing so would undoubtedly provoke Russia.

Israel faced a stark choice. On the one hand, Iran was nuclear and an atomic arms race in the Middle East had begun. A nuclear strike on Israel would allow religious leaders in Iran to create an apocalypse that they believed would usher in their messiah. Furthermore, the Iranians' religious beliefs stated that the Islamic Armageddon would include the destruction of Israel.

On the other hand, Israel could not risk a preemptive strike against Iran failing. If Israel, a tiny nation the size of New Jersey, took a retaliatory strike from Iran, it would be wiped out with a single nuclear weapon. If a preemptive Israeli strike wasn't 100% successful, it had no guarantee that Iran would not be able to hit Israel with an atomic bomb.

Israel's only option for surviving was to wipe out Iran and its plan for an apocalypse that would summon the Islamic messiah the Mahdi.

The only way to eradicate Iran's obsession would be the Samson

Option, Israel's deterrence strategy of massive retaliation with nuclear weapons before Russian planes began protecting Iranian airspace. The name is a reference to the biblical Israelite, Samson, who pushed down the pillars of the Philistine temple to destroy his enemies.

Sixteen to twenty million people would die in the initial nuclear strikes. Millions more could be expected to die slower, agonizing deaths by radiation poisoning afterward. Given the level of radiation that would come from a modern, high-yield, all-out nuclear strike, very few medical personnel and aid from other nations would be able to enter Iran to provide humanitarian assistance.

It was a terrible thing to contemplate, and Israel's senior leadership prayed fervently for some other alternative to present itself.

The doomsday clock was now seven seconds to midnight. God created the world in seven days. Either Iran's world would end in seven days or Israel's.

Israel's time to make a decision was up. It was now or never to take action to save itself. Eighty nuclear warheads would be launched, the Israeli Air Force planes were in the skies, F-151 and F-161s with atomic bombs along with Jericho 2 and 3 ballistic missiles along with submarine-launched nuclear-capable cruise missiles.

The End Times had arrived, and the final countdown to Armageddon had begun. . .

AUTHOR'S NOTE:

THE PERIOD OF TIME we may be staring in the face is a 2,500-year-old prophecy by a prophet found in Ezekiel 38. It speaks of Rosh which is a shortened version of Russia. Ezekiel and Daniel both describe the end times using the phrase "king of the north" to describe the commander of an alliance in that time (Daniel 11:5-35; Ezekiel 38:6, 15). Russia is the only modern nation to match this description. Persia, modern Iran, is also mentioned in Ezekiel with regard to the End Times and about 35 more times in Scripture.

This Russia-Ukraine war is leading to astonishing alliances between Russia and Iran. This unlikely and unholy alliance would not have been possible were it not for the seismic events set in motion by Russia's invasion of Ukraine.

In Revelation 16:12-16, it describes a battle called Armageddon. It says:

> "The sixth angel poured out his bowl on the great river Euphrates, and its water was dried up to prepare the way for the kings from the East... demonic spirits that performed signs.... go out to the kings

of the whole world to gather them for battle on the great day of God Almighty. . . then they gathered the kings together to the place that in Hebrew is called Armageddon."

There is no doubt in my mind that if the Russia-Ukraine war goes on for an extended period, Russia will ultimately grant Iran's atomic ambitions with Russian planes protecting Iran's airspace. This will inevitably usher in a Gulf States nuclear arms race.

I was told by the former head of Israel's atomic energy commission that if a Middle East arms race happens, "We will have Armageddon in a decade."

The Ukrainians are beautiful people who are only trying to defend themselves. They've gone through a living hell. Through my son's leadership, my ministry delivered 8 million pounds of food in the first year of the war to the frontlines of the Jewish community and to churches filled with refugees.

It is my prayer that what I am writing about in this fictional scenario docs not come to pass. But one thing is for certain: some of it will if the West refuses to give Ukraine the needed weapons to win the war. Also, prayer changes things. It is my prayer that believers will pray hard concerning these prophetic warnings.

This book is a prophetic wake-up call for all of us.

Mike Evans
Spring, 2023

PART II: RUSSIA AND THE UKRAINE WAR

PART III: UNHOLY ALLIANCES

PART IV: TO WIPE ISRAEL FROM THE MAP

PART VI: A NUCLEAR IRAN

PREFACE

I HAD A DREAM. IN THE DREAM, I was at a four-way stop-light. I noticed all the lights were green and yet no one seemed to be alarmed.

I thought, "This is horrible. It's going to be a massive tragedy."

Then I looked to one of the corners of the street to cry out, and I saw people celebrating idols, drinking champagne, and partying. It was a huge political party celebrating their candidate. On the other corner, I saw more idols and a huge crowd and an auctioneer auctioning off stuff, boats, cars, vacation packages, and homes, and I saw more idolatry. Then I looked on the third corner and it was unspeakable immorality and idolatry.

Then I looked on the fourth corner and it was religious people. They had on religious robes but they were all worshipping idols and there were stones in their hands. They were circling someone. And when I looked at the center of the circle, I saw the person in the center was Jesus.

Suddenly out of nowhere, a cloud appeared with the words on it "final warning."

But nobody was alarmed. They wouldn't even look up.

Then all the green lights turn red. And when they turned red, there was something inside of each light. It was a hammer and a sickle. The hammer and the sickle touched each other. And when they did, the lights ignited and huge mushroom clouds started coming up from the red lights.

When I woke up, I started praying about the interpretation of the dream, and the interpretation came. I remembered the former head of the Israel Atomic Energy Commission telling me that if a nuclear arms race begins among the Gulf states, in ten years the world would experience Armageddon.

I have been going to Ukraine for over a decade, bringing food to impoverished Holocaust survivors and Jewish orphans. When the Ukraine-Russia war broke out in 2022, we ramped up our operation. On my first trip in after the war began, I was stuck at the border between Poland and Ukraine for many hours because of miles and miles of camouflaged military trucks going into Ukraine.

I turned to my companion and said, "Viktor, World War III is being fought right now between the West and Russia with plausible deniability."

More than a quarter million Ukrainian and Russian soldiers were casualties in the first year of the war. The U.S. has provided billions of dollars in aid to Ukraine since the war began. As I'm writing to you, Ukrainians are in Oklahoma being trained to use Patriot missiles.

The Russian-Ukrainian war has been the deadliest in Europe since World War II. The war quickly became a proxy war between the U.S.-led West and Russia. The roots of the conflict extend back to the collapse and disillusionment of the Soviet Union in the early 1990s.

I had lunch with Ronald Reagan shortly after he was elected and asked him what he was going to do about communism. He smiled and in his trademark whisper said, "Oh, I think I'll bankrupt it."

He did indeed. Russia has watched NATO steadily expand eastward, with most of the former USSR republics in eastern Europe joining NATO. The West has provided military assistance for Ukraine to continue waging war but not enough for Ukraine to win the war. The West continues to bleed Russia's economy of men, machinery, and resources.

Russia knows this. Russia has been fighting in Syria now going on 12 years. The architect of this Russian-Syrian alliance was General Qasem Soleimani who was in charge of Iran's foreign military strategy. He traveled to Moscow to see President Vladimir Putin and ask him if Russia would save the Syrian regime. The Syrian patriarch also appealed to Putin, saying that he could be the savior of Christianity.

As Russia loses troops and massive amounts of weaponry in the war in Ukraine, Iran is returning the favor by giving Russia thousands of drones, along with the support of the Iranian Revolutionary Guard in Crimea to train Russians on how to use them. Soon, surface-to-surface and surface-to-air missiles will also start arriving in Russia from Iran.

Iran believes that Russia will return the favor by guaranteeing the Islamic terrorist state a nuclear umbrella. That umbrella would not only mean Iran going nuclear but that Russia would protect Iran from any attacks against it as Russia has done in Syria.

If this were to come to pass, it would precipitate a Sunni, Gulf State nuclear arms race that will result in Armageddon within a decade, exactly as the former chairman of the nuclear atomic commission of Israel told me it would.

Approximately 2,500 years ago, Ezekiel predicted specific events concerning Russia's future. He begins in Ezekiel 38 with a long list of nations that will attack Israel. The reference to Rosh in verse 2 is a shortened version of the word Russia. The Bible describes Russia as being far to the north. Both Ezekiel and Daniel describe Israel's end-time aggressors as the being from the North.

The use of the phrase "king of the north" to describe the commander of the lions, Daniel 11:5, 35 seems to refer to Russia as well. Ezekiel's prophecy lends support to Daniel's, indicating a very large army will arrive in Israel from the far north, Ezekiel 38:6, 15. Russia is the only nation that fits this description well.

One name on Ezekiel's list, Gog, is the name of a national leader. We find this in Ezekiel 38:1-2. Second, Persia is mentioned in Ezekiel 38:5 and about 35 more times in Scripture. In 1935, Persia changed his name to Iran. Then, in 1979 it became the Islamic Republic of Iran. Today, Russia is Iran's strong strongest ally and Israel's strongest enemy.

Israel has been ostracized by the Biden administration for not sending weapons into Ukraine, but Israel knows what I am telling you, that the Ukraine war will ultimately release an atomic Islamic State with a nuclear umbrella that is hell-bent on ushering in the 12th Imam.

Iranian religious leaders consider the 12th Imam, the Islamic Messiah, one who can only come after an apocalypse. The mullahs who run Iran believe a nuclear attack on the Little Satan, Israel, will usher in the Mahdi—the Islamic apocalypse—and the entire world will surrender and become Islamic.

That may sound totally nuts, but I've met with the former President of Iran, Mahmoud Ahmadinejad. He told me the exact same thing concerning the Mahdi and an apocalypse. What the mullahs believe is what the Iranian government's leaders—the people with the power to launch a nuclear strike—also believe.

Ahmadinejad told me that when he spoke to the U.N., nobody blinked for 26 to 28 minutes and that a green light filled the room. He also told me that Zionists lived to be 82 and Iranians 62 because Zionists send rats into Iran to poison its crops and people eat the poisoned food and die 20 years younger.

And these are the people on the verge of getting themselves a nuclear arsenal and protection from Russia for themselves and their nuclear weapons.

My son Michael is risking his life going to the frontlines of Ukraine, preaching the gospel, praying for the sick, and providing food to starving refugees. He has delivered more than 8 million pounds of food and supplies in twelve months. He and I have nothing but the deepest compassion and sympathy for the plight of the Ukrainian people.

The one person whom I believe has the ability to negotiate a resolution to this growing world war is Israeli Prime Minister Benjamin Netanyahu. Otherwise Israel, America, and the rest of the world will face our gravest national security threat ever.

To receive Mike Evans' prophetic intelligence reports contact events@drmichaeldevans.com.

PART I:

KNOW THINE ENEMY: IRAN AND WHERE IT COMES FROM

CHAPTER ONE:

MODERN IRAN'S ROOTS IN ANCIENT PERSIA

"And then that day when we attack Israel, even the trees and
the stones will have mouths. They will cry out. They will say,
"There is a Jew hiding behind me. Come, O Muslim. Come, O slave of
Allah. Come and kill him till not one male Jew is left."

—Walid Shoebat,
Former Palestinian terrorist recounting the teaching
he received as a child "terrorist-in-training"

*"Tell us, when will these things happen? And what will
be the sign that they are all about to be fulfilled?"*

*Jesus said to them: "Watch out that no one
deceives you. . . When you hear of wars and rumors
of wars, do not be alarmed. Such things must happen,
but the end is still to come. Nation will rise against
nation, and kingdom against kingdom. There will be
earthquakes in various places, and famines. These are
the beginning of birth pains. . .*

*"Brother will betray brother to death. . . All men
will hate you because of me, but he who stands firm to
the end will be saved." (Mark 13:4-5, 7-8, 12-13)*

Almost all students of prophecy believe the End Times will begin with a great battle. Centered in the Middle East. It will be a conflict between Isaac, the Jew, and Ishmael, the Arab, and it will grow until it engulfs the entire world.

However, it doesn't take being any great biblical scholar or student of prophecy to look at the world today and know that this battle is growing closer, much closer, to us all.

The apostle John received a vision on the Isle of Patmos in A.D. 95 that became the Book of Revelation. In it, he saw the four riders commonly known as the Four Horsemen of the Apocalypse. They galloped across the earth, bringing to mankind deceit, destruction, pestilence, and devastation. I wrote years ago that if you listened closely, you could hear the hoof beats of those four horses across newspapers, magazines, and news channels.

Today, the sound of those hoof beats is deafening. It's impossible to listen to any news channel, open any newspaper, or consume any social media without hearing their ominous clatter. It's entirely possible they are nearly upon us, those four horsemen.

The Book of Revelation begins with the unveiling of a scroll sealed with the seven seals. Those seals would have been made in biblical times with wax or possibly clay that, when broken, would reveal that someone had opened that scroll. One by one, the seals in John's vision were broken to reveal the contents of the scroll.

And, as John broke each seal, another portion of God's revelation about the final days of the earth was disclosed, each one a worse horror than the revelation before.

Daniel, the prophet who lived in ancient Babylon (modern-day Iraq), wrote this of the mystery of the End Times:

At that time Michael, the great prince who protects your people, will arise. There will be a time of distress such as has not happened from the beginning of nations until then. But at that time your people— everyone whose name is found written in the book— will be delivered. Multitudes who sleep in the dust of the earth will awake: some to everlasting life, others to shame and everlasting contempt. Those who are wise will shine like the brightness of the heavens, and those who lead many to righteousness, like the stars for ever and ever. But you, Daniel, close up and seal the words of the scroll until the time of the end. Many will go here and there to increase knowledge.

I heard, but I did not understand. So I asked, "My lord, what will the outcome of all this be?"

He replied, "Go your way, Daniel, because the words are closed up and sealed until the time of the end. Many will be purified, made spotless and refined, but the wicked will continue to be wicked. None of the wicked will understand, but those who are wise will understand. (Daniel 12:1-4, 8-10)

It's difficult to look around oneself today and not believe that such an apocalyptic time threatens us now, from Iran, which was Persia until 1935, and Russia, referred to as Rosh or the kingdom of the north in biblical writings. Even the existence of modern Israel which was reborn in 1948 in the very lands promised by God to Abraham and his descendants, points at the coming of the end days.

IRAN IS PERSIAN, NOT ARAB

The predominant Iranian culture is Persian, not Arabian. The Persians consider Arabs in a pejorative sense, thinking of them as desert nomads. To many Persians, Arabs are mere "Bedouins," a migratory people known for packing their tents and moving across the sands on camels.

The Persian people by comparison think of their culture as more elevated. The Persians of history lived along the ancient silk routes. They were traders who established shops in a tradition of entrepreneurial "bazaars." The traditional religion of the Persian people is Zoroastrianism, which some claim traces back 600 BC. Zoroaster preached monotheism. While few Americans know much about this religion, Zoroastrianism was one of the first religions to identify a duality between good and evil.

Theologians argue that Jewish and Christian ideas of God and Satan, as well as Heaven and Hell, trace back to Zoroastrianism. Islam was founded in what is now Saudi Arabia by Mohammed, who was born in 570 AD and received his first revelation of Allah in 610 AD. For the Persians, Islam is an Arab religion, not a Persian religion.

The Arabs invaded Persia around 650 A.D., bringing with them Islam. Over time, Islam supplanted Zoroastrianism as the predominant religion of Persia. Many Zoroastrians fled to India when the Arabs invaded, introducing their religion. These distinctions are well-appreciated in the Middle East, even today. To call a "Persian" person an "Arab" may be taken as an insult. That Islam is not the original religion of Iran remains a tension even today just below the surface.

There are a few more distinctions that are important in understanding Iran. The vast majority of Iranians are Shiites, a minority sect within Islam wherein worldwide most Muslims are Sunnis. In the 1970s, the mullahs prepared the way for the return of Ayatollah Khomeini by preaching radical revolution and a fundamentalist reform version of Shiite Islam in Iran's mosques. Ayatollah Khomeini's revolution began in Iran's vast peasant countryside. The revolution moved into the poor urban mosques first because the peasants who moved to the city settled in the poorer, inner-city areas.

In many ways, Ayatollah Khomeini's revolution was fueled by Iran's rural peasant communities and urban poor who wanted a return to fundamental Islam. Their goal was to throw out all the foreign influences, including the British, Russians, and Americans, who had been fighting one another for control of Iran's oil resources since before World War II began.

But at the end of World War II, Great Britain and the United States made sure Stalin pulled Soviet troops out of Iran. Throughout the time the Shah was in power, Russia longed to get Iran back into its sphere of influence. Maybe that time has finally arrived. But let's not get ahead of ourselves.

PERSIA'S ORIGIN

A quick review of the history and biblical background of Persia can help us understand the context we—and the world—find ourselves in today with Iran. It can also help us see just how great the threats are upon whose precipice we stand.

Ancient Persia sat in the region most scholars believe to be the location of the Garden of Eden. Several of the oldest civilizations on earth formed in that exact area. It's not an exaggeration to call Persia the cradle of human civilization.

At its height, the Persian empire encompassed the land mass from India to Greece, from the Red Sea to the Caspian Sea. In modern-day terms, it would include the countries of Pakistan, part of India, Afghanistan, Iran, Iraq, Syria, Turkey, Jordan, Israel, and Egypt, plus small pieces of a half-dozen more modern countries along the north coast of the Mediterranean and into Africa.

For three thousand years, Persia (renamed Iran in 1935) has remained an autonomous territory—a fact the Iranian people are very proud of. Unlike its neighbors, Iran is not Arab. It is Persian, or more accurately, Indo-European. Although Iranians do use the Arabic alphabet, its official language is not Arabic, but Farsi.

Furthermore, Iran's history is not rooted in Islam. It begins much earlier, when kings were worshiped as gods and great temples, mausoleums, and religious buildings were erected in their honor. Zoroastrianism, which is credited with being the first monotheistic, or one-god, religion, originated in Persia up to two thousand years before Christ.

Islam, which came to Persia during the Muslim Conquest of 633 to 654 A.D., is a relative newcomer to Persian culture. However, Persia fully embraced the new religion and has been a devout Islamic nation since the introduction of the faith.

Despite being fully Islamified, even in modern times some of the ancient Persian traditions remain. For example, Iran celebrates *No Ruz (meaning New Day or New Year). This is not an Islamic holiday, but a holdover from the time before Islam became the main religion of Persia.*

PERSIA'S FIRST GREAT EMPEROR

Cyrus the Great, the first king to call himself "great" and the first Achaemenid ruler, established the Persian Empire by uniting two of the earliest tribes in the region, the Medes and the Persians, in 550 B.C.

Cyrus conquered Lydia, and its king, Croesus (of rich as Croesus fame) within a few years of becoming the Persian emperor. Cyrus took control of much of the coast of the Aegean Sea, controlling areas in Asia Mino, Armenia, and parts of Greece.

He also controlled an area called the Levant, which included the modern-day countries of Lebanon, Syria, Palestine, Jordon, Israel, and parts of Iraq and Saudi Arabia. Conquering eastward, Cyrus seized Parthia, Chorasmia, and Bactria—which comprised most of modern-day Afghanistan and Pakistan.

In spite of ruling one of the largest empires in early recorded history, he was known for his fairness, forbearance, and charitable posture toward those he conquered.

BABYLON AND THE JEWS UNDER CYRUS'S RULE

In 539 B.C., Babylon fell to Cyrus's army. He was greeted with cheers and roars of welcome from the Jews who had been taken prisoner by Nebuchadnezzar and transported to Babylonia as captive slaves. Following his conquest of the capital city, Cyrus permitted some forty-thousand Jews to leave and return to their homes in Canaan.

Indeed, under the leadership of Cyrus, the Persians exhibited great compassion for the religious tenets and cultures of other peoples. Cyrus was hailed as being upright, a great leader of men, generous, and benevolent. The Hellenes, whom he conquered, called him "Lawgiver", and the Jews referred to him as "anointed of the Lord."

Cyrus is first mentioned in the Bible in 2 Chronicles 36:22-23 and in Ezra 1:1-3.

> *In the first year of Cyrus king of Persia, in order to fulfill the word of the Lord spoken by Jeremiah, the Lord moved the heart of Cyrus king of Persia to make a proclamation throughout his realm and to put it in writing:*
>
> *This is what Cyrus king of Persia says:*
> *'The Lord, the God of heaven, has given me all the kingdoms of the earth and he has appointed me to build a temple for him at Jerusalem in Judah. Anyone of his people among you—may his God be with him, and let him go up to Jerusalem in Judah and build the temple of the Lord, the God of Israel, the God who is in Jerusalem."* (Ezra 1:1-3)

Not only did Cyrus allow the Jews to return to their homes in Judah and Jerusalem, but he also provided them with everything they would need to rebuild the temple and the walls of the city. Furthermore, he returned to the Jews all of the treasures from the temple that the Babylonians had stolen when they conquered Jerusalem some seventy years before.

Cyrus was unique, not only because he allowed the Jews to return to Israel, but also because his birth and his name were foretold by the prophet Isaiah almost one-hundred-fifty years before he was born. God also revealed Cyrus's mission to the prophet. Isaiah recorded that Cyrus would accomplish specific tasks under God's direction during his lifetime. He was destined to carry out God's plan as it related to His chosen people:

> *Who says of Cyrus, "He is my shepherd*
> *And will accomplish all that I please,*
> *He will say of Jerusalem, 'Let it be rebuilt,'*
> *And of the temple, 'Let its foundations be laid.*
> (Isaiah 44:28)

Although Cyrus was a practicing pagan, a worshiper of the god, Marduk, he would achieve noble feats as an instrument in the hands of Jehovah God. He would contribute, albeit indirectly, to the coming of the Messiah, God's anointed One.

> *Moreover, King Cyrus brought out the articles belong-*
> *ing to the temple of the Lord, which Nebuchadnezzar*
> *had carried away from Jerusalem and had placed*
> *in the temple of his god. Cyrus king of Persia had*
> *them brought by Mithredath the treasurer, who*
> *counted them out to Sheshbazzar the prince of Judah.*
> (Ezra 1:7-8)

> *However, in the first year of Cyrus king of Babylon,*
> *King Cyrus issued a decree to rebuild this house of*
> *God. He even removed from the temple of Babylon*
> *the gold and silver articles of the house of God, which*
> *Nebuchadnezzar had taken from the temple in Jeru-*
> *salem and brought to the temple in Babylon.*

Then King Cyrus gave them to a man named Sheshbazzar, whom he had appointed governor, and he told him, "Take these articles and go and deposit them in the temple in Jerusalem. And rebuild the house of God on its site. So this Sheshbazzar came and laid the foundation of the house of God in Jerusalem. From that day to the present it has been under construction but is not yet finished.

Now if it pleases the king, let a search be made in the royal archives of Babylon to see if King Cyrus did, in fact, issue a decree to rebuild this house of God in Jerusalem. Then let the king send us his decision in this matter. (Ezra 5:13-17)

In the first year of King Cyrus, the king issued a decree concerning the temple of God In Jerusalem:

Let the temple be rebuilt as a place to present sacrifices, and let its foundations be laid. It is to be ninety feet high and ninety feet wide, with three courses of large stones and one of timbers. The costs are to be paid by the royal treasury. Also, the gold and silver articles of the house of God, which Nebuchadnezzar took from the temple in Jerusalem and brought to Babylon, are to be returned to their places in the temple in Jerusalem; they are to be deposited in the house of God. (Ezra 6:3-5)

Cyrus's name is recorded in the Bible over twenty times. It is ironic that the descendants of the very nation that were instrumental in returning the Jews to Jerusalem during the reign of King Cyrus now want them wiped off the map.

THE JEWS UNDER DARIUS AND XERXES

Another great ruler of Persia who had an outsized influence on the history, and very survival of the Jews, was Darius. He took the Persian kingdom from the descendants of Cyrus and used its small army intelligently to solidify his rule over the entire Persian Empire.

He produced the "Ordinance of Good Regulation" to create a uniform code of law throughout the empire. He also created a system of mail transport similar to the Pony Express. He built a system of roads that extended 1,500 miles from east to west.

Darius's son Xerxes I succeeded him and notably took the Jewess Hadassah (better known as Esther) as his queen. She was a beautiful young Jewish girl torn from her homeland and taken as a captive to Persia. Xerxes had recently banished his queen, Vashti, from the royal throne for disobeying him. He initiated a search for her successor and, captured by Esther's beauty, married her.

Esther's cousin and guardian, Mordecai, offended Xerxes' grand vizier, Haman, by refusing to prostrate himself before Haman. Infuriated, Haman plotted to convince Xerxes to kill all the Jews:

> *Then Haman said to King Xerxes, "there is a certain*
> *people dispersed and scattered among the peoples in*
> *all the provinces of your kingdom whose customs are*
> *different from those of all other people and who do not*

obey the king's laws; it is not in the king's best interest to tolerate them." (Esther 3:8)

Esther's cousin, Mordecai, challenged the queen to approach the king, a move that could be punishable by being banished like Vashti or being put to death. Mordecai entreated her to ask for the salvation of her people:

"For if you remain silent at this time, relief and deliverance for the Jews will arise from another place, but you and your father's family will perish. And who knows but that you have come to royal position for such a time as this?" (Esther 4:14)

Esther's response to Mordecai is magnificent:

"Go, gather together all the Jews who are in Susa, and fast for me. Do not eat or drink for three days, night or day. I and my maids will fast as you do. When this is done, I will go to the king, even though it is against the law. And if I perish, I perish." (Esther 4:16)

Undoubtedly with great trepidation, Esther approached Haman and asked for an audience with the king. Xerxes granted her request to spare the Jews, Haman's plan to eradicate the Jews was thwarted, and Esther was not punished by her husband. Esther's people were allowed to live in peace in Shushan.

Yet again, the Jews were saved by the decision of a great Persian king.

ISLAM COMES TO PERSIA

By the year 628, Persia was weakened after decades of warfare with the Byzantine Empire. The Parthians in the north of Persia were embroiled in internal struggle with the Sassanians in the south and west for control of the empire. In 633, the Muslim general, Khalid ibn al-Walid invaded Mesopotamia (a southwestern province controlled by the Sassanians.) Although his forces were eventually repelled, the fight for control of Persia was continuous from then on.

In 642, Umar ibn al-Khattab, then-Caliph of the Muslims, executed a series of well-coordinated, multi-pronged attacks that led to the nearly complete annexation of Persia by the Arabs. The Parthians in the north refused to fight to defend the Sassanian territories and elected to convert to Islam, avoiding bloodshed in their lands.

The Islamization of Persia was gradual. Muslim rulers offered fair treatment and relative religious tolerance if local populations would convert to Islam. All bureaucrats were required to be Muslim, and the Arab alphabet was imposed across the region.

The result of this relatively bloodless transition to Islam was that the culture, beliefs, and customs of Persia were blended with those of Islam as opposed to being replaced by Islam entirely. Over the ensuing centuries, the Persians worked hard to preserve their language, history, and culture.

Historian, Bernard Lewis describes it like this:

> "Iran was indeed Islamized, but it was not Arabized.
> Persians remained Persians. And after an interval of

silence, Iran reemerged as a separate, different and distinctive element within Islam, eventually adding a new element even to Islam itself.

Culturally, politically, and most remarkable of all even religiously, the Iranian contribution to this new Islamic civilization is of immense importance. The work of Iranians can be seen in every field of cultural endeavor, including Arabic poetry, to which poets of Iranian origin composing their poems in Arabic made a very significant contribution.

In a sense, Iranian Islam is a second advent of Islam itself, a new Islam sometimes referred to as Islami Ajam. It was this Persian Islam, rather than the original Arab Islam, that was brought to new areas and new peoples: to the Turks, first in Central Asia and then in the Middle East in the country that came to be called Turkey, and of course to India. The Ottoman Turks brought a form of Iranian civilization to the walls of Vienna."

All was not proceeding so bloodlessly within Islam at this same time, however. Hussein, the grandson of Prophet Muhammed, and forces loyal to Caliph Yazid met in battle on the plains of Karbala—today one of the holiest cities in Iraq. This proved to be a watershed even in Islam, for it was here that Hussein died, and it was here that an irreparable division between the Sunnis and Shiites began.

MUHAMMED

Muhammed was born in 570 A.D. He was orphaned in childhood and raised by an uncle. He married and had three sons and four daughters. All three of Muhammed's sons died in childhood. Shiites believe that only Muhammed's daughter Fatima, was his biological child, but Sunnis dispute this.

Ali ib Abi Talib was Muhammed's cousin and married Muhammed's daughter Fatima. They had two sons, Hasan and Hussein.

Muhammad called Ali his *brother, guardian, and successor*, and he was the flag bearer in most of the wars and became famous for his bravery. On his return from the Farewell Pilgrimage, Muhammad uttered the phrase, "Whoever I am his *Mawla*, this Ali is his Mawla." But the meaning of Mawla became disputed. Shiites believed that Ali was being appointed by Muhammad to lead Islam, and Sunnis interpreted the word as friendship and love.

At this time, Arab politics and religion were tightly intertwined. Caliphs were both political leaders and religious leaders. Muhammed was both in his lifetime.

Upon Muhammed's death, Ali was elected as the next Caliph. However, other factions—those of Umar and Abu Bakr, close companions of Muhammed's—were unhappy about this development, and strife followed.

When Ali's wife, Fatima, died after a miscarriage, he relinquished the caliphate to Abu Bakr. Shiites insist that Abu Bakr's followers attacked the house of Ali to force him to pledge allegiance to Abu Bakr and were responsible for Fatima's death, a claim Sunni's strongly dispute.

Abu Bakr (one of Muhammed's companions) ruled for only two years. On his deathbed, he appointed Umar to be his successor. After being stabbed, a dying Umar appointed Uthman to succeed him. These two were also companions of Muhammed's.

Shiites hold that Ali (Muhammed's son-in-law) was wrongly deposed as the rightful heir to the Muslim caliphate in a backroom deal between Umar, Abu Bakr, and their supporters after Muhammed's death.

Without delving too deeply into early disagreements between Shia and Sunni, the two factions are in agreement over the two functions of prophets: to reveal God's law to men, and to guide men toward God.

Sunnis believe these roles both ended with the death of the prophet, Muhammed. Shiites believe that while revealing God's laws ended with Muhammed, the function of guiding and explaining divine law continued through the line of religious leaders they called imams.

FOUNDING OF SHIA

Shia Islam was founded in 661 A.D. by Ali ibn Abi Talib, Muhammed's son-in-law. It was from his name that the name Shia evolved. It's a derivation of the phrase *Shiat Ali*—partisans or followers of Ali. Ali's followers believed him to be the last of the true caliphs.

Although he decided to, or was forced to—depending on which sect of Islam one listens to—swear allegiance to Abu Bakr, he remained wildly popular and led the army of the Arab caliphate.

In 661, he entered into battle with the army of the governor of Damascus. The Damascene soldiers attached verses of the Quran to the tips of their spears. When faced with a fighting force hiding behind the words of Muhammed, Ali's army declined to fight. Ali was forced to negotiate with this enemy. Although he escaped death in open combat, one of his followers subsequently murdered him.

Upon Ali's death, the governor of Damascus, Mu'awiya, declared himself caliph. Ali's son, Hassan, the rightful heir, died under suspicious circumstances while the next in the line of succession, Hussein, agreed to take no action to take back the caliphate until the governor died.

However, when Mu'awiya died, his son, Yazid, claimed the title of caliph and sent his army of a thousand men into battle against Hussein and a small group of his followers. The bloody battle of Karbala resulted in Hussein and most of his men dying. Only Hussein's baby boy survived the carnage to carry on the line of Ali.

The Yazidis continued to hold the political title of caliph, but they could not stop the descendants of Ali from declaring themselves the religious heirs to Muhammed's legacy and using the title Imam to indicate they were the religious leaders of Islam. The title was passed down for nearly two hundred years to successive descendants of Ali.

THE MAHDI

The Eleventh Imam after Ali, named Hasan al Askari, was poisoned and died, leaving behind his young son, Muhammed, as his heir to the title of Twelfth Imam.

Immediately after Hasan's death, young Muhammed disappeared. Another man, Uthman ibn Sa'id, claimed that the young boy had been hidden away for his own safety and assumed control of the Shi'a community. However, it was widely reported at the time that the four-year-old boy fell down a well and disappeared.

Uthman, followed by three more imams, collectively called the Four Deputies, claimed over a period of seventy years following that incident, that the child Muhammed was being held in a state of occultation—a state of being hidden from view—by God.

Refusing to believe he was dead, the child's followers imbued him with timelessness. They declared him to be merely "hidden" and that on some future date he would suddenly appear to reestablish an Islamic caliphate worldwide.

Over time, the belief evolved. His followers claimed that how he would reappear would involve an apocalyptic upheaval necessary for the Mahdi, or Hidden Imam, to ascend to his rightful place of leadership. These Twelvers, who awaited the return of the Twelfth Imam of Shia, championed the belief that every individual, regardless of their religious beliefs, would one day bow to Islam—or die.

As more time passed and the Mahdi failed to make an appearance, authority passed to the *ulema*, a body of mullahs endowed with the power to appoint a supreme leader. Perhaps one of the best-known imam was Grand Ayatollah Ruhollah Khomeini.

The Sunnis went their own way, developing an Islamic religion and state in Arabia, while Shiites, the Twelvers among them, developed their own beliefs in parallel under the broader umbrella of Islam.

The Safavid dynasty ruled Persia from 1501 to 1736. It was

under them that Shia Islam became Persia's official religion. It was also during this time that Persia was once again reunited as a single sovereign entity that ultimately evolved into what we now know as modern-day Iran.

A MESSIANIC VISION OF IRAN'S FUTURE

During more than twenty-five centuries of history, Persians have maintained their unique sense of identity. Though they converted to Islam, they have not always followed the accepted views of that religion. To an extent, Zoroastrianism, the religion of the early Persians, Persian culture, ancient Persian traditions, and an early schism within Islam itself, color the Iranian variety of Islam.

Iran is now one of the largest countries not only in the Middle East, but also in the Islamic world. Because of its past history and the efforts of outsiders to change it, Iran has developed a thorny sense of separatism. Invaded during both World Wars and later set upon by its neighbor Iraq, modern Iran still has reason to fear foreign influence.

Although the borders of Iran remained largely unchanged during the twentieth century, a desire to recapture the glory of the vast and ancient Persian Empire may be reemerging once more. Perhaps this is a driving force behind Iran's seemingly sudden emergence as a budding player in the world's nuclear superpower game. And perhaps Iran has a special understanding of and affinity for Vladimir Putin's obsession with restoring the Russian Empire to its former glory as well.

While it might not be a cause for great concern if Iran merely wanted to reassert itself on the world stage and regain lost national pride, it is the obsession of Iran's supreme leaders—both political and religious—with ushering in the return of the Mahdi that makes Iran's ambitions dangerous.

What raises Iran's messianic ambitions from dangerous to an existential threat to mankind is the other obsession of Iran's supreme leaders, namely obtaining a nuclear weapon at the earliest possible opportunity.

CHAPTER TWO:

RECENT HISTORY IN IRAN. . . AND WHY IT MATTERS

"We shall export our revolution to the whole world.
Until the cry 'There is no god but Allah' resounds
over the whole world, there will be struggle."

—Ruhollah Khomeini

"Americans are the great Satan, the wounded snake."

—Ruhollah Khomeini

"There is no room for play in Islam. . .
It is deadly serious about everything."

—Ruhollah Khomeini

IRAN'S MESSIANIC AND NUCLEAR ambitions matter for one simple reason: with its history of contempt for the United Nations and the IAEA (International Atomic Energy Agency), the timetable for an apocalyptic event provoked by that nation could escalate at any moment. We literally stand poised on the precipice of a catastrophic nuclear event in the name of bringing back Iranian religious extremists' Mahdi.

If we want to understand Iran's ambitions and where they came from, we can learn a lot about its motives and end goals by taking a look at how Iran became an Islamic revolutionary state hotly pursuing nuclearization.

JIMMY CARTER BETRAYS THE SHAH OF IRAN

An Islamic revolution was birthed on April Fools' Day in 1980 as Ayatollah Khomeini proclaimed it the "first day of the government of God." This revolution has now become an apocalyptic, tsunami-like wave that will turn into a mushroom cloud if we close our eyes and ears at this most critical moment in history.

In 1980, I wrote *Israel, America's Key to Survival.* The premise of the book was that terrorism was spreading like a plague, and America was in the crosshairs. While writing the book, I interviewed many of America's top generals. One of the most memorable interviews took place just outside of Washington, D.C. at the home of General Robert Huyser, head of the Strategic Nuclear War plan for all U.S. nuclear forces. Huyser was sent to Iran to work with the prime minister and generals. This plan was part of President Carter's bid to destabilize the Shah's government.

Huyser, a man of principal and moral clarity, believed that his mission was to support the Shah's generals and the Bakhtiar government. Little did he realize that Carter had no desire to see a pro-Shah regime in power; instead, he preferred the Ayatollah. Carter was, in fact, pressuring the Shah to make what he called "human rights concessions" in the country.

The President promised the Iranian generals and Iranian Prime Minister Bakhtiar that the U.S. would protect and provide all assets needed to shore up their government. General Huyser told me that he had awakened in shock with the realization that the orders given to him by Jimmy Carter were not the President's real intentions.

Huyser was stunned to learn that Carter had no intention of supporting the Shah's regime but was instead working through the U. S. Embassy and the State Department to put Khomeini in power. Carter saw Khomeini as a Gandhi-like figure whose ascension to power was the most suitable course for the U.S. to pursue.

Bakhtiar could have stabilized the country with the unconditional support of America. Instead, the U.S. betrayed those who trusted it, and as a result, was the midwife that helped birth the Islamic revolution.

REVOLUTION COMES TO IRAN

On Thursday, February 1, 1979, over one million people filled the streets of Tehran. The hordes had been organized to greet a triumphal Khomeini as he returned to Tehran. A military guard at the airport stood ready to receive him with the full support of President Jimmy Carter.

On Saturday, February 3, the Ayatollah told the masses gathered that his goal was to replace the 28-year-old government headed by Prime Minister Bakhtiar with an Islamic revolutionary government. The crowds chanted, "Death to Carter! Death to Huyser!, and Khomeini predicted that the newly launched Islamic revolution would spread far beyond Iran's borders.

Little did the world know that the Islamic revolution would give birth to the Osama bin Ladens of the world. Many of the generals who'd worked to stabilize the country were assassinated. After fleeing to France, Dr. Shapour Bakhtiar was murdered in his home. This was just the beginning.

The Shah was overthrown and forced to flee for his life. Radical Iranian students overran the U.S. embassy and took 52 American diplomats and citizens as hostages. The hostages were held for 444 days, through the failure of delicate political negotiations and an ill-fated and abortive attempt by the Carter administration to rescue the prisoners. These events would ultimately signal the end of Jimmy Carter's political career.

The crisis with Islamic fascists that America faces today can be laid at the feet of Jimmy Carter and his liberal, Leftist policies designed to undermine the Shah of Iran. President Carter contributed to the birth of the revolution.

REVOLUTIONARY IRAN PLAYS CHESS WITH THE WEST

Iran, the inventors of the game of chess, has waged a war of terror against America for decades. In 1981, they engineered the release of the U.S. embassy hostages in Tehran to end Jimmy Carter's career and launch Ronald Reagan's. In 1983, they bombed the Marine barracks in Beirut, killing 241 U.S. Marines.

Iran succeeded in driving America out of Lebanon through that attack and the threat posed by its terrorist organizations there. Iran even orchestrated a scenario so diabolical that the President of the United States provided protection for the world's most fearsome terrorist organization at the time, the PLO. When the PLO made a deal to move more than 10,000 of its terrorists on ships for Tunisia, the United States told Israeli General Ariel Sharon to stand down and let them go in peace.

The United States was naïve and didn't understand Iran's game back then. Iran was more than happy to take advantage of our ignorance to advance its own interests, foremost of which were driving the U.S. out of the region, leaving Israel alone and exposed to Iran-backed terrorists, and leaving Iran alone to do as it wished. For this, too, the United States bears responsibility in helping give birth to the crisis facing us today.

IRAN RAISES THE STAKES

Iran is serious. . . dead serious. Their intentions can neither be taken for granted nor minimized. The Islamization of Palestine was orchestrated through Iran. Palestinians were nationalists, not Islamic fundamentalists, before Iran's influence came to hold sway. It was the Iranian mullahs who indoctrinated the children of Palestine with the dogma of the Islamic revolution and persuaded them to become human bombs.

Hamas, which controls the Palestinian Territory, is a pawn of Iran, as is Hezbollah in Lebanon with its ten thousand missiles. The world saw Iran's true intentions the day Israelis intercepted a Palestinian ship, the *Katrine-A*, in the Red Sea on January 4, 2002. The ship was loaded with Katusha rockets with a maximum range of 12 miles, assault rifles, anti-tank missiles, mines, ammunition, and explosives. Most of the weapons were Iranian. They were bound for Hamas.

In August 2004, John R. Bolton, then-Under Secretary for Arms Control and International Security, said:

"We cannot let Iran, a leading sponsor of international terrorism, acquire nuclear weapons and the means to deliver them to Europe, most of central Asia and the Middle East, or beyond. Without serious, concerted, immediate intervention by the international community, Iran will be well on the road to doing so."

In January 2005, IDF Intelligence Branch head Major General Aharon Ze'evi Farkash spoke to a group assembled at the National Security Studies Center at the University of Haifa. According to Farkash, "If Iran's uranium enrichment activities [were] not halted, it could develop its first atomic bomb at some point between 2007 and 2009." He opined that Iran was about six months from being able to enrich uranium, a step he described as the "point of no return."

Global onlookers seemed certain that Iran's actions were aimed at moving forward with the development of a nuclear weapon in noncompliance with IAEA accords. The question was: Had Iran already reached the "point of no return" in the negotiation process? If so, would military action be necessary to prevent Iran from developing nuclear weapon capabilities?

These twin problems of Iran supporting terrorists and pursuing nuclear weapons are not new. They've been around for two decades. But the United States largely ignored them both.

ISRAEL SOUNDS A WARNING

Israel, on the other hand, has been deeply concerned for a long time that Iran's nuclear activities will spell disaster worldwide.

All the way back on May 24, 2005, at the Washington Convention Center I sat across the table from Prime Minister Ariel Sharon during his last trip to Washington, D.C. I asked him specifically: "How dangerous do you consider Iran and its nuclear threat to be?"

Sharon's response, "Iran is an insane regime, and the center of world terror. Iran will make every effort possible to possess nuclear weapons. This is a danger to the Middle East, a danger to Europe, and a danger to America."

Sharon said to me in that meeting, "Israel cannot accept a nuclear Iran nor can America. We have the ability to deal with this, and we are making all the necessary preparations to be ready."

Thank goodness Israel was on top of it, for the United States surely was not. Israel commenced a low-level campaign of sabotage and assassinations aimed at slowing down and disrupting Iran's nuclear development program. At the same time, Israel launched countless surgical attacks against terrorists in the region, some were airstrikes, others were missile attacks, some were special forces operations. These attacks were designed to weaken and destroy terror networks and prevent imminent attacks upon Israel.

Iran became a top priority for Israeli intelligence operations. It took many years, but Iran has finally become a top priority for U.S. intelligence operations, as well.

I met with Sharon's former Chief of Staff, Moshe Ya'alon, and I asked him why Iran was threatening Israel with a nuclear attack. He replied:

> "Iran is the main generator today of terrorism against Israel. We continue to see Hezbollah attacks

from Lebanon. Hezbollah is an Iranian-made organization supported by Iran. They get about $18 million annually. Iran armed Hezbollah for attacks against Israel, using Lebanon as a platform.

Iran also supports the Palestinian Islamic Jihad. They fully finance this organization. In the Palestinian Authority, Iran finances Fatah activists. They finance the families of those who commit bombing attacks. Families of suicide bombers get $25,000–$40,000 for suicide bombings. That's a lot of money in the Palestinian Authority."

Equally concerned was my good friend, Israeli Prime Minister Benjamin Netanyahu through the long years of American inaction and disinterest in what Iran was up to. In one of our discussions, Netanyahu cautioned that Hamas represented a major threat. "Hamas is a second Iran," he explained. "Hamas is backed by Iran and they agree with Iran that Israel has no right to exist."

Netanyahu's comments concerned me deeply. Over the last two decades, I have known him to be a man of level-judgment, a tough supporter of Israel, but not a man prone to exaggeration. "With Hamas controlling the Palestinian Authority," Netanyahu explained, "we are in a vice with Iran pressing and Hamas closing in around us."

He went on to say of Hamas and other Iranian-backed terrorists:

> "They will try to create a much larger Iranian state from the outskirts of Iran to the outskirts of Tel Aviv.

If such a state came into being. . . it would be not merely a threat to Israel, but a threat to the entire region and to the safety of the world."

General Ya'alon indicated another reason for Iran's hostile determination. He said,

"Shiite Muslims believe that the Twelfth Imam, or Mahdi, the last in a line of saints descended from Ali, the founder of their sect, vanished down a well (near Jamkaran, Iran) in 941 A.D. According to their beliefs, he went into a state of 'occultation,' like the sun being hidden behind the clouds. After a stormy period of apocalyptic wars, the clouds will part, and the sun (the Mahdi) will be revealed. They believe that when he is released from his imprisonment, the entire world will submit to Islam."

The words would not have been so startling except that they fell from General Ya'alon's lips.

General Ya'alon was not talking about Palestine; he was not talking about Saudi Arabia; he was not talking about Iran; he was talking about the entire world. The war that is being waged by the *jihadists* exported from Iran is not a war against Israel. It's not a war against Sunni Islam; it is a war against the West. . . Western culture and Western values. This war would eradicate the Jews and the Christians, all infidels, and would establish the Nation of Islam worldwide the Middle East.

This sounds like a ridiculous dream, but armed with nuclear weapons, Iran's dream would have to be reckoned with. The spirit of the Grand Ayatollah Khomeini lives on in Iran. This is the same Khomeini who said in 1981, "I say let Iran go up in smoke, provided Islam emerges triumphant in the rest of the world."

PRESDIENT AHMADINEJAD: TWELVER TRUE BELIEVER

Just days before I interviewed General Ya'alon, I watched a DVD recorded shortly after Mahmoud Ahmadinejad returned from the U.N. General Assembly meeting in New York in September 2005. The President is seen entering a house with Ayatollah Javadi Amoli, a senior conservative figure in Qom. They sat on a carpet and were served tea while talking about the money the government has allocated at the shrine at Jamkaran.

Then Ahmadinejad turns to his recent U.N. address:

> "On the last day when I was speaking, one of our group told me that when I started to say *"bismullah Muhammad"*, he saw a green light come from around me, and I was placed inside this aura. I felt it myself. I felt that the atmosphere suddenly changed and for those twenty-seven to twenty-eight minutes, all the leaders of the world did not blink. When I say they didn't move an eyelid, I am not exaggerating. They were looking as if a hand were holding them there and had just opened their eyes."

The world may smirk as they hear the President of Iran talking of the return of the Mahdi and dismiss his beliefs as just a bunch of religious foolishness. But he is dead serious. Not only does he believe it, but the tens of thousands of mullahs controlling ancient Persia—now modern Iran—believe it also. It is their mission from God.

When the hardline, then-mayor of Tehran, Mahmoud Ahmadinejad, walked across American and Israeli flags painted on the pavement of a mosque, and voted in Iran's ninth presidential election, the world was convinced there was no possibility of his election. They were stunned when proven wrong.

An ideologue emerged triumphant; Ahmadinejad is, without question, fueled by messianic religious fervor. He has rekindled revolutionary fires long extinguished. He believes that Iran's redemption will come through a combustible mixture of this Islamist ideology and Ahmadinejad's deep suspicion of a world conspiracy propagated by the Crusaders and the Zionists.

When Ahmadinejad came on the scene, I was shocked to hear a repeat of the exact anti-Semite hate rhetoric that first poured out of Hitler's pre-war Nazi Germany. Not only did the president of Iran challenge the validity of the Holocaust, he said that Israel must be "wiped off the map." How could Ahmadinejad dare to doubt the Holocaust or suggest that Israel should be moved from the Middle East to be relocated somewhere in Europe? Yet none of this was fiction. Ahmadinejad was serious and his rhetoric was government policy.

NAMES CHANGE BUT THE FANATICISM
REMAINS THE SAME

The West believed that when Ahmadinejad's term as president of Iran ended in 2013, the next man to hold the office would surely be less fanatical and more reasonable to deal with. But what the West failed to understand is every government official in Iran, every mullah, every ayatollah, shares Khomeini's fanatical vision with the same fervor Ahmadinejad did. He was not the exception to the rule. He was the norm.

Years earlier, when the Grand Ayatollah Ruholla Khomeini died in 1989, the West naively hoped that a more moderate religious leader might take his place, one more friendly to the West, more concerned with restoring the rights of women in Iran, and even slightly interested in human rights. The West believed that *surely* the new leader would be less fanatical in his beliefs regarding the Mahdi, and the obsession with eradicating Israel, and frankly, the desire to eradicate infidels everywhere.

The West was wrong.

Ali Khamenei, who served as president of Iran from 1981 to 1989, was elected Supreme Leader of Iran by the Council of Experts. Shortly before his death, Khomeini had a serious disagreement with his chosen heir to the position, and there was no agreed upon successor when Khomeini died. According to Akbar Hashemi Rafsanjani, Khamenei was the man Khomeini had chosen as his successor before dying. No surprise, the newly elected Khamenei promptly chose Rafsanjani to be the next president of Iran.

The Supreme Leader is officially Iran's head of state, the commander-in-chief of its armed forces, issues decrees, and makes the

THE END TIMES and ARMAGEDDON

final decisions on the main policies of the government. Supreme Leaders generally dictate policy regarding the economy, foreign policy, most domestic policy (ignoring only the most trivial aspects of the government), even the environment.

As Supreme Leader, Khamenei has direct control over the executive and legislative branches, the military, and the media, and has indirect control over the judiciary branches—not that any judge who hopes to live very long would dare go against the Supreme Leader.

All candidates for the Assembly of Experts (a religious advisory council), the Majlis (Parliament), and the Presidency and are vetted by the Guardian Council, whose members are selected directly or indirectly by the Supreme Leader.

This is all to say the Supreme Leader in Iran is all-powerful within that country. Whatever he wants, he gets. It's ironic that Jimmy Carter actually thought by replacing the Shah he would loosen the controls on the people of Iran. By installing Khomeini as the Leader of the Revolution and ultimately as Supreme Leader, Carter flung Iran backwards by hundreds of years in absolute religious control over the country.

Khamenei was president from 1981 to 1989, Rafsanjani from 1989 to 1997, Khatami from 1997 to 2005, Ahmadinejad from 2005 to 2013, Rouhani from 2013 to 2021, and Raisi from 2021 to now. They have each been more or less cookie cutter versions of one another, dutifully doing whatever the Supreme Leader tells them to.

Although, each president has been slightly different—one known as a reformer, one slightly more moderate than the others, another a return to hardliner presidents—each one has been a fervent Twelver in his own right. Each president has despised Israel with a fiery passion matched only by his burning hatred of the United States, and each one has believed in the eventual supremacy of Iran on the world stage.

Presidents of Iran may come and go, but they are all cut from the same cloth. And, as long as the Supreme Leader is calling the shots, Iran will never change its political, religious, or ideological stance.

The only option for any meaningful change in Iran is revolution from within—an overthrow of not only the president but the Supreme Leader as well. This, however, would require the defection or defeat of the Revolutionary Guards, a tall order for an unarmed civilian populace.

THE REVOLUTIONARY GUARD

The Iranian Revolutionary Guard Corps (IRGC), founded by Khomeini in 1979, is technically a branch of the Iranian armed forces. However, it operates completely independent from the rest of the armed forces. IRGC has its own ground forces, air forces, navy, special forces, and intelligence units.

Within the IRGC is a paramilitary group of volunteers called the Basij militia. This plainclothes militia spies on Iranian citizens, infiltrates resistance groups, suppresses protests, and intimidates the civilian population as needed to maintain control over the population.

Whereas the Iranian Army defends Iranian borders and maintains internal order, according to the Iranian constitution the Revolutionary Guard is intended to protect the country's Islamic republic political system, which supporters believe includes preventing foreign interference and coups by the military or "deviant movements".

The Revolutionary Guard typically stands at around 250,000 military personnel. Its naval forces are now the primary forces tasked with operational control of the Persian Gulf. The Basij militia has about 90,000 active personnel and claims to be able to activate up to 600,000 men at a moment's notice.

The IRGC's media—which is to say propaganda—arm is Sepah News.

On March 16, 2022, the IRGC formed a new independent branch called the Command for the Protection and Security of Nuclear Centers.

Expansion of the IRGC's social, political, military, and economic power has led many Western analysts to argue that its political power has surpassed even that of the country's Shia clerical system.

As long as the IRGC remains loyal to the Supreme Leader, it will be extremely difficult to unseat whoever holds the position.

ANOTHER WORLD WAR?

To stop Hitler's Nazi Germany, the world suffered over 60 million deaths, including the Holocaust and the murder of 6 million Jews. If a new world war were occasioned by Iran's pursuit of nuclear weapons, how many would have to die this time? This time will 600 million have to die?

The consequences of a nuclear conflagration set off in a Middle Eastern war are horribly unimaginable. Yet, unfortunately, this is the abyss into which we are forced to look. If the world does nothing to stop Iran, it's only a matter of time before Iran has nuclear weapons.

According to retired colonel Eran Lerman, director of the Israel office of the American Jewish Committee and a former intelligence officer in the Israeli army who oversaw military intelligence gathering on both Iraq and Iran, "The point is that Iran is in breach of the will of the international community. We shouldn't play its game. . . We dare not let our children live under the shadow of a nuclear Iran."

I can't help wondering if we aren't living in a period just like the 1930s. A great power nation has invaded its smaller neighbor, declaring its intent to annex it (Russia's invasion of Ukraine). That conflict has potential to spread across Europe and involve many countries. Development of nuclear weapons by a hostile power looms, and the survival of the Jewish people, and perhaps the world, hangs in the balance.

Hitler shared his intentions clearly in *Mein Kampf,* but nobody believed him. The thought that Hitler might engage in a Holocaust to rid Germany and Europe of millions of Jews who had lived there peacefully for generations was seen as unlikely. Rather than oppose Hitler when he was weak, the world appeased him.

Are we doing the same today with the Iran? Do we take its radical anti-Semitic ravings as serious statements of its foreign policy intent? Do we really think the ayatollahs would be insane enough to use nuclear weapons should they be able to develop them?

We might be on the verge of the first truly nuclear international war, yet we discount the possibility. Will hatred of Jews lead the world once again down this dark abyss? The thought is truly frightening. But I cannot get the thought out of my mind. The nightmare of a nuclear Holocaust continues to haunt me.

U.S. INACTION

Why the United States refused to impose sanctions early in the development of Iran's nuclear program upon nations that supplied nuclear technology to Iran, i.e., Russia, is a question that has never been adequately answered. Why America didn't impose diplomatic and economic sanctions on countries that financed Iran by purchasing its oil, i.e. China to the tune of $60 billion, must also be asked.

In a high-level meeting with a member of the Israeli Atomic Energy Commission, I was asked why the U.S. does not cancel the credit cards (American Express, Visa, MasterCard) of the thousands of millionaire mullahs in Iran, and why the U.S. continues to fund the International Atomic Energy Agency (IAEA) to the tune of thirty-five cents out of every IAEA dollar when Iran is a card-carrying member. I had no answer for him.

Iran was behind the marine barracks bombing in Beirut that killed 241 U.S. Marines. The 9-11 Commission proved that Iran was complicit in the devastating events of September 11, 2001. Iran played a direct role in the 1996 attack on the U. S. military base in Dhahran, Saudi Arabia that killed 19 U.S. troops. And yet, we took no action against Iran. The death of the vast majority of American troops killed in Iraq can be attributed to money, intelligence, and improvised explosive devices from Iran. And we still did nothing to Iran.

In a rally in New York City, a group calling themselves "Islamic Thinkers Society" waved banners and flags symbolizing their desire to bring the entire world under Islamic rule. Here are just a few excerpts from this chilling radical group:

The leader of the group cries in Arabic, and those gathered respond in kind:

"With our blood and our lives we will liberate al Aqsa!"
Leader: *"Israeli Zionists, what do you say?*
The real Holocaust is on the way. Takbeer!"
Response: *"Allah Akbar!"*

Another verse of this demonic chant issues this warning:

"Zionists, Zionists, you will pay! The Wrath of Allah is on its way!

Israeli Zionists you shall pay! The Wrath of Allah is on its way!

The mushroom cloud is on its way! The real Holocaust is on its way!"

This diabolical tirade ends with:

"Islam will dominate the world.

Islam is the only solution!

Takbeer. . . Another mushroom cloud right in the middle of Israel!"

To paraphrase another great quotation: We have met the enemy, and he is in our midst. And perhaps the original quotation from long-ago "Pogo" comic strip writer Walt Kelly is applicable as well: "We have met the enemy, and he is us."

Will the desire for peace at any price enslave us to those whose desire is domination at any price?

CHAPTER THREE:

IRAN'S BRUTAL THEOCRACY

"Kill him. Next."

—Ayatollah Sadeq Khalkhali, 1981

NOW AND THEN, someone asks me, "Is Iran really that bad? Surely, the media is exaggerating what it's like to live there. After all, the people of Iran supported the overthrow of the Shah and the return of Ayatollah Khomeini. They wanted the Islamic Revolution."

Ayatollah Khomeini imposed upon Iran a strict version of fundamental Islam that included a set of religious laws known as *sharia law.* This version of divine law imposed a medieval morality upon the Iranian people.

Banned were all western music, western movies, western sexual freedom. In Khomeini's Iran, young lovers could be severely punished for holding hands in public. Women could be beaten if they did not cover themselves in black veils and long, heavy dresses. Female flesh was not to be seen in public, only female eyes. This was the religious orthodoxy that Khomeini imposed.

THE HANGING JUDGE

Ayatollah Sadeq Khalkhali died at 77 years old, marking the end of an era. He was known as the hanging judge, appointed to head the Revolutionary Courts as soon as Ayatollah Khomeini took over. Khalkhali was a farmer's son who attended religious schools and fought as an Islamic resistance fighter against the Shah.

In an obituary written in *The Guardian* on December 1, 2003, the British newspaper noted that Khalkhali was "at the forefront of the reign of terror that followed the Iranian revolution in 1979 and was a founding member of the Militant Clergy of Tehran who was committed to Islamification at all costs."

He was known for ordering execution by hanging for defendants who had no lawyers and were given no trials. Many of the Shah's lieutenants were given summary hearings that sometimes lasted less than a minute. The defendants were inevitably sentenced to death. Once convicted, the helpless victims were immediately taken to the school rooftops where they were hanged.

The killings started by purging Shah loyalists from the government and the state police, the Savak. Soon, the trials and summary judgments began to be imposed on the citizens themselves. People were executed for "moral violations." Suspected drug dealers were rounded up and hung. Others were killed for their political views, simply because they wrote something critical of the revolution in the newspaper. Any offense the Revolutionary Courts found to be distasteful to the revolution could end up in a death sentence.

Khalkhali ordered summary executions for Kurdish activists who fought for the independence of Kurdistan. He is remembered for the execution of General Mehdi Rahimi who was one of the generals most loyal to the Shah.

So too, Khalkhali ordered the death of Prime Minister Amir Abbas Hoveyda, one of the Shah's last diplomats. Hoveyda had become Prime Minister in February 1965 when his predecessor, Hassan Ali Mansur, was assassinated by revolutionary Islamic extremists. Hoveyda had legal papers and documents to defend himself at his trial, but they were not needed. His trial too was a formality.

According to one report, "Khalkhali read off a list of some 'crimes' Hoveyda had committed and did not allow Hoveyda to defend himself. On April 7, Hoveyda was executed, shot twice on the same roof where many others had been put to death. Many say that it was Khalkhali, the 'judge' himself, who proudly executed Hoveyda."

NO REMORSE

In an interview given to the French newspaper *Le Figaro* on January 14, 2000, Khalkhali defended himself, arguing that he had personally condemned fewer than 1,000 to death. He claimed he was not an extremist. "I carried out the laws of Islam. All those whom I condemned to death were according to the Koran."

Still, the French text of the interview that was not translated into English for publication was more direct. Here is how *Le Figaro* introduced the interview:

> "The butcher of the Iranian Revolution grants an
> audience at his house, in the heart of the holy city
> of Qom, between the end of a siesta and the start of

evening prayers. In 1979, only the name of Ayatollah Khalkhali was enough to generate terror. His signature equated with firing squads, public whippings or death by stoning.

Thousands of men and women were executed after a process that hardly lasted a few minutes or without proper trial. Today, as Iran seeks to surface from years of revolution, war and clerical tyranny, it prefers to forget Ayatollah Khalkhali. This figure embarrasses everyone, the conservatives who applauded him and the reformers whom he has just rallied to support.

But he is the only one not aware of what is happening. At 73, struck by Parkinson disease, this little bearded man with big eyeglasses leads a happy and peaceful life teaching the Koran, always escorted by two armed soldiers. He regrets nothing: "If my victims were to come back on earth," he says often, "I would execute them again, all of them, without exception."

At the height of the revolutionary frenzy, Ayatollah Khalkhali proclaimed that every citizen had the right to be an executioner. Gallows were hastily set up in the streets of Tehran. Sometimes as many as eight people were hanged at a time. Children as young as nine years old were executed.

Thousands were killed indiscriminately until Ayatollah Khomeini spoke out as the supreme spiritual leader of the Islamic

Republic. He ordered that the reign of religious violence by reckless judicial terror must come to an end. Khalkhali remained powerful, however, even as he retreated to Qom. There he resumed his apparently pious life of religious studies.

When Ayatollah Khomeini died in 1989, Khalkhali was reportedly the first to propose Ali Khamenei to be his successor as the spiritual leader of Iran. This was a surprising choice since Khamenei did not have the years of religious study and training that could anywhere near establish him as an Imam. No one could argue that Ali Khamenei was one of the best Islamic scholars in Iran.

Khalkhali's motive was to select someone to succeed Khomeini who would preserve the Ayatollah's legacy. He believed this was the best way to protect the role played by Khalkhali himself in establishing the brutal theocracy.

In their reign of terror, Khomeini and Khalkhali had firmly established the principal that the Islamic Republic could imprison, torture, and kill virtually "at will." The legal procedures were conducted without due process or even the semblance of a fair trial. As long as the victims were defined as enemies of the revolution or violators of Islamic law, they were convicted to death.

THE HARSH REALITY OF IRAN'S REVOLUTION

In the 1980s, the joyous exhilaration that welcomed the revolution turned into a harsh reality, often edging on despair. In the long and disastrous eight-year war against Iraq from 1980 through 1988, Iran lost between 450,000 and 960,000 in near suicidal battles. Iranians sent wave after wave of their own children into combat ahead of soldiers, sometimes without weapons, often just to clear the minefields.

During this time, Ayatollah Khomeini pushed the Iranian people to have more children. He believed that a larger Iranian population would have a competitive advantage. Moreover, he wanted to bolster the ranks of "soldiers for Islam," as the Imam was proclaiming the need for an "army of 20 million."

In 1979, as the revolution began, Iran had a population of approximately 30 million. Today, that number has swelled to some 90 million, with the result that 60 percent of the population is under age 30.

This demographic reality has important political and economic consequences. Those born since 1979 have no personal memories of pre-revolutionary Iran or life under the Shah. The Islamic Republic has established new universities to educate the youth. Still, some 1 million Iranians enter the workforce each year, while only some 300,000 new jobs are created. Unemployment rates in Iran run as high as 15 percent, with the jobless rate for those in the 15- to 29-year-old age group as high as 50 percent. Most of the unemployed in Iran today are university graduates.

Iran holds oil reserves of approximately 125.8 billion barrels of proven reserves, approximately 10 percent of the world's total. Exporting 4 million barrels a day at an average price of $55 per barrel (which is a discount off global market prices, but all Iran is able to charge the few nations willing to buy its sanctioned oil), Iran receives approximately $220 million per day in oil revenue. Yet, little of this oil wealth reaches the Iranian people.

The World Bank estimates that two thirds of the urban

population of Iran lives in poverty. Moreover, Iran has undergone a rapid process of urbanization since the revolution that has emptied many small villages and created a new urban underclass that lives in dire poverty, prostitution and international crime. More than 1.3 million people in Iran earn less than $1 a day.

The number of women engaged in prostitution in Iran is estimated at approximately 1 million; the number of hard drug addicts is estimated at about 2.5 million people. A growing sex slave trade in Iran is considered one of the country's most profitable businesses. Poor families may have no financial alternative but to sell a daughter into the sex trade. But those parents have no choice; if one child is not sold into sex slavery, the other children may not eat.

Since Khomeini took power on April Fools' Day in 1980 and established the "government of God", the *madressas* (religious schools known for intense indoctrination, a la brainwashing) in Iran have been turning out *shadeen*, suicide bombers by the thousands. Iranian leaders are preparing the entire nation for a world Islamic revolution, the second coming of the Twelfth Imam.

Most westerners think—wrongly—that, given a chance, the youth and university students of Iran would revolt against the ruling party. The opposite is true; this generation is the most dangerous yet because of the indoctrination they have received through the *madressas* and mullahs of Iran.

IRANIANS FLEE IRAN

Not surprisingly, since the revolution millions have fled Iran for safety and superior economic opportunities in other countries.

The International Monetary Fund estimates that every year

approximately 150,000 educated Iranians leave Iran in hopes of finding a better life abroad. This brain drain is one of the highest experienced by any country in the world. The situation is particularly serious among Iran's best-educated young people. As many as four out of five who win scientific awards attempt to emigrate.

Since the Islamic revolution, the population of Iranian expatriates in America numbers over 1 million people. California, especially Los Angeles County, has one of the largest Iranian expatriate communities in the world. The expatriates maintain strong contacts back in Iran.

Many Iranians living in the United States work with dissidents back home and work to help other family members escape. Expatriates in California operate private radio and television stations that daily broadcast in Farsi back to Iran. These radio and television stations provide Iranians with news not available through the censored media controlled by the mullahs.

Internet discussions have become a widespread phenomenon, supplementing the illegal satellite radio and television broadcast by the expatriate community. These serve as links to the outside through which the Iranian people are able to find out what is happening in the world. Iranians found hiding illegal satellite receivers are subject to arrest without notice, imprisoned without legal representation, and tortured or killed without notice to their families or friends.

The utopia of the Islamic revolution brought forth by Ayatollah Khomeini has turned into a nightmare for millions of Iranians. Even those who consider themselves friends and allies of the ultra-conservative theocracy can never live in quiet assurance. At any moment, the religious or political winds might suddenly shift. No one is safe from the whims of false accusation, imprisonment, torture, and even death that the radical clerics might impose upon them.

THE MULLAHS GET RICH

The only sure winners in the radical Islamic Republic of Iran are the mullahs themselves. These harsh clerics continue to preach hatred of America and Israel from the mosques. Meanwhile, they live as a criminal mafia.

Today, the mullahs are firmly in control of Iran's government-run businesses, including the oil industry. The top mullahs hide away millions in foreign bank accounts and foreign-controlled business ventures. In the past few years, the mullahs and their cronies have stashed nearly $400 billion in bank accounts in Dubai. Over 500,000 Iranians now make the United Arab Emirates their home, many with luxury high-rise apartments on Dubai's world class beaches.

Even the former president, Rafsanjani, has become a billionaire. Rafsanjani emerged from poverty before the revolution, starting out as a poor pistachio farmer in rural Iran. He began his political career by preaching Islam in the rural mosques. Today he is one of Iran's wealthiest citizens.

The Iranian theocracy can be profitable, providing you are one of the honored mullahs or one of their best friends. Holding top government positions and traveling internationally have benefited Iran's new religious rich. Yet their formula depends on the theocracy continuing to rule the people of Iran with an iron hand.

CHAPTER FOUR:

IRAN'S NUCLEAR AMBITION

"The nation of Islam will sit on the throne of the world,
and the world will be full of remorse."

—Khaled Mashaal, Hamas leader

"When the day comes that Tehran can announce its nuclear capability,
every shred of international law will have been discarded.
The mullahs have publicly sworn—to the United Nations and
the European Union and the International Atomic Energy
Agency—that they are not cheating. As they unmask their batteries,
they will be jeering at the very idea of an 'international community.'
How strange it is that those who usually fetishize the United Nations
and its inspectors do not feel this shame more keenly."

—Christopher Hitchens, British-American journalist

AS EARLY AS THE 2005, Meir Dagan, the head of Mossad, the Israeli Intelligence Agency at the time, told the Knesset that Iran was one to two years away, at the most, from having enriched uranium. Unfortunately, that estimate is less now. Much less.

IRAN IS DEFIANT FROM THE START

In an announcement that temporarily sent the U.S. stock market plunging in April 2006, Iran's former president, Akbar Hashemi

Rafsanjani, reported to the Kuwaiti news agency, JUNA, that Iran was producing enriched uranium from 164 centrifuges. These statements were confirmed in a televised speech on the same day by President Ahmadinejad.

On April 13, 2006, a request by the United Nations nuclear agency chief to halt uranium enrichment was rebuffed by Iran's president who said, "Uranium enrichment is a line in the sand from which my nation shall not retreat."

Just one day after the President of Iran challenged the U.N. nuclear agency over uranium enrichment, Ahmadinejad proclaimed that Israel was a permanent threat to the Middle East that would soon be liberated.

The setting was an Islamic fundraising conference which Ahmadinejad was hosting for the Palestinian terror organizations, Hamas and Islamic Jihad, with Iran's supreme leader Ayatollah Ali Khameini and smiling Hezbollah members sitting on the front row as he said:

"Like it or not, the Zionist regime is headed toward annihilation. The Zionist regime is a rotten dry tree that will be eliminated by one storm. Palestine will be liberated soon. The existence of the Israeli regime is a permanent threat to the Middle East. Its existence has harmed the dignity of Islamic nations.

The Great Satan, the United States, has hatched plots against Iran, Iraq, Syria and Lebanon to bring the entire region under Israeli control. The chain of plots by the American government against Iran, Iraq, Syria and Lebanon is aimed at governing the Middle East through the control of the Zionist regime, and it will not succeed."

ISRAEL AND THE U.S. RESPOND

Former Prime Minister Shimon Peres of Israel, responding on Israeli radio to Ahmadinejad's Hitler-like threats stated, "Iran's president represents the devil, not God. His extreme remarks are reminiscent of remarks made by ousted Iraqi dictator Saddam Hussein. Whoever has acted in such a manner has suffered the same fate," said Peres.

The *Washington Post* reported on April 9, 2006 in an article titled, "U.S. is Studying Military Strike Options on Iran" that Pentagon planners were studying how to penetrate eight-foot deep targets and are contemplating tactical nuclear devices. "The targeteers honestly keep coming back and saying it will require nuclear penetrator munitions to take out those tunnels," said Kenneth M. Pollack, a former CIA analyst.

According to the *Post* article, "Retired Air Force Col. Sam Gardiner, an expert in targeting and war games who teaches at the National Defense University, recently gamed an Iran attack and identified 24 potential nuclear-related facilities, some below 50 feet of reinforced concrete and soil.

At a conference in Berlin, Gardiner outlined a five-day operation that would require 400 "aim points," or targets for individual weapons, at nuclear facilities, at least 75 of which would require penetrating weapons. He also presumed the Pentagon would hit two chemical production plants, medium-range ballistic missile launchers and 14 airfields with sheltered aircraft. Special Operations forces would be required, he said.

Gardiner concluded that a military attack would not work but said he believes the United States seems to be moving inexorably toward it, and we are "very close to being left with only the military option."

If General Gardiner said that in 2006, what would he think of how close we are to having only a military option today?

One of my sources told me that a nuclear laser-guided bomb could penetrate a bunker under granite without killing the surrounding civilian population, would minimize the collateral damage, and make them acceptable tools. The problem, I was told, was that no earth-penetrating nuclear missile's blast can be contained. It would blow out radio-active dirt that would rain down on the local region.

There is currently no known way to knock out Iran's entirely underground nuclear development program without resorting to nuclear weapons ourselves.

IRAN'S MARTYRS

Training martyrs, which is another way of saying, brainwashing people into committing suicide for the Iranian government, is not a new tactic for Iran.

Almost two decades ago, in 2006, Reuters reported that some "200 Iranians had volunteered to carry out martyrdom missions against the U.S. and Britain interests if Iran was attacked over its nuclear program. They signed a document called 'registration form for martyrdom-seeking operations' and pledged to defend the Islamic republic's interests.

Since then, some 52,000 people have signed up to be involved in possible attacks. The Sunday Times in London has quoted unnamed Iranian officials as saying that Iran has 40,000 trained suicide bombers prepared to strike Western targets if Iran is attacked.

I hear you asking, but is Iran really willing to use these martyr volunteers?

During the Iran-Iraq War, Iran sent over 100,000 martyrs into the battle, many of them children under the age of 15 years. They were tied to one another to form long lines, a martyr's badge was given them, and they were sent out ahead of the troops to clear the mine fields.

It's one thing for United States to encourage Israel to be the one to launch a nuclear strike on Iran, but we much understand it will be Israel that pays the price for such an attack. We'll talk more later on the various forms of retaliation and the scale of them that Israel can expect if it attempts to take out Iran's nuclear program, but waves of suicide bombers are sure to be one of them.

THE U.S. HINTS THAT ISRAEL SHOULD STRIKE IRAN

At the onset of President George Bush's second term, Vice President Dick Cheney dropped a bombshell. He indicated that Iran was at the top of the list of the rogue enemies of America. Israel would, so to speak, be doing us a favor if they took out Iran's nuclear program, particularly if we didn't have to be involved militarily ourselves and without us being seen putting pressure on Israel to do it.

Indeed, what country wouldn't want its dirty work done by someone else, leaving itself free of blame and free of the inevitable retaliation by Iran?

My long-time friend and Prime Minister of Israel, Ehud Olmert offered this summation of Israel's position regarding a first strike against Iran:

> "As the one who has to make the decision, I can tell you that I genuinely don't think Israel should be on the forefront of this war. I don't know why people think this is first and foremost a war for Israel. It's a problem for every civilized country.
>
> Iran is a major threat to the well-being of Europe and America just as much as it is for the state of Israel. I don't think America can tolerate the idea of a leader of a nation of 30 million people who can openly speak of the liquidation of another country.
>
> And therefore, it is incumbent upon America and Europeans to form a strategy and implement it to remove this danger of unconventional weapons in Iran. To assume that Israel would be the first to go into a military confrontation with Iran represents a misunderstanding of this issue."

Are we surprised that Israel declined Cheney's invitation to take out Iran's nuclear program by itself... and suffer all the terrible consequences afterward by itself as well?

Over and over again, my Israeli friends stress to me that Iran is not an Israeli problem. "Iran is a world problem," I am told again and again.

"This is a clash of civilizations," is a constant theme of my discussions, regardless of who I speak with in Israel. "You in

America are the 'Great Satan' to the radical zealots in Iran," I am reminded, over and over again. "We in Israel are only the 'Little Satan.'"

Each time I return from the Middle East, I am more determined than ever that I must find a way to communicate to America the seriousness of the Iranian nuclear crisis. A showdown with Israel is coming, and America will be at the center of the conflict, whether we like it or not.

IRAN ENTERS THE SECOND PHASE
OF ITS GRAND PLAN

The first phase of the Islamic Revolution was to establish strict rule over Iran and institute a religious state focused on preparing for the coming of the Mahdi. The second, more ruthless phase of its revolution—the spread of radical Islam—has been underway for some twenty years, now.

The regime has expanded its version of radical Islam throughout the Gulf region—into Iraq and through Syria into the Palestinian territories as well. It has sent infiltrators, moles, and sleepers throughout the Middle East. It has and continues to fund, train, and arm terrorist groups.

At the same time phase two was happening, it commenced the third phase of its grand plan: doing its level best to obtain nuclear weapons.

Truly, obtaining nuclear weapons at any cost is the final insurance policy the ayatollahs and the mullahs may ever need. If dealing with Iran today is difficult for Israel and the United States, dealing with a nuclear-armed Iran will be impossible.

I fear the radical clerics ruling Iran are aware that their time is short unless they can firm up their position with nuclear weapons. Once Iran is nuclear-armed, Israel or the United States will have to go to the brink of a thermonuclear exchange if either country is to push a regime-change agenda in Iran.

It was President John F. Kennedy in a speech to the United Nations in 1963 who said:

> "Never before has man had such capacity. . . to end thirst and hunger, to conquer poverty and disease, to banish illiteracy and massive human misery. We have the [nuclear] power to make this the best generation of mankind in the history of the world—or make it the last."

If Iran is boldly supporting terrorism today, how outrageous will Iran be once the mullahs can protect terrorists with a nuclear umbrella? The possibilities of extortion by a nuclear Iran are enormous. We'll talk about those more later. . .and prepare to be horrified.

SANCTIONS AGAINST IRAN

In an effort to force Iran to modify its belligerent behavior, the United States and other western nations have imposed a number of sanctions against Iran.

- ✦ The first set was imposed in 1979 in response to the storming of the U.S. Embassy in Iran and the taking hostage of 44 Americans. These sanctions were lifted in January 1981 after the hostages were released.

+ A new set of sanctions was imposed by the United States in 1987 in response to Iran attacking U.S. ships and vessels of other countries in the Persian Gulf. Also cited as a cause for the second round of sanctions was Iran's support for terrorism around the world.

+ These sanctions were expanded in 1995 to include companies dealing with the Iranian government.

+ A third round of sanctions were imposed in December 2006 by the United Nations after Iran refused to comply with United Nations Security Council Resolution 1696, which demanded that Iran halt its uranium enrichment program.

+ These sanctions also restricted banking and insurance transactions (including with the Central Bank of Iran), shipping, web-hosting services for commercial endeavors, and domain name registration services.

+ Additional U.S. sanctions targeted investments in oil, gas, and petrochemicals, exports of refined petroleum products, and business dealings with the Islamic Revolutionary Guard Corps (IRGC).

+ A host of later UN Resolutions expanded sanctions against Iran as the countries of the world tried to twist the Iranian government's arm until it gave up its nuclear ambitions.

Over the years, sanctions have taken a serious toll on Iran's economy and people. Since 1979, the United States has led international efforts to use sanctions to influence Iran's policies, including Iran's uranium enrichment program, which Western governments fear is intended for developing the capability to produce nuclear weapons.

Of course, Iran counters that its nuclear program is for civilian purposes, including generating electricity and medical purposes.

But to Iran, this is not a matter of economics or even politics. To them, pursuing a nuclear weapons program is a holy endeavor. Through nuclear weapons, they believe they can eradicate Israel from the earth in an Armageddon-like conflict that will usher in the coming of the Mahdi, who will bring Islam to the entire world.

No amount of sanctions or arm-twisting is going to deter the Supreme Leader, and through him the entire Iranian government, from its holy mission to obtain a nuclear bomb.

A NUCLEAR ARMS TREATY WITH IRAN

Despite their determination never to give up on a nuclear weapon, the leadership of Iran eventually felt enough pressure from the sanctions regime to go to the negotiating table with the United States, Russia, China, The United Kingdom, and France, plus Germany together with the European Union, jointly referred to as the P5+1—the Permanent 5 +1.

In 2015, Iran signed the Joint Comprehensive Plan of Action, also called the JCPOA. It went into effect in January, 2016. Under its terms, Iran would dismantle much of its nuclear program and open its facilities to more extensive international inspections in returns for billions of dollars' worth of sanctions relief.

Middle Eastern states were upset by the JCPOA. They said they should have been consulted or included in the talks since they would be the most affected by a nuclear-armed Iran. Israel opposed the agreement, saying it was too lenient.

The P5+1's stated goal was to turn back Iran's nuclear program far enough that, if Iran decided to pursue building a nuclear weapon, it would take at least one year to complete the weapons, thereby giving world powers time to respond.

Israel had already taken preemptive military action against nuclear facilities in Iraq and Syria, and it was expected to do the same against Iran, perhaps triggering reprisals by Hezbollah and Hamas, and disruptions in oil transport in the Persian Gulf by Iran itself.

Saudi Arabia signaled that if Iran got a nuclear weapon, it would take steps to obtain nuclear weapons of its own. It was this escalation into a nuclear arms race in the Middle East that the P5+1 hoped to give themselves time to avoid.

In return, Iran received hundreds of billions of dollars. International sanctions from 2012 to 2014 alone cost Iran more than $100 billion in revenues. A timeline for lifting all sanctions was developed, and the most onerous sanctions regarding sale of oil were lifted immediately.

Under the terms of the JCPOA, Iran agreed not to produce the highly enriched uranium or plutonium necessary to build a nuclear weapon. Iran also agreed to restrict its Furdow, Natanz, and Arak facilities to only medical and industrial research.

Many of the JCPOA's restrictions on Iran's nuclear program had expiration dates. For example, restrictions on the number of centrifuges Iran can operate would be lifted gradually. After fifteen years, the amount of low-enriched uranium (suitable for nuclear power plants) that Iran can possess would also be lifted.

Most experts agree that, if all parties had adhered to the pledges, the deal almost certainly could have achieved the goal of keeping nuclear armament at bay for a decade or more. Critics pointed out that the JCPOA merely delayed Iran obtaining a nuclear weapon and did nothing to permanently stop Iran from getting a nuclear bomb.

U.S. WITHDRAWS FROM THE JCPOA

Two inspections in 2017 confirmed that Iran was in compliance with the JCPOA, and the bulk of sanctions were lifted. In May 2018, the United States withdrew from the JCPOA, and the Trump administration reinstated devastating banking and oil sanctions against Iran.

President Trump said the agreement failed to address Iran's ballistic missile program and its proxy warfare in the region and pointed out that the sunset provisions would enable Iran to pursue nuclear weapons in the future. He pledged that he could and would negotiate a better deal. He left office without fulfilling that pledge.

Following the U.S. withdrawal from the JCPOA, several countries continued to import Iranian oil under waivers granted by the Trump administration, and Iran continued to abide by its commitments to the JCPOA and allowing inspections of its nuclear facilities.

But, in 2019, the United States ended the oil waivers with the aim of halting Iran's oil exports completely.

Claiming breaches in the deal by its signatories, Iran immediately started to exceed agreed upon limits to its stockpile of low-enriched uranium and began enriching uranium to higher concentrations, although still far short of the purity required for weapons.

Iran also developed new centrifuges to increase uranium enrichment, resumed heavy water production at its Arak facility, and enriched uranium at Fordow, making the isotopes there unusable for medical purposes.

In 2020, The U.S. killed a top Iranian general, Qasem Soleimani. In response, Iran announced that it would no longer limit its uranium enrichment at all. In October of that year, it began building a new centrifuge facility at Natanz to replace the one destroyed several months earlier in an attack it blamed on Israel.

In November 2020, in response to the assassination of a prominent Iranian nuclear scientist (which Iran blamed Israel for), Iran's parliament passed a law that led to even more uranium enrichment.

In 2021, Iran announced new restrictions on the International Atomic Energy Agency's (IAEA's) ability to inspect Iranian facilities. Soon after, Iran ended its inspection agreement with the IAEA completely.

FATE OF THE JCPOA

In April of 2021, the P5+1 began talks with Iran to bring the United States and Iran back into the agreement. The talks have been off and on, but the election of conservative cleric Ebrahim Raisi as president of Iran and Russia's invasion of Ukraine have complicated matters.

Iran is insisting that United States must remove the Iranian Revolutionary Guard from its list of terrorist organizations. Iran also insists that its ballistic missile program should not be part of the negotiation, and it's insisting on restoration of its ability to bank internationally. And of course, Iran is insisting that all sanctions on sales of its oil must be lifted before it will sign anything, let alone scale back its nuclear program.

While all parties agree there is no better alternative than the terms of the current JCPOA, neither side is willing to sign the agreement again. Talks remains stalled, and Iran continues to charge full speed ahead with developing its nuclear program.

A LOOMING NUCLEAR ARMS RACE IN THE MIDDLE EAST

How many countries in the Middle East will demand nuclear weapons the moment Iran announces that they have succeeded in developing their own?

Certainly, Turkey will feel insecure and a NATO security guarantee may not be sufficient to relax its fears. Will Sunni Saudi Arabia be confident that the United States will protect it against a radical Shiite regime armed with nuclear weapons in Iran? Saudi leaders have been quoted as recently as 2022 saying with regards to a possible Middle East nuclear arms race, "If Iran gets nuclear weapons, all bets are off." Meaning, they absolutely plan to get nuclear weapons of their own in response.

Iran getting nuclear weapons will inevitably set off a nuclear arms race in the Middle East and Asia. Right now, only India and Pakistan have nuclear weapons in near East Asia. If Iran gets nuclear weapons, the number of countries pursuing nuclear weapons may instantly go to six or seven.

How about Egypt? Or even Syria? Who is to say Lebanon should not have nuclear weapons? Preventing a nuclear war between India and Pakistan has been difficult enough. Will a nuclear war be preventable when a half-dozen countries in the region have nuclear weapons capabilities? Particularly when a few of those countries are ruled by unstable, violent regimes?

Never before has the world stood at a moment where a nuclear holocaust could be occasioned by radical Islamic zealots who were committed to the elimination of Israel. Nuclear terrorism was the material for novels and Hollywood movies. How could nuclear terrorism be permitted in today's world?

The Israeli people are tired of terrorism. Israelis want nothing more than to come to peace with their Arab neighbors. But for this to happen, the Muslim world will have to accept Israel's right to exist. Saudi Arabia and the other Gulf States share a common interest with Israel in that all of them see Iran as their enemy. As the old saying goes, "The enemy of my enemy is my friend."

Is this the moment when Israel and its neighbors will finally come together in unity against a larger threat? Or will religious differences, old enmities, and long-held grudges keep the Gulf States at one another's throats while Iran gets nuclear weapons?

In coming years, it will be vital for Israel to form, if not full alliances with its Arab neighbors, at least friendly relations with them, and vice versa. If the regional powers do not come together, they will all find themselves held hostage by a nuclear Iran.

Of course, even if the entire Gulf region unites against Iran, we could still be in for the type of apocalypse that only radical zealots could anticipate with enthusiasm.

QUESTIONS MOUNT

A confrontation with Iran is building toward an inevitable crisis. Will Israel survive? This is a question we can no longer avoid asking, not in the face of a growing nuclear threat from an increasingly defiant Iran that grows more determined, more emboldened, and more belligerent with each passing day.

Mohammad Samadi, spokesperson for an Iranian group, the Committee for the Commemoration of Martyrs of the Global Islamic Campaign, stated Iran's determination to eliminate Israel with crystal clarity:

> "The first target is Israel. For us, that is the battlefield. All Jews are targets, whether military or civilian. It's our land and they are in the wrong place. It's their duty to pay attention to the safety of their own families and move them away from the battlefield [Israel]."

The Mossad (Israel's intelligence service) is advising the United States that the Iranians may be closer to possessing nuclear weapons capabilities than many thought, and Israel's political leadership echoes the warnings, saying that Iran's ability to build a nuclear bomb may be as little as a few months away.

The questions posed by this news are very real and very disturbing:

- Why did the U.S. agree that Iran could begin enriching uranium as long as they could show the U.N. it was for peaceful purposes?

- Why has the U.S. not implemented specific measures to force Russia to stand down providing Iran educational and technical assistance with its nuclear program?

- Iran boasts of having graduated 50,000 suicide bombers; where are they? Are they already in America?

- How will the world respond to Iran's threats to blow up the Strait of Hormuz if attacked?

- How does belief in the 12th Imam (The Mahdi) influence the Supreme Leader and president of Iran?

- Are the Iranians willing to precipitate an apocalyptic event with worldwide repercussions to achieve their goal of preparing the world for what they believe to be the return of the Mahdi?

- Is there a way to thwart Iran's advance in the nuclear arms race?

- How will the United States respond if sanctions against Iran are ineffective. . .which they already are?

+ What would happen if Israel were to attack Iran's nuclear facilities?

+ What would happen if the U.S. were to attack Iran's nuclear facilities?

+ What are Russia's and China's roles in Iran?

+ If Vladimir Putin resorts to using nuclear weapons in Ukraine, will he go ahead and give Iran the nuclear technology it has been asking him for?

+ Has Iran's massive military aid to Russia in its invasion of Ukraine earned it repayment in the final nuclear technology it seeks?

+ Will Iran use black gold and nuclear blackmail to subjugate the world?

+ How much time do we really have to wait for the answer to these questions?

+ The question above all other questions is this: How close are we to World War III?

Although I will attempt to answer to these questions and more in the pages of this book, the real answer lies in the pages of another Book. I've said many times that this scenario being played out on the world stage is a battle between two spirits and two books.

With the advent of the Russia-Ukraine War, I can now add that this scenario is also being played out over two wars: one a cold war for nuclear dominance in the Middle East, and the other on the killing fields of Ukraine. The two are inextricably linked, and the outcome of one will likely determine the outcome of the other.

The battle will ultimately be won, not by conventional weapons, but by the One who sits upon the throne and judges in righteousness.

A COMING WAR WITH IRAN?

No matter what lies it tells, Iran is pursuing a secret nuclear weapons program, in defiance of world diplomats and the United Nation's International Atomic Energy Agency (IAEA).

Israel and the United States have both announced that Iran will not be permitted to develop a deliverable nuclear weapon. If current diplomatic attempts to bring Iran into compliance with the inspection requests of the International Atomic Energy Agency do not work, then a pre-emptive military strike by Israel or the United States becomes increasingly likely.

This is not science fiction. Iran is governed by radical Shiite zealots who believe in a messianic Islamic religious figure, named the "Mahdi." In 941 A.D., the Mahdi disappeared down a well, passing into Islamic fame as the "Lost Imam."

The Supreme Leaders of Iran have declared to the world that they have a "mission from Allah" to bring about the Apocalypse needed as a precondition to occasion the Second Coming of the Mahdi. The return of the Mahdi, also known as the "Twelfth Imam," is predicted in Shiite Islam to be the dawn of a new era. With the Second Coming of the Mahdi, Shiite Muslims expect to realize the final triumph of Islam worldwide.

Iran's leadership has declared that its divine mission on earth is to set the stage for the Mahdi to return. This will fulfill the prophecies of Ayatollah Khomeini who foretold that Iran's destiny was to destroy Israel and the United States in a final religious war. Iran truly believes it is fated to fulfill a mission that has been foretold in Islam since the days of Prophet Muhammed.

The problem is that the cult of the Mahdi believes a worldwide Apocalypse must happen before Islam triumphs globally. So, Iran's mission may well be to bring about the Apocalypse as a precondition to the Mahdi's Second Coming. Nothing could be dearer to the hearts of Iran's Twelver rulers. The Mahdi destiny, they believe, is to lead Islam in defeating all other religions, ushering a new era of Islamic justice upon the world.

The moment the mullahs in Iran have nuclear weapons, world politics will forever be changed. So, how can Iran be stopped?

One option involves diplomacy, possibly even tougher sanctions than ever before. However, with the recent alliance between Russia and Iran, support from Russia could keep Iran's economy afloat for years, if not decades. Add in China and India to the group of powers willing to bust Western sanctions, and Iran will be able to shrug off and largely ignore sanctions from the West, now.

If diplomacy fails, the only recourse may be war. Will Israel launch a pre-emptive strike? Or will the United States attack Iran, possibly with a coalition that includes Israel?

War against Iran is not an option the United States or Israel wants to pursue. Yet, the religious zealots in Iran are single-minded in their determination to export their radical revolution. The world has never before experienced a terror-supporting state in possession of nuclear weapons.

When Ayatollah Khamenei says he wants Israel wiped from the map, we should all listen. When President Raisi says he wants America destroyed, he is not ranting fantasies; he is stating official regime policy.

The world has not witnessed a head of state proclaiming a declaration of war against the Jews since Hitler became chancellor in Germany. World War II eliminated Hitler, but at a cost of sixty million deaths, including the genocidal Holocaust in which six million Jews were killed. How many will need to die to rid the world of the nuclear weapons threat in Iran? Today, a world thermonuclear war could kill hundreds of millions.

Is this a price we will have to pay? With Iran defying the world community and pushing for nuclear weapons, the time grows short.

IRAN'S PLAN TO CHECKMATE THE WORLD

We should never forget that the Persians invented the game of chess. The intent of Ayatollah Khamenei, Iran's current Supreme Leader, is for Iran to get nuclear weapons in a way that the mullahs can announce to the world "checkmate in three moves." The Iranians intend to play the chess match such that there is nothing the United States or Israel can do to stop them from developing nuclear weapons.

Remember, Ayatollah Khomeini has affirmed that Iran is on a mission from God to extend its revolution worldwide. Iran's ultimate goal is for its version of Shiite Islam to set an agenda of submission for non-believers around the globe. The ayatollahs and the mullahs currently ruling Iran have the conviction of their religious fervor that Allah has pre-ordained their destiny. They believe that nothing any of us may do can deter them from the path of success.

From the day Ayatollah Khomeini returned to Tehran, the religious radicals in Iran believed they would win because we are weak. Khomeini inspired the mullahs in their conviction that the Western nations, including the United States, lacked Iran's religious zeal. Since February 1, 1979, Iran has never deviated from the goal of wiping Israel off the map. With a zealot's intensity, the Iranian mullahs believe the destruction of Israel is a divinely intentioned goal they are destined to fulfill.

Khomeini taught that while the Western nations supported Israel, the United States lacked Iran's unwavering resolve. The Iranians calculate that western nations, including the United States, will stop short of war to protect Israel. Iran also knows that America and Europe have an insatiable desire for oil with which Iran is well endowed. Indeed, the mullahs see Iran's ample oil endowment as part of God's plan for their victory.

The Russia-Ukraine War may have reminded the West of the urgency of moving away from petroleum as its primary source of energy. But the West is still decades away from complete independence from oil. The first year of the Ukraine War saw oil reserves in the West dip precipitously as leaders released their national oil reserves to stabilize the price of oil and heat homes across Europe. At some point, those reserves will no longer exist, and Iran's chess piece labeled oil will become extremely powerful.

With abundant oil, Iran can recruit oil-poor nations including China and India, both massive consumers of oil, as allies. These powerful nations would turn against America and Europe for oil. Oil-greedy nations would likely turn a blind eye to Iran's militaristic intentions. The pay-off for looking the other way would be ready access on a preferred basis to continued supplies of Iranian natural gas and oil.

Ayatollah Khomeini preached that the old guard ruling Russia were still communists in their hearts and that the Russians felt the Cold War had been stolen from them. Khomeini rightly predicted that Russia would be a ready ally for Iran.

IRAN'S SECRET PLAN

Still, Iran could only obtain nuclear weapons by pursuing a stealth plan. If Iran openly announced its intention of develop nuclear weapons, the world would have intervened to prevent this from happening.

By using deception and claiming that it wanted nuclear power only for peaceful purposes, Khomeini realized the West would be hoodwinked. Countries such as France, Germany, and the United Kingdom would be cautious but desirous of obtaining favored access to Iran's oil and natural gas reserves. The French and Germans could also be bought with lucrative contracts to help build Iran's "peaceful" nuclear infrastructure.

The strategy Iran put in place was brilliant. By remaining a signatory to the Nuclear Non-Proliferation Treaty (NPT), Iran could claim a right to pursue nuclear energy for peaceful purposes. This lie would not be discovered until too late.

From the beginning, Ayatollah Khomeini calculated his radical revolutionaries would ultimately be able to checkmate the world.

Then no country would be able to stop Iran from realizing its cherished goals—goals that Ayatollah Khomeini had predicted were destined by Allah to be fulfilled.

Now Ayatollah Khamenei is in place as Iran's Supreme Leader, his mission: fulfill Khomeini's dream of ushering in the Mahdi. Religious zealots in Iran know without a doubt that the day is growing close when a surprise nuclear attack to destroy Israel can be launched successfully.

NETANYAHU EXPRESSES CONCERN

Prime Minister (again), Benjamin Netanyahu, has been deeply apprehensive from the very beginning concerning the threat a nuclear Iran poses to Israel:

> "We must take whatever action is required to prevent Iran from getting nuclear weapons. I hope we can get effective action in the United Nations. But if Iran does succeed, the Islamic international militancy will have a nuclear umbrella under which they will continue carrying out their terrorist activities. We also cannot rule out that Iran would use nuclear weapons to destroy the State of Israel, to wipe Israel off the map, as Iran has threatened."

I asked my friend the next obvious question, does Netanyahu see a nuclear-armed Iran as a threat to America?

"Absolutely," Netanyahu answers very seriously. "A nuclear-armed Iran is a threat to the whole world and it must be prevented."

Netanyahu believes that, to prevent Iran from getting nuclear arms, we must "puncture their hope." And just how does he think the U.S. can do that?

Netanyahu explains it this way:

> "We must take whatever preventative action is necessary, but we must convince Iran once and for all that the responsible world will never allow the Iranian regime to possess nuclear weapons—not while Iran openly threatens to destroy Israel and America."

CHAPTER FIVE

IRAN DECIDES TO GO NUCLEAR

"War is a blessing for the world and for every nation."

—Ayatolloh Khomeini,
December 12, 1984

"The application of an atomic bomb would not leave anything in Israel."

—Hashemi-Rafsanjani,
Former Prime Minister 2001

IRAN HAS MOVED with great determination to become a nuclear weapons power as fast as possible. Make no mistake about it. The strategy employed to get to this goal has been both subtle and brilliant.

IRAN NUCLEAR FACILITIES WERE BUILT TO BE ATTACKED

Why, if a nation's intentions for its nuclear program were completely peaceful, would any nation go to the trouble and expense of building nuclear facilities underground, in hidden locations, in concrete and steel reinforced bunkers hardened to withstand bunker buster bombs and even direct nuclear strikes?

This question has kept me up at night for many years, and it has surely kept many senior Israeli government and defense officials awake at night also. Unfortunately, there's only one logical answer: Iran's nuclear program is not now and never has been peaceful in purpose.

We can go all the way back to 1981 to the earliest days of Iran's nuclear program, and even then, their interest in nuclear development was clearly military in nature. It was never focused on developing civilian nuclear power plants. Indeed, Iran went to school studying how Israel launched a military strike against Iraq's nuclear reactor at Osirak in June 1981.

The Israeli attack was relatively simple because Iraq had only one major nuclear facility. So, Iran resolved not to make this same mistake. As a defensive move, Iran decided to decentralize their nuclear facilities around the country. Many nuclear facilities could be embedded in population centers. Thus, to attack successfully, Israel or the United States would have to launch a multi-pronged strike that would be more tactically difficult to plan and implement successfully.

With nuclear facilities inside Iran's cities, a military strike by Israel or the United States would cause civilian casualties. Would Israel and America be willing to kill tens of thousands of Iranian civilians to take out Iran's nuclear facilities in a pre-emptive military attack? Clearly, this would raise the stakes against Iran's enemies.

Iran further determined that each separate nuclear installation would be devoted to a single purpose, a piece that could be fitted into the puzzle. This way, if a particular facility were attacked and destroyed, Iran would lose only the functionality fulfilled at that location.

Some operations would be duplicated in more than one facility. Others might be replaced by outsourcing the fulfillment of the function to a friendly country, perhaps to Russia or to Pakistan.

So, the principle of decentralization was reinforced by the principle of compartmentalization. No successful attack on any one facility could knock Iran's nuclear capabilities offline for long.

Iran's nuclear facilities were designed from the beginning with the expectation that they would be attacked and that the system as a whole would need to remain operational. Even if particular components were destroyed or were temporarily put out of service as a result of a military strike, Iran could rebuild the nuclear system quickly.

IRAN'S "FULL FUEL CYCLE" NUCLEAR PLAN

Iran's nuclear program has been built to create a "full fuel cycle," going all the way from raw uranium ore to weapons-grade uranium. Iran's ability to create its own weapons grade uranium is entirely housed inside its own borders. Its program is designed to be completely self-sufficient.

Each facility is separate, compartmentalized, handling only one step in the uranium enrichment process. All the facilities work together in an elaborate plan, designed so attacking any one piece will not put the entire system out of operation.

URANIUM ORE AND INITIAL PROCESSING

So, where does Iran get its raw uranium ore from?

Since 1988, Iran has opened an estimated 10 different uranium mines inside Iran. It's estimated that the uranium resources of Iran are in the range of 20,000—30,000 tons throughout the country, more than enough to fuel Iran's civilian nuclear power plants well into the future.

Iran's main uranium processing facility is located at Isfahan, a central Iranian city, some 250 miles south of Tehran.

The Nuclear Technology and Research Center in Isfahan is said to employ as many as 3,000 scientists, in a facility constructed about 15 kilometers southeast of central Isfahan, at a research complex constructed by the French under a 1975 agreement with Iran.

On the eastern outskirts of Isfahan is the Uranium Conversion Facility, a cluster of buildings, surrounded by razor wire fencing, and protected by anti-aircraft guns and military patrols.

In a connected, underground facility, the uranium ore, commonly known as "yellowcake" ore, is processed into uranium hexafluoride gas (UF4), the first step required to convert uranium ore to the enriched state needed to run a nuclear power plant or to provide the weapons-grade uranium needed to make an atom bomb.

URANIUM ENRICHING

From Isfahan, the uranium hexafluoride gas is transported to yet another facility, this one at Natanz, about 90 miles to the northeast of Isfahan.

Here the uranium hexafluoride gas is enriched in centrifuges to the higher-grade uranium-235. This completes the "full fuel cycle," ending with enriched uranium. At lower grades of enrichment (3 to 5 % enriched), the uranium can be used to fuel peaceful power plants. Uranium enriched to uranium-235 can also be fashioned into the metallic form needed for the fissile core of an atom bomb.

The Fuel Enrichment Plant at Natanz is located about 10 miles to the northeast of the town of Natanz. It houses two large underground halls built 8 meters below ground. The halls are hardened by thick underground concrete reinforcing walls built to protect the facility. The construction was designed to house an advanced centrifuge complex of as many as 50,000 centrifuges.

As of the September 2022 IAEA quarterly report, Iran had 2782 advanced centrifuges of various types installed at its three enrichment facilities at Natanz and Fordow as well as 7110 installed IR-1 centrifuges. Most of these advanced centrifuges are IR-2m, IR-4, and IR-6 centrifuges.

Some reports place the current number of advanced centrifuges operating in Natanz and Fordow at closer more than 4,000 as of the writing of this book.

Operating at full capacity, the Natanz centrifuges reported in 2022 were capable of producing enough weapons-grade uranium to build over 20 weapons per year. It's thought that, with the new centrifuges rumored to have been built, Natanz could produce enough weapons grade uranium for one nuclear warhead in as little as five days.

The underground facilities have no visible above ground signature, a move designed to complicate precise targeting of any munitions that could be used to attack the facility. Even publicly available satellite photos show plentiful military defense and anti-aircraft installations designed to provide security for these sites.

The Iranians paid careful attention to facility design both for the professional operation of nuclear activity and for the military preparedness needed to protect the facilities from attack.

WHY IRAN HALTED URANIUM PROCESSING

In November 2004, Iran agreed to stop all processing of uranium at both Isfahan and Natanz. Iran made this decision to comply with a pre-condition set by the EU3 (the European Union countries of France, Germany, and the United Kingdom) for negotiations to begin.

The goal of the EU3 was to settle with Iran the IAEA requirements for facility inspection. The IAEA wanted to determine that Iran was compliant with the provisions of the NPT prohibiting the development of nuclear weapons. The IAEA was obligated to hold Iran to a standard of "transparency," meaning that all Iranian nuclear facilities and operations should be open to IAEA inspection at times and places of the IAEA's choosing.

The IAEA and the EU3 believed that Iran was using inspection restrictions to conceal nuclear weapons activities. If Iran were allowed to limit inspections to certain times and to certain facilities or particular areas within facilities, the "advanced warning" limitations would give workers the opportunity to "sanitize" operations prior to inspection.

International skeptics argued that Iran only agreed to suspend uranium processing because Isfahan and Natanz were not yet complete and more time was needed by Iran to finish facility construction and resolve technical problems.

By agreeing to "stop" operations Iran was truly not ready

to begin, they merely seized the opportunity to appear cooperative. Skeptics argued Iran's primary goal was simply to buy more time.

Thus began a pattern that has continued to this day of obfuscating and appearing to cooperate while actually hiding the full extent of Iran's progress toward weapons-grade nuclear enrichment.

HOW IRAN CHEATED

In September 2004, Iran told the IAEA in a report little noticed at the time that the country planned to process some 40 tons of uranium into uranium hexafluoride gas. This notice was largely forgotten as soon as Iran announced in November 2004 that uranium processing and enrichment were being voluntarily suspended.

Then in February 2005, an IAEA report was leaked to the Associated Press suggesting that Tehran was planning on processing 37 tons of yellowcake uranium oxide, estimated to be enough to make about five small atomic bombs.

The report caused a blow-up in the press. Ali Akbar Salehi, a senior Foreign Ministry advisor, was forced to admit:

> "That we want to process 37 metric tons of uranium ore into hexafluoride gas is not a discovery. The IAEA has been aware of Iran's plan to construct the Uranium Conversion Facility in Isfahan since it was a barren land. We haven't constructed the Isfahan facility to produce biscuits but hexafluoride gas."

This type of reluctant, forced admission raised concerns in the international community that Iran was deliberately lying about its nuclear intentions. Was Iran going to process uranium or not? The answer to that question was not clear.

Then, in May 2005, international rumors circulated suggesting that Iran had gone ahead with processing the 37 tons of uranium ore, suggesting that work at Isfahan had never been suspended after all, or that after completing construction there, Isfahan was now fully operational.

To resolve this controversy, Mohammad Saeedi, the deputy head of the Atomic Energy Organization of Iran (AEOI), was forced to come forward and explain to the international press, "We converted all the 37 tons of uranium concentrate known as yellowcake into UF4 at the Isfahan Uranium Conversion Facility before we suspended work there."

Again and again, Iran admitted to nothing until it was caught, and then it shrugged and casually admitted to what there was already outside evidence confirming.

IRAN OPENLY RESUMES URANIAUM PROCESSING AT ISFAHAN

On June 25, 2005, Ahmadinejad was elected president and construction of Iran's nuclear processing facilities was complete. Ayatollah Khamenei had everything in place needed to take the regime in the ultra-conservative direction he believed would fulfill Ayatollah Khomeini's prophecy. Never had the moment been so right for Iran and so wrong for the United States and Israel.

In August 2005, Iran openly resumed processing uranium at

Isfahan, defiantly breaking its earlier promise to suspend uranium processing while the EU-3 negotiations were proceeding. Iran's aggressive defiance was met with confusion and inaction from the United States and the Europeans.

Iran knew its unilateral move to resume uranium processing at Isfahan would throw a monkey wrench into the U.S. plan to corner it. Yet even here, the Iranians were calculating carefully, taking one step at a time.

By not opening Natanz, which housed the second half of the enrichment process, the Iranians technically were not engaging in uranium enrichment. Carefully, the Iranians were moving their pieces on the chessboard, always with a view to being able one day to declare a surprise checkmate.

In response to Isfahan's opening, the IAEA began a series of crisis meetings. On September 24, 2005, the International Atomic Energy Agency voted at the urging of the United States to hold Iran in non-compliance with the Nuclear Non-Proliferation Strategy.

In Tehran, Foreign Minister Manouchehr Mottaki called the IAEA resolution "political, illegal, and illogical." On state-run television, Mottaki portrayed the EU-3 as puppets of the United States, claiming that "the three European countries implemented a planned scenario already determined by the United States."

That same week, John Bolton, the U.S. Ambassador to the UN, told the House International Relations Committee that Iran had a choice to make:

"Right now, in the aftermath of the IAEA resolution, it's unmistakably up to Iran to decide whether it's going to continue a policy of pursuing nuclear weapons or whether it's going to give it up, as did the government of Libya."

Apparently, Tehran wasn't impressed with that warning shot across the bow by Bolton when he invoked the massive air raid and bombing of Libya the United States had launched (in retaliation for the Khaddafi regime bombing a night club in West Berlin, killing three, including a U.S. serviceman, and injuring 229). Iran continued on with its nuclear program unabated.

IRAN THREATENS TO RESUME URANIUM ENRICHMENT AT NATANZ

Reuters next reported on November 17, 2005, that Iran was preparing to process a new batch of 250 drums of yellowcake uranium at Isfahan. This left no doubt about Iran's intentions. Iran evidently did not want to resume negotiations with the EU-3 if resuming negotiations meant forfeiting the right to process uranium.

The Iranian decision was particularly defiant, given that the IAEA was expected to meet on November 24 to vote on the September resolution to take Iran to the Security Council.

Immediately, Russia put a proposal of its own on the table. To break the impasse, Russia offered to establish a joint venture with Iran to operate a uranium enrichment facility located in Russia. Once again, the IAEA postponed a decision to take Iran to the

United Nations Security Council for additional sanctions, preferring instead to give Russia time to develop more fully the alternative and to win Iranian acceptance of the idea.

Once again, Iran had calculated correctly. By taking the defiant path, Iran had thrown the IAEA and the EU-3 into confusion. Rather than confront Iran, the first impulse of the IAEA and the EU-3 was to retreat, hoping they could still work out a diplomatic solution.

THE IRANIAN'S ATOMIC STRATEGY

Skillfully, the Iranians had gone from enriching uranium, to not enriching uranium, to maybe enriching uranium, and finally to enriching uranium again. They played the same dance in their negotiations—first the Iranians refused to negotiate, then they began negotiating, only once again to break off negotiations.

Now the Iranians said they would negotiate again, but Iran would not give up the right to enrich uranium in their own country, not even to Russia. The Iranians would talk, but only as long as the talks were on their terms.

With every move, Iran bought more time. With every start and stop, confusion deepened in the United States and among the Europeans, just as Ayatollah Khomeini had foretold decades earlier.

With his team of radical true believers more firmly in command than ever and the West in disarray over his nuclear program, Khamenei could see his path to the end game and winning his chess match with the world. Iran would have the nuclear weapons it needed to fulfill the vision to wipe Israel off the face of the earth.

CHAPTER SIX:

TWO DECADES OF CONCEALMENT

"For the last three years we have been doing intensive verification in Iran, and even after three years I am not yet in a position to make a judgment on the peaceful nature of Iran's nuclear program."

—Mohamed ElBaradei,
IAEA Director-General, January 2006

"Unless and until Iran provides technically credible explanations for the presence of uranium particles of anthropogenic origin at three undeclared locations in Iran and informs the Agency of the current location(s) of the nuclear material and/or of the contaminated equipment, the Agency will not be able to confirm the correctness and completeness of Iran's declarations under its Comprehensive Safeguards Agreement. Because it has not yet done so, the Agency is not in a position to provide assurance that Iran's nuclear programme is exclusively peaceful."

—Rafael Mariano Grossi,
IAEA Director-General 12 Sept 2022

FOR SOME 20 YEARS, the Islamic Republic of Iran has pursued a policy of concealment and deception regarding the development of their nuclear industries. Iran's strategy was to obfuscate and lie about their nuclear plans, while all the time pressing forward quietly, but with determination.

THE RUSSIAN-BUILT REACTOR AT BUSHEHR

In 1992, Russia agreed to build a nuclear reactor for Iran at Bushehr, for a cost of between $800 million and $1 billion. Bushehr is located in southern Iran, along the Persian Gulf, a location consistent with Iran's plan to decentralize their nuclear facilities.

The Russians finally finished the Bushehr nuclear reactor in October 2004. "We're done," was the statement of a spokesperson for Russia's Atomic Energy Agency (Rosatom). "All we need to do now is work out an agreement on sending spent fuel back to Russia."

In spite of initial construction being completed in 2004, it wasn't until 2013 that Bushehr finally began to produce power for the Iranian power grid.

A reasonable argument can be made that the plant was never intended to produce electricity. Instead, the real goal may have been to create a subterfuge. . .and lots of spent uranium, which could be diverted to Russia to make nuclear bombs.

IRAN'S HEAVY WATER FACILITY AT ARAK

Little noticed in this ongoing drama over Iran's uranium enrichment program was the quiet resolve with which Iran continued to work on building its heavy-water facility located at Arak, yet another nuclear plant. Arak is in central Iran, 150 miles to the southwest of Tehran.

The only reason Iran would need a heavy water facility is if the country were planning to build a plutonium bomb. The Russian-built reactor at Bushehr does not use heavy water. Heavy water is required to moderate the nuclear chain reaction needed to produce weapons grade plutonium.

Fission bombs requiring plutonium are more sophisticated to design and detonate than bombs using uranium-235. But the explosive magnitude of plutonium bombs is many times greater.

By focusing the discussion on uranium enrichment, the Iranians were telegraphing their decision to build first a simpler, more reliable uranium bomb. Even when the first nuclear bombs were designed by the Manhattan Project in World War II, scientists have always known that the mechanics of building a gun-type uranium device were simpler and more reliable.

The first atomic bomb ever exploded in combat, the bomb dropped on Hiroshima, was a simple gun-type design uranium-235 atomic bomb. That weapon was considered so reliable that no prototype was ever tested.

Building a heavy water facility at Arak suggested that Iran was on the same path. First, Iran would build a simple, gun-type design uranium bomb. Yet, not far behind, Iran evidently planned to be able to build a plutonium device of higher yield and greater destructive power.

OPPOSITION FROM INSIDE IRAN

Iran has typically kept nuclear activities secret until details of those activities were reported by others.

One group that has hounded Iran is the National Council for Resistance on Iran (NCRI), the political arm for the People's Mujahedin of Iran (also known as the Mujahadeen Khalk, or the People's Mujahedin, the MEK).

The MEK was formed in Tehran in the 1965, as a far leftist, anti-imperialist organization dedicated to the overthrow of the

Shah. Their communist sympathies never fit into Ayatollah Khomeini's view of radical Islam. The mullahs forced the MEK to leave Iran, causing the organization to split up, with factions settling in the United States, France, and Iraq.

The National Council of Resistance of Iran has formed a coalition with a number of anti-government groups and is today considered to be the largest political opposition to the Iranian government. The NCRI has long called for an end to human rights abuses inside Iran and an end to financing terrorist groups such as Hamas, Hezbollah, and other militant groups. It also strongly opposes Iran obtaining nuclear weapons.

The nuclear facility at Natanz was clandestine and completely unknown to the outside world until the National Council of Resistance for Iran (NCRI) revealed the site in a press conference held in Washington, D.C. in mid-August 2002.

The NCRI press release was highly detailed, and none of the information in it was known to the IAEA. Afterwards, the IAEA investigated and confirmed the accuracy of the NCRI report, and then declared Iran in breach of the Nuclear Non-Proliferation Treaty.

The NCRI issued another press release on November 14, 2004 disclosing a major nuclear site in Tehran that had been kept secret. According to the document, the Iranian Ministry of Defense had set up "The Modern Defense Readiness and Technology Center" (MDRTC) on a 60-acre site previously occupied by three heavy transport battalions operating under the Ministry of Defense.

The report explained that "activities in nuclear and biological warfare" that had previously been performed elsewhere were moved to the MDRTC. This was an important report. For the first time, it was revealed that the Iranian government had assigned nuclear work to the military, keeping the military operation secret from Iran's own atomic energy agency.

The NCRI information was obviously obtained from MEK undercover agents operating in Iran. Much of what was reported had previously not been known by the IAEA, or by American intelligence units, including the CIA. Not all aspects of the NCRI's reports have been fully accurate, but the vast majority of what they have exposed has subsequently been verified by the IAEA or one of the major intelligence agencies around the world.

IAEA MISSES SEEING IRANIAN NON-COMPLIANCE

Reading IAEA reports starting as early as 2005 and continuing until today, it is clear that Iran has actively engaged in extensive concealment behavior and intentionally took steps to mislead IAEA inspectors.

What the diplomatic language of the various IAEA reports through the years takes pains to gloss over is the international embarrassment caused to the IAEA every time Iran's deception is revealed by someone else.

A long string of third party disclosures and international press reports have forced IAEA inspectors to go back and look for what they've missed over the years. Each time this happens, the IAEA is forced to issue new, corrected reports. The embarrassment to the IAEA is immediate as the world realizes that the Iranians have fed the IAEA lies, half-truths, and outright deceptions. . .and the IAEA has swallowed them.

It took the release of the truth by opposition groups such as the NCRI to finally expose publicly Iran's clandestine nuclear activities. The obvious conclusion is that the IAEA still cannot be relied upon to do its job.

THE IAEA DOCUMENTS LEAK

In 2018, the Mossad seized a large cache of stolen IAEA documents that the Iranian government had accessed as early as 2003 and used to create cover stories for its nuclear program. The documents were circulated among senior Iranian military, government, and nuclear officials, and constituted a serious breach of internal security at the IAEA.

Using these documents, Iran designed answers to IAEA inquiries where it admitted to what the IAEA already knew, offered up information that the IAEA would likely discover on its own, and hid what the IAEA did not yet know. Iranian officials were able to change dates on their own records, change corporate registration records to show a civilian company owning a government-operated uranium mine, and obfuscate other parts of their nuclear program in this fashion.

The Iranians also got advance notice of IAEA inspections through the same intelligence methods used to obtain the confidential records. In one example, a planned inspection of the Arak Heavy Water Production site was reported to officials at Arak well before the visit, giving them plenty of time to set up the site to look as if it was only being used for medical and research use.

The Iranians used their inside information to hide a container of radiation-monitoring equipment from IAEA inspectors, to hide uranium conversion research Iran was carrying out, to hide nuclear material Iran has received from China, and to obfuscate its Green Salt project, which aimed to produce tetrafluoride, an intermediate material used in producing feed material for uranium enrichment.

The exposure of Iran's systematic program to deceive the IAEA should have been a wake-up call to the IAEA and to the world. And yet, the IAEA never received a satisfactory explanation from Iran regarding the stolen documents and information, let alone punished Iran for its egregious deceptions.

The exposure of the widespread theft of IAEA documents removed any lingering doubt that Iran's systematic policy of fraud, theft, obfuscation, and concealing evidence from the IAEA and the world is real. The facts of the matter are no longer in question.

IRAN'S SHAHAB MISSILES

It's not enough for Iran to develop weapons-grade uranium. It also has to have a missile system to deliver nuclear weapons fueled by that uranium to its enemies. Not surprisingly, at the same time Iran set about building a nuclear materials program, it also set about designing and building a new missile system.

On September 21, 2004, a Shahab-3 missile was first paraded in Tehran with banners proclaiming, "We will crush America under our feet" and "Wipe Israel off the map."

In July 2005, Iran announced that a solid-fuel engine had been successfully tested for the country's mainstay missile, the Shahab-3. The significance of equipping the Shahab-3 with a solid-fuel engine is that less time is required to prepare the missile for firing. Also, solid fuel technology generally adds greater reliability and accuracy to the missile's performance.

The Shahab-3 is a single-stage, medium-range ballistic missile based on the North Korean "Nodong" missile series, with a reliable range of approximately 995 miles (1,600 kilometers) and a maximum range estimated at 1,250 miles. This is more than enough to hit Tel Aviv or U.S. military troops stationed in Turkey.

Anti-missile systems are most effective if they can detect early preparations to fire a missile and if they can hit the missile when it is first leaving the launching pad before it accelerates to high speed or reaches high altitude. Missiles in full flight are more difficult to hit. Think of the difficulty of hitting one bullet in flight with another bullet fired at it.

Exercises conducted by United States and Israel tested the ability of their respective missile defense systems, the U.S. Patriot Missile Defense System and Israel's Arrow-2 system, to knock down incoming ballistic missiles. One such exercise, Operation Juniper Cobra, demonstrated that the missile defense systems were reliable against a single missile attack, but the reliability was far less assured if the attack involved a barrage of missiles launched simultaneously.

On June 14, 2005, the NCRI held another press conference in Washington, D.C. to announce that Iran had just completed Shahab-4 missile tests at a firing range within Iran. The Shahab-4 is also a single-stage missile but with a greater range, approximately 1,250 miles (2,000 km), comfortably reaching into Europe.

When Iran's ICBM development program is eventually completed, it will be able to strike anywhere on the globe.

IRAN'S PURSUIT OF AN ICBM

The Emad missile, tested in 2015, is a modified, medium range version of the medium-range Ghadr and Shahab-3 missiles. The modification fitted it with four-small winglets at the base of the warhead, similar to those usually used to steer a warhead during re-entry into the atmosphere. While it is not known if Iran has successfully transformed the Emad into a precision-guided missile, its changes are a clear indication of Iran's ambitions.

Sajjil missiles are a class of medium-range missiles that use solid fuel, which offers many strategic advantages. They are less vulnerable to destruction before they fire because the launch requires shorter preparation than liquid fueled launchers—minutes rather than hours. Iran is the only country to have developed missiles of this range without first having developed nuclear weapons.

The Sajjil-2 surface-to-surface missile is made inside Iran. It has a range of about 1,200 miles (2,000 km) when carrying a warhead. Brigadier General Abdollah Araghi, a Revolutionary Guard commander, describes the Sajji-2 this way: "[it] would allow Iran to "target any place that threatens Iran."

The *Sajjil*-2 appears to have encountered technical issues and its full development has slowed. Its last known test flight was during the Great Prophet 15 War Games on January 15, 2021, when other solid fueled missiles also appear to have been tested. Also of note in these particular war games, Iran flight tested kamikaze drones for the first time.

If *Sajjil*-2 flight testing resumes, the missile's performance and reliability could be proven within a year or two. It is the most likely nuclear delivery vehicle. But it would need to build a bomb small enough to fit on the top of this missile, which would be a major challenge. Indeed, warhead miniaturization is usually the final and most difficult development stage for any nuclear weapons program.

A Sajjil-3 missile is also in development. It would reportedly have three stages, a maximum range of around 2485 miles (4,000 km). It has an improved engine, upgraded guidance system, and better survivability. It's more maneuverable than previous Iranian missiles, making it harder for anti-ballistic missile systems to intercept.

A TIMELINE OF IRANIAN MISSILE DEVELOPMENT

Take a look at the following timeline of just a few highlights of Iran's exceedingly active missile development program for the past ten years. . .

Early 2014: Iran deployed cruise missiles aboard its naval vessels and coastal defense sites.

August 2014: Iran successfully tested fired a Bavar-373 missile, a version of the Russian S-300 surface-to-air defense system built in Iran.

Early 2015: Iran began mass production of Qadir cruise missiles with a range of around 300 KM (196 miles).

August 2015: Iran revealed the Fateh-313, a solid fueled missile with a range of up to 500 KM (330 miles).

October 2015: Video of an underground missile launch facility is released by Iranian news agencies. Reportedly, the military base is

500 meters underground and one of hundreds located throughout the country.

November 2015: Iran signs a contract for delivery of the S-300 air defense system from Russian. They will arrive in Iran by September 2016 and Iranian military personnel will receive training on them at the Mozharsky Academy in St. Petersburg.

November 2015: Iran tests the liquid-fueled, medium-range Ghadr-110, an improved version of the Shahab-3, with a reported range of about 1,900 km. U.S. Ambassador to the U.N. Samantha Power said that "the U.S. is conducting a serious review of the reported incident" and would bring the matter to the U.N. Security Council if it determined the test violated U.N. resolutions.

January 2016: Iranian missile technicians from the Shahid Hemmat Industrial Group (SHIG) traveled to North Korea to work on an 80-ton rocket booster jointly developed with the North Korean government. Iranian officials also coordinated shipments of missile technology from the Korea Mining Development Trading Corporation (KOMID) to Iran.

March 2016: According to *Reuters*, a joint U.S., British, French, and German letter to U.N. Secretary General Ban Ki-moon and Spain's U.N. Ambassador calls Iran's ballistic missile tests in March 2016 "inconsistent with" and "in defiance of" U.N. resolution 2231. The letter states that the missiles are "inherently capable of delivering nuclear weapons" and asks the Security Council to discuss "appropriate responses" to Iran's actions.

NOTE: The Security Council did nothing, and Iran continued its missile research, development, and testing.

April 2016: Iran reportedly conducts its first test launch of the Simorgh space launch vehicle, which is judged partly successful by U.S. intelligence agencies.

September 2016: Iran test-fires a new short-range ballistic missile, the Zolfaghar (Zulfiqar), for the first time. The Zolfaghar is reportedly a variant of the solid-fueled Fateh-110 ballistic missile series, with a range of 700 km. Coinciding with the test, Iranian Defense Minister Brigadier General Hossein Dehqan announces that the Zolfaghar has entered the production line.

February 2017: U.S. National Security Advisor Michael Flynn condemns Iran's January missile test and announces that the U.S. has officially put Iran "on notice." Flynn's statement follows Iranian Defense Minister Brigadier General Hossein Dehqan's confirmation of the test.

NOTE: Iran ignored Flynn's statement.

February 2017: The IRGC tests several missile systems during the "Defenders of the Velayat Skies" aerospace drills, according to Iranian news outlets. The missile systems reportedly tested include the Khordad-III, which has a reported range of 75 km and the ability to hit multiple targets at once; the Tabas, which is also capable of engaging multiple targets and has a reported range of 60 km; and the Sayyad-II, which has a reported range of 75 km and the ability to counter electronic warfare.

NOTE: MRV's or Multiple Re-entry Vehicles use a single missile—a rocket—to deliver multiple warheads—bombs—to the same general geographic location. They are force multipliers, if you will, and require sophisticated guidance systems for each warhead to send the individual warheads accurately to separate locations. This represents a significant upgrade to the Iranian's nuclear weapons program.

July 2017: Iran inaugurates the production line of the Sayyad-3 (Hunter-3), a long-range surface-to-air missile (SAM) that will reportedly be used with the Talash-2 air defense system.

September 2017: Iran displays its Khorramshahr medium-range ballistic missile at a military parade. The commander of the IRGC Aerospace Force claims the missile is capable of carrying multiple warheads and has a range of 2,000 km. The Khorramshahr is based on North Korea's BM-25 Musudan.

October 2017: A German intelligence report finds that Iran made 32 attempts in 2016 to procure technology that could be used for its ballistic missile program from the state of North Rhine-Westphalia, down from 141 attempts in 2015.

March 2018: The commander of the IRGC Aerospace Force, Brigadier General Amir Ali Hajizadeh, claims that Iran has tripled its missile production.

February 2019: Iran tests a submarine-launched cruise missile for the first time as part of its "Velayat 97" war game exercises in the Strait of Hormuz.

NOTE: This is another significant upgrade to Iran's military capabilities. Any self-respecting nuclear triad relies on three means of delivery: airplane-delivered nuclear weapons, ballistic missile delivered nuclear weapons, and submarine-based nuclear weapons, which are highly mobile and nearly impossible to detect. Submarines can approach enemy shores very closely, and when they launch their missiles, the enemy has very little time to attempt an intercept.

August 2019: Iran unveils three new precision-guided air-to-air missiles: the Yasin, the Balaban, and an updated variant of the Qaem. The missiles are developed by the Iranian Defense Ministry and Iran Electronics Industries (IEI).

March 2020: The commander of U.S. Central Command estimates that Iran possesses between 2,500 and 3,000 ballistic missiles.

April 2020: The IRGC announces that it has successfully put the Noor military satellite into orbit from a base in Semnan Province with a three-stage Ghased space launch vehicle that uses both liquid and solid fuel. According to independent analysis, the Ghased likely uses a Ghadr medium-range ballistic missile for its first stage and a solid-fuel motor designed by the IRGC Research and Self-Sufficiency Jihad Organization (RSSJO) for its second stage.

August 2020: Iran announces the development of two new missiles: the Martyr Hajj Qassem surface-to-surface ballistic missile, with a reported range of 1,400 km (870 miles), and the Martyr Abu Mahdi anti-ship cruise missile, with a reported range of 1,000 km (621 miles).

November 2020: The Iranian Army announces the development of an underground facility for ballistic missiles capable of a simultaneous launch or consecutive launches. The base uses a rail system enabling Iran to fire Emad missiles from a single silo in quick succession.

January 2021: The Iranian Navy claims to have established a "missile city" consisting of a column of missiles and launching systems on Iran's Persian Gulf coast. During a military exercise, the Iranian Navy tested solid-fueled ballistic missiles and kamikaze drones.

February 2021: The Iranian Ministry of Defense announces that Iran has conducted a test of a new space launch vehicle using a solid-fuel motor with a 5-foot diameter and a thrust of 75 kilotons.

March 2021: A U.N. panel of experts on North Korea documents allegations from a U.N. member state that Iran and North Korea "have resumed cooperation on long-range missile development projects," which "included the transfer of critical parts" in 2020.

June 2021: According to the U.S. Defense Department, Iran unsuccessfully attempts to launch a satellite, making it the fourth consecutive launch failure.

December 2021: The Iranian Ministry of Defense announces another failed launch of three research devices into space.

February 2022: Iran unveils the solid-fuel "Kheibar Shekan" surface-to-surface ballistic missile, which Iran claims is produced by the Iranian military and has a range of 1,450 km.

March 2022: Satellite imagery indicates that yet another space launch failed. The Zuljanah Space Launch Vehicle, or SLV, used a combination of solid and liquid fuel.

May 2022: Iran unveils the Heidar-1 and Heidar-2 cruise missiles. The Heidar-1 is reportedly Iran's first drone-launched cruise missile and has a claimed range of 200 km. The reportedly helicopter-launched Heidar-2 relies on a turbojet engine apparently copied from the Czech-made PBS TJ100 turbojet that has been found on Houthi missiles in Yemen.

June 2022: The Iranian Ministry of Defense announces a second (successful) suborbital test launch of the Zuljanah SLV. It also says Iran will study the results of the test to prepare for a third Zuljanah launch at an unspecified date.

On June 17, 2022, The U.S. State Department issued this chilling statement:

> "Last month, Iran's nuclear program entered dangerous new territory: Tehran now possesses enough highly enriched uranium for a nuclear bomb. That material, enriched to 60 percent, would need to be further enriched to roughly 90 percent—so-called weapons-grade uranium—before it could be used in a nuclear weapon. But that process, known as

'breakout,' will now take just weeks because of Iran's advances since 2019, when Tehran began casting off the constraints of the 2015 Iran nuclear deal following the U.S. withdrawal from the agreement. Although this action alone would not give Iran a bomb, it is the most important step in building one."

IRAN SELLS MISSILES TO TERRORISTS

Let's not forget that, throughout this period of rapid research and development, Iranian-made, conventional ballistic missiles have:

+ been found in the possession of Hezbollah

+ been intercepted enroute to Gaza, likely bound for an unknown terrorist group

+ been intercepted enroute to, successfully shipped to, and been fired by Houthi rebels in Yemen

+ been found at the site of an oil field bombing in Saudi Arabia

+ been fired at American troops at military bases in Iraq

+ been fired at what Iranian officials called a secret Israel military base in Iraqi Kurdistan and at other Kurdish targets.

+ been deployed along the entire length of the Persian Gulf

- been fired by Houthi rebels at targets inside Saudi Arabia, including the Saudi Defense Ministry, Abha Airport, and an Aramco oil facility

- been fired by Houthi rebels at targets inside the United Arab Emirates

- been fired by Iranian Quds Force soldiers from Damascus at the Golan Heights

The U. S. State Department imposed new sanctions on Iran or entities in other nations who supply missiles, missile components, or technology in:

July 1998
January 1999
April 2000
May 2003
January 2005
June 2006
December 2006 (United Nations sanctions)
January 2007
March 2007 (further United Nations sanctions)
June 2007
March 2008 (yet more travel and financial sanctions by the United Nations)
August 2008
September 2008 (twice that month)
June 2010 (United Nations Security Council)
September 2010
January 2011
February 2011
July 2012
January 2013
May 2013

December 2013
January 2016
March 2016
February 2017
May 2017
July 2017 (twice)
August 2017
October 2017
January 2018
May 2018
August 2019
September 2019 (twice)
February 2020
September 2020
December 2020
January 2021
August 2021
September 2021
October 2021
May 2022
June 2022
July 2022
August 2022
September 2022
October 2022
November 2022
December 2022
January 2023

NOTE: In January 2016, with the implementation of the JCPOA, some of these sanctions were terminated. However, most were subsequently reinstated as the United States withdrew from the JCPOA and Iran flagrantly violated the agreement.

I won't make you count. That's 51 rounds of sanctions imposed by the United States and United Nations against Iran, various Iranian companies, allies of Iran's, and companies attempting to sell or send aid in developing long-range missiles to Iran. Over the course of twenty years, one would think we would figure out that sanctions don't work against Iran.

Appeasement and wholly ineffective sanctions have been the only serious western response to Iran since the very beginning of its nuclear program. No wonder it's so close to having a nuclear arsenal now.

Regardless of the cost, regardless of the damage to its economy, and regardless of threats by other nations, Iran's nuclear program is charging full speed ahead. When one Iranian spy is caught trying to purchase components or missile technology, they merely send out another spy. When one country or company is prevented from selling them what they need, they find another country or company to do it. Iran is obsessed with developing an ICBM.

IRAN'S "SPACE" PROGRAM

The multi-stage, solid-fueled rocket technology that takes satellites or astronauts into space is essentially the same technology that sends a nuclear weapon up into space and halfway around the world, where it re-enters the atmosphere and delivers its warhead to a specified target location.

Over and over in the past decade or more, Iran has attempted launches of "satellite launch systems." All of their early tests failed. But over the years, they've gotten closer and closer to a successful launch.

In one test, two of the three stages of the rocket fired successfully, and they achieved low orbit. In another test, they got partial firing of all the stages. In a third test, they used two solid-fueled stages and a third liquid-fueled stage. (They will need a third solid fueled stage to lift the weight of a nuclear weapon into orbit.)

Bit by bit, Iran's "satellite" program is approaching success. In March of 2022, the Iranian military announced that it had successfully launched a second reconnaissance satellite into low-earth orbit using a mixed fuel rocket from a truck-based launcher.

The good news: reconnaissance satellites are very small and light. Iran still can't lift a heavy bomb into orbit. The bad news: why would any peaceful "satellite launch program" need to launch their satellites from a *truck*? The only reason to launch anything from a truck is so you can move it and hide it. That truck launcher is good for one thing, and one thing only—launching a weapon.

The most recent test launch of an Iranian orbital rocket system, in June of 2022, was declared a success. In it, a suborbital test launch of the Zuljanah Satellite Launch Vehicle made it to the hoped-for height above the earth and will be studied in preparation for another launch in the near future.

Keep in mind, that air bursting a nuclear weapon (detonating it in mid-air) high above the ground results in a massive electromagnetic pulse (EMP) being released outward in all directions. This EMP burst destroys every electronic device and electrical power system within its line of sight. The higher above the earth the bomb explodes, the further the electromagnetic pulse can travel, and the wider the damage area.

"Achieving sub-orbital flight" is another way of saying, "our future nuclear weapon delivery system achieved an appropriate nuclear air-burst height."

ADVANCES IN PRECISION GUIDANCE AND RANGE

It's not enough for Iran to have weapons-grade uranium and missiles that can fire it at their enemies. They also need to be able to aim their missiles with at least some degree of accuracy.

By 2015, Iranian missile guidance systems were able to achieve a fairly high degree of accuracy at ranges approaching a thousand miles. In 2017, Iran introduced a new guidance system they probably developed with the help of North Korea, although some intelligence sources think it may be entirely imported from North Korea. At any rate, Iran is now believed to have a steerable warhead that will increase missile accuracy even more.

CEP—Circular Error Probable—is a measurement of how precise a weapon is. It describes how close a weapon is generally able to come to hitting a specific point. With the North Korean upgrades, Iranian Chairman of the Armed Forces, General Mohammad Bagheri, claimed that Iran can now achieve a CEP of 60 meters at a ranged of 1300 km (807 miles).

In the world of precision missile strikes, a consistent CEP of 10 meters or less would put Iran's weapons in the same class and the best military weaponry in the world. Iran has yet to achieve this with its current medium range missiles, but it has definitely achieved it with several of its short-range missiles.

A September 2018 missile strike on a meeting of Iranian dissidents with Kurds, a September 2019 strike on a Saudi Aramco facility, and the January 202 strike on U.S. troops at al-Asad Air Base in Iraq demonstrated CEP's of 10 meters or less.

Of course, one must ask oneself if missing a target by 10 meters or 60 meters is going to make any difference whatsoever to the people in the blast radius of an incoming nuclear weapon. Nonetheless, Iran's improvements in precision targeting are yet another puzzle piece in its nuclear weapon and missile development programs.

THERE'S ONLY ONE REASON FOR MISSILES

The speed and urgency with which Iran is developing long-range missiles, improving their payload capacity (meaning how much weight they can lift), and improving their targeting accuracy gives the lie to Iran's claims that they are only interested in developing "satellite delivery" systems.

The sheer scale of Iran's missile development program makes no sense at all for a nation with peaceful intentions toward its neighbors.

Plus, the appearance of Iranian missile remains (debris, fragments, and serial-numbered parts) at attacks across the Middle East is hard evidence that Iran has no such peaceful intentions. Iran is shamelessly arming terrorist groups who have shamelessly used those missiles and will continue to do so.

Iran shows no interest whatsoever in slowing down or halting further development of its missile program. The West must conclude that at some point, probably sooner rather than later, Iran will increase its missile capabilities until it can fire a nuclear weapon at medium or even long range.

Iran already has missiles with the range to strike Israel. In the near future, Iran is likely to obtain or build missiles with the range to strike targets further abroad—across the entire Middle East, Mediterranean, and into Europe and Asia.

All Iran lacks now is an atomic bomb small enough to mount on the tip of one of its missiles. . .

CHAPTER SEVEN:

A DEFIANT IRAN PRESSES AHEAD

Iran's expansion of its uranium enrichment program drastically shortened its breakout time. When Iran was fully complying with the JCPOA between 2016 and 2019, the breakout time [the time required to create enough weapons grade uranium for one nuclear weapon] was about 12 months. By late 2022, breakout time was down to less than a week. . . More troubling, Iran's advances mean that it could produce enough uranium to fuel three or four weapons in about a month.

—Mariano Grossi,
IAEA Director General Rafael, December 2022

"Iran could have nuclear weaponry [full-blown nuclear missiles] within five years. Such progress would be unaffected by its current talks with world powers on a new deal to cap its nuclear technologies."

—Avigdor Lieberman,
Israeli Finance Minister, November 2022

SURELY, AS IRAN COMMENCED processing uranium all the while professing loudly that it was doing so for peaceful means, the governments of the world were not so naïve as to believe them. Iran was only granted permission by the IAEA to enrich uranium to 3.67%, appropriate for fueling civilian nuclear power plants. And yet, the world stood by and watched Iran enrich uranium first to 20% and then to 60%.

What then, was the West and the IAEA doing to stop the Iranians from moving forward toward obtaining a nuclear arsenal?

THE UNITED STATES IS CONFUSED AND BEMUSED

In August 2005, the *Washington Post* published a report on a leaked classified document that claimed Iran was yet 10 years away from having enough enriched uranium to make a nuclear weapon. The actual intelligence estimate was more like 5 years.

The story criticized the Bush administration for "hyping" intelligence estimates to create a nuclear weapons scare. The administration pushed back, saying there was, indeed, a real problem. The squabbling muddied the entire situation for the American public, who didn't know what to believe.

Unfortunately, definitive proof was lacking that Iran was building a bomb. This uncertainty was crippling to any decision to take military action against Iran:

> The new National Intelligence Estimate includes what the intelligence community views as credible indicators that Iran's military is conducting clandestine work. But the sources said there is no information linking those projects directly to a nuclear weapons program. What is clear is that Iran, mostly through its energy program, is acquiring and mastering technologies that could be diverted to bomb making.

All this confusion in the U.S. confirmed the brilliance of the Iranian strategy. Without more precise intelligence, how could the

United States design a clear response, either diplomatic or military?

In its nuclear chess game, Iran had paralyzed the U.S. government with indecision.

HINDSIGHT IS 20/20

With the administration under heavy pressure from the political left over the war in Iraq—and over the inaccurate intelligence that led us into the war—President Bush was blocked from taking military action against Iran, even if that had been his first choice. Without reliable intelligence estimates, President Bush would look unreasonably aggressive if he were to pursue a military solution instead of a diplomatic solution.

Despite evidence which suggested Iran's nuclear program *was* a weapons program, the argument was inferential and circumstantial at best. The administration lacked definitive proof that Iran was planning to build a bomb soon and that their likelihood of success was high.

In this book, we have the luxury of hindsight. I can outline exactly what Iran was, in fact, doing from the early 2000's until very recently to develop nuclear weapons. But back then, Iran's shell game of concealment, misdirection, and lies was working perfectly. Nobody was sure of anything Iran might or might not be doing.

Back then, we could infer that Iran was pursuing nuclear weapons because the country had more than enough natural gas and oil to provide cheap energy because nuclear power was more expensive and because Iran had concealed its nuclear efforts and lied about nuclear technology.

Still, these arguments were inferences, not proofs—not as long as the mullahs kept insisting that their nuclear goals were strictly peaceful.

ELBARADEI RAISES CONCERNS

On December 5, 2005, *The Independent,* a British newspaper, published an interview with Mohamed ElBaradei, the Director General of the IAEA. In it, ElBaradei argued that once Iran opened Natanz to complete uranium enrichment, the nuclear crisis with Iran would reach a new level.

Here is what ElBaradei said:

> "If they start enriching, this is a major issue and a serious concern for the international community. I know they are trying to acquire the full fuel cycle. I know that acquiring the full fuel cycle means that a country is months away from nuclear weapons, and that applies to Iran and everyone else. If Tehran indeed resumes its uranium enrichment in other plants, as threatened, it will only take several months to make a bomb."

This statement sent shocks through the international press and diplomatic community. Lulled by the earlier *Washington Post* report than Iran might be as much as 10 years away from having an atomic bomb, a statement by the head of the IAEA that Iran could be only months away was alarming.

ElBaradei carefully added a caution that he considered

military action against Iran unadvisable: "On the other hand, any attempt to resolve the crisis by non-diplomatic means will open a Pandora's box."

ElBaradei's statement also hit a nerve worldwide because Iran was not taking steps to gain the trust of the international community. Had Iran truly been pursuing only a peaceful nuclear program, many steps could have been taken that were not.

This point was forcibly made by Phillippe Errera, a French diplomat, in a speech given in Tehran in March 2005. His words are as true today as they were then:

> "Iran has lost this trust not because of any dis-criminatory attitude toward it, nor because of any instrumentalization by "third parties," the United States or Israel, for example, but simply because of the revelation of close to 20 years of clandestine activities dealing with highly sensitive nuclear matters, and of secret cooperation with an international proliferation network linked to nuclear proliferation programs in Libya and North Korea, coupled with the absence of any civilian justification to its nuclear fuel cycle program; there is no functioning reactor in Iran today."

ElBaradei's interview set off a round of intensive diplomatic negotiations with Iran. The IAEA and the West had bent over backwards in these talks, offering Iran every imaginable concession if only Iran would agree not to enrich uranium. Iran ignored them all.

Iran claimed that national security concerns demanded that its government maintain a strong military. . .for defensive reasons only. The West and the IAEA offered to negotiate a multi-national security agreement with Iran, promising a non-aggression pact would be signed by any and all countries Iran felt were potentially threatening their national security. Iran declined.

Then the West and the IAEA offered to promote Iran's entry into the World Trade Organization, under the premise that such a major economic incentive might tempt Iran to step away from its nuclear weapons ambitions. Iran said no.

Russia's proposal to enrich uranium in Russia for Iran was still on the table and was renewed. This offer would permit the Iranians to gain technical knowledge regarding uranium enrichment while making sure the process remained under Russian control. Iran refused the offer.

Tehran would never give up its ambitions to acquire the full nuclear fuel-cycle on its own soil. It was only a matter of time before Iran fulfilled its stated threat to open Natanz and begin enriching uranium.

Once Iran began completing uranium enrichment at Natanz, even the IAEA's own head Mohamed ElBaradei agreed Iran was only months, maybe 4 months, maybe 5 months, away from being able to enrich enough uranium to make a bomb.

In response to all these intense diplomatic overtures, Iran became even more belligerent. The Associated Press reported on December 3, 2005, that Iran's Guardian Council had accepted a bill passed by the Majlis, Iran's parliament, affirming that if the IAEA voted to refer Iran to the UN's Security Council, the Iranian government would respond by blocking any further international inspection of its nuclear facilities.

This amounted to a threat: if Iran were sanctioned, all cooperation with IAEA inspections would be terminated.

EARLY WARNINGS THAT SANCTIONS WON'T WORK

In December 2005, a report issued by the United States Institute of Peace said:

> Iran's leaders appear to have calculated that they can withstand the diplomatic pressure they are facing from the United States, the Europeans, and many members of the International Atomic Energy Agency (IAEA), and that even if sanctions are imposed, Iran has the will and financial resources to ride them out.

Israel came to the same conclusion. Speaking at Tel Aviv University at the end of November 2005, Israeli Defense Forces Chief of Staff Lt.-General Dan Halutz told the audience:

> "A state like Iran that has accumulated just in the past two years $150 billion beyond what it planned because of the rise in oil prices is not so sensitive to economic sanctions."

Separately, Halutz was quoted as despairing that a diplomatic solution would be found:

> "The fact that the Iranians are succeeding time after time to get away from the international pressure

either under the IAEA Board of Governors or the UN Security Council is encouraging them with their nuclear project. I believe that the political means that are used by the European countries and the Americans to convince the Iranians to stop their project will not end in stopping the Iranian project."

The Israelis' frustration was evident. The West and the IAEA had offered Iran virtually every concession imaginable, including security assurances and trade agreements, yet Iran was not interested in incentives. Iran was clearly prepared to ignore the sanctions the West was counting on to bring Iran to heel.

On December 1, 2006, Prime Minister Ariel Sharon spoke officially about the Iranian threat. Sharon said in no uncertain terms that Israel "can't accept a situation where Iran has nuclear arms." He affirmed that Israel was "making all the necessary preparations to handle a situation like this," a comment that conveyed a thinly veiled threat of military action.

Sharon repeated that Israel did not want to be seen as leading the charge, preferring to see a united international coalition take the issue to the UN Security Council to neutralize "this great danger." However, if the international community continued not to step up and address the threat directly, Sharon was leaving no doubt that Israel was not ready to accept the risk that Iran could have nuclear weapons soon.

RUSSIA COMPLICATES THE IRAN DILEMMA

As Iran was hardening it foreign policy into nuclear defiance and an overt anti-Israel posture, its alliance with Russia appeared to grow stronger. In October 2005, Russia launched Iran's first-ever satellite into space, aboard a Kosmos-3M rocket.

The satellite, named Sina-1, was described by Iran as intended for monitoring natural disasters in Iran, an earthquake-prone country, and to improve telecommunications. Many credible international observers disagreed, arguing that the Sina-1 was designed to spy on Israel.

Russia agreed to launch a second Iranian satellite, a move that allowed Iran to join the global satellites surveillance race without diverting time or money to make their Shahab missiles capable of delivering satellites into orbit.

The First Gulf War in 1990-91, saw the United States roll out the Patriot Missile Defense System. For the first time ever, the world witnessed ballistic missiles being knocked out of the sky, mid-flight toward their targets and harmlessly blown up in the air. Although the concept had been in development since the 1950's the concept was unproven until then.

Immediately upon Patriot batteries being used against incoming SCUD missiles, the race was on for every major military power in the world to duplicate the Americans' feat and develop their own missile defense system.

On December 2, 2005, Russian newspapers announced a military agreement with Iran under which Russia agreed to sell Iran $1 billion worth of the recently developed Russian TOR-M1 antimissile defense system.

Operating on a mobile platform, the TOR-M1 can track multiple targets and is capable of firing at two targets simultaneously. The TOR-M1 functions very effectively as an anti-aircraft missile system as well, operating much like a SAM (Surface-to-Air-Missile) system.

By deploying Russian TOR-M1 anti-missile batteries around its nuclear facilities, Iran hoped to harden these facilities against air attack by the United States or Israel. Once the TOR-M1 systems were operational, loss estimates increased dramatically for aircraft involved in strikes on Iran.

This agreement between Iran and Russia escalated the arms race in the Middle East. Now Israel had to be concerned about countermeasures. Were Israeli military aircraft capable of fighting the TOR-M1 system? Was a missile attack on Iran's nuclear facilities the only viable alternative? Would Russian military be assigned in Iran to train Iranians to use the system; or would Russian military be permanently stationed in Iran as advisors regarding the systems operation?

Ultimately, Russia chose to train Iranian soldiers inside Russia on how to operate the system. In subsequent exercises over the next several years, the Iranian military was at pains to demonstrate that its soldiers knew how to use the TOR-M1 system correctly and effectively.

Among others, the United States strongly objected to the sale, reminding Russia of various international agreements not to sell arms to any nation that openly supported terrorist organizations, referencing Iran's ongoing financial support for the Lebanon-based terrorist organization Hezbollah.

Israel was alarmed enough at the sale to engage in a little saber rattling of its own:

On Friday, December 2, 2005, as the news of the TOR-M1 missile sale was being reported by Russian newspapers, Israel openly and publicly carried out a successful test firing of an Arrow interceptor missile, hitting and destroying a test enemy missile that was fired from an airplane over the Mediterranean Sea, and aimed east, back toward Israel. The simulated enemy missile was designed to mimic an Iranian Shahab-3 missile.

The point of the demonstration was to put Iran and the world on notice that Israel was alarmed that Iran's nuclear program now had Russia's backing, with both Iran and Russia playing a "wink-wink" game in claiming Iran had only peaceful nuclear purposes. With the Arrow missile test-firing, Israel was sending Iran, and Russia, a warning message.

CHAPTER EIGHT:

HOW SOON WILL IRAN HAVE A NUCLEAR WEAPON?

———

"Iran's nuclear program is galloping forward. . .
The longer this goes on, the more the breakout time gets down. . .
it's now down, by public reports, to a few months at best.
And if this continues, it will get down to a matter of weeks."

—Anthony Blinken,
U.S. Secretary of State, June 2022

THE NUCLEAR CLOCK is ticking in Iran. Of this there is no longer any doubt. The question of the hour, then, is how soon is Iran likely to have a nuclear weapon?

THE DOOMSDAY CLOCK IS RESET TO 90 SECONDS TO MIDNIGHT

The Doomsday Clock was first conceptualized in 1945 by Albert Einstein, Robert Oppenheimer, and other nuclear scientists involved in the Manhattan Project. Alarmed by the awesome and terrible potential of nuclear weapons to end the world, they felt a need to warn mankind of how close we really were to nuclear annihilation. The Doomsday clock was a metaphor for how close humanity was coming to ending itself.

Initially, the clock was set at seven minutes to midnight. It has advanced and retreated in the decades since its inception. The furthest from midnight it has ever been is 17 minutes, following the end of the Cold War in 1991.

The Science and Security Board of the *Bulletin of the Atomic Scientists* is the body responsible for maintaining the metaphorical clock, and each year it updates the time remaining before midnight. This group currently includes 10 Nobel laureates

In 2017, the Doomsday Clock advanced a full half-minute to 2 ½ minutes until midnight, because of reckless approaches toward nuclear weapons and climate change.

In 2018, the Doomsday Clock moved forward 30 seconds more, to 2 minutes until midnight. Major nuclear actors were declared to be on the cusp of a new arms race, one that would be both very expensive and significantly increase the likelihood of a nuclear accident or outright nuclear conflict.

In January of 2020, the clock was moved to 100 seconds from midnight, the closest it had ever been to midnight in its history. It was moved for two reasons: climate change and increase in the threat of nuclear war.

The group responsible for the clock noted that national leaders had ended or undermined several major arms control treaties in the previous year, particularly ones pertaining to nuclear weaponry. It was deemed that in 2020 an environment conducive to a renewed nuclear arms race, to the proliferation of nuclear weapons, and to lowered barriers to nuclear war was significantly more likely.

Additionally in 2020, the keepers of the Doomsday Clock pointed out that political conflicts regarding nuclear programs in Iran and North Korea remained unresolved and were, if anything, worsening. They also cited that US-Russia cooperation on arms control and disarmament was all but nonexistent and little to no meaningful discussion on these topics was underway.

On January 23, 2023, the team responsible for the Doomsday Clock moved it forward to just 90 seconds to midnight.

The Science and Security Board of the *Bulletin of the Atomic Scientists* said the move—the closest to widespread calamity humanity has ever been judged to be—was "largely, though not exclusively" because of the war in Ukraine. Much of the 2023 announcement focused on Russia, President Vladimir Putin's threat to use nuclear weapons, and his refusal to accept anything other than victory in Ukraine, saying:

> "Russia's thinly veiled threats to use nuclear weapons remind the world that escalation of the conflict—by accident, intention, or miscalculation—is a terrible risk. The possibility that the conflict could spin out of anyone's control remains high."

RUSSIA BREAKS DOWN THE NUCLEAR TABOO

When the top nuclear scientists in the world are alarmed about how close to nuclear annihilation we are, the rest of us would be wise to listen. They, more than anyone, understand just how close Iran is to obtaining a nuclear arsenal of its own, not to mention how close Russia may be to destroying the long-standing taboo against using nuclear weapons.

When the United States dropped nuclear bombs on Hiroshima and Nagasaki in 1945, the world did not understand the true destructive capability of nuclear weapons. While the scientists who built them had some inkling of the devastation they would unleash, it took the world seeing the aftermath in those two devastated cities to fully grasp the danger of nuclear weapons.

Although a nuclear arms race followed World War II, there was a general, global revulsion toward the notion of ever using nuclear weapons again. As various political crises have come and gone in the many decades since World War II, politicians have always recoiled when they approached the brink of a nuclear exchange and ultimately abided by an unspoken understanding that we must not ever break the taboo and use nuclear weapons.

This has become an even more important line in the sand in the years since 1945 because the size and yield of nuclear weapons have increased exponentially since the first—tiny by modern standards—nuclear bombs were dropped. The destructive capability of a single modern nuclear weapon dwarfs the devastation of the Hiroshima bomb. Plus, nuclear arsenals for the largest countries in the world number in the thousands of nuclear devices.

Occasionally since 1945, politicians have threatened to use a nuclear weapon. Instead of turning this book into a history text, suffice it to say they all backed off of their threats fairly quickly.

This happened because other nations reacted strongly to the threat and promised or imposed severe penalties for making a nuclear threat, or because the politician's own citizens rose up in protest, or because the threat of retaliation by other nuclear-armed nations was swift and strong enough to deter the politician from following through on the threat.

But time seems to have dulled mankind's memories of the true horror of nuclear war. Politicians in Russia are engaging freely in nuclear saber-rattling—freely enough that western analysts are left with no choice but to accept that the threats may be real.

As of the writing of this book, Vladimir Putin has not launched a nuclear strike in Ukraine. But he has made it crystal clear he plans to do so if there is no other way for him to win a war in Ukraine. While this poses a whole series of dilemmas for the United States, NATO, and their allies that we will discuss elsewhere in this book, Putin's threats have had one more deeply chilling effect.

His threats have removed some or all of the sense of taboo surrounding the use of nuclear weapons by other aggressive, unprincipled world leaders. Kim Jung Un in North Korea is moving full speed ahead with developing his nuclear program as are the ayatollahs in Iran. Neither seems to have any compunction about using nuclear weapons on their enemies (perceived or real) going forward, and this is a very, very serious problem.

The United Nations, the International Atomic Energy Agency, dozens of concerned governments around the world, and other groups are imploring Putin to stop this dangerous brinksmanship that is having such a damaging effect on the entire nuclear environment globally. But their pleas have fallen on deaf ears. If anything, Putin and his henchmen's nuclear rhetoric has increased as the Ukraine war drags into its second year.

Even if Putin does not ultimately use nuclear weapons against Ukraine, world leaders including those in Washington

D.C. and in Israel fear the damage is done. His wildly irresponsible threats to use nuclear weapons have challenged and broken down the long-standing world order with regard to use of nuclear weapons.

Putin's constant talk of using nuclear weapons in Ukraine threatens the entire system of treaties, accords, agreements, and understandings that prohibit crossing the nuclear Rubicon.

In February 2023, Putin went so far as to suspend Russia's participation in the START (Strategic Arms Limitation Treaty) with the United States in a move that appears to be clearing the way for himself to use nuclear weapons. . .and possibly to share nuclear weapons with another nation, namely his new best friend, Iran.

75 years of work to limit the dangers of nuclear war, to build and maintain a deep and abiding taboo against using these weapons, has been systematically destroyed by Vladimir Putin. Worse, the leadership of Iran stands ready, eager even, to leap into that gap and not only build, but use, nuclear weapons to destroy its enemies.

BREAKOUT TIME

Nuclear breakout is defined as the crossing over of a nation from incapable of building nuclear weapons to capable of building them. How long it will take Iran to break out is another way of stating the question, "How long until Iran has a nuclear weapon?

There are three measures of time we need to think about as we take a look at Iran's breakout time:

- ✦ First, how long will it take Iran to produce enough weapons grade uranium to fuel a nuclear weapon?

+ Second, how long will it take the rest of the world, by means of international inspectors or intelligence operations, to detect that Iran is moving forward with the final preparations to build a nuclear weapon?

+ Third, how long will it take the rest of the world to respond to this news?

Each of these three timeframes will affect how long it actually takes for Iran to go operational with a nuclear weapon.

In the past, it would take Iran longer to produce enough fissionable nuclear fuel than it would take for the West to figure out Iran was making that fuel and to respond. But that is no longer the case.

Iran can now create enough weapons grade uranium for a nuclear weapon in something like five days. The reality is that Iran is at or near the end of its breakout. Now. Not in a few months, not in a few weeks. Right now.

We have run out of time for diplomacy. If the United States gets word that Iran has commenced the final enrichment process to create nuclear fuel, Iran will finish that operation in no more than five days and potentially less time than that.

How long will it take for inspectors to figure out that breakout has commenced?

In a best-case inspection scenario, IAEA inspectors would visit Iran's enrichment sites about once a week—which they're not doing at all right now, I might add. Even if the IAEA resumed a full inspection regimen, Iran now has the capability to fully process all the weapons grade uranium it needs for a weapon *between* regularly schedule visits of inspectors.

It's possible that intelligence sources might hear that Iran is commencing breakout, but such reports need verification and that verification takes time.

If we're all *very* lucky, the world might get notified that Iran is moving ahead with breakout perhaps 24 hours after it starts. Which leaves the world more like four days to respond instead of five.

This brings us to the final timeline question: how long it will take the world to respond to this disastrous news?

How long will it take the United States, the United Nations, other governments, and other international agencies to analyze the reports, convene crisis meetings to discuss options, to engage in negotiations over how to respond, and to coordinate a response?

Can the United States decide upon and coordinate a military response to a crisis of this magnitude in five days or less? The White House does maintain contingency plans developed in advance to help it respond quickly to crises it might face. However, each situation is different and has its own intricacies and special considerations, not to mention each administration will have its own take on how the United States should respond to a crisis of such magnitude.

Of course, the U.S. military also has contingency plans already in place to respond to a wide variety of military crises, including this one. And, the U.S. has forces deployed in various locations around the world that would significantly speed up our response time. But the wheels of the U.S. government tend to turn slowly. It is designed to be a slow-moving, cumbersome bureaucracy that intentionally slows down the biggest decisions of all to guard against precipitous and ill-thought-out reactions to crises.

It remains to be seen if the U.S. government is even capable of responding nimbly enough to a crisis of this type to take any action at all before Iran would go operational with a nuclear weapon.

What if the United States needs to strike multiple targets inside Iran to prevent it from assembling and launching its first nuclear weapon? Can the U.S. scramble a broad enough array of attack aircraft and weapons at many targets fast enough to stop completion of Iran's breakout?

Remember, Iran has significant air defense systems, compliments of Russia. Not all the U.S. planes would make it to their targets. There would need to be back-up planes and secondary strikes. While the first wave of U.S. bombers might have the element of surprise on their side, the second wave would not. The Iranian military would be ready and waiting for them to arrive.

If the United States doesn't find out about an Iranian breakout in time to respond and stop the breakout, then the U.S. will face yet another dilemma. Should it respond at all? Would the risk of Iran retaliating against us or our allies be high enough (and nuclear, to boot) that we would be better off doing nothing in response to Iran's breakout?

Since February of 2021, IAEA inspectors have had no access to the cameras monitoring Iran's centrifuge facilities. We have no way of knowing if any of those centrifuges have been dismantled and moved to a secret facility or facilities elsewhere in Iran. It's possible that the United States could get evidence of an Iranian breakout, launch its bombers, destroy all the known Iranian enrichment facilities, and still not stop the breakout from finishing.

Why can Iran break out so fast now?

In the past, Iran had to start with raw uranium ore that had to be enriched over and over to increase its concentration. Iran also started out its enrichment program with old, first-generation centrifuges that were slow. The process was tedious and time consuming, which meant breakout for Iran was a minimum of two years or more away.

However, Iran has significantly upgraded its centrifuges to more advanced and faster models with help from Russia. It also has a lot of them—some 4,000 or more of the fastest type. Plus, Iran has been in the enrichment business for decades, now. It has large stockpiles of 60% and 20% enriched material. That 60% material can be enriched up to the 90% level of enrichment very, very quickly.

Because IAEA inspectors are no longer being allowed into various Iranian enrichment facilities in the aftermath of the JCPOA's breakdown, the West has no way of knowing how exactly much 60% enriched material Iran currently possesses. Nor can we be certain that Iran does not have any new, clandestine enrichment locations.

BEYOND BREAKOUT

Of course, Iran can have all the 90% enriched, fissionable uranium it wants and not have the means to build a bomb or deliver a warhead to its enemy targets. Because weapons grade uranium is the easiest to detect and track, because of its significant radiation signature, it is usually the component of a nuclear bomb that is the most closely tracked and monitored. But, with Iran's uranium stored deep underground, weapons grade uranium is nearly impossible to detect.

Also of concern, the Iranian facilities that build missiles and the other components for nuclear warheads are much less closely watched than its enrichment facilities and are scattered across Iran. Not to mention, Iran has allies, namely North Korea and Russia, who seem prepared to ship parts, manufacturing equipment, technological information, and even scientists and technicians to Iran to help it build long-range missiles and miniaturized warheads.

Current estimates place the time it would take Iran to actually build a deliverable nuclear missile from scratch at a year or more. But it's entirely possible that Iran has purchased and smuggled into Iran at least a few ICBMs (Intercontinental Ballistic Missiles) and/or a few empty nuclear warheads lacking only the uranium to make them operable. If this is the case, the United States has no way of detecting the final arming operations necessary to make such a nuclear warhead and long-range delivery system ready to use.

The short answer to the question of how long will it take Iran to have a usable nuclear weapon is that we don't know. The worst-case scenario, which is not all that far-fetched, is that Iran can have the uranium it needs for a bomb in under a week. If it has a warhead and a missile from an ally, it can fuel the warhead and be ready to fire it in perhaps another week or two.

Even if Iran doesn't obtain a warhead and ICBM from a friend, we are perhaps a year away from breakout. A nuclear Iran is close. Very close. And it poses a threat that looms over us all.

IRAN DOESN'T EVEN NEED TO BUILD A BOMB

The reality is that even if Iran never chooses to build a nuclear weapon, the United States and its allies, particularly Israel face some difficult and serious decisions. If Iran continues to develop its "space" program, which is undoubtedly a flimsy cover story for its efforts to develop ICBMs, the threat of long-range missiles that could deliver a nuclear weapon is extremely serious.

In that case, should the United States intervene to stop construction of long-range missiles or not? Do they technically pose a threat in the absence of nuclear warheads being built? Should the West sit back and do nothing as long as there's no evidence of breakout, or should there be other markers that provoke western intervention?

For example, if Iran successfully launches a multiple stage solid-fueled rocket into orbit, is that cause for Western retaliation? How about if Iran develops miniaturization technology necessary to build nuclear warheads but doesn't go ahead and build actual warheads?

In a related conundrum, if Iran continues to advance the technologies necessary for building a nuclear weapon without actually crossing over into a breakout, how are the other countries of the Middle East likely to react?

Most experts believe that a nuclear- or nearly nuclear-Iran will provoke a massive arms race across the Middle East as other nations scramble to approach or achieve nuclear breakouts of their own. How should the United States respond to a renewed round of nuclear proliferation in several countries with whom we've had deeply strained relationships over the past several decades? Do we trust all the leaders of the Middle East to behave responsibly in the face of an aggressively posturing Iran?

Iran is already taunting the West with the possibility of break-out. Ayatollah Khamenei routinely talks about how eager he is to launch a full out nuclear assault on the Little Satan of Israel and one day upon the Great Satan of America. In this saber rattling, Iran is taking its cues directly from Vladimir Putin.

The United States is already trapped between two unsavory options. Should we dive into deeper alliances and military commitments in the Middle East even though we would much prefer to allocate our military resources and diplomatic efforts in other parts of the world, or should we stay out of development in the Middle East, even if it means uncontrolled nuclear proliferation bursts out across that sensitive and strategically vital region of the world?

CAN THE WEST ROLL BACK THE DOOMSDAY CLOCK?

Unfortunately, Iran has little or no incentive to slow down or stop its nuclear weapons development program. In the past year, it has gained significant military and diplomatic cover from Russia, not to mention significant technical and scientific support from Russia and North Korea to continue developing its nuclear capabilities.

The United States and a number of other nations are putting as much diplomatic pressure as they can on Iran to try to bring it back to the negotiating table and back into some sort of nuclear arms limitation treaty. Whether it's a return to the JCPOA or an entirely new, and hopefully better, arms limitation accord with Iran, the West doesn't much care. It just needs to get Iran back to the negotiating table and get it to agree to halt research and development of all the components necessary to construct a nuclear arsenal. (Not that I think Iran will actually agree to this as long as Twelvers rule Iran.)

Iran is surely enjoying the pressure it has put on the West and the terrible choices it is forcing upon America and its allies. Meanwhile, in the complete absence of inspections and outside monitoring, Iran can proceed full speed ahead toward its nuclear objectives.

The one thing the West still may have a chance to control is the monitoring and detection of Iranian activity aimed at weapons grade uranium enrichment, long-range missile development, and warhead miniaturization.

The West also has the capacity to decide right now what its response will be when the time comes that Iran achieves breakout. The White House assures reporters that it has a plan in place to respond to such an event, and we should all sincerely hope it does. If and when Iran finally breaks out into nuclear armament, we may have to respond very quickly and very decisively if we're to stand any chance at all of neutralizing the threat.

The United States desperately needs to push its allies into supporting our position that the IAEA should be allowed back into all Iranian Uranium enrichment facilities and nuclear material storage facilities *on a daily basis* going forward. We should also push for Iran to reactivate all the online, automated monitors that watch and report continuously on enrichment levels of the uranium Iran is currently refining.

In addition, the United Nations, IAEA, United States, and their allies should increase their intelligence gathering efforts sooner rather than later. It's critical to us all to know precisely what's going on inside Iran and where.

We must spot breakout as soon as humanly possible if we're to stand any chance at all of thwarting Iran's nuclear ambitions. Hours or even minutes may make the difference between stopping Iran from achieving breakout and having to face a fully nuclear Iranian regime and the consequences of that.

WILL IRAN AGREE TO RENEWED INSPECTIONS?

It's not an entirely unreasonable request to let IAEA inspectors back into Iran. It would significantly get the global community off the Iranians' backs. And it isn't as if Iran didn't know for years what the IAEA was going to do well in advance of the agency ever setting foot in any Iranian enrichment or storage facility.

Letting the IAEA back into Iranian nuclear facilities might also reassure the rest of the world that Iran is not racing as fast as it can toward developing a nuclear arsenal. Iran is the only country in the world currently producing highly enriched uranium that doesn't already have nuclear weapons.

Calming global fears of an Iranian breakout might significantly reduce the chances of a military strike by Israel, the United States, and others against Iranian enrichment facilities. Surely this is an appealing option to the ayatollahs.

But of course, we must ask ourselves, even if Iran allows inspections of its nuclear facilities to resume, what reason do we have to believe that the leopard has changed its spots? The world has no reason to believe Iran will honestly and forthrightly reveal the full extent of its nuclear program. It never has before—why would it start now?

Also, the world has no way of knowing what new facilities Iran has built in the years the JCPOA and inspections were suspended. Why should we expect that Iran will openly and honestly tell us where all those facilities are and that's happening inside them? The good news is it's very difficult for Iran to build any major new facility without Israeli or American intelligence or surveillance assets detecting it. They may have a few new facilities, but they probably don't have a lot of them.

The truth is the fox is already in the henhouse. While renewed inspections might tell us a little more about how advanced Iran's nuclear program is today, the reality is Iran is so close to breakout that it won't much matter what any future inspectors find.

SPEEDING UP AMERICAN RESPONSE TO A BREAKOUT

The U.S. State Department has suggested that the National Security Council establish a committee at the very top levels of the government that would convene immediately upon receiving reports indicating an Iranian breakout. In the meantime, this committee should practice convening and should do test runs with various degrees of ambiguity in the data it receives. Thus, the committee can test run various options well before the actual crisis comes.

The most important step the United States can take in response to an Iranian breakout will be to shorten the military response time significantly from where it is today. We might need to permanently position aircraft, missile defense systems, and bunker buster bombs much closer to Iran, perhaps somewhere in the Middle East. This might also include deploying American troops on a rotating basis to maintain and operate this forward-deployed equipment.

American assets in or near the Middle East would send a strong signal to our allies in the region that we stand ready to assist and defend them from an Iranian breakout and the serious threats to follow such an event.

Along with this stick, the United States and its allies must continue to offer carrots to Iran. Behave with restraint and transparency regarding uranium enrichment, storage, and monitoring, and the West will lift sanctions, perhaps in some sort of rolling timetable dependent on continued Iranian cooperation. The end goal is not to bomb Iran. It is to prevent Iran from bombing its neighbors and for the West not to have to bomb Iran.

At the end of the day, Israel and the United States cannot pin all their hopes on the notion that Iran will, out of the goodness of its heart, up and choose not to continue its nuclear weapon program until it finally breaks out into a full-blown nuclear regime.

PART TWO:

RUSSIA
AND THE
UKRAINE
WAR

CHAPTER NINE:

THE RISE OF VLADIMIR PUTIN

"To understand the Putin regime's enmity toward the United States, you must understand the man himself, as well as those around him. Ever since becoming the president of Russia in 2000, Putin has been on a messianic quest to restore Russia's lost Soviet-era power."

—Mike Pompeo,
former U.S. Secretary of State

"Having sat across the table from Vladimir Putin, it's pretty clear when you meet him that he has an almost limitless ambition for power. And he's been very good at acquiring it—political power, economic power, military power, territorial power."

—Carly Fiorina,
CEO Hewlett-Packard

LET'S SHIFT OUR FOCUS now to Vladimir Putin and the Russia-Ukraine War. While the two may not seem at first to be related to Iran's nuclear ambitions, they are inextricably linked. Before I show you how, let's take a look at who Vladimir Putin is and how Russia and Ukraine came to be at war with each other.

It's all well and good to know that Vladimir Putin was born in 1952 in Leningrad, that he attended law school at Leningrad State University, that he served as a KGB officer for sixteen years before entering local politics, and that he climbed rapidly through the political ranks until Boris Yeltsin appointed Putin his successor in 1999. But it's just as important to understand what was going on in Russia that shaped Vladimir Putin into the man—or monster as the case may be—that he is today.

PUTIN'S EARLY LIFE

Vladimir Putin was born into a family with long and tight connections to socialism. His grandfather, Spirodon Putin, was the personal chef of both Vladimir Lenin and Joseph Stalin. You have to understand—having access to the food these men ate was tantamount to holding their lives in his hands. Spiridon had to be unshakably, fanatically loyal to both men lest he be tempted, paid, or coerced into poisoning them. This was a fanaticism Putin grew up seeing and probably absorbing.

Vladimir Putin's parents were working class people. His mother worked in a factory, and his father served on a submarine in the Russian navy in the 1930's and worked for the NKVD (the precursor of the KGB and FSB). Putin was the youngest of three sons born to Maria Ivanova Shelomova and Vladimir Spirodonovich Putin. The first son, Albert, died as a baby. The second son, Viktor, born in 1940, died of starvation and diptheria during the siege of Leningrad by Nazi Germany.

Yes, that siege. The one that lasted 872 days, where by 1942, 100,000 civilians a month were dying. The Germans lost some 85,000 men in the siege, and 1.4 million Russian civilians died. The total death toll for Russians on the northern front, of which the siege was the centerpiece, added up to over 3.4 million casualties.

Putin's father was severely wounded in 1942 fighting the Nazis while a tank driver. It is no doubt from him that Putin learned his love of tanks, his admiration for tank battalions, and his belief in the indomitable will of Russian infantry soldiers. We'll discuss this in more detail later as we examine Putin's inexplicably World War II-style strategy for invading Ukraine.

Putin's maternal grandmother was killed by Nazis in the Tver region in 1941, and both of his uncles disappeared on the Eastern Front and were never seen again. Undoubtedly, they died and were buried in one of the thousands of hasty mass graves strewn across western Russia.

Suffice it to say the war took a terrible toll on Putin's family. This is almost certainly the origin of Putin's deep and abiding hatred of Nazis. It also probably explains why he resorts to calling anyone he thinks of as "bad" a Nazi or neo-Nazi. To him, Nazis are the boogeyman he was terrified of as a child.

Putin grew up in a tough, communal housing block. It's reported he often got into fights with boys bigger than him, which drove him to take up martial arts. He studied judo and sambo, a Russian combat-wrestling martial art form. He also studied German and speaks it fluently to this day.

He graduated from law school in 1975 and joined the Communist Party. While at Leningrad State University, he met Anatoly Sobchak, an assistant professor of business law who would later help Putin enter Moscow politics.

When asked why he wanted to join the KGB, Putin answered that, in the KGB:

"One man's effort could achieve what whole armies could not. One spy could decide the fate of thousands of people."

Immediately after law school, Vladimir Putin achieved his dream of joining the KGB and trained in counterintelligence. He was eventually transferred to the directorate that monitored foreigners and diplomatic officials in Leningrad (now St. Petersburg).

Although it has never been proven, it's believed he served in New Zealand for some time, allegedly undercover as a shoe salesman in Wellington.

DRESDEN GALVANIZES PUTIN

From 1985 to 1990, Putin was stationed in Dresden, East Germany, working undercover as a translator. His wife at the time, Ludmilla, accompanied him to Dresden, and they lived a comfortable life in East Germany. The standard of living was substantially better there than in Russia, and it was a plush assignment. He and his wife socialized with members of the KGB and Stasi—the East German Secret Police—and probably considered themselves untouchable elites within that police state.

A former KGB colleague, Vladimir Usoltsev, described Putin spending hours leafing through Western mail-order catalogues, to keep up with fashions and trends.

He also enjoyed the beer, purchasing a weekly supply of the local brew, Radeberger.

A journalist who covered the KGB in East Germany at that time says of Putin, "He enjoyed very much this little paradise for him. East Germany is his model of politics especially. He rebuilt some kind of East Germany in Russia now."

Although East Germany was a communist state (in technical point of fact it was socialist, as was Russia), East Germany differed from Russia in that it allowed multiple political parties. Nonetheless, the East German regime ruled with an iron fist and seemed in firm control of the nation.

And then the uprisings of 1989 swept across most of Eastern Europe.

In June of 1989, the people of Poland voted out their own Communist regime, electing the Solidarity Trade Union in its place. In August of 1989, Hungary opened a border gate between it and Austria. In December of 1989, a violent uprising in Romania overthrew the communist regime there as well.

In what must have seemed like an overwhelming cascade failure, one communist regime after another collapsed suddenly, and in some cases, almost without warning. The Fall of the Berlin Wall and the opening of East Germany's borders took place in the middle of that wave of democratic uprising across eastern Europe.

Political unrest erupted in East Germany in the summer of 1989, growing steadily louder and more popular into the autumn. The East German government reversed itself without warning, declaring on November 9, 1989, that its citizens could cross the country's borders, notably with West Germany, freely. Jubilant crowds rushed the Berlin Wall and physically toppled it on the evening of November 9, 1989.

By December of 1989, the entire East German regime neared collapse as the people of that country rose up in even more protests.

PUTIN IS FOREVER CHANGED BY THE FALL OF EAST GERMANY

The night the East German regime fell, December 5, 1989, crowds stormed the Stasi headquarters in Dresden. A small party of protestors peeled away from the main crowd and decided to head across the street to the house holding the local KGB office, where Putin and his cronies worked and spied from.

Siegfried Dannath, who was present in that crowd described it like this:

> "The guard on the gate immediately rushed back into the house. But shortly afterwards an officer emerged—quite small, agitated."

NOTE: That officer was Vladimir Putin.

Dannath continues:

> "He said to our group, 'Don't try to force your way into this property. My comrades are armed, and they're authorized to use their weapons in an emergency.' That persuaded the group to withdraw."

But that KGB officer knew how dangerous the situation remained. Putin described later how he went back inside and immediately called the headquarters of a Red Army tank unit to ask for protection.

The answer Putin received was a devastating, life-changing shock.

> "We cannot do anything without orders from Moscow," the voice at the other end replied. "And Moscow is silent."

As forceful and confident as Putin appeared to those protestors, he could do nothing more in the face of silence from Moscow. Putin's idyllic time in the "paradise" of East Germany collapsed around him as abruptly as the Berlin Wall came crashing down.

Left completely on their own, the KGB officers in Dresden frantically destroyed evidence of their espionage activities. Putin later recalled, "I personally burned a huge amount of material. We burned so much stuff that the furnace burst."

Two weeks later, the West German Chancellor, Helmut Kohl, came to Dresden to make a speech offering rapid reunification to East Germany and praised Mikhail Gorbachev. Kohl referred for the first time since World War II to Germany as the *vaterland*—fatherland—a term that had been taboo since the end of the war, but now drew huge cheers from the crowd. It had to be a chilling site to a Russian man whose family had been so devastated by the Nazi Army.

Putin's wife Ludmilla described the implosion of East Germany likewise imploding their lives as well:

> "We had the horrible feeling that the country that had almost become our home would no longer exist. My neighbor, who was my friend, (and a fellow

KGB wife) cried for a week. It was the collapse of everything—our lives, our careers."

One of Putin's closest colleagues, a Stasi Major General Horst Boehm, was humiliated by a crowd demonstrating against him and committed suicide in January of 1990. It was the final blow to Putin. He returned to Moscow with only a 20-year-old, secondhand washing machine given to them by German friends and nothing more to show for his time in Germany.

This experience taught Putin a valuable lesson in just how fragile any regime can be in the face of a popular uprising against it. Scholars agree he probably developed his deep paranoia of being overthrown from his Dresden experience.

Putin himself said later that he was haunted by the military's failure to support the KGB when called upon to do so. It is probably in this time period that Putin's ideas regarding the political leadership of Russia needing to assert absolute control over the Russian military developed.

PUTIN COMES HOME TO THE USSR'S COLLAPSE

If his experience in Dresden wasn't traumatic enough, the Russia Putin came home to was also on the verge of collapse. The old Soviet Union he'd known was moving rapidly toward dissolution. The economy was in freefall, and Gorbachev was struggling to implement domestic reforms and keeping a dying economy on life support.

The West was openly exultant at the collapse of communism in East Germany and other Warsaw Pact nations—all satellite states of

Russia and important geopolitical buffers between it and Western Europe. A new atmosphere of freedom, opportunity. . .and rebellion. . .was in the air.

Disillusioned, Putin decided to leave the KGB and considered becoming a taxi driver, but he was talked into staying in the KGB by the "profitable business opportunities" for people as connected inside the government as he was. Initially upon his return to Russia, he worked at Leningrad State University spotting and recruiting students for the KGB.

In late July of 1991, a group of hardliners called the Gang of Eight attempted a coup d'état to oust Prime Minister Gorbachev. They were all cabinet members in the Soviet government and were about to be stripped of most of their power by reforms proposed by Gorbachev. At that time, Boris Yeltsin was the Chairman of the Parliament and fast becoming the most popular politician in the USSR. He supported Gorbachev throughout the coup, as did Putin.

The slow-moving coup lasted several weeks with the public split on the matter. By August 22, 1991, the coup had been put down, largely because the military refused to back the hardliners.

Gorbachev returned to Moscow where he reluctantly admitted that the Communist Party of the Soviet Union—whose senior members had attempted the coup—must be disbanded. Gorbachev resigned as General Secretary of the CPSU, and the Supreme Soviet (the parliament) suspended the party.

And then, the USSR literally disintegrated:

> **August 25, 1991:** Belorussia declared itself a sovereign nation.

August 27, 1991: Moldova declared itself independent.

August 30, 1991: Azerbaijan declared independence.

August 31, 1991: Kyrgyzstan declared independence.

September 6, 1991: the newly created Soviet State Council recognized Latvia, Lithuania, and Estonia's independence.

September 9, 1991: Tajikistan left the USSR.

99% of voters in Armenia voted for independence in September, and it left.

October 27, 1991: Turkmenistan left the USSR.

December 1, 1991: Ukraine held a referendum in which more than 90% of voters supported Ukraine declaring independence, and it left as well.

On December 8th, 1991 Boris Yeltsin signed the Belovezha Accords, declaring that the Soviet Union had ceased to exist. The Russian Soviet Socialist Republic renamed itself the Russian Federation, and on Christmas Eve, 1991, informed the United Nations that it would inherit the Soviet Union's membership in the UN, including the USSR's permanent seat on the UN Security Council. Nobody in the United Nations nor in the Security Council objected.

On December 25th, Gorbachev resigned as President of the Soviet Union and Boris Yeltsin took over ruling the brand-new Russian Federation.

PUTIN ENTERS POLITICS

As early as 2005, Putin said in a speech,

> "First and foremost, it is worth acknowledging that
> the demise of the Soviet Union was the greatest
> geopolitical catastrophe of the century. As for the
> Russian people, it became a genuine tragedy. Tens
> of millions of our fellow citizens and countrymen
> found themselves beyond the fringes of Russian ter-
> ritory. The epidemic of collapse has spilled over to
> Russia itself."

Here, we see the first seeds of his awareness that ethnic Russians and those who had supported the old USSR were still scattered
among the former Soviet republics, which were now independent
nations, and furthermore that they might be useful pawns for him
in his political chess games.

Following the dissolution of the USSR, Putin declined to work
in the intelligence community within the new government. He
didn't agree with the USSR having been allowed to collapse, and
he had no intention of supporting the new, weak regime. He did,
however, take a job in the Leningrad Mayor's Office and began
working his way up through the political ranks of the renamed city
of St. Petersburg (formerly Leningrad).

In June 1996, Putin's mentor Anatoly Sobchak lost his re-elec-
tion bid in the St. Petersburg government and moved to Moscow,
taking his protégé with him. By March of 1997, Putin had caught
the eye of President Boris Yeltsin, who appointed him Deputy Chief
of the Presidential Staff.

In the summer of 1997, Putin defended his doctoral dissertation and was awarded a PhD in economics. His thesis was on strategic planning of Russia's mineral economy. Which is to say, he knows what he's doing when he attempts to manipulate global oil prices.

NATO EXPANSION

Throughout the 1990s Russian officials repeatedly expressed concerns about NATO expanding eastward toward Russia. American officials offered verbal assurances that NATO would not expand into Eastern Europe, and the Russian leadership appeared to believe them.

However, the West's promise eroded over a period of years. Poland, Hungary, and the Czech Republic were admitted to NATO in 1999. Then, in 2004, Estonia, Latvia, Lithuania, Bulgaria, Romania, Slovakia, and Slovenia were admitted to NATO. Since then, Croatia, Albania, Montenegro, and North Macedonia have also been admitted to NATO's ranks.

This development is said to have infuriated Putin, who railed against allowing the enemy to come so close to Russia's borders.

Before we leave the topic of NATO's expansion into Eastern Europe, it's worth noting that in 2008, NATO issued a declaration that it welcomed Ukraine and Georgia's aspirations to join NATO. These were Russia's most prosperous former republics, and the two Russia most desired to retake and absorb back into the Russian Federation.

NATO's invitation to the two nations to apply to NATO enraged Russian leadership. Putin was reported to have been nearly apoplectic with rage over NATO making overtures at luring away two of the crown jewels of the old Russian empire. Putin was (and is) a proud man and proudly Russian, and he viewed NATO's advances as a humiliation of Russia...a humiliation that called for retribution.

Many point to NATO's declaration of welcome to Ukraine and Georgia as one of the main reasons Russia ultimately invaded Georgia. Russia was trying to forcibly prevent Georgia from applying to NATO.

For that matter, clauses within the NATO charter requiring clear territorial control and rule of law are preventing Ukraine from applying for NATO membership right now. Indeed, since 2014, Russia's illegal seizure of the Crimea and occupation of Luhansk and Donetsk has blocked Ukraine from eligibility for NATO membership, a fact which Putin is undoubtedly vividly aware of, and which was likely a major factor in Putin's decision to commence chipping away at Ukraine's territorial integrity when he did.

Foreign policy scholar, George Kennan, warned in 1998 that NATO expansion would lead to a new Cold War, and he turned out to be prescient. For someone like Putin, who saw the collapse of the Soviet Union as a blunder of epic proportions, the expansion of NATO into multiple former Soviet Republics and right up to Russia's borders had to be salt in the wound to his Russian patriotic pride.

PUTIN'S METORIC RISE

In July of 1998, Yeltsin appointed Putin director of the FSB, the new intelligence and security organization of the Russian Federation and successor to the KGB.

The following year, on August 9, 1999, an ailing Yeltsin appointed Putin to be one of three first deputy prime ministers. Later that *same day*, Yeltsin appointed him acting Prime Minister of the Government of the Russian Federation, making it crystal clear he wanted Putin to be his successor as President of the Russian Federation. Putin agreed to run for the office permanently the following year.

In the fall of 1999, a series of Russian apartment bombings, and the invasion of Dagestan rattled the Russian public. In spite of Yeltsin's main opponents campaigning hard against the almost completely unknown Putin, his strong, law-and-order image proved popular as the presidential campaign got under way.

Yeltsin unexpectedly resigned on December 31, 1999, forcing the presidential election to happen several months early. Already acting president of the Russian Federation after Yeltsin resigned, Putin won the presidency outright with 53% of the vote.

THE TOUGH GUY EMERGES

The brand-new President Putin promptly made criminal charges levied against several old friends of his and against Yeltsin family members disappear. Putin also made a lawsuit against his own alleged corruption in metal exports evaporate. He wasted no time exerting control over the judicial system and over the FSB—his old stomping grounds.

During Putin's first term in office, with the Russian economy shifting from a government-controlled, command economy to a largely privatized economy, the great money grab was on. Business and industry leaders seized control of everything they could get their hands on—factories, supply lines, domestic and foreign production contracts, bank accounts—and built private business empires for themselves.

Putin won a power struggle with these new oligarchs, reaching what he described as a "grand bargain" with them. They could maintain their power, wealth, and income in exchange for explicit and unwavering support for him and his government. Take one step out of line, however, and he would strip them of everything they and their family owned. In those cases, he had an overwhelming tendency to keep all the seized businesses, wealth, and power for himself or to hand them over to a close friend in return for substantial kickbacks.

One by one, Putin ousted oligarchs who strayed from utter loyalty to him and replaced them with his friends and cronies, most of whom he'd known since his days in Dresden.

And then he started killing journalists. Political dissidents began to die. And the State Security Force was formed. This group reported (and still does report) directly to Putin and to him alone. This personal police force's primary jobs are to keep order in the streets, spy on civilians, arrest troublemakers, and let everyone know exactly who's in charge in Russia.

PRIME MINISTER AND BACK AGAIN

The Russian Constitution forbade Putin from running for a third term in office in 2008 as President, so he arranged for first deputy prime minister Dmitry Medvedev to be elected President and immediately appoint Putin Prime Minister, allowing him to go right on running the country.

In 2012, Putin ran for President again and won by a suspiciously large landslide. Protests broke out over election fraud and were viciously suppressed by his State Security Force. He won a fourth presidential term in 2018, and in 2020 changed the Russian Constitution to allow himself to run for two more six-year terms, assuring himself of remaining in office until at least the year 2032.

On December 22, 2020, Putin signed a bill giving lifetime immunity from prosecution to all Russian ex-presidents.

WHAT KIND OF LEADER IS PUTIN?

In a word, he's tough. He has always portrayed himself as a tough guy ruling a tough country. His shirtless poses on horses or martial arts videos are quintessential Putin.

He has gradually done away with various freedoms—of the press, of political opposition, of speech by anyone criticizing him or his regime. In fact, it has recently been made a crime to *think* negative or treasonous thoughts about him or his regime.

Bit by bit, he has returned the Russian Federation to a close approximation of the bad old days under the Soviet Regime.

Putin swiftly and violently suppresses all opposition to him and puts down anything even remotely resembling rebellion, or even opposition, anywhere within Russia's borders. A shocking number of his would-be political opponents have found themselves poisoned or irradiated to death in recent years. The lucky ones are merely jailed indefinitely on trumped up charges.

He has worked diligently to rebuild the Russian economy, managing to restore it to a position as the world's 11th largest economy by about 2015. Russia's economy going into the Ukraine war was about the same size as Italy's. He has worked equally hard to rebuild the Russian military, massively expanding spending on modernizing and increasing the size of it. But more on that in a bit.

He openly promotes the return of the Russian Orthodox Church to Russia. The USSR was officially an atheist nation, and practice of religion of any kind was against the law. Soviet officials were willing to look the other way as long as Russian Orthodox priests did not cross the government, but only a tiny percentage of Russians—1 to 2%—formally belonged to an active church parish when Putin took office.

Today, 70 to 80% of all Russians do profess to be Orthodox, but less than 15% attend church services more than once a month, and only about 5 percent once a week. This state of mostly "unchurched believers" persisted until the death of Patriarch Aleksii in 2008.

Patriarch Kirill of Moscow replaced Aleksii as head of the Russian Orthodox Church. He was and is fanatically loyal to Putin, and Putin has made Kirill a very wealthy man. The two of them have pushed hard to rebuild the church inside Russia, increasing the number of physical churches and parishes. They've both worked to centralize the Orthodox Church's authority away from parishes, return it to traditional conservative views, increase church membership, and aggressively support Putin from the pulpit in spite of an official policy of not involving itself in politics.

Above all, Putin desires to rebuild and reconstitute the USSR. Some scholars speculate that he has expanded his vision beyond even that and may have a secret ambition of rebuilding the entire Russian Empire, which once stretched across most of Central Asia, parts of Northeast Asia, Alaska, Hawaii, parts of California, the Baltic states, and parts of Poland and Finland.

Putin makes no secret of being determined to reverse what he sees as the humiliation of Russia through the 1990's and 2000's, and this may be his biggest ambition of all.

He's also dead set on returning Russia to its former status internationally as one of the Great Powers on earth. That means building an intimidating army, engaging in expansionist actions abroad, interfering in global politics, squeezing as much income out of global oil and mineral markets as he can, and throwing his weight around on the world stage.

Famously in a meeting with the German Prime Minister at his dacha in Sochi, Crimea on July 7, 2017, Putin brought his black lab dog, Koni, into the meeting. Angela Merkel was known to have a severe phobia of dogs.

The New Yorker described the moment:

> "As the dog approached and sniffed her, Merkel froze, visibly frightened. She'd been bitten once, in 1995, and her fear of dogs couldn't have escaped Putin, who sat back and enjoyed the moment, legs spread wide. 'I'm sure it will behave itself,' he said. Merkel had the presence of mind to reply, in Russian, 'It doesn't eat journalists, after all.' . . ."

Merkel commented after the incident, "I understand why he has to do this—to prove he's a man,' she told a group of reporters. "He's afraid of his own weakness. Russia has nothing, no successful politics or economy. All they have is this.'"

CHAPTER TEN:

EXPANSIONIST PUTIN

"Vladimir Putin wants to, in fact, reestablish the former Soviet Union."

—President Joe Biden,
February 2022

"If someone decides to destroy Russia, then we have a legal right
to respond. Yes, for humanity it will be a global catastrophe,
for the world there will be a global catastrophe. But still, as a citizen of
Russia and the head of the Russian state, then I want to ask myself the
question, why do we need such a world where there is no Russia?"

—Vladimir Putin

VLADIMIR PUTIN inherited from his predecessors an ongoing conflict in Chechnya. His response to this conflict gave the world its first peek at the aggressive expansionist Putin was going to become.

CHECHNYA BACKGROUND

If you look at a map of Russia, it is shaped like a large oval lying on its long side. At the western end of that oval, a chunk of land called the Caucasus projects down to the south between the Black Sea and the Caspian Sea. In the southern center of that land mass lies a small region officially called the Chechen Republic and informally called Chechnya.

This region is about 6,700 square miles (17,300 square km) in size and has a population of about 1.5 million people, about 96% native Chechnyans. They are mostly Muslim in faith. 95% of citizens polled in the capital city, Grozny, call themselves Muslim.

The Chechnyans are indigenous to the Caucasus. They have their own language, Chechen, and are ethnically part of the Nakh peoples who have inhabited the Caucasus for millennia.

The Caucasus fell under Persian rule for many centuries and was first invaded by Peter the Great. This region bounced back and forth between Persian (and later Ottoman) rule and Imperial Russian rule for several hundred years. It was finally absorbed into the USSR in 1921.

The northern two-thirds of Chechnya is flat plains with several major rivers and is heavily agricultural. The Southern third of Chechnya is mountainous and inhabited by indigenous Chechnyans who have lived in the Caucasus Mountains for centuries.

In 1991, in the midst of all the Russian republics declaring independence from Russia, Chechnya declared independence from the USSR as well. In 1994, however, Russian forces attempted to regain control of the region and force it back under Russian rule.

From 1994 to 1996 the First Chechnyan War was fought, killing 100,000 Chechnyans. In spite of numerical and technological superiority in equipment and troops, the Russian army was unable to defeat the Chechnyans in the mountainous south and never managed to assert permanent control over the region.

Boris Yeltsin declared a ceasefire in 1996, signed a peace treaty later that year with the Chechnyan government, and withdrew Russian forces from the region. Chechnya was unstable with a weak regime, a devastated economy, and kidnapping became one of the primary sources of income inside the fledgling nation over the next two years.

Islamist insurgents in Chechnya invaded neighboring Dagastan in 1999 in an effort to help Muslims there declare independence from Russia and break away from the Russian Federation. Russian military forces fought back, driving the insurgents out of Dagastan and pursuing them back into Chechnya.

PUTIN INHERITS THE CHECHNYA PROBLEM

Vladimir Putin was elected Prime Minister for the first time in August of 1999. He came to power in the middle of this ongoing fight to put down the Chechnyan insurgency.

In the fall of 1999, a series of apartment building bombings struck several major Russian cities, including Moscow, killing some 300 people. These bombings were blamed on Chechnyan separatists.

Putin struck back hard. In retaliation, Russia launched a series of airstrikes inside Chechnya followed by a ground invasion. This invasion was much better planned and equipped than the first invasion in 1994 and quickly swept across Chechnya's flat northern region.

Although Russian forces took control of most of Chechnya, they again failed to gain control of the rugged mountains in the south. The invasion and takeover of Chechnya were marked by extremely brutal tactics by the Russian Army. Putin himself has taken credit for ordering these tactics.

Putin described the conflict in Chechnya like this:

"The Chechnya problem is a centuries old problem. The thing is that today, fundamentalists and terrorists are exploiting those centuries-old problems to accomplish their own objectives that have nothing to do whatsoever with the interests of Chechnya."

He also said:

"International terrorists who pursue completely mad objectives such as establishing a world caliphate or something of the sort, are quite adept at disguising their real aims as a struggle for independence in Chechnya."

The United States and other nations, also deep into fights against terrorists at home and abroad, didn't disagree with Putin's observations and looked the other way as Putin invaded Chechnya, which had throughout the 1990s been an independent, sovereign nation.

The West also looked the other way as Putin engaged in war crimes and genocide against the Chechnyan people. Because they were Muslim and because a few of them were engaging in terrorist attacks, apparently they all were fair game for annihilation.

Meanwhile, Chechnyan insurgents operated out of the southern mountains, engaging on terrorist attacks against Russian forces inside Chechnya and against Russians outside the region.

Human Rights Watch Emergency Researcher, Peter Boukaert, said in testimony before the U.S. Senate Committee for Foreign Relations on February 29, 2000:

"The evidence we have gathered in Chechnya is disturbing: Russian forces have committed grave abuses, including war crimes, in their campaign in Chechnya. In Grozny, the graffiti on the walls reads "Welcome to Hell: Part Two," about as good a summary as any of what Chechen civilians have been living through in the past five months.

"Russia talks about fighting a war against terrorism in Chechnya, but it is Chechen civilians who have borne the brunt of the Russian offensive in this war, as in the first Chechen conflict. Most abuses we have documented have been committed by Russian forces; we have also documented serious abuses by Chechen fighters."

He went on to describe in detail the atrocities, war crimes, and human rights abuses being perpetrated by Russian Forces in Chechnya against civilians.

Although this is a lengthy passage, take note of how exactly it could be describing the behavior of Russian forces in Ukraine today:

"Since the beginning of the conflict, Russian forces have indiscriminately and disproportionately bombed and shelled civilian objects, causing heavy civilian casualties. The Russian forces have ignored their Geneva convention obligations to focus their attacks on combatants and appear to take few safeguards to protect civilians:

It is this carpet-bombing campaign that has been responsible for the vast majority of civilian deaths in the conflict in Chechnya. The Russian forces have used powerful surface-to surface rockets on numerous occasions, causing death tolls in the hundreds in the Central Market bombing in Grozny and in many smaller towns and villages.

Lately, Russian commanders have threatened to use even more powerful explosives, including fuel-air explosives which could have a disastrous casualty count if used against civilian targets. The bombing campaign has turned many parts of Chechnya to a wasteland: even the most experienced war reporters I have spoken to told me they have never seen anything in their careers like the destruction of the capital Grozny.

Russian forces have often refused to create safe corridors to allow civilians to leave areas of active fighting, trapping civilians behind front lines for months. The haggard men and women who came out of Grozny after a perilous journey told me of living for months in dark, cold cellars with no water, gas, or electricity and limited food: their little children were often in shock, whimpering in the corners of their tents in Ingushetia and screaming in fright whenever Russian war planes flew over, reminding them of the terror in Grozny.

Men especially face grave difficulties when attempting to flee areas of fighting: they are subjected to verbal taunting, extortion, theft, beatings, and arbitrary arrest.

On several occasions, refugee convoys have come under intense bombardment by Russian forces, causing heavy casualties. Currently, tens of thousands of civilians remain trapped in the Argun River gorge in Southern Chechnya, stuck behind Russian lines without a way out from the constant bombardment and rapidly running out of food supplies.

For many Chechens, the constant bombardment was only the beginning of the horror. Once they came into contact with Russian forces, they faced even greater dangers. Human Rights Watch has now documented three large-scale massacres by Russian forces in Chechnya.

In December, Russian troops killed seventeen civilians in the village of Alkhan-Yurt while going on a looting spree, burning many of the remaining homes and raping several women.

We have documented at least fifty murders, mostly of older men and women, by Russian soldiers in the Staropromyslovski district of Grozny since Russian forces took control of that district: innocent civilians shot to death in their homes and their yards. In one case, three generations of the Zubayev family were shot to death in the yard of their home.

On February 5, a few days after Secretary of State Albright met with President Putin in Moscow, Russian forces went on a killing spree in the Aldi district of Grozny, shooting at least sixty-two and possibly many more civilians who were waiting in the street and their yards for soldiers to check their documents. These were entirely preventable deaths, not unavoidable casualties of war. They were acts of murder, plain and simple.

Refugees are returning to Grozny to find their relatives or neighbors shot to death in their homes. And most disturbing of all, there is no evidence that the killing spree has stopped.

In the past month, the Russian authorities have begun arresting large numbers of civilian men throughout Chechnya. These men, numbering well over a thousand, and some women, have been taken to undisclosed detention facilities, and their relatives are desperately trying to locate them.

I have spoken to men who have been able to pay their way out of these detention facilities, and they have given me consistent testimony about constant beatings, severe torture, and even cases of rape of both men and women. One of the men suffered from a back injury after being hit with a heavy metal hammer; a second man had several broken ribs and suffered from kidney problems from the severe beatings."

Vladimir Putin made no secret of these tactics. In fact, he was known to brag about them. He took pride in the violence, war crimes, and atrocities of his forces.

His brutality was in plain sight for all the world to see if we had just paid attention. It should be no surprise to anyone that he employed the exact same tactics in his invasion of Ukraine. He got away with it in Chechnya. Why shouldn't he get away with it in Ukraine as well?

THE MOSCOW THEATER HOSTAGE CRISIS

Russians captured Grozny, the capital city of Chechnya, in 2000, marking the end of open hostilities in the region, However, Chechnyan insurgents (whom the Russians labeled terrorists) continued to fight back against Russia.

In October 2002, 40 to 50 Chechnyan rebels seized a theater in Moscow, taking around 900 hostages. A standoff ensued as the Chechnyans demanded the immediate and complete withdrawal of Russian forces from Chechnya. The rebels planted explosives all over the theater, including a very large explosive device directly in the middle of the theater among the hostages.

The layout of the theater would have forced Russian Spetznatz soldiers (Russian Special Forces) to fight down a long corridor and up a flight of stairs to reach the hostages in the main theater. These approaches were heavily defended and heavily booby trapped with explosives.

Four days of negotiations took place, with the Russian people increasingly demanding that Putin order tough action to rescue the hostages and take down the terrorists.

Very early on the fifth morning of the siege, Russian Spetnatz troops piped toxic gas into the theater. The Chechnyans opened fire on Russian troops surrounding the theater. Some of the Chechnyans had gas masks and continued to engage in a firefight with Spetznatz forces who stormed the theater. Eventually, all the Chechnyans—awake or unconscious—were shot, and the Russians began evacuating hostages from the theater.

The final casualty toll is unknown. Official reports place it at 118 hostages and all of the Chechnyan rebels. However, a full month after the incident, of the 645 surviving hostages, 150 were still in intensive care with 45 listed in critical condition. 73 hostages were never rendered medical aid and subsequently died, although they were removed from the theater alive. Estimates range between 200 and 300 hostages ultimately perished in the attack and rescue operation.

Later analysis of gas residue on the clothing of two British hostages whose bodies were returned to Britain indicated that two derivatives of fentanyl gas were used to incapacitate the rebels and hostages. However, no medical units outside the theater were informed of this. Had they known the composition of the mystery gas, they could have administered antidotes and potentially saved most or all of the hostages.

Later that morning, after the Spetznatz assault, Vladimir Putin went on national television to praise the assault, saying that Special Forces had "achieved the nearly impossible, saving hundreds of people." He went on to declare that the rescue "proved it is impossible to bring Russia to its knees."

Yet again, he openly and proudly resorted to the most violent possible response to a crisis. He applauded the Special Forces for murdering many of the civilian hostages in the theater if that was what it took to kill a handful of filthy Chechnyan terrorists.

Putin showed no interest in protecting innocent lives. In fact, he casually treated the theater hostages as relatively meaningless collateral damage. Again, Putin did not hesitate to display his core brutality.

There can be no doubt Putin sleeps perfectly well at night knowing that his army is murdering tens of thousands of innocent civilians in Ukraine. He never has shown the slightest concern for protecting innocent lives, and indeed, openly approves of terrorizing and brutalizing them into submission to him.

PUTIN DOUBLES DOWN IN CHECHNYA

The same evening as the assault to rescue the Moscow theater hostages, Putin released one last televised statement, declaring:

> "Russia will respond with measures that are adequate to the threat to the Russian Federation, striking all the places where the terrorists themselves, the organizers of these crimes and their ideological and financial inspirations are. I stress, wherever they may be located."

It was generally believed that Putin was referring to the now independent, former Soviet Republic of Georgia just to the south of Chechnya. Analysts believed he was issuing a veiled threat that Georgia was next on the invasion chopping block. The analysts were not wrong.

But first, Putin crushed Chechnya.

In response to the Moscow theater crisis, Putin launched large-scale military operations against Chechnyan separatists across Chechnya. By early 2001, the president of Chechnya offered to start peace talks with Russia, which Putin dismissed out of hand.

The Russian Parliament, the Duma, passed a number of strict new anti-terrorism laws, among which were sweeping new laws controlling how the Russian media was allowed to report on terrorism and anti-terrorism operations by Russia. Putin commenced aggressively enforcing these laws.

This was the first time that real fear was widely expressed in Russia that Putin was systematically taking control of the Russian media, much in the same way the USSR had completely controlled the state media during its authoritarian rule.

In words that proved to be prophetic, the leader of the liberal opposition party in Russia, Sergei Yushenkov, was quoted as saying:

> "On a wave of emotion, we have in fact legitimized censorship and practically banned criticism of the authorities in emergency situations."

PUTIN REFUSES TO LEAVE OFFICE

At the end of his second term as president of Russia, Putin faced a problem. The Russian Constitution prohibited him from serving a third term as president. So, in the final days of his presidency, he realigned the rules and procedures of the federal government to give most of the power in the country to the prime minister.

Then, in the 2008 presidential election, he backed Dmitry Medvedev, all but handing the election to him. No surprise, Medvedev immediately appointed Putin Prime Minister, and Putin didn't miss a step. He went on ruling the country from his new office.

The Great Recession of 2007 to 2009 hit Russia hard. But, due to high oil prices and a Russian Stabilization Fund previously established by Putin, the country weathered the recession reasonably well. This allowed Putin to turn his attention to his greatest ambition, reconstituting the old USSR into a single nation, ruled by him.

RUSSIA INVADES GEORGIA

The Republic of Georgia is a skinny triangle of land that lies along the eastern shore of the Black Sea at the southern tip of the Russian Caucasus between Russia to the north and Turkey to the southwest. It is a mountainous region of significant strategic importance, acting as the first barrier to invasion of the motherland from the south. Georgia also shares its southern border with Armenia to the direct south and Azerbaijan to the southeast.

Georgia is a largely Christian region with its own language, Georgian. It became part of the Russian Empire in 1800 and was incorporated into the USSR in 1921 when Bolshevik forces overran it. On April 9, 1991, it declared independence from the USSR, the first non-Baltic republic to break away from the Soviet Union.

Two regions inside Georgia—Abkhazia in the far northwest corner of Georgia, and South Ossetia along the northern border with Russia in the middle of the nation—were not thrilled to break away from Russia. These two areas both had large minority populations of ethnic Russians who wanted to leave Georgia and join Russia (much as the Luhansk and Donetsk regions of Ukraine did).

Conflict between pro-Russian separatists and Georgian nationalists erupted into civil war by 1992. By 1993, some 250,000 pro-Georgians had been expelled from Abkhazia and around 23,000 pro-Georgians were forced to flee South Ossetia.

Supported by Russia (in much the same way Russia has supported Luhansk and Donetsk) with Special forces troops in civilian clothing, money, weapons, training, and intelligence information, Abkhazia and South Ossetia achieved unofficial independence from Georgia.

When a treaty signed between Russia and Georgia required all Russian troops to withdraw from former Soviet military bases, Russia did not withdraw its troops from military bases in Abkhazia. Tensions between the two nations escalated rapidly.

In August of 2008, a carful of Georgian peacekeepers was blown up by South Ossetian separatists and open hostilities broke out between Georgian forces and the separatists. Russia accused Georgia of aggression against South Ossetia and launched a full-scale invasion of Georgia under the guise of a "peacekeeping operation."

During the invasion, Russia engaged in a large-scale ethnic cleansing operation of Georgians living in South Ossetia. The French government negotiated a peace treaty, but Russia currently recognizes Abkhazia and South Ossetia as separate republics and not part of the country of Georgia. Georgia, however, maintains that both regions are occupied Georgian territories.

While the invasion of Georgia was relatively short and sharp, it provides a blueprint for Putin's later invasion of pro-Russian separatist regions of eastern Ukraine, his support of those separatists with covert operations, and his insistence that those regions are independent despite international law and unanimous international opinion disagreeing with Putin's assertions.

Georgia is a representative parliamentary democracy. Since its war with Russia, it has focused on growing its economy and corralling corruption within the government, and it has shown steady improvement in education and quality of life. It has been described as being well on its way to becoming a European democracy. Its foreign policy points squarely toward the West, and it's currently working on becoming a full member of NATO. It has been classed as an aspirant-country by NATO since 2014.

Russia strongly opposes Georgia becoming a NATO member.

PUTIN RETURNS TO THE PRESDEINCY AND ANNEXES CRIMEA

In 2012, after serving one term as Prime Minister, President Medvedev formally asked Vladimir Putin to run for President of Russia again. Medvedev let it slip that he and Putin had cut a deal long ago that Putin would run for president again in 2012. The Russian media dubbed it "Rokirovka", the Russian term for castling in chess, a move where two important pieces on the board swap positions.

There actually was a fair bit of pushback inside Russia to Putin running for a third term. Protests erupted in the major cities and had to be put down with riot police from the State Security Force. Counterprotests with pro-Putin supporters were organized with some attendees claiming they were forced by their employers to attend and others saying they were told they were being bussed to a folk music festival.

At any rate, Putin won election to a third term in office. He immediately reversed the rules and procedures of the government he had changed in 2008 that had made the prime minister all-powerful, and he restored the lion's share of power back to the presidency.

In 2014, Putin invaded and annexed Crimea. This will be discussed in much more detail in a later chapter. But Putin continued his pattern of small, fast, illegal land grabs in former Soviet republics. He didn't attempt to take over any entire former republics. Rather, he was content to take back key portions of them.

Perhaps he was concerned that invading and taking over an entire nation wholesale would cause international backlash. Or perhaps he was content to chip away at his neighbors a little at a time. But that would change by the time 2022 rolled around.

RUSSIA INTERVENES IN SYRIA

The Syrian Civil War began in 2011 when Islamist and anti-government groups joined forces to attempt to take down the regime of Bashar al-Assad.

General Hafez al-Assad was president of Syria from 1971 to 2000 and transformed the country from a republic into a dynastic dictatorship. The military and Mukhabarat (Syria's secret services) were intensely loyal to the Assad family and helped the general remain in power. When the general died in June of 2000, his son Bashar succeeded his father. Every seven years since then, elections are held, and Bashar al-Assad wins them with overwhelming majorities that voting observers unanimously call rigged and sham elections.

By 2014, a significant portion of Syria's territory was claimed by ISIL. In northwest Syria, an Al-Qaeda linked group, the al-Nusra Front was active. Other smaller militant groups worked together under the moniker, Free Syrian Army, and this coalition was supported by the United States and other allies in the region.

ISIS/ISIL/DAESH/IS

A quick side note: ISIL stands for the Islamic State of Iraq and the Levant. The Levant is a historical term that refers to a broad region at the east end of the Mediterranean, including Libya, Egypt, Cyprus, Greece, Israel, Palestine, Jordan, Lebanon, Syria, Turkey, and Iraq. ISIS stands specifically for the Islamic State of Iraq and Syria, although this has become the most commonly used name for them globally and is most widely recognized in the United States.

The two names, ISIS and ISIL, do in fact refer to the same group of terrorists. In Arabic, their lengthy, full name is shortened to Daesh. However, this moniker is insulting to members of the group because it is thought to sound ugly and ignores the meaning of the group's full name.

Internally, members of the group now refer to themselves merely as IS—Islamic State. ISIL/ISIS/Daesh/IS claims to have religious authority over all Muslims everywhere. The bottom line: despite many names, it is one group, with one main goal, namely establishing and ruling a religious, Shiite caliphate in the Middle East and eventually across the entire world.

At any rate, ISIL had become widely active in Syria, exploiting the civil war inside that country to seize lands and expand its caliphate. ISIL seized a number of villages and cities, establishing strict and violent rule over them according to extremist Shiite religious beliefs. ISIL's leaders had already been expelled from Al-Qaeda by the time they attacked Syria and were acting independently.

Meanwhile, the al-Nusra Front acted as Al-Qaeda's surrogate inside Syria. Al-Nusra was a jihadist group whose goal was to overthrow the Assad regime and establish its own Islamic state ruled under sharia law. (Sharia law is a body of law derived from Muslim religious documents and teachings based on the scriptures of Islam).

BASHAR AL-ASSAD ASKS RUSSIA FOR HELP

The Assad regime, assailed on all sides, was in imminent danger of collapse by late 2015. In September of that year, the Syrian government formally asked Russia for help. Before then, the Assad government had been receiving military supplies, humanitarian aid, advisors, and other miscellaneous help from Russia.

Putin immediately sent in Russian Special Operations forces, military advisors, and the Wagner Group, a private military contractor infamous for the atrocities it committed across Africa and elsewhere. In addition, Putin sent in a sizable force of aircraft, missiles, and other military equipment to assist the Assad regime.

Putin stated that his goal in Syria was to stabilize the regime and set up an environment for negotiations to end hostilities. What he actually did was indiscriminately bomb civilian targets, including schools, hospitals, and markets. He employed a double-tap airstrike strategy wherein a location was bombed and then, after rescue workers and volunteers gathered to help the wounded, the location would be struck a second time.

Putin achieved broader objectives of rolling back U.S. influence within Syria and in the region, gaining strategically significant access to warm-water ports in the eastern Mediterranean Sea, and perhaps most important of all, he blocked construction of any oil pipelines from the Middle East to Europe, projects that had been proposed by Turkey and Qatar. These proposed pipelines would have put a serious dent in Russia's dominance of European oil markets.

The Russians spent the end of 2015 and much of 2016 carpet bombing the city of Aleppo, specifically targeting infrastructure and civilian targets, including underground hospitals, which had been moved below ground for safety after above-ground hospitals, health clinics, and ambulances were specially targeted.

Hezbollah and Iranian fighters coordinated with Russian airstrikes to invade Syria and attack the Free Syrian Army and other moderate rebel groups. Russia operated up to 60 airstrikes a day, claiming the attacks were specifically targeted at ISIS. In reality, only a tiny fraction of those airstrikes ever hit ISIS targets.

The United Nations condemned the intervention and found Russia guilty of war crimes there, which Russia scoffed at and denounced. No serious action was ever taken against Russia for the atrocities committed in Syria.

Putin, the Wagner Group, and senior Russian military officials learned one particularly important lesson in their Syrian invasion—if they committed enough brutal atrocities against civilians, the population would buckle under the horror of it and surrender. This was a lesson they all carried forward into the invasion of Ukraine with disastrous results for the Ukrainian people, and one might argue, disastrous results for Russia. But more on that later.

Russian airstrikes in Syria continued into 2017, and the United States also commenced launching airstrikes of its own against various terrorist groups inside Syria. A careful effort was made between American and Russian military commanders to deconflict the region, meaning we went out of our way to notify each other when and where an airstrike was planned so the other's military could be well out of harm's way before the airstrike occurred. There were a few mistakes, but for the most part, the deconfliction strategy held.

In 2017, Russia declared Syria mostly back under the control of the Assad regime and withdrew the main force of its soldiers. However, Russia also announced that it would be establishing a permanent military presence in Syria.

Using those bases and troops, Russia has continued a campaign of airstrikes against rebel forces inside Syria and continues to launch airstrikes in that country to this day.

RUSSIAN REPORT CARD IN SYRIA

Russian airstrikes were particularly effective against ISIS-held oil pipelines and ISIS supply lines in the expanse of desert that comprises the eastern half of Syria. Military experts generally agree that Russia maintained an impressive pace of attack and showed the will to sustain the attack. Everyone agrees that without Russia's intervention, the Assad regime would have fallen. Putin's intervention allowed the Syrian military to shift from scrambling on defense to taking the offense aggressively.

The Russian Navy performed with mixed results, criticized for the small size of its air assets, problems with the MiG-29K, and a lack of aircraft catapults on its only aircraft carrier in the region that would have allowed it to launch heavier aircraft.

The Russian army used a small number of precision munitions relatively effectively in Syria, but it relied mostly on much cheaper unguided munitions. When launched from airplanes, those unguided munitions were nearly as accurate as guided missiles. However, when launched from the ground, unguided munitions were woefully inaccurate on the whole.

Russian Defense Minister, Sergei Shoigu, claimed that Russia got a chance to test some 300 different weapons systems in Syria. Which begs the question of why the Russian military has performed so abysmally on the whole in Ukraine.

Nonetheless, when faced with no serious military opposition in Syria, a deconfliction agreement with the U.S. forces in the region that insured Russian forces would never come up against American forces, and no opponent inside Syria with the money or resources to field any modern military equipment to speak of, the Russian army appeared to be a competent, modern fighting force.

Vladimir Putin seems to have believed his own press releases that the Russian military had reasserted itself as a serious global military power in light of its generally effective performance in Syria.

Since the invasion of Ukraine, the bulk of Russian troops have been withdrawn from Syria and redeployed to the Ukraine, but airstrikes in the Syrian theater of combat continue.

PUTIN EYES OTHER FORMER SOVIET REPUBLICS: MOLDOVA AND BELARUS

While we're about to spend a fair bit of time taking a look at Putin's attempt to reclaim Ukraine and absorb it back into the Russian federation, I would be remiss if I didn't mention that on February 14, 2023, Moldova's president, Maia Sandu, claimed that Moscow was plotting to overthrow her government with the aid of external saboteurs "at the disposal of Russia."

President Sandu said her nation's intelligence service had confirmed plans, intercepted by Ukraine, that were developed by the Russian secret services to destroy her country's democracy.

She ended her statement with these words to the Moldovan people:

> "I want to ask you to stay vigilant, be attentive and trust the official information, as the most aggressive form of attack is the information attack. The Kremlin's attempts to bring violence in our country will fail. We should keep calm. We should trust the Republic of Moldova."

On February 14, 2023, a leaked internal strategy document from Vladimir Putin's executive office was handed to western news outlets. In it, plans are laid out to take full control of Belarus in the next decade under the pretext of a merger between the two countries.

The document describes in "granular detail" a creeping annexation by political, economic, and military means, including an expansion of Russian military presence in Belarus. This is sure to alarm Belarus's immediate neighbors, Poland, Estonia, Latvia, and Lithuania, all of whom are NATO members.

The leaked document also advocates the "formation of pro-Russian sentiments in political and military elites and the population," while "limiting the influence of nationalist and pro-Western forces in Belarus." It outlines "harmonization" of Belarusian laws with those of Russia, coordinated foreign and defense policy, and trade and economic cooperation:

> "ensuring the predominant influence of the Russian Federation in the socio-political, trade-economic, scientific-educational, and cultural-information spheres."

According to the document, the end goal is the formation of a so-called "Union State of Russia and Belarus" no later than 2030.

Michael Carpenter, U.S. Ambassador to the Organization for Security and Cooperation in Europe commented on the leaked plans, saying:

> "Russia's goals with regards to Belarus are the same as with Ukraine. Only in Belarus, it relies on coercion rather than war. Its end goal is still wholesale incorporation."

Rainier Saks, former head of Estonia's Foreign Intelligence Service responded:

"Of course, Russia will take control of Belarus, but the question is if it does so at the cost of independence. It is surprising to me why this target—2030—is set so far ahead. Why should Russia wait so long?"

Belarus's opposition leader, Svetlana Tsikhanovskaya, described the plan contained in the document this way:

"It is not a union of equals. It is a roadmap for the absorption of Belarus by Russia. Since our goal is to return Belarus to the path of democracy, it will be impossible to do so in a Union State with Russia."

PUTIN'S PLAYBOOK FOR INVASION

Over the course his invasions and successes in Chechnya, Georgia, and Syria, Putin developed a personal playbook for how to invade a nation, how to take only the portions of it that were amenable to rejoining the Russian Federation, and avoiding biting off and gobbling up such a large chunk of any one sovereign nation that the global community would squawk too loudly.

Putin had every reason to believe that his brutal, scorched earth tactics against civilians, that had worked so well already, would continue to work everywhere, every time, to cow and frighten civilian populations.

He also had every reason to believe the West had no stomach for any kind of direct confrontation with him, no matter how boldly he stole land from a small neighbor or marched into an ally's nation and threw his weight around.

He upped the stakes a little bit more each time from Chechnya to Georgia to Syria. Each time, he got away with grabbing more land, asserting Russian military dominance a little more forcefully, and establishing permanent Russian military presences in each place.

Indeed, why should he have any reason to expect that anyone would care too much if he upped the stakes a little bit more and, instead of just stealing a few provinces in eastern Ukraine, he decided to take the whole country this time?

The stage was set for a Russian invasion close to home. . .this time with an eye to achieving Putin's long-held dream of bringing back together the USSR under his rule.

CHAPTER ELEVEN:

UKRAINE AND RUSSIA IN CONFLICT

ON THE EVE of Russia's full-scale invasion of Ukraine, Putin ordered the West not to interfere in what he described as Russia's "special military operation" in eastern Ukraine. . .

> "To anyone who would consider interfering from outside:
> If you do, you will face consequences greater than
> any you have faced in history. All the relevant decisions
> have been taken. I hope you hear me."
> —Vladimir Putin, Feb, 24, 2022

And so began the first major war on the European continent in 75 years and possibly the greatest, and final, existential threat to the world in its history.

A reasonable person might ask why a book about the End Times and Armageddon launched by Iran against Israel includes a discussion of the Russia-Ukraine War. It is because this war forms a critical backdrop for the crisis emerging right now in the Middle East.

It is under the cover of this war that Putin is forming a close military alliance with Iran through which he can arm Iran with nuclear weapons. . . the very weapons Iran needs to annihilate Israel in its own Islamic version of Armageddon that will usher in its Mahdi, its Islamic messianic figure.

And, it is the West's naïve response to the Russia-Ukraine War that is allowing Russia, Iran, Syria, North Korea, and even China to position themselves to potentially destroy western civilization, starting with nuclear Armageddon against Israel.

THE ORIGINS OF THE RUSSIA-UKRAINE WAR

Like most wars, the 2022 Russia-Ukraine war began some years earlier as a smaller conflict, initially contained in the relatively small geographic area of Crimea and spreading outward gradually from there.

On August 24, 1991, Ukraine gained its independence from a post-USSR Russia as the Soviet Union fell apart. Ukraine declared itself a neutral nation but that didn't sit well with all of its population. Some wanted closer ties to Europe, and some wanted a closer partnership with or even return to being part of Russia.

Nonetheless, the Ukrainian people established a constitution, formed a government, and set about building a nation. But they struggled to find their place in the world, particularly while living in the shadow of their much larger and stronger neighbor, Russia.

Ukraine declared itself a neutral nation to appease Russia. At the urging of President Clinton, who guaranteed its safety in return, the Ukrainian government gave back to Russia the entire arsenal of nuclear weapons Russia had deployed in Ukraine while it was still part of the USSR.

Voluntarily disarmed in this manner, Ukraine was left largely undefended and without a military of its own. Strained by the growing pains of creating its own economy and international trade relationships, Ukraine didn't spend a great deal of its national budget building a robust military. After all, the U.S. had promised to protect it.

Furthermore, why should Ukraine bother to arm itself? Russia was in disarray. Its military was aging and without funding to modernize, its economy was in full collapse, NATO was dominant on the world stage, and the Cold War was, at long last, over.

The days of a belligerent USSR looming over its smaller neighbors and using them as buffers against any potential land invasion from Western Europe were over. The great world wars of the past were obsolete. Conflict was solved at the negotiating table or in the halls of the United Nations these days.

THE EARLY 2000'S IN UKRAINE

As the 2000's came, simmering polarization grew in Ukraine between those who favored Ukraine reaching west for trade partnerships and political alliances and those who favored forming a closer relationship with the new Russia.

After all, Ukrainians had all, until recently, been Russian themselves. Many had family and friends across the border in Russia, almost all of them spoke Russian (the Ukrainian language was mostly spoken in the west while Russian was the primary language in the east, but every student studied Russian in school), and many Ukrainians worked for companies that did extensive work or trade with Russian companies.

However, the early 2000's financial corruption and phenomenon of ultra-rich, ultra-powerful oligarchs in Russia bled over into Ukraine. Historically, Ukraine was an important segment of the Russian economy, and many rich, powerful Russians had their fingers in or outright ownership of important Ukrainian businesses, factories, and other enterprises. They exerted outsized, and typically corrupt, influence on the Ukrainian government.

Meanwhile, the Russian intelligence services developed numerous assets inside Ukraine and deep within the Ukrainian government. If they couldn't own Ukraine outright, they certainly wanted to influence it to lean more toward Russia and away from Europe. These Russian intelligence assets made no secret of stirring dissent and polarization inside Ukraine. They provided money, resources, and training to a small but growing group of pro-Russian separatists who advocated the return of some or all of Ukraine to the control of Russia.

In late 2004, the Ukrainian presidential election was rife with massive corruption, voter intimidation, and voting fraud engineered by Russia. Kyiv, in the western, pro-European part of Ukraine exploded in protests and demonstrations. Both domestic and foreign election monitors declared the election rigged in favor of the pro-Russian candidate, Viktor Yanukovych.

Yanukovych claimed he'd won the run-off election and tried to assume power, and a general uprising ensued. Called the Orange Revolution, it ultimately succeeded in getting the results of the first election annulled. A second election was held under intense international scrutiny, and ultimately declared to be a free and fair election. In the second ballot, the pro-western, anti-Russian candidate, Viktor Yuschenko won by a 52% to 48% margin.

It was a victory for Yuschenko, but the sharp divisions within Ukraine were clearly drawn. The country was about evenly split pro-Europe vs pro-Russia.

Discontent over the corruption inside the Ukrainian government continued to grow, and the Yuschenko government was as riddled with bribery, influence peddling, under the table deals, and corruption as the previous governments. Protests by one side or the other became a common part of daily life in Kyiv, the Ukrainian capital.

A CHANGE OF GOVERNMENT IN UKRAINE AND REVOLUTION

In 2010, in another closely watched election, Yanukovych defeated Prime Minister Yulia Timoschenko in another tight election.

Calls for parts of Ukraine to break away from Ukraine and rejoin Russia became louder, and occasional acts of sabotage and separatist vs non-separatist clashes began to occur. Rumors abounded that Russian security forces and infiltrators were helping stir up this violence.

In late 2013, President Yanukovych refused to sign the agreement for Ukraine to join the European Union, which had been in the works for years. Instead, he signed a trade deal and political alliance agreement with Russia. This infuriated the pro-Europe half of the Ukrainian population, and they took to the streets again in protest.

Whereas the Orange Revolution had been peaceful and bloodless, these protests grew increasingly violent. Protestors barricaded themselves into a central square in Kyiv and camped there, demonstrating daily. Security forces clashed with protestors in an effort to force them to vacate central Kyiv.

In February of 2014, thousands of protestors wearing helmets and carrying riot shields of their own marched on the parliament in an effort to oust the president.

On February 21, use of live ammunition was authorized by the Yanukovych government against the protestors. Police snipers fired on the crowd and over 100 people were killed in two days. The crowd eventually reached the Parliament building, where opposition leaders in the parliament were finally able to force Yanukovych to sign a deal to form an interim unity government.

The police withdrew and, unprotected from outraged protestors, Yanukovych fled Kyiv for eastern Ukraine and its heavy concentration of pro-Russian activists. The following day, the Ukrainian parliament voted to remove Yanukovych from power by a vote of 328-0.

RUSSIA SEIZES CRIMEA

A new, interim government was established. Notably, it declared itself anti-Russian and immediately signed an arrest warrant for Yanukovych. In the meantime, Yanukovych declared the vote to oust him illegal and asked Russia for help. Putin refused to recognize his overthrow, either, calling it an illegal coup d'état.

This new interim government did not sit well with the many pro-Russians in Ukraine, and clashes erupted across eastern and southern Ukraine, including in Crimea. The worst of the conflict centered in the wealthy Luhansk and Donetsk regions, both of which sit in the vastly rich farmlands of the Don River Basin—nicknamed the Donbas.

Nor did this new anti-Russian regime sit well with Vladimir Putin, particularly since Ukraine controlled the vital port of Sevastopol, situated on the Crimean Peninsula, which juts down into the Black Sea from southeastern Ukraine. Although Russia has a lease on the port until 2042, concerns began to arise in Moscow that this new Ukrainian government might consider kicking the Russians out of Crimea and their vital port.

Sevastopol is a warm water port, one of only a handful Russia has access to. From there, Russian goods can be shipped south across the Black Sea, through the Bosporus Strait that divides Turkey and its capital, Istanbul in two, and from there into the Mediterranean Sea and the rest of the world.

But more importantly, Sevastopol is the home port of Russia's Black Sea Fleet, a naval force Russia has been aggressively upgrading in the past decade. It includes a fleet of modernized destroyers, frigates, missile ships, and submarines, among others. From Sevastopol, Russia can project force all the way into the Mediterranean with its Black Sea Fleet, a mission that was added to this naval fleet in the aftermath of the seizure of Crimea from Ukraine.

Amidst the violence and chaos in the immediate aftermath of Yanukovych's ouster, Russian troops invaded Crimea. They captured strategic sites, particularly the port of Sevastopol, evicted Ukrainians from their military bases, and installed a pro-Russian government in Crimea. Shortly thereafter, a referendum was held in Crimea and independence declared from Ukraine. On March 18, 2014, Russia formally—and completely illegally, according to international law—annexed Crimea and incorporated it back into the Russian Federation.

Control of Crimea provides Russia with important strategic defense options. The Black Sea fleet, air forces, and air defenses in Crimea can intercept threats from other nations attacking from the Black Sea.

And let's be honest. By controlling Crimea, Putin poked a giant stick in Ukraine's side. He hoped it would serve as a symbol to encourage pro-Russian forces inside Ukraine, and he probably believed the strong Russian military presence in Crimea would deter western nations from growing any closer to Ukraine.

Not to mention, Putin's occupation of Crimea not only blocked Ukraine from applying for NATO membership but probably stopped western nations from selling military equipment and weapons to Ukraine.

Lastly, Crimea would make an excellent staging point for a future invasion of Ukraine. A military offensive coming up from the south out of Crimea could cut Ukraine in half and potentially trap Ukrainian forces engaging against pro-Russian forces in eastern Ukraine.

The cost to Russia of seizing Crimea was very low. The operation was fast, effective, and bloodless because Russia already had troops on the ground at its naval base in Sevastopol and because the local population of Crimea was largely pro-Russian. The strategic rewards of controlling Crimea were very large, however.

Although Ukraine and many other countries condemned the annexation, it was a done deal. Ukraine did not have the military resources to retake the peninsula, nor was the West willing to supply it with the weapons and resources it would need to eject Russia from Crimea.

The West had no stomach for engaging in direct military conflict with Russia. The West imposed sanctions upon Russia, but Putin insisted he was merely honoring the referendum voted upon by the admittedly largely pro-Russian population of Crimea.

Resentment over the seizure simmered among anti-Russian Ukrainians, who maintained that the peninsula was illegally annexed. In the absence of direct combat to retake the region, however, the Russians moved in and asserted full control of Crimea.

DONETSK AND LUHANSK ATTEMPT
TO BREAK AWAY

Emboldened by the annexation for Crimea, pro-Russian activists in the Donetsk region seized control of the provincial government and declared independence from Ukraine in April of 2014. In May of 2014, pro-Russian separatists in Luhansk followed suit, seizing control of the local government in that region as well.

The Ukrainian military struck back, shelling various pro-Russian controlled targets. Undoubtedly with the help of Russian Spetznatz and FSB forces, the pro-Russian contingent retaliated with military-style strikes of its own.

Meanwhile, Ukraine accused Russian intelligence agents and military provocateurs of posing as local pro-Russian separatists and stirring up progressively more trouble and violence, particularly in the Luhansk and Donetsk regions. There were periodic calls for independence votes by those who wished to break away from Ukraine, and tensions mounted.

The crisis came to a head when Malaysian Air Flight 17 was shot down by Russian forces over eastern Donetsk on July 17, 2014. In the months leading up to that tragedy, various Ukrainian and Russian aircraft had been shot down by the opposing forces in eastern Ukraine.

Russian Separatists in the region claimed they had no training to hit such an aircraft at high altitude. Russian security forces claimed they had no equipment in the area that could fire an SA-11 missile, which was determined by Dutch investigators to be the source of the crash. Russia vetoed a measure in the U.N. Security Council to open a criminal investigation into the crash.

Some months later, exhaustive intelligence research by western nations indicated that MH17 was shot down by a Buk surface-to-air missile launcher operated by the 53rd Anti-Aircraft Missile Brigade out of Kursk, Russia.

(In November of 2022, three Russian FSB officers were sentenced to life in prison in absentia by a Dutch criminal court for the murder of 298 people in the shooting down of Malaysian Air Flight 17. To date, none of the men have been extradited from Russia to The Hague to serve their sentences.)

STATIC CONFLICT IN THE DONBAS

By 2015, the Donbas region settled into a static conflict between the Ukrainian army and pro-Russia separatists. It's estimated that about one-quarter of the pro-Russia forces were actually Russian soldiers and special forces troops. The hostilities continued with neither side gaining an advantage over the other.

Although two sets of peace deals, the Minsk Accords I and II, were signed, neither was ever implemented. Various ceasefires, some 29 of them, were negotiated, but none ever held more than two weeks. Both sides were determined to prevail and unwilling to budge.

No further resolution was sought or obtained for the conflict in the region. Both sides seemed prepared to continue fighting indefinitely with no end in sight. An actual line of contact was drawn, and literal trenches dug on each side of it. Shelling across that line went on for the next seven years along with the occasional special forces operation across one side of the line or the other.

From 2014 to the beginning of 2022, the tensions in eastern Ukraine only continued to rise, with countless incidents of violence, sabotage, accusations, and retaliation for real or perceived insults and aggression.

Ukraine was a country at war with itself, and Russia did everything it could to stir up that violence and tear Ukraine apart from the inside out. Corruption in the government was rampant and there was little the population could do about it. The pro-Russian government in Kyiv took ever more repressive measures to stop any kind of protests.

A CHANGE IN THE STATUS QUO

Russia's plan to weaken Ukraine until it could sweep in and take the country back for itself seemed to be working until a young, charismatic comedian and television actor ran for president of Ukraine in

2019. Volodymyr Zelensky ran on a platform of anti-corruption and a promise to end the long-running conflict with Russia. He won the election in a landslide, garnering 73% of the vote.

Zelensky successfully negotiated prisoner swaps with Russia but was unable to arrive at a negotiated peace settlement with the Russian government. European leaders attempted to help the two nations arrive at a settlement in a peace conference held in Paris in December of 2019, but to no avail.

Zelensky insisted on the return of Crimea to Ukraine and the withdrawal of all Russian troops from the Donbas region, and Putin insisted on keeping both Crimea and the Russian occupied regions of the Donbas and incorporating them into Russia.

The negotiations failed.

Through 2020 and 2021, Russia engaged in a large-scale military build-up of forces around Ukraine. Zelensky grew increasingly alarmed and asked the West repeatedly for assistance in building up his own military.

However, his pleas fell on deaf ears. Western governments made it clear they wanted no part of engaging in direct military conflict with Russia.

THE LEAD UP TO RUSSIAN INVASION

By December of 2021, however, American intelligence sources were releasing multiple, detailed reports outlining the Russian invasion plan for Ukraine.

Russia commenced a disinformation campaign, mostly for internal Russian consumption, claiming genocides of Russians in Ukraine, questioning the legitimacy of the Ukrainian state, and accusing the Ukrainian government of being run by Nazis.

These claims were absurd, of course. Zelensky, although not religious himself, was Jewish by birth. Although Ukraine does have a tiny, far-right fringe within its population, neo-Nazis by no means dominated the Ukrainian government as Putin claimed.

Putin then put forward a conspiracy theory that cast Russian Christians, rather than Jews, as the true victims of Nazi Germany. He told the Russian people that those same Nazi forces were alive and well in Ukraine and coming for the Russian people again.

It's worth nothing that Putin increasingly seems to see himself as the savior of Christianity, the Russian Orthodox church being the true Christian church, and himself the person who will restore it to its rightful place of prominence in the world.

Putin then demanded that Ukraine, the U.S., and NATO sign a legally binding deal that Ukraine would never join NATO. The U.S. and NATO rejected the demand in part because the NATO treaty has in it an open-door policy that allows for any nation to apply for NATO membership. For its part, Ukraine promptly requested to join NATO, infuriating Putin.

In early 2022, fighting escalated sharply in the Donbas as the crisis reached a tipping point.

On February 21, 2022, Putin announced that Russia formally recognized Donetsk and Luhansk as republics of Russia.

On February 22nd, the upper house of the Russian government—the Federation Council (its Senate)—authorized Putin to use military force outside of Russia.

On the night of February 23rd, Zelensky gave a speech in Russian appealing to the Russian people to stop a war from happening. That same day, the pro-Russian leaders of Donetsk and Luhansk sent letters to Russia asking it for help.

The pieces were all in place. The next day, Vladimir Putin officially invaded Ukraine.

CHAPTER TWELVE:

WAR IN UKRAINE

"Stop the enemy wherever you see it. The fate of Ukraine depends only on Ukrainians. No one but ourselves will control our lives. We are on our land. The truth is on our side. It will not be possible to destroy our character. This morning we are defending our state alone, as we did yesterday. The world's most powerful forces are watching from afar."

—**Volodymyr Zelensky,** President of Ukraine,
February 25, 2022, day 2 of the invasion

RUSSIA INVADES

The Russian invasion of Ukraine was envisioned by Putin and his military advisors as a blitzkrieg-style attack with multiple major columns of tanks, armored vehicles, and infantry sweeping across Ukraine from several directions to converge on Kyiv at lightning speed to crush the capitol.

It was widely expected that the Ukrainian president, a political lightweight, would flee the country immediately, leaving Ukraine rudderless and easy prey. Just in case, however, Russian black ops teams were sent to Kyiv to capture or kill Zelensky.

Vladimir Putin's own intelligence service had spent years forwarding glowing reports of how effectively FSB operations had cultivated pro-Russian cells all across Ukraine that would be loyal to the motherland and eagerly awaited the return of Russian rule.

Putin was told these Russia loyalists would welcome Putin's triumphant tank columns with armfuls of flowers and parades in their honor. Indeed, Ukrainian troops and international press reported finding parade uniforms in the gear carried by all Russian soldiers who participated in the initial invasion force.

Recent reports indicate that the FSB had a huge budget, for a decade or more, dedicated to recruiting, funding, and secretly arming pro-Russian separatist groups throughout Ukraine. These same reports indicate that almost all the money ended up in the pockets of corrupt FSB officers who wrote false reports about fake separatist groups and fabricated wildly exaggerated numbers of Ukrainians eager to rejoin the Russian Federation. It's entirely possible Putin was wildly misled by his own intelligence service as to how easily he would be able to overrun and seize Ukraine.

Only in the Donetsk and Luhansk regions in the far eastern end of Ukraine did a significant number of residents actually show any affinity for the idea of rejoining Russia. Those regions were populated mostly by ethnic Russians, and Russian Special Forces troops had been actively agitating in that area since before the beginning of open hostilities in 2014. Estimates at the time of the invasion place around 40% of the population of each oblast (the equivalent of a state in America) polling in favor of breaking away from Ukraine and rejoining Russia.

At any rate, Putin invaded Ukraine with high expectations of a fast win. He was undoubtedly excited at the prospect of bringing one of the wealthiest, most developed former Soviet republics back into the fold. He and the other kleptocrats in his government had to be salivating at the idea of taking control of Ukraine's rich mineral, agricultural, and industrial resources for themselves.

DAY ONE OF THE INVASION

In the early hours of February 24, 2022, seven major columns of tanks, armored personal carriers full of infantry, trucks, and fuel tanker trucks invaded from the north, east and south, all heading in the general direction of Kyiv, the capitol of Ukraine. If Ukraine is shaped like an oval lying on its long side, Kyiv is located in the north central section of the oval.

The Russian forces targeted military sites, important infrastructure, and shelled some 40 cities, including in Kharkiv, Ukraine's second largest city. It is located in northeastern Ukraine and is the capitol of the Kharkiv oblast, which sits just to the west of the Luhansk oblast.

The Pentagon announced that it was clear Russia intended to sweep into Kyiv and "decapitate the government." Most western powers expected Russia to succeed, and furthermore, to do so easily and quickly.

However, western military security experts were already in place and helped the Ukrainian military ensure their president's safety. Furthermore, top military strategists from around the world were also already in place inside Ukraine, standing by to help the Ukrainian government plan and wage a defensive action against the Russian invaders.

Tens of thousands of Ukrainians fled their homes, mostly heading west, away from the advancing Russian forces, causing enormous traffic jams and a more than two-day long wait at border crossings into neighboring nations. The fleeing populace did pause long enough, however, to remove all of the road signs, which left advancing Russian forces unable to use the paper road maps they'd been given to navigate toward their goals.

By the end of day one, Spetznatz troops had seized the Chernobyl nuclear site and Russian forces had advanced to within 15 miles of Kyiv. Heavy fighting was reported in the suburbs of the capitol.

President Biden announced heavy sanctions against Russia, declaring Russia the aggressor in the invasion. In Moscow, thousands of people, mostly young, took to the streets to protest and were met with heavy State Security and many hundreds of beatings and arrests.

Oil prices skyrocketed, stock markets across the world fell sharply, and the Russian ruble declined very sharply.

That evening, Putin warned ominously:

> "Russia remains one of the most powerful nuclear states and has a certain advantage in several cutting-edge weapons." He went on to threaten, "consequences you have never faced in your history for anyone who tries to interfere with us. There should be no doubt that any potential aggressor will face defeat and ominous consequences should it directly attack our country."

Nobody missed the implication that he was threatening a nuclear attack upon any nation who interfered with his invasion and capture of Ukraine.

DAY TWO OF THE INVASION

For months, the West and NATO had been insisting they would not send troops into Ukraine to protect it from an impending Ukrainian invasion. U.S. and other western intelligence sources, and intelligence sources inside Ukraine itself, had been warning with increasing urgency that Russia was planning an invasion at any moment.

Nobody was surprised by the invasion. . .merely by the timing of it. Winter in Ukraine is very cold, can be very muddy, and is miserable for troops trying to live in the field in rough conditions. However, if Putin believed his troops were literally going to drive into Kyiv unimpeded on wide-open roads, welcomed by the locals, winter field conditions would not have been a serious consideration for him.

For several months prior to the invasion, the U.S. and other NATO countries had finally started pouring tons of equipment, weapons, and ammunition into Ukraine. But on day two of the invasion, the United States announced that it was sending some 7,000 more troops to Europe to bolster the Poland, Romania, Estonia, Latvia, and Lithuania borders with Russia. All of them had joined NATO in the aftermath of the collapse of the Soviet Union and as such, are entitled to the full support and protection of all the other NATO nations.

In Russia, Putin insisted to his shocked nation that it was not war against Ukraine, but merely a "special military operation." He declared without any proof that the Ukrainian government was controlled by neo-Nazis whom he intended to destroy.

In response, the German government put out a statement stating:

"We know Nazis. And the Ukrainians are not Nazis."

In a surprise move, Volodymyr Zelensky did not flee Kyiv. Instead, he remained in the capitol and forcefully urged the Ukrainian people to stand and fight against the invaders. For the moment, the Ukrainian people seemed prepared to rally around him.

THE FIRST WEEK OF THE INVASION

It didn't take long for the impressively long columns of Russian tanks, trucks, and other military vehicles to bog down and come to a humiliating standstill on roads across Ukraine because...

...they ran out of gas.

Literally. The Russian army did not bring along enough fuel trucks and fuel to keep its advance moving. Not to mention, the Russians filled both lanes of two-lane roads heading toward Kyiv with military equipment and did not leave a clear lane for fuel trucks to move forward to refuel equipment. Fuel trucks that tried to go around the columns quickly bogged down in mud and got stuck, further compounding the traffic jam. It is one of the most basic concepts of column advances: leave room for the fuel trucks. And yet, the Russians failed to do so.

The advances were also stalled by huge numbers of tires failing on wheeled vehicles. Later analysis revealed that funds earmarked for maintaining and replacing rubber tires were largely embezzled by military officers and tire manufacturers. The Russian army was rolling on old, rotted tires that had been exposed to years of sunlight and weather that had aged and weakened them.

In the absence of a clear road lane for maintenance vehicles and trucks carrying spare tires to move forward to replace failed tires, the columns were left to limp along on destroyed tires until the vehicles had to stop altogether.

And then there were the dreadful Russian communications. Captured Russian soldiers complained that they had no communications whatsoever, no walkie-talkies, no radios, nothing. Evidence suggests that money meant to replace and modernize communications up and down the chain of command in the Russian army were also misappropriated and misused.

Russian troops were reduced to using their cell phones—on towers controlled by their enemy. Their calls were listened to and decrypted in nearly real time. From the very beginning, Ukrainians were able to listen to targets being relayed to the Russian Air Force. By the time Russian planes arrived to strike, the targets had nearly always moved and were no longer at the relayed coordinates.

In one extreme example of how totally communications broke down, a Russian Air Force officer had to fly by helicopter to units to deliver orders in person.

Not only were the individual communication units a disaster, but communications across services was terrible. The Russian army, air forces, and naval forces were still using old and unreliable command and control systems that were outdated a decade previously. Ground forces had all but no means of communicating with the air forces providing close air support for them and who were conducting bombing missions on targets spotted by the ground forces.

To make matters worse, battalion tactical groups quickly outran their command posts that could provide secure communications, and special detachments quickly outran the battalion tactical groups.

Even Russian generals turned to their unsecured cell phones to communicate in the midst of the invasion. In one instance, the Ukrainians were able to geolocate and kill a Russian general based on a cell phone call he made.

Meanwhile, Ukrainians shocked the Russians by turning out in force to shoot at the stalled Russian columns, which were sitting ducks. The Ukrainian military moved swiftly into the countryside to attack and retreat, attack and hide. Civilian volunteers joined in, helping the Ukrainian military navigate local areas, hide in homes and villages, and harass the Russian columns.

After a full week of attacking Ukraine, the Russians managed to capture only a single city, Kherson, in the south very near the Crimean Peninsula. The Russians failed to establish air superiority, they ran low on food and fuel, logistic support was nearly non-existent, and communications had broken down. By all accounts, Russia failed to send in enough troops to support three major, simultaneous military thrusts, and Putin's lightning invasion had stalled.

Publicly, Putin insisted the invasion was going according to plan. However, rumors persisted from inside the Kremlin that he was frustrated, furious, and embarrassed by how dismally the Russian army was performing.

Putin continued to insist that his goal was the "demilitarization and denazification" of Ukraine—a statement widely disputed and scoffed at, a transparent attempt to vilify the Ukrainian leadership.

Begging to differ with Putin's propaganda on Russian progress in the invasion, former CIA Director Gen. David Petraeus declared that Putin's war was "going terribly" and that "at the strategic level, he has essentially united most of the rest of the world."

Petraeus went on to say that Russia was "stretched beyond its logistical and mechanical capabilities, its troops, some of whom are less-experienced conscripts, are likely to be extremely tired and inexperienced in the face of a determined opponent, as Ukraine is proving to be."

Male Ukrainian volunteers by the thousands stayed behind in Ukraine even as their wives and children created days-long traffic jams at border crossings fleeing the country. These volunteers picked up weapons and commenced engaging in guerilla warfare, popping up to shoot at Russians, then disappearing into the countryside.

Western military analysts were unanimous in thinking that Ukrainian resistance to Russian occupation would be determined, stubborn, and unrelenting, whether Russia occupied Ukraine partially or completely, for one year or five or ten.

And yet, Putin seemingly failed to take into account the patriotism and national pride of the Ukrainian people. For his part, Putin seemed to think of them as former Soviet citizens who would consider it an honor to rejoin Russia. He was gravely mistaken in underestimating the willingness of the Ukrainian people to stand and fight, even to the death.

A single week into the war, this mistake was patently obvious. Reports surfaced of a Ukrainian grandmother approaching Russian troops and handing them sunflower seeds to put in their pockets, then telling the soldiers, "There. Now when you die, sunflowers will grow to mark your graves."

THE FIRST MONTH OF THE INVASION

As the invasion dragged into a second month, countries around the world joined the United States in freezing Russian assets in banks and financial institutions, said to amount to some 650 billion dollars. More sanctions were imposed upon Russia, a long list of Russian oligarchs, military generals, and government officials were distressed and angered to have their assets frozen abroad, and a hunt commenced to find and seize the mega yachts of various oligarchs, friends, and family members of Putin.

Increasingly enraged at the poor performance of his armed forces, Putin pushed his military to be more aggressive, more forceful, and ultimately, more brutal. Reports began to surface of war crimes in a village called Bucha, and journalists and humanitarian aid groups began to report war crimes across the country on a breathtaking scale. (One year into the war, some 65,000 war crimes have been reported.)

Casualties began to mount at an alarming rate, particularly on the Russian side. In the early days of the war, up to a thousand Russian casualties per day were being estimated by military analysts and western intelligence agencies. Russia refused to report any casualty numbers, of course.

Russia didn't seem to have sent much by way of medical support or transportation to the front lines for its wounded. Eventually, it would be estimated that close to half of all wounded Russian soldiers were dying from their wounds. This ghastly mortality rate was undoubtedly because of a lack of proper care for wounds where most of them should not have been fatal.

Ukraine doesn't really have an air force to speak of, and Russia's Black Sea fleet remained firmly in control of the southern coast of Ukraine. Which meant those thousand casualties a day were happening on the ground, in infantry combat, often in close quarters. Not only was this turning into a high-intensity war, but it was turning ugly on a horrific scale.

The Russian propaganda machine went into high gear, swearing that all was going well in Ukraine and encouraging the Russian people to get on with everyday life. And for the most part, they did. Western restaurants, stores, and fast-food chains were shutting down and pulling out of Russia in droves, but life went on in Russia. The majority of the population didn't seem particularly aware that they were at war, and furthermore, that the war was not going well at all.

President Zelensky, a master of using video and social media effectively, continued to stay in Ukraine, leading his nation with courage and resolve—to the shock of nearly everyone. Ukrainian resolve hardened and the Ukrainian people dug in.

Zelensky continued to win the media war, endearing himself to most of the world with his pluck, intelligence, and bravery. He and western intelligence sources continued to anticipate Putin's moves, revealing Russia's military strategy and upcoming gambits often before Russia executed them. It was embarrassing to Putin, who began to purge his intelligence services.

Right around this time, a shocking number of Putin critics commenced falling out of high windows, falling down staircases to their deaths, having mysterious heart attacks, and flat-out dying of poison. Meanwhile, the number of active thugs in the Russian State Security Service swelled to some 440,000, more than the number of soldiers active in the Russian army.

Meanwhile, the West rushed military supplies, food, humanitarian aid, and money into Ukraine at a staggering pace. Billions of dollars poured into Ukraine to keep it alive and in the fight. Millions of Ukrainian refugees were absorbed into Europe, and tens of thousands of Ukrainian men headed for the front lines and received hasty training.

Although most people in the West did not understand immediately that we, too, were at war, western leaders understood that it was vital to stop Putin in Ukraine or else face the specter of a third world war in Europe. If Putin won in Ukraine and became emboldened in his victory, he would undoubtedly move on to invade Moldova, Georgia, Albania, and eventually the Baltic states—Latvia, Lithuania, and Estonia—in his obsession with recreating the old Soviet Union.

Article 5 of the NATO Alliance treaty promises that if one NATO country in invaded, they all have been invaded and will respond together to the attack. The choice facing the West and NATO was stark—stop Putin in Ukraine or fight him in Europe, with the understanding that NATO would easily crush this weak, ineffective Russian army, leaving Putin with no choice but to resort to nuclear weapons.

Between them, Ukraine and Russia produce about 30% of all the wheat in the world. They produce 75% of the sunflower oil in the world, as well. But, instead of planting crops in the fertile farmlands of Ukraine as the war stretched into early spring of 2022, farmers made international news by hitching their tractors to abandoned Russian tanks, often merely out of gas, and towing them to the nearest Ukrainian military units.

An interesting side note: The Russian army figured out fairly quickly that most farmers store diesel fuel on their farms to run tractors and other equipment. The Russian army started raiding Ukrainian farms to steal the fuel. Ukrainian farmers retaliated by putting chemicals in their fuel storage tanks to foul the diesel fuel and destroy any engine that burned it. This may account for some of the massive rate of equipment failure in the Russian forces.

Poor nations around the world, many of whom rely heavily on Russian and Ukrainian grain to stave off famine, began to rumble warnings that this war needed to stop and soon if they were to avoid humanitarian crises of their own. Globally, emergency stores of grain were dipped into, and for the moment, mass starvation was held at bay.

RUSSIAN OIL BECOMES A FRICTION POINT

Russian oil isn't of great quality and contains sulphur and impurities that require it to be refined at specific refineries. This limits its ability to be sold to just anyone, anywhere. Both China and India have plenty of refineries that can handle it, however. As arguments commenced over whether or not to sanction Russian oil, those two nations made it clear they would not go along with any oil sanctions.

Europe was deeply concerned that its factories would stop operating and homes would go cold and dark in the absence of

Russian oil. The United States argued that it was necessary to starve Russia of oil income to keep financing its war and propping up its economy as sanctions began to take effect.

As the war entered its second and then third month, Russia's oil sales dropped from roughly 6 million barrels per day to 5 million or so barrels per day. About 1.7 million barrels per day went to China and about 2.5 million barrels still went to Europe. Most of the rest went to India, Japan, and South Korea.

Russia offered China deep discounts on the price of its oil, and China responded by greatly increasing the amount of Russian oil it imported. This dropped China's purchases of Norwegian, Saudi, and American oil, and world markets shifted to buying oil from those three nations.

The net result of the early oil sanctions was that oil sales and consumption didn't drop much. However, oil had to be transported to new and more distant locations than before, which kept the price of oil high. Uncertainty about the oil market also contributed to high oil prices.

The United States leaned hard on Saudi Arabia to try to get it to release more of its oil reserves and bring down global oil prices, but the Saudis flatly refused to do so.

Russia threatened to shut down natural gas pipelines to Europe, which would have a strong negative effect on German manufacturing (particularly heavy industries like steel production). In response, German engineers went to work at top speed building liquid natural gas download points at various ports, which would enable it to import plentiful liquid natural gas from the United States and other sources. But in the short term, Germany felt the crunch of higher prices and threats from Putin to restrict natural gas flow.

As stridently as Putin threatened to cut off oil to the West, at the end of the day he couldn't afford to cut off oil exports if he was to keep his war going and his economy afloat. He continued to sell oil at a massive pace to China for as long as China was willing to continue buying it.

As the war headed into spring, it fell into a predictable pattern. The battle lines stagnated into a definable front in eastern Ukraine. Russia inched forward, taking over the Donetsk oblast bit by bloody bit.

Russia brought in heavy artillery and concentrated it in the Donbas region. They shelled a single, small area, concentrating fire until everything in that area was pulverized and reduced to rubble. Only then would Russia advance infantry troops a block or two forward to take possession of the destroyed area. Then, it re-aimed its artillery a few blocks ahead and repeated the maneuver over and over. The Russian army's progress was extremely slow and costly.

Ukrainians engaged drones and used civilian spotters (reporting to the Ukrainian army on handy phone apps) to find Russian positions and call in artillery strikes of their own. Casualties began to mount on both sides, although Russian casualties outnumbered Ukrainian ones at a nearly six to one pace.

In return, Ukrainians mounted attacks on Russian supply lines and railroads under the control of Russia to disrupt already terrible logistics and supply chains. Morale was reported to be dismal among Russian troops who reported being reduced to having to hunt and fish for food to eat.

One of the alarming early developments in the war was the siege of the Zaporizhzhia Nuclear Power Plant. Located in south-eastern Ukraine, the facility was surrounded by Russian forces that proceeded to shell the plant itself. It's a sprawling facility, and the Russians for the most part fired at the non-critical nuclear portions of the facility.

The Ukrainians shut down the reactors as much as they could, but nuclear power plants don't ever actually turn off fully. Cooling water must continue to circulate around the power rods even when the nuclear reactions are as shut down as it's possible to make them. The Russians repeatedly cut electric power lines and shelled power transformers that supplied emergency power to the water pumps inside the plant and kept it from overheating.

The International Atomic Energy Agency and the United Nations urgently negotiated with Putin to allow inspectors and nuclear engineers into the facility to help keep it safe, and they urged Putin to create a no combat zone around the nuclear plant. Putin refused for months and continued playing with nuclear fire by letting his forces continue to shell the plant and attack the electric grid supplying power to it.

Eventually, the Ukrainian army was able to push back the Russian forces enough to stabilize the situation at the plant, and Russia finally let in a team of IAEA inspectors who hunkered down and remained inside the plant, using themselves as human shields to prevent further Russian attacks on the facility.

Throughout the Zaporizhzhia crisis, Putin seemed to relish scaring the world with the idea of causing a nuclear melt-down. It was the first time in the Ukraine War that we saw

Putin's flirtation with causing a nuclear event. It would not be the last.

AIRPLANES AND FINLAND

Inside Russia, major western companies abandoned factories and assets, closed their doors, and vowed never to come back. Airbus and Boeing complained that Russia was refusing to return some 50% of its aviation fleet (including 80% of its passenger airplane fleet), leased from the two companies, back to them. In retaliation, Boeing and Airbus refused to provide any spare parts for the stolen aircraft.

Russia doesn't historically maintain a huge backlog of spare parts, and in a matter of weeks, the inspections and airworthiness certificates on many passenger jets began to expire. Russian aircraft were prohibited from flying in foreign airspace—even China refused to allow Russian jets over its territory and warned its citizens to avoid flying on Aeroflot and other Russian airlines.

Russia is a REALLY big country. Large swatches of it have no roads and rely only on rail and air transport for supplies and commerce. As its aviation industry slowly ground to a halt, supply chains began to falter and inconvenience mounted for the population. For the most part, Russian airlines used outside ticket sales systems, and as those were shut down by America's SABRE system and Spain's Amadeus ticket app, even Russians struggled to buy tickets on the planes that were flying.

Meanwhile, Finland began reporting that Russia was jamming its GPS navigation system, used by commercial airliners to identify where they are and to fly on designated flight routes. Then, Finland reported that Russia was using GPS confusion systems sending out false signals that told airlines they were in different locations than they actually were.

Speculation mounted that Russia was trying to lure an aircraft into Russian airspace to shoot it down and then blame Finland for shooting it down. The Finns were convinced Russia was looking for an excuse to invade Finland, and the entire country went onto a wartime footing. Moreover, the Finnish people were outraged.

For decades, the Finns have lived relatively peacefully with their gigantic and powerful neighbor by adhering to a strict policy of political and economic neutrality. Finland, which lies on the northern border of Russia between it and the Arctic Ocean, shares a 830 mile (1340 km) border with Russia.

But all of a sudden, the Finnish people began to rumble about the possibility of applying for membership in NATO. Since the end of World War II, the Finns have steadfastly refused to break their neutrality and seek NATO membership. But public opinion inside Finland began to shift rapidly over continued Russian provocations and threats, as the Finnish people watched in horror what Russia was doing to another country it shared a border with.

Sweden is Finland's next-door neighbor to the west. It has no land border with Russia, however it has a long shoreline along the entire west side of the Baltic Sea and overlooks important shipping and military naval lanes that Russia relies on. It, too, has long maintained a largely neutral relationship with Russia. However, in light of Russia's invasion of Ukraine, the Swedes also began to rumble about applying for application to join NATO.

One of the main reasons western analysts believe that Putin invaded Ukraine was because he was afraid Ukraine might join NATO. Historically, Russia has depended on its enemies being a thousand or more miles away from its capitol over land to give it a sense of safety. Putin, raised on studying World War II and hearing stories of its tank battles from his father, surely shares a strong sense of alarm at the idea of having NATO forces within a few hundred miles of Moscow.

The distance from the Ukraine border to Moscow is a mere 300 miles, and the distance from the Finnish border to Moscow is about 550 miles. These numbers must send chills down Putin's spine when he contemplates them. For a nation that historically relies on grinding tank battles and slogging infantry warfare to survive invasions of it, the more land between its heart and its enemies, the better.

THE PROXY WAR COMMENCES

For its part, NATO also settled into a pattern—send Ukraine enough aid, supplies, military equipment, and training to survive, but don't send enough for Ukraine to win the war. As of the writing of this book, this pattern continues to hold. NATO, wary of provoking Putin to resort to nuclear weapons, still refuses to send NATO troops into Ukraine and refuses to send the most advanced and long-range weapons to Ukraine that it needs to force Russia to retreat.

Finland and Sweden shocked the world when referendums in both countries to seek NATO membership passed by wide margins. Putin reacted by engaging in more serious nuclear saber rattling.

Putin showed an eagerness to go nuclear that hasn't been seen since the Cuban Missile Crisis. On a daily basis, he talked about his willingness to use nuclear weapons in Ukraine, and his willingness to use nuclear weapons on NATO countries in Europe if they continued to interfere in Ukraine.

Inside Russia, it takes a fairly lengthy sequence of approvals from various military and government officials to authorize use of a nuclear weapon. Western analysts watched with alarm as Putin began to systematically fire and retire the men in that nuclear approval chain who were likely to oppose use of nuclear weapons. No surprise, he replaced these cooler heads with sycophants and ultra-nationalists guaranteed to approve use of nuclear weapons.

Alarmed, NATO responded cautiously, eking out weapons and supplies to Ukraine in the absolute smallest amounts it could get away with and not have Ukraine lose the war.

Putin continued to taunt NATO, all but daring it to intervene directly in Ukraine. It's worth remembering that, as a former KGB officer, he has excellent training in how to manipulate emotions and maneuver others into doing what he wants them to. He applied these skills to frustrate and irritate Russia's adversaries as summer came to Ukraine.

His war was not unanimously popular at home. The Russian people are estimated to be split about 50/50 on supporting versus opposing the war. Younger, urban, educated people poll strongly against the war while older, rural, uneducated citizens poll strongly in favor of it.

However, if Putin can draw NATO directly into the war, odds are good he can invoke Russian patriotism to get most of the population behind his war. Possibly more importantly, if he can lure NATO into a direct fight against him, his own popularity will soar at home on a wave of Russian patriotism. With his own prestige, judgment, and leadership increasingly tarnished, this may be the single largest motivator for Putin to taunt NATO into attacking his troops—and by extension, him—directly.

Certain NATO member states, namely Poland and the Baltic states, have been eager from the very beginning of the war to enter the fight directly. They have hundreds of years' worth of bones to pick with Russia, and with the might and resources of NATO behind them this time, this fight is one they can finally win against the once mighty Russian empire.

Germany, the United States, France, and the UK worked hard over the summer of 2022 to convince Poland in particular that its best means of defeating Russia would be to continue absorbing massive numbers of refugees from Ukraine, housing and feeding them.

DRONE WARFARE PROVING GROUND

The war in Ukraine marks the first time we've seen drones employed in a conflict involving major powers and modern armies on both sides, and the first time they've been used so extensively and over an extended period of time.

It's fair to say Ukraine has emerged as a guinea pig for drone warfare. A wide array of unmanned aerial vehicles produced everywhere from the US to China and from Turkey to Iran have been used in battle there.

In the early days of the fighting, Ukraine saw success using the Turkish-made Bayraktar TB2 drone to rain hell from above on key Russian assets like armored vehicles. A Bayraktar—which has a range of 186 miles, is the size of a small plane, and is capable of carrying laser-guided bombs—was involved in the attack that sank the Moskva, the flagship of Russia's Black Sea fleet.

Later in the war, Russia began launching swarms of Iranian-made Shahed-136 "kamikaze" drones, striking targets across Ukraine. The Shahed-136 is a loitering munition—designed to linger or loiter before locating a target and crashing into it.

It's less than 12 feet long, can fly at 115 mph, contains an explosive warhead in its nose, and explodes on impact. These single-use drones are relatively cheap ($20,000 each) and have been used by Russia to destroy vital civilian infrastructure and make life even harder for Ukrainians.

The U.S. has also provided Ukraine with hundreds of Switchblade drones, a type of loitering munition or kamikaze drone, which can be carried in backpacks. Switchblades can be used to strike infantry, armor, and artillery. This war has seen the first use of swarm drones as well—clusters of many small drones flying in unison like a flock of birds. A lot of people have pointed to drones as the future of warfare.

To date, Iranian production has tipped the balance of power in the budding drone war to Russia's favor. However, the West is greatly stepping up supplying drones to Ukraine as 2023 commences.

Plus, Ukraine has manufactured some of its own drones, notably those used to strike Russia's Engels-2 air base more than 350 miles inside Russia. While the damage from the drone attack was minimal, the psychological effect on Russia was spectacular. It sent shock waves through the stunned Russian people and forced Russia to reallocate some of its resources to defending domestic military assets.

PUTIN HINTS AT USING CHEMICAL WEAPONS

When caution and reason prevailed and NATO refused to be drawn into the war, Putin switched tactics. He accused Ukrainians of dropping chemical weapons on his troops.

A standard disinformation technique, and one that most Americans are undoubtedly familiar with, is to accuse your opponents or critics of doing exactly the thing you're actually doing or contemplating doing. It diverts attention from your actions and gives you a ready-made excuse to retaliate in kind.

Hence, when Putin started making accusations of chemical attacks against Russian soldiers, the West and Ukraine both saw this as a huge red flag. They believed it signaled that Putin was preparing to use chemical weapons in Ukraine. Deeply alarmed, the West and Ukraine swung into action fast to counteract Putin's absurd claims.

United Nations and humanitarian observers, plus journalists from all over the world on the ground in Ukraine were recruited en masse to refute Putin's claims. They all did so forcefully. Unanimously, they declared that absolutely no chemical weapons had been used against Russian forces.

Zelensky again won the propaganda war, getting word out quickly that no way, no how, had the Ukrainians used chemical or biological weapons on the Russian invaders.

If Putin was, in fact toying with the idea of dropping chemical weapons in Ukraine in "retaliation" for these alleged attacks against his own forces, global media squashed any notion of Ukraine having done it first. He lost his plausible justification for using his own chemical weapons.

I suspect that, on a regular basis, Putin privately curses the invention of the Internet. With the entire international press corps and global social media shouting to high heaven across the Internet that Ukraine had never used chemical weapons, he didn't stand a very good chance of convincing his population of that lie.

For the first few months of the war, the Russian state propaganda machine, also known as Russian State News, managed to partially suppress awareness in the Russian population of what was going on in Ukraine.

Young, educated people with money and access to the Internet that bypassed Russian censorship were widely aware of the war from the beginning. They knew Russian forces were performing badly and were seeing reports of war crimes committed by Russians against Ukrainian civilians.

That said, multiple women were interviewed on Russian State News giving their husbands permission to rape as many Ukrainian women as they could. The fact that the Russian army was committing serious war crimes in Ukraine didn't seem to bother the Russian people. This probably speaks more to the inhumanity and brutality of the regime to which they are accustomed rather than to their own individual lack of humanity.

As the summer of 2022 aged, three things happened inside Russia:

1) The economic sanctions became impossible to ignore and living conditions got significantly worse inside Russia, to the extent that the general population could not fail to see it.

2) No announcement of a victory in the "special military operation" inside Ukraine was forthcoming. Which, by the way, shocked Russians to their core. They'd just assumed their mighty military would crush Ukraine out of hand.

3) Body bags started coming home. Lots of them. Tens of thousands of them.

As a side note, dropping chemical weapons on Ukrainians in the summer of 2022 would in no way have broken their spirits or will to fight. Although this tactic worked swimmingly well against Syrians who buckled quickly in the face of horrific poison gas attacks, there's no question it would have served to enrage Ukrainians further. They viscerally loathed the Russians by then and would have only dug in harder.

Putin seemed to have forgotten that Ukrainians were cut from the exact same cloth as Russians. If Russians are stubborn, so are Ukrainians. If it is a Russian strength to endure suffering as long as necessary to prevail in war, the Ukrainians possess the exact same strength and willingness to endure.

And he forgot that, as patriotic as Russians are at their cores, Ukrainians are fully as patriotic and loyal to their homeland.

Perhaps this was Putin's biggest miscalculation of all. He failed to understand how stubbornly the Ukrainian people would resist him. In the face of horrendous war crimes, indiscriminate shelling of civilians, total destruction of the country's infrastructure, the Ukrainians simply are not going to submit to Russian rule.

I believe it's not an overstatement to say the Ukrainians will die to the last man, woman, and child before they ever accept Russia as their overlord.

Even if at some future date, as of the writing of this book, Russia overruns Ukraine and takes control of the entire country, you can be sure the Ukrainian people will continue to resist. They will engage in guerilla warfare, insurgent attacks, and sabotage for as long as it takes to drive the Russians from their homeland.

Mark my words. The hatred of Russia that Putin has planted in the hearts of the Ukrainian people will last for decades, if not centuries.

CHAPTER THIRTEEN:

SETBACKS FOR RUSSIA

"The result of this war and the war crimes being committed
by the Russians will now be a Russia where even fellow Slavs
will hate Russian guts for decades to come."

—Tom Nichols, journalist, The Atlantic

UKRAINE'S BEND BUT DON'T BREAK TACTICS

As the war dragged on, Russia very gradually took possession of most of the Luhansk and Donetsk regions. However, as soon as Russian troops advanced forward to attack new villages, the old villages they'd just conquered welcomed back Ukrainian forces that moved in behind them, and the villages declared themselves Ukrainian once more.

And then Russia ran into the city of Severodonetsk, on the bank of the Siversky-Donets River. The first attempt by Russians to cross the river on a pontoon bridge was foiled by a drone attack that destroyed the bridge and washed a dozen or more armored personal carriers and Jeeps down the river, drowning several hundred soldiers.

Putin concentrated almost all of his artillery forces in the Donbas region on this one city, pummeling it for weeks with massive artillery shelling. The vast majority of civilians fled the city, and the Ukrainian forces who remained hunkered down in underground bunkers to wait out the shelling, suffering relatively few casualties.

When the Russians finally did enter the city of Severodonetsk, they encountered stiff resistance from Ukrainians who were much more familiar with the city. Furthermore, most of the Russian infantry being sent in was not trained in urban combat and Russian casualties skyrocketed as house-to-house street fighting broke out. The Ukrainians had a massive home court advantage and the full support of the few civilians left in the city, and they used both to their benefit.

A THOUSAND BEE STINGS

Ukraine was content (and wise) not to confront the Russian army in a head-to-head battle with tanks and infantry duking it out. This sort of battle would have greatly favored the Russians. Better for the Ukrainians to melt away into the forests and private homes around Russian encampments, coming out only to strike quickly in guerilla fashion and then fade away into the local area once more.

Analysts began to call the Ukrainian strategy "Death by a Thousand Bee Stings." It was an apt description.

Even in cities like Severodonetsk, Lysychansk, Kherson, and Bakhmut where lengthy artillery bombardments, glacially slow infantry advances, and lengthy sieges are the norm, the Ukrainians avoided direct confrontation as much as possible, preferring to rely on drone attacks, snipers, and small units that attacked fast and then moved away quickly.

The problem for the Russians is there's little to no way to tell who is attacking them. It could just as easily be a farmer driving by on his tractor as a grandmother weeding her garden. All Ukrainians who remain in Ukraine consider themselves enemies of the Russians and will take any opportunity they can to hit the Russians themselves or to help and hide the Ukrainian soldiers and volunteers doing the attacking.

This in no way makes it okay for the Russians to commit war crimes against and slaughter civilians the way they are. It merely means that the Russians can trust no one inside Ukraine and that the remaining populace is unanimously opposed to their presence and happy to see as many Russians as possible die.

Of note: fairly early in the war, pro-Russian residents of Luhansk and Donetsk were offered transportation free of charge into Russia, where they were provided with permanent housing, jobs, and Russian passports. It is estimated that the vast majority of pro-Russian separatists in the Donbas region took Russia up on this offer and got out of the way of the war. Those who remain in Ukraine pretty much unanimously support Ukraine's independence.

RIVERS GET IN THE WAY

Rivers continued to prove difficult for the Russian army to cross as bridge after bridge was blown up by the Ukrainians, and pontoon bridge after pontoon bridge was scouted out by drones and then hit with precision western artillery.

Not only was the Siversky-Donets River a problem, but the large Dniepro River proved just as difficult to cross. Every major bridge across it was blown up by the Ukrainians, and any time the Russians attempted to build pontoon bridges, the Ukrainians gleefully struck the exposed trucks and personnel carriers using the temporary bridges. Dozens of vehicles and hundreds of Russian soldiers at a time were lost as crossing after crossing was hit by the Ukrainians.

Even smaller rivers also posed challenges for the Russians, paranoid after their terrible experiences trying to cross the larger rivers. Soldiers were forced to walk across pontoon bridges on foot, afraid of drowning trapped inside heavy vehicles. As for the vehicles themselves, the Russians were reduced to driving one vehicle at a time across temporary bridges lest they draw an attack by the Ukrainian forces.

Given that the rail bridges across the rivers were also blown up, trucks became a vital source of weapons, food, supplies, and medical evacuations for the Russians. Trying to keep hundreds of thousands of Russian troops supplied one truck at a time made the Russian logistic nightmare even worse than it already was.

A LINE OF CONTROL

On maps, the Russian army advanced across eastern Ukraine and appeared to be taking control of the Donbas region. But in reality, as soon as the front lines moved ahead, there were few to no Russian troops being left behind to keep control of "conquered" areas.

Instead of asserting an area of control, the Russians were only able to establish a line of control associated with their front lines. The Russians only maintained control of a thin strip of territory at and just behind their line of advance, but the Ukrainians retook most of the territory behind the Russians quickly after the Russians moved through.

This meant that what supply lines still existed to the front were under constant attack by Ukrainians. The Ukrainian military didn't necessarily do this attacking. Civilians and volunteer resistance fighters were happy to shoot at the random passing truck or put a few sticks of dynamite on a train track to hit a passing train. Even if all the Ukrainian locals did was text the location of a truck convoy, a few Ukrainian military troops could quickly pounce on it and hit it with shoulder-held rocket-propelled grenade (RPG) launchers.

The Russians did station clusters of troops at important supply dumps, rail depots, and road crossings to protect them, but the Ukrainians rapidly figured out these spots were prime targets for missile attacks and sabotage by special forces troops. These supply hubs were decimated over the summer and fall, and the chaos within Russian logistics and supply chains was complete.

This failure to control the territory behind their front lines also meant that Russian retreats of any kind were problematic. Perhaps more importantly, it made withdrawing the wounded and taking them to field hospitals nearly impossible. Russian soldiers bled and died where they fell with little to no medical help.

THE RUSSIAN NAVY GETS A BLOODY NOSE

And then the Moskva was sunk. The state-of-the-art (for Russia) cruiser-class ship was the flagship of the entire Black Sea fleet and shook Russian naval commanders to their cores. Its ammunition room was struck by two Ukrainian Neptune anti-ship missiles and a major explosion ensued that suck the ship quickly and violently.

Just one week later, the frigate Makarov was attacked and set on fire, although the ship survived the attack. The Makarov is Russia's most advanced frigate and carried a large supply of guided missiles. After the back-to-back attacks, the Russian navy withdrew most of its vessels some eighty miles offshore into the Black Sea and refused to come any nearer to the Ukrainian coast.

Until then, Russian naval bombardment had been pulverizing the southern coast of Ukraine. Not only did the sinking of the Moskva rattle the Russians and give Putin quite a bloody nose in news coverage back home, but it ended the highly successful bombardment of Kherson and other major Ukrainian port cities.

Western analysts couldn't understand why the Russian Navy backed off like that and never did really engage fully in the war again. Were they really that poorly trained and equipped and that afraid of losing vessels that apparently could not be replaced?

THE RUSSIAN AIR FORCE GETS A BLOODY NOSE

As the West sent high-tech, western, anti-aircraft artillery to Ukraine and trained the Ukrainian military on how to use it, the Russian Air Force all but stopped flying over Ukraine. What few planes did venture into Ukrainian airspace did so at very high altitude and for very short periods of time. There was no meaningful bombing campaign and the number of Russian combat helicopters flying sorties dropped precipitously over the summer.

Granted, the Ukrainians had plenty of shoulder-held ground-to-air missiles and were having excellent success knocking down helicopters. But western military analysts looked on in shock as the Russian Air Force inexplicably refused to establish air superiority or provide close air support for its ground forces in any meaningful way. Was the Russian Air Force really that poorly trained and equipped?

Putin was embarrassed at the annual Victory Day parade in May when no flyovers of any aircraft occurred. Putin claimed low cloud ceilings had grounded all aircraft, including a much vaunted "doomsday plane" he'd been bragging about showing off to the world. This doomsday plane is a flying command post designed to keep Putin safe and in charge in the event of a nuclear attack.

There were rumors of an effort to sabotage the plane when it flew over the Victory Day parade. One wonders just how much protection such an aircraft would be to Putin if clouds and rumors were enough to ground it. Despite making a fiery speech that day, Putin had no big victories to announce in Ukraine, and his bluster didn't impress anyone, including his own population.

CASUALTIES AND WAR CRIMES MOUNT

The casualties continued to climb for Russia, passing 40,000 and heading rapidly toward double that number. For its part, the Ukrainian army suffered about 1,500 deaths in the same time frame and a total of around 5,000 casualties. Many of the roughly 3,500 injured Ukrainian soldiers were able to return to combat before summer's end.

Civilian deaths were difficult to count and not reported by the Ukrainian government, but the death toll among them was much higher than in the Ukrainian military. Perhaps as many as 20,000 civilians died in the first six months of the war.

Accusations of war crimes against Russia continued to mount. Scenes of massacres, mass graves, tortured and raped corpses became commonplace in media coverage of the war. Some 458 bodies of civilians were recovered in the town of Bucha, most executed and many tortured first. Investigators for various international criminal courts and the United Nations went to work collecting evidence of the widespread brutality and war crimes committed by the Russian army.

Anyone who paid attention to Russia's invasions of Chechnya and Syria was not surprised by the sheer brutality of the Russian forces against civilians. In both of the previous conflicts, such animalistic brutality had proven wildly effective at breaking the will of the local populations to fight.

Putin has long espoused the idea of war as total conflict. He openly encouraged his forces to take war to every single Ukrainian they encountered. He also moved the military commanders responsible for the decimation of Syria into positions of power over the invasion force in Ukraine.

THE INVASION STALLS

As the summer of 2022 aged, forward movement largely stopped for the Russian army, and in fact, Ukraine began to claw back land that Russia had fought hard for and suffered high casualties for. The Ukrainians took back villages and small towns by the dozens as the demoralized Russians were forced time and again to fall back from motivated and increasingly well-armed Ukrainian military forces.

And then another humiliation for Putin: the twelve-mile-long Kerch Bridge, a four-lane automobile bridge and double-track rail bridge to Crimea from Russian territory to the east was bombed and badly damaged. Putin himself had ordered construction of the bridge shortly after Russia annexed Crimea, and Putin personally drove the first truck across the bridge when it opened. The bridge had been a triumphant political statement for him, and he was enraged when Ukrainian saboteurs blew it up.

Putin retaliated with a spate of missiles and artillery shelling that, while impressive in scale, showed the inaccuracy of Russian artillery in general. Not that Putin seemed to care if his shells hit their targets or not. In that moment, he seemed more concerned with shock and awe than precise tactical damage.

RUSSIAN MANPOWER PROBLEMS

Since the 1980's demographers (people who study populations of countries) have been warning that Russia was headed toward a serious population collapse. The birth rate among white Caucasians plummeted even back then, and Russia resorted to restricting access to abortions and issuing shoddy birth control measures that failed more often than they worked.

The only places where the Soviet birth rate remained high were in the Baltic states (which remained deeply Russian Orthodox in spite of official state atheism under Soviet rule) and in the largely Muslim republics of southern Russia—Kazakhstan, Kyrgyzstan, Turkmenistan, Tajikistan, and Uzbekistan. However, when the Soviet Union dissolved, all of these high-birth rate areas peeled away from the Russian Federation and became independent states, leaving Russia to deal with its own dismal birth rate.

Before the invasion of Ukraine, Russia was already staring down a crisis wherein there are not enough young men to field a full army and also to work in heavy manufacturing jobs. The war has only made this crisis worse. Much worse.

Russia has a mandatory draft for all men ages 18-27, although volunteers as young as 16 are allowed. It happens twice a year in April and October, and conscripts serve one year. They get 1-2 months of basic training followed by 3-6 months' worth of advanced training. By law, they're not allowed to go into combat until they've had four months' worth of training.

There are lots of exemptions for the draft, and only about 11% of Russian men serve in the military. Which is to say, the educated and wealthy don't send their sons to the Red Army, a source of resentment in poor, rural areas, and a source of morale issues within the army itself.

As the war commenced, about 25% of the soldiers in Ukraine were these one-year conscripts. The rest were "professional soldiers", which is to say, they had extended their enlistments for some period of time. In the face of high unemployment in rural areas and lack of opportunities for education or advanced vocational training, some young men opted to remain in the army rather than return home. But the majority of them were by no means committed to long-term careers as true professional soldiers.

On February 18, 2022, Russia called its spring conscription two months early. (Sure. They weren't planning an invasion of Ukraine.) This move surprised Russians and alarmed western military intelligence experts. It was, in fact, one of the decisions analysts pointed at when warning that Russia was about to invade Ukraine.

Less than one month into the war, Putin extended the conscription period of all current Russian conscripts by six months. There's no way this improved troop morale, particularly of the conscripts already in Ukraine. A good chunk of them were a few weeks from heading home. And now they were stuck in Ukraine for six more months, dealing with terrible conditions, a severe lack of food, ammunition, and decent leadership, watching the high casualty rate and the near total lack of medical care for those who did get injured.

This was not a recipe for good morale. Not to mention, those conscripts had no reason to believe they would be allowed to return home in another six months. (They turned out to be absolutely correct about that.)

Most of the Fall 2021 conscripts were sent to Ukraine at the beginning of the war and took many of the casualties. At the rate of soldier attrition suffered in Ukraine over the summer of 2022, February 2022's batch of conscripts, at best, replaced the initial troop numbers but did not expand the number of troops engaged in Ukraine significantly from when it first invaded.

The Russian Reserve has over two million soldiers (mostly former conscripts) on paper. But less than 10% of them have ever received any refresher training. The Rand Corporation estimated that only 4,000 to 5,000 soldiers were maintained in what westerners would consider an active reserve status—meaning regularly trained. This does NOT include equipping them, integrating them into active units, or keeping them ready to deploy on short notice.

In the spring of 2022, the Red Army actually solicited dona-tions of socks, coats, hats, and food from Russians near the Ukraine border. They couldn't provide basic clothing or food for their army, and that was before Putin greatly expanded the number of troops participating in the war.

In August of 2021, Putin started a new program to recruit vol-unteers for a Russian Combat Army Reserve that would get some regular training. Significant signing bonuses were offered, and the plan was to raise a 100,000-man force. Western estimates are that about 10% of that number were actually recruited. They were never trained or integrated into active-duty units, however. Yet again, they were only paper soldiers.

When the Russian Defense Minister, Sergei Shoigu, (who is Putin's childhood friend and has NO military experience whatso-ever) claimed the country had 100,000 reserve troops ready to go, it was this hypothetical Combat Army Reserve he was referring to. It never existed in any meaningful way.

Undoubtedly Shoigu's boss wanted to be told these reserves did exist, though, and more importantly, Putin wanted everyone to believe they were real. Therefore, Shoigu gave a number of speeches making reference to the 100,000 reserve troops Russia could throw into the Ukraine war at a moment's notice.

Putin and Shoigu also spent a fair bit of time in the summer of 2022 talking about 40,000 volunteers from the Syrian army who were enroute to Ukraine and 10,000 Chechnyan commandos who were on their way to Ukraine.

Those 40,000 alleged Syrian troops? They never material-ized. Those 10,000 brutal Chechnyan commandos? They took a shellacking in their first week in Ukraine and their warlord boss, Ramzan Kadyrov, pulled them back to Chechnya.

Kadyrov, who is wildly unpopular in Chechnya, couldn't afford for all his strongmen to be slaughtered because they were and are the only reason he remains in power in Chechnya. The Chechnyan people loathe Kadyrov and will depose him the minute they can overwhelm his private army.

And what of Belarus's super-soldier brigade that President Lukashenko of Belarus promised to Putin? 70 of them were killed in the first 48 hours of their incursion into Ukraine and Lukashenko promptly withdrew them all because, like Kadyrov in Chechnya, he couldn't afford to lose his strongman-thugs if he wanted to remain in power.

PUTIN HIDES HIS DEAD

As Putin's losses mounted in Ukraine, he resorted to shipping corpses on trains to Belarus in the dead of night to hide the real numbers of Russian soldiers killed in action. He also is reported to have sent many of his wounded to Belarus for treatment so the Russian people would not catch wind of how many soldiers were being injured.

I will say it again. Russia is a really big country. The eastern ¾ of the nation is rural and isolated with tiny villages dotting the steppes stretching from the Ural Mountains all the way to Alaska. As young men, many hailing from these widely scattered villages, started coming home in body bags, a few to each village at a time, it took a while for the Russian people to begin to get a sense of just how many young men were dying.

In the initial invasion, Putin sent 190,000 troops into Ukraine. In the first 30 days of the war, NATO estimated that Russia suffered 40,000 casualties, including 15,000 dead. Not all of that 190,000 were front line infantry soldiers, of course. There would have been medics, cooks, truck drivers, back line staff and officers, communications technicians, and the like. But even if every one of those 190,000 troops was a frontline fighter, Putin lost 21% of his combat troops in a single month.

The Russian military was forced to combine fragmented and decimated units into new operating groups. Even under the best of circumstances, this would have been difficult as new chains of command had to be formed, new communications structures built, and new leadership had to establish authority over troops unfamiliar with them.

In the midst of this organizational chaos, Ukrainian snipers were having a field day taking out Russian officers from junior field commanders to senior generals. By July of 2022, 14 Russian generals had been killed using a combination of western intelligence information, spotter drones, cell phone data, and Ukrainian spotters on the ground to locate them.

THE RUSSIAN MANPOWER PROBLEM
BECOMES DESPERATE

To give you an idea of just how desperate the Russian senior military leadership situation became, in July 2022, an obese, visibly unhealthy Russian Special Forces general was called out of retirement. He made his surprise at being called up known to anyone who would listen to him. Nonetheless, he was sent to Ukraine to take command of the Spetnatz forces in Ukraine after the current Spetnatz commander there was badly injured in an ambush.

This retired general was reported to consume five meals and a liter of vodka a day, and he'd been out of action for twenty years. His knowledge of military doctrine and strategy was two *decades* old, and he was the best Putin could find to lead his elite troops in Ukraine. One can only wonder at the effect his clearly unwilling reactivation, age, and horrible physical condition had on the morale of the troops he took command of.

We're jumping ahead a bit here, but in the first nine months of the war, some 1,500 Russian officers were killed. Such a large leadership vacuum would be a challenge for any military to recover from, but the Russian military is deeply authoritarian with little real power extended down to senior enlisted personnel. In the absence of officers to give orders to Russian ground troops, the Russian infantry was practically paralyzed by mid-summer, and that problem only grew worse into the fall.

In July, rumors started to fly that Russia was about to call up its reserves and send them to Ukraine. Yes. . .those in name only reserves of 100,000 ready reserves, who were actually only about 10,000 men. Rumors also flew that some of the two million men who'd ever served in the Russian military might be subject to a call-up to active duty.

It's worth noting that fitness is not a craze in Russia the way it is in the West. Life is hard in Russia and work is often hard. The average life expectancy for men in Russia today is around 68 years of age, although that number has probably gone down a bit in the wake of the Covid crisis. The officially reported life expectancy in

Russia is 73 years of age, but demographers worldwide believe age 68 to be much closer to accurate.

Alcoholism in adult Russian men is reported officially to be around 36%. Again, demographers believe the real number to be much higher, but nobody knows exactly by how much. About 27% of adult Russian men smoke, as well. While there may be plenty of overlap with those who also drink to excess, it's fair to say that at least one-quarter (and more likely, closer to half) of all Russian men are drinkers and smokers who would struggle to perform up to the minimum standards required of soldiers.

So. If Putin were to call up some of the two million men who've served in the Russian army in the past, say, thirty years, a significant percentage of them are likely to be out of shape, alcoholics, smokers, or just plain unhealthy. Infantry work involves walking long distances and carrying heavy gear, occasional running, and long periods of high stress.

This does not even begin to take into account how many of those called-up men wouldn't want to be there in the first place. Morale is critical to military success, and no military functions well when morale is terrible. It's a military maxim that bad morale tends to be contagious. If 100,000 men with mostly miserable morale were to be injected into an already beleaguered Russian invasion force, it was inevitable that morale would not improve and would, in fact, degrade even further.

Putin might be able to force a lot of warm bodies into Ukraine but that would by no means ensure his army would fight hard and valiantly for him.

THINGS GO FROM BAD TO WORSE FOR RUSSIA

Russia finally took control of the rubble of Severodonetsk and crossed the Siversky-Donets River to begin the whole process of artillery bombardment and glacially slow advances in the neighboring city of Lysychansk. Russian heavy artillery was effective at flattening cities, but it took time.

And that time spent in one place firing artillery shells gave the Ukrainian military and resistance fighters plenty of time and opportunity to make hit-and-run strikes against Russian forces for weeks on end.

When Russian forces finally advanced within the city of Lysychansk, they again encountered stiff resistance in the form of street fighting, snipers galore, and hit-and run tactics that greatly favored the hometown Ukrainian forces. Casualties continued to pile up for Russia. Casualty rates rain in the neighborhood of 600 or so per day for the Russians. 18,000 men per month was a high price, indeed, to pay for a few square miles of rubble. But Putin insisted that his military pay it.

For their part, the Ukrainians kept just enough soldiers hanging around in the city to force Russia to continue its expensive bombardment. And, when Russian infantry advanced a block or two, the Ukrainian forces came out just long enough to hit with snipers and harassment tactics to kill a few more Russian soldiers.

The casualty rates in these sieges were wildly lopsided against the Russians. The Ukrainians stung like bees and retreated over and over, bending, but never breaking, attacking and fleeing, never confronting directly.

In July, Putin made a speech to the Russian Parliament in which he warned the rest of the world to look out. If they refused to negotiate peace with him in Ukraine, he warned that he was coming for all of Europe. This led scoffing western military experts to ask, "With what army?"

The only real threat buried beneath Putin's bluster was that of using chemical or nuclear weapons against European targets, a fact that was not lost on western leaders. Again, when the going got bad, Putin turned to threats of nuclear war.

Lysychansk eventually fell to Russia when it had been literally reduced to rubble and a bunch of Russian soldiers had been killed. Ukraine eventually withdrew and let Russia take the city which had no remaining strategic value. It did, however, complete Putin's invasion of the Luhansk region. (Keeping in mind that Russian troops had moved on from much of the oblast and large areas behind the Russians were already back under Ukrainian control).

Putin declared it all a great victory and gave a series of triumphant speeches. For their part, the Ukrainians shrugged, unimpressed with his empty boasts. They were well pleased with what they had managed to cost Putin before handing him his pyrrhic victory.

CASUALTIES AT THE ONE-YEAR MARK

One year into the war, conservative Western analysts place the number of Russian casualties at approximately 200,000, with at least 60,000 of those soldiers having been killed and possibly as many 150,000 dead. In early 2023, Russia lost an average of 500-700 soldiers per day, losing up to 824 soldiers in a single day.

If this pace of casualties continues, Russia can expect to lose another 150,000 men in the second year of the war, effectively wiping out the entire 300,000 men called up to bolster Putin's war effort.

Putin announced in late January that he was calling up another 500,000 men to bolster the war effort. He's going to need those half-million men. For the moment, however, their mobilization is on hold due to inability to equip, train, or integrate them into existing units.

We're left to wonder just how many men Putin is willing to kill in this war of his. By comparison, Russia lost 15,000 troops in its entire ten-year war with Afghanistan. As for the Wagner Group, British intelligence services estimate its casualty rate stand at 50%.

For Ukraine, an estimated 13,000 troops have died. If we extrapolate typical death to injury rates, something like another 60,000 Ukrainian soldiers have been injured. The United Nations reports that more than 7,000 civilians have been killed and another 12,000 have been injured—although the real civilian casualty rate is probably *much* higher. For example, an estimated 65,000 war crimes have been reported to date, and many of those resulted in as yet uncounted murders. It's likely that tens of thousands of Ukrainian civilians died in the first year of the war.

The U.N. also reports that at least 6,000 Ukrainian children have been kidnapped and taken to camps and other facilities where they have been prevented from contacting their families and sub-jected to "re-education." Infants are reportedly being given to families inside Russia, some as young as 4 months old.

CHAPTER FOURTEEN

RUSSIA REGROUPS

"As of today, there are four new regions of Russia. The results [of a series of illegal, sham referendums staged by Russia in various Ukrainian held areas] are known. Well known. These results are due to the will of millions of people who have the right to self-determination: Luhansk, Donetsk, Kherson, and Zaporizhzhia. Russia has the right to use nuclear weapons to defend its territory and citizens if we feel there is an existential threat, even if it is attacked by conventional weapons."

—**Vladimir Putin**, September 30, 2022

UKRAINE TAKES CONTROL OF LYMAN, a strategically important city in Donetsk October 1, 2022, driving out the last 5,000 Russian troops. . .

"As of 1230 today, Lyman is fully cleared of Russian Forces."

—Volodymyr Zelensky , Oct 2, 2022

So much for Putin's great victory in taking Luhansk and Donetsk and making them part of Russia. It lasted all of one day before Russia suffered a humiliating defeat in an important Donetsk city that made a mockery of Russia's referendum and annexation of the Donbas.

After the costly campaigns to take Severodonetsk and Lysychansk, Russia called a halt in attacking the Donbas region to regroup. Which was to say its forces had taken such staggering and debilitating losses in men, equipment, and supplies that it could not continue on until it took a break to physically regroup and resupply its military units.

While Russia massed almost all of its heavy artillery on the edge of the Donetsk region in preparation to finish conquering that oblast, the Ukrainians surprised everyone by launching an aggressive offensive of their own in the south to take control of the Kherson region. This oblast borders the Crimean Peninsula and provides critical access to Crimea, particularly in light of the heavy damage suffered by the Kerch Bridge, which stretched toward Crimea from the east.

Only one major railway remained usable by the Russians to reach their forces in Kherson and conditions among the Russian forces in the south became dire quickly. Attempts were made to bring in Russian ships to resupply and reinforce the beleaguered troops, but attacks by drone boats and saboteurs in the Black Sea nixed that idea quickly.

The Russians found themselves backed up against the Dniepro River which is a large body of water, with no easy means of retreating across it. They dug in and fought hard, but Russian casualties were very high in that battle. Again, the Ukrainians hunkered down in bunkers and basements while the Russians expended massive numbers of missiles and artillery shells attempting to push the Ukrainians back.

RUSSIA TRIES TO REGAIN THE ADVANTAGE

Russia went ahead with its attack on the Donetsk region, relying on its tactic of heavy artillery shelling to flatten everything in the Russian army's path before finally advancing infantry troops on the ground. To give you an idea of how slowly the Russians were moving, in the month of August, the Russian army advanced a grand total of six miles. Six.

For their part, someone launched a sneak attack on a Russian air base in Crimea. The Ukrainian government denied responsibility for the attack, pointing at disaffected Russians living in Crimea as the culprits. Perhaps it was a Ukrainian Special Forces team that sabotaged the ammunition dump at the airbase and blew up a number of buildings around it. Or perhaps it really was local Russians. Either way, many frightened Russian civilians and Russian sympathizers fled Crimea, causing massive traffic jams on the remaining bridge off the peninsula.

The sinking of the Moskva and retreat of the Black Sea Fleet from the coast of Ukraine months before took on new significance as Ukraine steadily pushed Russian ground forces in the Kherson region back toward their one remaining rail line and lone means of retreat.

Back home in Russia, dissenters and those who criticized Putin continued to die, including the daughter of a prominent journalist who was blown up in a car bombing. She also was a journalist, and it's unknown if she was the target or her father was. Either way, Putin's State Security Forces continued to crack down on and jail anyone who said anything that could be construed as negative about the Russian regime. It became a crime punishable by 10 to 15 years in jail to even call the invasion of Ukraine a 'war'.

RUSSIA RESORTS TO SHELLING

In the absence of ground forces able to make significant advances against the technologically superior Ukrainian forces, Putin shifted to a new tactic. Aerial bombardment. . .and lots of it.

The Russians quickly figured out it was most effective to fire a large barrage of different types of missiles together at the same target, say, a major city. They might group cruise missiles, traditional ballistic missiles, drones, and air defense interceptors on nearly identical ballistic trajectories.

This method poses a challenge to air defense systems because radars focus on certain sectors of the sky. So, if attention is on the horizon, defenses might be neglecting threats at a higher altitude, and if the attention is focused up high, threats could approach from a lower level. Diversity of missile types and flight profiles can help overcome a stiff air defense.

Missiles and artillery shells began to rain down on Ukraine by the thousands. Sometimes as many as thousand strikes a day poured down on Ukraine. The attacks targeted major military installations, cities, and infrastructure. Especially infrastructure. Russia set out to destroy the electrical power grid, dams, bridges, highways, rail lines, water pumping stations, sanitation facilities, cell phone and wireless towers across the country.

Cruelty was the point of Putin's massive artillery attacks in Ukraine. His aim was to make life as miserable as possible for the Ukrainian people and to cripple the Ukrainian military. He no doubt hoped that the burden of repairing damage and caring for the 5 million or more internally displaced Ukrainian civilian refugees would weaken the Ukrainian war effort and break the will of the Ukrainian people.

I know I'm repeating myself, but it bears repeating: The Ukrainian people are not going to surrender. However, Putin seems to be counting on the Russian military and the Russian population back home to endure more suffering and loss than their Ukrainian cousins to the south.

The Ukrainian people share the exact same history with the Russians. They've both endured massive wars on their territories over the centuries. They both fought the Nazis in World War II. They've both endured sieges, tank battles, and infantry battles in their lands with staggering casualties.

But here's the thing. The Ukrainians are fighting on their home soil for their country. Their children, wives, and mothers live where they're fighting. The Russians, however, are the foreign invaders this time. Unlike in World War II, the Russians are *not* patriotically fighting on their own turf for their homeland. Ukraine is. And that makes all the difference.

If the last Ukrainian man died and Ukraine was still at war with Russia, you can be sure that Ukrainian women and children would take up arms and continue the fight where their men left off. This is total war for Ukraine, war for survival. Russia has no such stakes on the line.

At the very beginning of the war, many of the first captured Russian soldiers reported not even knowing they were in Ukraine, and most reported having no idea why they were fighting against

Ukraine. Many expressed confusion over why they were fighting Ukrainians. The soldiers reported having relatives, family and friends in Ukraine, and knowing many Ukrainians with deep family and friend ties inside Russia. What was there to fight over?

In spite of Putin's efforts to restrict press coverage of the war and the deluge of pro-war, anti-Ukrainian propaganda Russian state television spews in an unending stream, Russian soldiers for the most part seem to understand they are in the wrong in this conflict.

Unlike the Russian population at home, the Russian forces in Ukraine are confronted daily with the violent reality of the war they started. They know up close and personal that they provoked this war, and they know what it's costing the Ukrainian people.

This understanding of being in the wrong within the Russian military is strongly reflected in poor morale, numerous surrenders and defections by Russian troops, and poor overall performance by Russian forces on the battlefield. Russian commanders can bully and threaten their troops all they want, but if a soldier's heart isn't in it, it's impossible to force a man to perform courageous acts above and beyond the call of duty upon which victories often depend.

RUSSIA RUNS OUT OF MISSILES

Russia launched so many missiles at Ukraine in October and November 2022 that it literally ran out of them. Western analysts know this because Russia resorted to converting surface-to-air missiles normally used for defense of its military bases inside Russia into makeshift surface-to-surface missiles that got shot at Ukraine.

They rained down on Ukraine daily for months, anywhere from a few hundred to a thousand or more strikes every day. The city of Kherson reported taking 16 incoming attacks in 24 hours, and Kyiv sometimes reported new barrages of incoming missiles once an hour.

Russia shot artillery shells by the thousands, it launched cruise missiles out of Russia that flew over Belarus to reach Ukraine, and it launched guided missiles from its ships in the Black Sea. It threw everything it had at Ukraine.

While the high-tech missiles it used were, for the most part, accurate, the same cannot be said of its ballistic artillery shells and converted surface-to-air missiles. Attacks hit civilian targets more often than they hit their intended military or infrastructure targets, and civilians died from one end of the country to the other in the bombardment. Schools and hospitals were hit. Apartment buildings and supermarkets were struck. Nowhere was safe from the shelling.

And then Russia started using what became known as kamikaze drones. Small and inexpensive, these drones loitered passively at low altitude until a target was spotted. Then they came in low— well below radar—and slow—too slow for aircraft to target—delivering a relatively small explosive charge. In particular, the Russians used these drones against electric power grid targets to great effect.

IRANIAN KAMIKAZE DRONES

But the Russians quickly ran out of their own drones, as well. They turned to Iran to buy HESA Shahed 136 drones. They're about 11 feet long with a wingspan of about 8 feet and weigh about 200 kg (440 pounds). They can carry an explosive charge of between 30 and 50 kg (66 to 110 pounds). Their maximum forward speed is only about 115 miles per hour.

Russian forces in the Crimea, Iranian-trained and "supervised", which is to say helped by Iranians, guided these Iranian-made kamikaze drones to targets across Ukraine. In October of 2022, Russia fired as many as 50 Shahed drones a day. These drones have bedeviled Ukraine since their introduction to the war.

In November 2022, Iran admitted that it had sent "a small number" of drones to Russia before the war. Western experts believe Russia purchased an estimated 2,400 Shahed 136 and other models of Iranian drones.

Over the course of October and November 2022, Russia exhausted its entire stockpile of Iranian suicide drones, as well. By December, they were absent from the ongoing aerial bombardment by Russia.

Russian Security Council secretary, Nikolai Patrushev visited Tehran in November of 2022, allegedly to purchase more drones. However, Russia wanted the deal to include a transfer of technology that would enable Russia to produce the drones on its own, and Iran would not agree to that. To date, no new deal for drones from Iran to Russia has occurred.

Ukrainian defense officials are quick to point out that internal problems inside Iran may be contributing to the delay or failure of such a deal. The Iranian government may be losing its grip on Iranian society to the extent that it just doesn't have time for dealing with Russian drone manufacturing. One can only hope this is correct.

While they were in use, the Iranian kamikaze drones were not only effective but highly cost effective. A single Shahed drone costs about $20,000 to manufacture, and Ukraine was expending expensive, western-provided guided missiles that cost up to $140,000 apiece, sometimes two per drone, to knock them out of the sky.

The Ukrainians report an approximately 70% success rate in knocking all missiles, shells, and drones out of the sky. However, the effect of the prolonged bombardment by Russia has been catastrophic on the ground.

At any given time, at least half of the Ukrainian power grid is down, and sometimes up to 70% of the country is without power of any kind. Cities have had to resort to creating warming and electronic recharging centers, and civilians go days at a time with no electricity or running water, let alone flushing toilets or working cell phones. Rechargeable car batteries and portable generators are *everywhere* in Ukraine, filling in as emergency power sources.

Winter in Ukraine is not gentle. Nighttime temperatures are below freezing—sometimes falling to below 0 degrees Fahrenheit (-18 C). Obtaining clean drinking water or cooking food can turn into heavy labor as water must be hauled from trucks or centralized wells, and what food is available is largely cooked over wood fires made up of scavenged wooden debris. Life in the absence of basic infrastructure is harsh at best. And yet, it has only hardened the determination of the Ukrainian people to persevere.

PUTIN CALLS UP 300,000 MORE TROOPS

At the end of August, with his military stagnated and Ukraine actively beginning to take the offensive and drive his army back, Putin signed an order to call up 300,000 more men to active duty, effective immediately.

An interesting aside, the day Putin was scheduled to make the announcement, Russian state television stations were notified at noon that he would be making a major speech at eight o'clock that evening. The airways were cleared and the speech was announced on all major news outlets.

But 8 p.m. came and went with no interruption of regular broadcasting and no speech. There was no sign of Putin and no statements out of the Kremlin about where he was or what was going on, not to mention why the speech hadn't happened. Putin didn't surface until nearly six p.m. the following evening. He made the speech without getting the wide national coverage that had been arranged the day before.

Putin would have had to go to the Kremlin to make such a major speech. Since the outbreak of the war, he preferred to spend all his time at his heavily fortified, two-billion-dollar private palace outside of Moscow with its extensive and deep underground bunker system. Western intelligence sources believe an attempt was probably made on Putin's life after he arrived at the Kremlin and he was emergency evacuated back to his estate and stashed in a bunker for over twenty-four hours.

Putin is nothing if not paranoid. He trusts nobody and only an extremely tiny cadre of servants and advisors are even allowed into the same room with him. An ex-KGB officer himself, Putin is obsessive about his personal security. It appears he may indeed have good reason to be paranoid. And, it also appears that he does not enjoy the unanimous support of everyone inside his government.

At any rate, Putin eventually called up 300,000 men immediately to active duty. Current college students and men in various critical jobs were exempted from the order, which was only supposed to affect men who'd formerly served in the Russian military.

THE CALL-UP FIASCO

That's not how the draft went down. Thousands of men were randomly snatched off the streets by the State Security Force, thrown into vans, and shipped to recruitment centers where they were offered a choice: sign up to serve in the military or go to jail. In more than a few cases, men reported being told to sign up or be shot.

The logistics and supply fiasco that had dogged Putin since the very beginning of the Ukraine War only intensified as his military struggled to provide weapons, ammunition, and even uniforms for this new surge of troops. Russian men reported getting two weeks of "refresher training" wherein they fired a grand total of three rounds of ammunition from weapons shared three to five men to a single rifle. They were shipped to Ukraine, many wearing only armbands over their civilian clothes to indicate they were Russian infantry.

Once these unhappy recruits arrived at the front, they were told Spetnatz troops were positioned behind them. If they retreated even a little bit, they would be shot by the Spetnatz soldiers. They were ordered to advance or die. It's no surprise that the Russian recruits commenced referring to themselves as *myahsuh*, the Russian word for meat.

As forecast by western military experts, morale in the Russian forces went from dismal to abysmal. Reports started coming in of entire Russian units surrendering together for lack of coats, food, radios, or maps. In several cases, they appeared to have murdered their commanding officers before marching themselves into the nearest Ukrainian-held area to surrender.

Although Putin now had plenty of fresh troops, his forces continued to advance by feet and not by miles. The logistical and communication problems that had dogged him from day one, if anything, got worse. His war was going terribly. So terribly, in fact, that there began to be serious rumblings of discontent at home in Russia.

Ultra-nationalist commentators on State television began to criticize Putin's management of the war. They called for more brutality, more bombing of civilians, more violence, and above all, more successes. Putin fired a series of generals and advisors, no doubt in an attempt to right the ship, clean house, and look as if he was still firmly in control. But his façade of invincibility was slipping badly. He had to do something dramatic to get the war back on track. . .

THE WAGNER GROUP

PMC (Private Military Company) Wagner was formed in 2014 in St. Petersburg, Russia. Although a few of its senior commanders were known to the West, the founder and owner of the paramilitary company remained in the shadows and unknown for years.

The company started with about 250 men and grew steadily over the next several years into a force of some 8,000 mercenaries. They trained and operated largely in Africa and the Middle East, where they gained a reputation for viciousness and atrocities everywhere they went.

The crimes they have committed over many years in many countries are simply too heinous and sickening to describe in the pages of this book. They will surely go down in history as some of the worst war crimes perpetrated in human experience. Journalists who've witnessed the aftermath don't even try to report on the crimes because they defy comprehension or belief. I cannot overstate this point: the Wagner Group is evil incarnate.

Because they stayed abroad, never threatened him at home, and acted as his proxy in many foreign conflicts, Putin was willing to overlook their worst excesses. If anything, Putin seemed to embrace and rejoice in their brutality. Perhaps he saw it as manly or strong, a projection of the kind of power that made people tremble before him.

Putin seemed prepared to overlook the fact that private militias of any kind are illegal under Russian law. Despite that pesky legal issue, the Wagner Group operated as a de facto private army for Putin, following his orders to carry out all sorts of black ops and special forces-style missions, including kidnappings, torture, assassinations, and genocides. To put it bluntly, they did all the dirty work for Putin outside of Russia.

As early as 2014, the Wagner Group commenced helping pro-Russian separatist forces in Donetsk and Luhansk, taking part in training, sabotage missions, and stirring dissent against the Ukrainian government. They formed cells of local residents and trained them in para-military maneuvers, sabotage, and de-stabilization tactics. It's believed they led some or most of the attacks aimed at destroying the Ukrainian government in the Donbas region, including the shooting down of Malaysian Air Flight 17 over the Donetsk oblast, killing all 298 souls on board.

Even though they were an illegal outfit, the Wagner Group nonetheless was funded, supplied, and supported directly by the

Russian military. They were hired by the Russian government for most of their work, received intelligence directly from the GRU (the Russian military intelligence agency), and even used Russian military installations and instructors for training their "contractors." They are frequently considered to be a de facto fighting unit for Russia's GRU.

For much of the 2010's, the Wagner Group played a significant role in violence and civil wars in Libya, Mali, Sudan, the Central African Republic, and of course, Syria. These were areas of interest for Putin and places where he was looking to extend Russia's influence.

In Syria, particularly in the city of Aleppo, there were many international journalists, numerous human rights watchers, and observers from the International Criminal Court whose job was to document evidence of war crimes. For a change, the atrocities of the Wagner Group did not go unnoticed and unreported on, and the group gained global fame for its horrific attacks against civilians, particularly women and children. The global media declared them ruthless, and even monstrous.

The United Nations accused Russian forces in Syria (both military troops and the Wagner Group) of war crimes. Although an effort was made to censure Russia for its war crimes, Russia vetoed any such actions in the Security Council. It's worth noting that a number of small nations around the world, many of whom rely on Russian grain and Russian export of their natural resources also voted not to punish Russia for its war crimes in the Syrian conflict.

Putin literally laughed at the United Nations and declared that no war crimes had ever been committed by a Russian soldier.

I suppose, for a man who believes that the more brutal the better in war, it's easy to deny that war crimes even exist let alone were committed.

Russia benefits greatly from the fact that both NATO and Ukraine adhere to the Geneva Conventions and reject the idea of war crimes as a valid combat tactic. Russia is asymmetrically committing atrocities in Ukraine without any fear of retaliation in kind.

At any rate, use of the Wagner Group allows the Russian government, and Putin in particular, to claim no responsibility for the group's worst behavior. Putin throws up his hands and declares himself to have no part in what this private, civilian company does, even though the Wagner Group is without question doing its dirtiest deeds on his behalf and at his behest. Nobody believes Putin's protests of plausible deniability. He knows full well what the Wagner Group is doing and he approves of it all.

When things started going badly for Russia and the manpower crunch became obvious, a man named Yevgeny Prigozhin shocked the intelligence world by coming forward and declaring himself to be the founder, owner, and leader of the Wagner Group.

Prigozhin made his fortune in the 2000's as a restaurant magnate. He cornered all the catering contracts for the Kremlin and was given the moniker "Putin's Chef" in the western press. Apparently, he parlayed that fortune and his close contact with Putin into forming Wagner.

Immediately after coming forward as the owner of Wagner, Prigozhin commenced visiting Russian prisons in the summer of 2022 to recruit convicts to join the Wagner Group and go fight in Ukraine. He is estimated to have recruited in excess of 40,000 hardcore Russian convicts to join the Wagner Group. His offer: fight and kill for him for six months in Ukraine, and the Russian government would give them a full pardon.

Immediately, lawmakers inside Russia questioned his offer. As a civilian with no government affiliation whatsoever, how did Prigozhin have the authority to offer convicts their freedom, let alone pardons? Their questions were never answered by anyone official and Prigozhin continued to recruit killers out of the prisons.

In January of 2023, as the first Wagner recruits finished their stints in Ukraine, pardons were, indeed, forthcoming from the Russian government. Nobody seems exactly sure who authorized the pardons, nor who is signing them, but all indications are that Putin himself must have given the go-ahead to issue them. Putin is a dictator in every sense of the word and very little of significance happens in the Russian government without his approval.

The Wagner Group, numbering some 50,000 strong by late summer, headed for Ukraine. They were promptly put to use as shock troops, attacking ahead of the regular Russian forces. No surprise, they got up to their old tricks and commenced committing the worst atrocities yet against civilians in Ukraine.

In addition, Wagner troops were allegedly stationed just behind large units of newly deployed Russian recruits (the first of the 300,000 who'd been called up only a few weeks before). The Wagner men allegedly had orders to kill any recruits who fled or retreated from the field of battle. Whether or not this was true, the threat worked to freeze terrified and unhappy Russian soldiers in place on the front lines.

Prigozhin flung his convict-contractors into combat with abandon in an apparent pursuit of glory for the Wagner Group and for himself. These minimally trained convicts didn't perform much better than Putin's newly scraped up recruits did. Casualties of up to 80% were reported within Wagner's ranks.

Along with that exceedingly high casualty rate came discontent within the Wagner ranks. These were not highly trained, highly motivated, highly paid mercenaries who'd been brought over from the ranks of the Russian Special Forces. These were murderers and violent criminals who lacked discipline, training, and in many cases, basic education. They received only the barest minimum of indoctrination before being sent to Ukraine as cannon fodder. . .where they died like cannon fodder and resented it. Reports of Wagner troops turning on their commanders proliferated.

THE IGOR MANGUSHEV INCIDENT

Igor Mangushev was a one-time Russian soldier and former strategist for the Wagner Group. In 2012, he formed a small private military company called the E.N.O.T. Group, which he used to coordinate between multiple far-right, ultra-nationalist, patriotic groups inside Russia.

He was a neo-Nazi often seen to give Nazi hand salutes, and he was an extreme Russian nationalist. Beginning in 2014, he worked as a captain in the Luhansk People's Militia, a pro-Russian separatist group.

When the Ukraine War broke out, he led Russia's anti-drone platoon, using technology he and his men invented to jam and knock down Ukrainian drones.

In August of 2022, he famously appeared in a Moscow night-club holding what he claimed to be the skull of a Ukrainian soldier who died in the siege of the Azovstahl Iron and Steel Works siege. Mangushev proceeded to do a stand-up comedy routine using the skull as a prop.

On the night of February 4, 2023, Igor Mangushev was shot in the back of the head, execution style, at a Russian checkpoint in Ukraine well behind the front lines. He died several days later in a hospital. It's widely believed that the Wagner Group murdered him, and Yevgeny Prigozhin went uncharacteristically silent regarding the killing.

After the attack, the BBC quoted Russia expert Mark Galeotti saying the Mangushev assassination demonstrated that Russia was sliding back towards aspects of the 1990s, "when murder was a business tactic, and the lines between politics, business, crime, and war became near meaningless."

The incident is an interesting demonstration of the rivalries between Russian PMCs. It's reminiscent of the Russian mob violence of the 1990's and early 2000's, in fact.

As you'll recall, in August of 1991, the head of the KGB and several other high-ranking government officials attempted a coup d'état against Mikhail Gorbachev. When the coup failed, the KGB was officially disbanded by December of that year. It was replaced by the Federal Counterintelligence Service (FSK) of Russia, which Yeltsin also disbanded because it was "unreformable." (It was ultimately succeeded by the Federal Security Service of the Russian Federation, or FSB.)

At any rate, the disbanding of those intelligence services

dumped a bunch of analysts and operatives on the street with no job prospects, and many of them turned to the Russian mob for employment. Rival crews of highly trained and high-tech equipped former KGB officers vied for control of the Russian crime scene through the 1990s. Out of those ranks rose multiple crime bosses—and semi-legitimate business oligarchs—with vast wealth and power.

Hence, the current rivalries between private military companies inside Russia are not unfamiliar to Putin. He's seen this before with Russian crime families fighting among themselves. Putin is likely to let the fight for dominance among Russian PMCs play out as long as nobody turns against him. Indeed, he seems to relish internecine fights among his own people where the strongest and most brutal emerge victorious.

PRIOGOZHIN REVEALS POLITICAL AMBITIONS

Meanwhile back in Russia, Prigozhin commenced complaining about how the war was being run. Loudly. On State television. To the embarrassment of Putin.

Prigozhin is arguably the only man in Russia who could get away with doing such a thing these days, but Putin needs the Wagner Group whether he likes it or not. For the moment, they are the biggest dog on the block when it comes to private military companies.

Priogozhin criticized Russian generals, calling them weak, cowardly, and stupid, and straight up asserted that he could run the war better than the Russian army. Given that Putin has personally overseen the war from day one, Prigozhin was all but calling out Putin himself. Prigozhin even made a public statement that he would make a good leader of Russia, stronger than Putin, and that he would run the war much more aggressively.

I can't imagine how Putin must have reacted to that. A man in charge of some 50,000 trained killers paid by and loyal only to himself was showing interest in taking Putin's job from him. It's a sign of just how dependent on the Wagner Group Putin is that Prigozhin wasn't immediately arrested and very publicly executed—or at least pushed out of a very high window.

However, over the winter of 2022-2023, Putin began snubbing Prigozhin, turning down meetings with him and taking Russian army credit for wins in combat that Prigozhin claimed were the doing of his mercenaries. Putin was clearly worried by Prigozhin 's growing popularity with the Russian populace, particularly among right-wing nationalists who form the core of Putin's support.

Putin is clearly looking to clip his mercenary leader's wings. Whether or not it will work remains to be seen.

If nothing else, we should all take away the lesson that there are worse monsters than Putin inside Russia who would likely make a run at Putin's job if he were to die or be deposed.

PROLIFERATION OF PRIVATE ARMIES

On February 4, 2023, the Russian government gave Russia's largest energy company, Gazprom Neft, permission to create its own private security force. The pretext for approving this was to help secure vital energy sector resources.

It remains against the law for any private militia to exist inside Russia, and yet, Russia seems eager to enter into some sort of internal mercenary arms race. It's possible this move is meant to reduce

Wagner's monopoly on mercenary power inside Russia or perhaps to weaken Prigozhin to the point where he's no longer a threat to Putin or to Putin's job. It may also be a move by Putin to take partial control of Gazprom's vast wealth and apply it to international conflicts on Russia's behalf.

Also, several oligarchs are said to be forming their own private security forces. . .but much larger than are strictly necessary for their own personal security. Are they doing this to court favor with Putin? Or are they doing it to enhance their own power to the level that they can challenge Putin?

Nobody is sure at this point. Putin's mantra seems to be holding true, however: as long as you use your army to support my goals and you don't turn against me, you can form all the private armies you want.

Given the financial crunch that Russia is feeling from sanctions, funding the war, and trying to keep its economy afloat well enough that the Russian people don't revolt, Putin may see himself as having no choice but to let oligarchs use their personal riches to bolster the military capabilities of Russia. It's a risk on Putin's part. He could very easily lose control of those paramilitary forces, and they could turn on him in the end.

WHERE WILL WAGNER RECRUIT NOW?

The Wagner Group was said to be down to about 20,000 able-bodied fighters (almost all of whom are currently in Ukraine) as of February of 2023. Also in February, 2023, Prigozhin announced he was no longer recruiting in Russian prisons and penal colonies. Given that no soldiers are being released from active duty in the

Russian armed forces at this time, it does beg the question of where the Wagner Group plans to find new recruits to bolster its flagging numbers.

In the summer of 2022, before it commenced its prison recruiting campaign, the Wagner Group ran an aggressive ad campaign using TV commercials and billboards across all of Russia exhorting able-bodied men to join them. Which is to say, pretty much anyone inside Russia who wanted to volunteer for the Wagner Group already has.

Reports from inside Russian penal facilities indicate there are no more able-bodied prisoners left to recruit, and those few who do remain jailed in Russia would rather serve out their sentences than be subject to certain slaughter on the battlefield. Wagner is facing serious headwinds when it comes to recruiting new men.

Videos have surfaced of a deserter from the Wagner group (one of their prison recruits) being apprehended back inside Russia, where he was bludgeoned to death with sledgehammers by Wagner operatives. This, too, might be having a chilling effect on Wagner recruiting.

However, the Wagner Group appears to have its sights set on a new and unexpected source of military recruits to aid its struggling war efforts in Ukraine: United States veterans.

A 1½-minute long recruitment video began circulating on social media at the end of January 2023, in which a voice with a thick Russian accent speaks as Russian subtitles roll over images of US warfare that's not going well in the video, riots in America, burning swastikas, and violent images of the January 6th Insurrection. It says:

"You were a hero to your country, giving your best years in the army. You dreamed of defeating evil, you dreamed of doing much to make America great again. But in reality, you saw criminal orders, the destruction of nations, the death of civilians, and all for the will of a bunch of families who thought they were earthly gods—deciding who would live under their rule and who would be destroyed. You began to realize that this is the side of evil. This is not the America the founding fathers dreamed of. It has become the focus of the evil that is destroying the whole world."

The video shifts to images of the Russian military looking strong, organized, and victorious. Their uniforms are crisp and clean, and they march in a glorious parade. And then the video shows men in military camouflage wearing arm patches of PMC Wagner Group. The voiceover continues:

"And today, the only country fighting this evil is Russia. If you're a true patriot of the very future of great America, join the ranks of the warriors of Russia. Help defeat evil or it will be too late for everyone."

The video ends with an image of a city being annihilated by a nuclear blast.

In February 2023, Yevgeny Prigozhin claimed responsibility for the video.

ALL IS NOT WELL INSIDE WAGNER

In January 2023, disturbing video also surfaced, filmed by a Ukrainian drone, of Wagner troops carrying a wounded Wagner commander back from the front lines by the arms and legs. They carry him behind a barn, where they proceed to beat him to death with shovels. Morale doesn't seem to be much better inside the Wagner group units than it is inside the Russian army.

The once terrifying image of the Wagner mercenaries seems to have been badly tarnished in recent days. Progozhin's political star appears to be on the wane as Putin chips away at Prigozhin's personal image of strength and influence.

Recruitment for the company is way down and cracks are showing in the command-and-control structure of the group. Given the brutality of the men the company employs, it probably does not bode well for its senior leadership if those men are turning on their commanders.

Spetznatz troops currently on active duty in the Russian military not only aren't being released from active duty, but they currently have the full support of the Russian government. Why would they shift over to Wagner with its ridiculously high casualty rate and risk working for a company that may be well on its way out of favor or even heading toward collapse?

THE GAZPROM GAMBIT

Gazprom's new private army will undoubtedly erode the Wagner Group's status and financial support at least to some degree. How little or how much is yet to seen. Wagner already takes up a significant portion of Russia's budget for hiring military contractors, and it takes up significant training facilities earmarked for Russian army special forces use.

We must assume that Gazprom's training requirements will muscle aside at least some of Wagner's financial and facility agreements with the Russian military. It will be interesting to watch the two private armies compete for resources and see who comes out on top.

It's worth noting that Gazprom is, indeed, very rich and can fund much of its own training, but its wealth is not infinite and armies are very expensive to train, equip, and operate. At this time, it's unknown if funding its own army was Gazprom's idea or Putin's. The concept of forming an army may have been forced upon Gazprom by Putin, in which case, Gazprom may be reluctant to pony up any more of its own funds to pay for its army than it has to.

It's also possible that Gazprom CEO, Alexey Miller, is doing exactly what Prigozhin appears to be doing: putting himself in a position of such strength that he can one day challenge Putin for his job, or at least be in the running to replace Putin when he steps down or dies. At a minimum, Gazprom's move into the sphere of PMCs is likely to ingratiate the company and its CEO with Putin. . .for now.

Several other Russian oligarchs may have the exact same thing in mind: build a private army and dedicate it to Putin's use in the short term. Then, in the long term, use it to put themselves in a position to take control of the Russian government when Putin steps down, is deposed, or dies.

The formation of all these private military companies makes sense in the short-term context of Putin being in a fight for his survival in Ukraine. He needs all the manpower and resources he can muster to turn the tide in Ukraine in his favor.

But one does have to wonder what will happen after the war ends. Will the oligarchs and their private armies turn on Putin and take him down? It seems like a reasonable assumption that at least one of them will make a run at taking down Putin (politically or literally) at some point.

We must assume that these oligarchs have permission from Putin to build their private armies. Which leads us to an even larger and more disturbing question: has Putin completely abandoned the rule of law in favor of violent, criminal groups that, as long as they remain loyal to him, will have free reign to do whatever they want both inside and outside of Russia?

I cannot conclude any discussion of the Wagner Group without pointing out that the Ukrainian military has faced the Wagner Group and not buckled before it. It is Ukrainian soldiers inflicting those staggering casualties on the Wagner men. As fearsome as the Wagner Group's reputation was before it came to Ukraine and as horrendous as the war crimes it has committed against civilians in Ukraine have been, even the gory might of Wagner has failed to break the will and resolve of the Ukrainian people.

UKRAINE WILL NEVER SURRENDER

Without trying to give you a comprehensive, day-by-day, blow-by-blow history of the war in Ukraine, I hope you've gathered by now that the war has not gone well for Russia. In fact, practically nothing in the war has gone as Putin planned it would. He has had to resort to brutal tactics that pose a real danger to his long-term survival inside Russia, and still, the Ukrainian people refuse to surrender.

The reality is the Ukrainian people will never surrender. In a survey conducted by the Munich Security Report in November of 2022, 95% of Ukrainians advocate for continuing their military resistance if Ukrainian cities keep getting bombed.

And, in an eye-popping response, 89% of Ukrainians vote for continuing their military resistance even if Russia uses tactical nuclear weapons on the battlefield or against some Ukrainian city. In the case of Russia exploding a nuclear weapon over the Black Sea in a show of force—a move Putin and other Russian military advisors have threatened recently—91% of Ukrainians poll in favor of continuing their military resistance.

The survey went on to reveal that 93% of respondents are convinced that only a complete Russian withdrawal from Ukraine—including occupied Crimea—is necessary for ceasing fire. When questioned further, 10% of those surveyed were willing to take Crimea off the table and let Russia have it in exchange for peace, however 80% strongly disagreed with ceding Crimea to Russia.

Only 1% of Ukrainians surveyed believe it's necessary to leave everything as it is now and let Russia keep all the territory it has gained thus far in the war.

83% of Ukrainians think they will never be safe while Vladimir Putin is president. 75% of them believe they will not be safe without Western security guarantees. 65% of respondents think it will take membership in NATO to guarantee their future security while 71% say they must continue to receive western weapons and military support to remain safe.

THE WEST WILL NOT TOLERATE
A UKRAINIAN DEFEAT

In the West, an understanding between nations appears to have coalesced that defeat in Ukraine, meaning the defeat of the Ukrainian army, the fall of the Ukrainian government, and full reabsorption into the Russian Federation of the Ukraine, is not acceptable.

I do not believe the West thinks it to be in its best interest for Ukraine to win the war outright for one simple reason—nobody wants to see what Putin will do if he loses. But I do think the West will not accept an outright Ukrainian defeat. And this leaves Ukraine caught in a terrible, terrible situation.

The West is asking Ukraine to continue fighting Russia, to continue losing its citizens by the tens of thousands, to endure the utter annihilation of its country, and to act as the proxy for the West indefinitely.

The West is counting on its superior economic strength to eventually break the Russian economy. This is, of course, what the United States did in the Cold War of the 1960's through 1980's. The United States has enlisted most of the largest economies in the world to participate in devastating sanctions against Russia. The notable exceptions, of course, are China and India, but more on them in a bit.

Both Ukraine and the West are not seriously pursuing any options for a negotiated peace one year into this war and counting. Everyone lined up on Ukraine's side of this war seems to have decided that the only acceptable outcome for this war is a win at all costs. Unfortunately, Vladimir Putin has also decided he is prepared to win this war at all costs.

The war stands at a stalemate between Ukrainian will to survive/western technology and the massive numbers of soldiers Putin is flinging into battle. Diplomatic efforts to find a negotiated exit to the war for either side are also at a standstill. Nobody is willing to back down, and both Ukraine and Russia are prepared to let the slaughter continue for the foreseeable future in the belief that the other side will eventually have to blink.

A realistic and restrained foreign policy would see the world as it is, not as our diplomats and lawmakers wish it was. In Ukraine, this means keeping lines of communication open with Russia, no matter how deep our disapproval of its invasion. It means continuing to understand the real risks deeper involvement in this conflict involve and tailoring our policy going forward to put American safety and interests first.

This isn't a popular view, but it is a mature view. Pride is not a sufficient reason for hundreds of thousands of people, both Russian and Ukrainian, to die. At some point, one nation or both is going to utterly exhaust itself and its resources, and history will be left to wonder why the war went on so long with any serious effort to end it.

QUANTITY VERSUS QUALTIY IN WAR

The West is counting on its vastly superior military technology to hold off the massive numbers of soldiers Putin is willing to throw into Ukraine to fight and die.

In war, there are two major opposing forces: quantity of soldiers and quality of technology. If one side in a war has more soldiers than the quality of their enemy's technology can counteract, that side will win. Likewise, a combatant will win a war if it has better technology than its enemy can counteract through sheer numbers of soldiers. Of course, if one side in a conflict has both better technology and more soldiers, it is all but guaranteed to win.

It is this push and pull at work in the Ukraine war. Russia's technology has been shown to be woefully outdated and ineffective in comparison to western military technology. However, Russia's population of 146 million is vastly larger than Ukraine's 43 million (as of January 2023). Putin is counting on overwhelming Ukraine through the sheer number of soldiers he is trying to throw into the war.

Putin is being hampered in this effort by the spectacularly bad logistics and supply chains in his army that are failing to properly support his much larger army. Also, Putin failed to take into account that no matter how large an army is, if it doesn't want to be there, doesn't want to fight, and isn't willing to die for your cause, their performance will be tremendously degraded on the battlefield.

However, the military maxim still holds true: quantity of forces will always overwhelm quality of technology unless the technology gap is wildly lopsided against the larger force.

Remember, Putin was raised by survivors of World War II. His family participated heavily in that war, and he must have been raised on war stories of huge Russian armies holding out against the superior Panzer tank forces of the Nazis. Putin also studied military tactics in his youth and in his early government service. Russia has historically won all its major wars on the backs of huge armies that took massive casualties but endured at all costs to protect the motherland.

Putin has shown the world in the Ukraine War that this notion of Russian-style, grinding, tank-and-infantry warfare goes all the way down to his DNA. It's his identity as a military leader, and he believes it to be fundamental to the Russian identity, as well.

This is how he planned to fight the war before he ever sent the first tank into Ukraine, and it's how he plans to continue fighting the war. Hence the call-up of 300,000 additional troops in September of 2022, and the call-up of 500,000 more troops in January of 2023.

UKRAINE NEEDS TANKS

In response to Putin's clearly signaled intent to engage in a big, World War II style tank and infantry offensive in the Spring of 2023, Ukraine has been literally begging the West to give it heavy weapons, offensive weapons, it can use to push back this expected Russian offensive. In particular, Ukraine needs tanks.

The subject of giving Ukraine tanks has been a thorny debate for months. Ukraine insists it needs weaponry it can use not just to stand and hold its position against the Russian forces, but it needs weaponry it can use to push back the Russians. Zelensky points out that the war won't end until Russia leaves all Ukrainian soil; therefore, he needs weapons to drive Russia out.

Western nations have been hesitant to take the step of giving Ukraine state-of-the-art NATO weapons that could be perceived by Russia as offensive weapons (which they most certainly are). The West fears that, if NATO were to provide such aggressive weapons, Russia might declare itself to be directly at war with NATO and broaden the scope of the war.

A "broadened" Russia war might include Russian attacks on NATO nations bordering Russia and force NATO to send troops into combat directly against Russia. This, in turn, could escalate quickly into a third world war in Europe. Given the lopsided capability of NATO to crush Russia should NATO fully engage in such a war, this, in turn, would threaten to turn into a nuclear war.

In addition, sending heavy tanks to Ukraine in the quantity Zelensky is asking for would likely shift the balance of the war quickly and dramatically. If this occurs, the West fears Putin will become desperate and resort to chemical or nuclear weapons. To date, the West appears to be trying to slow roll the war, in other words, for the Russian forces to lose slowly enough not to panic Putin.

France became the first country to offer light tanks and Bastion armored fighting vehicles to Ukraine on January 4, 2023. These are not the heavy tanks Ukraine needs to push back the Russians, but they're a start.

The U.S. argues that its Abrams M-1 tanks are complicated machines. They're not easy to operate or to maintain, and they require extensive training and a robust supply chain for parts and maintenance. Instead, the U.S. suggested Germany should supply its simpler Leopard 2 tanks to Ukraine. German Chancellor Olaf Scholz refused, saying that the EU and NATO need to agree to it, first.

However, facing pressure from inside Germany to do more to support Ukraine and mounting pressure from the United States and NATO, Scholz finally relented. He agreed to send 40 Marder infantry fighting vehicles to Ukraine and to train Ukrainian troops on Leopard 2s.

On January 13, 2023, Britain's Prime Minister, Rishi Sunak announced that the United Kingdom will send a small number of Challenger 2 tanks to Ukraine. This powerful tank will easily outmatch any current Russian battle tank. The UK hopes that its example will encourage other western countries to step up and provide tanks to Ukraine, as well. The initial commitment is for about a dozen tanks.

Some military experts say a dozen tanks are a "token gesture" by the UK because tanks need to be numerous to be truly effective in battle. However, Ukraine hopes the move will open the way for other western nations to send more tanks, particularly more Leopard 2 tanks that several European countries currently use.

Poland announced a few days after the UK commitment to send tanks that it plans to send 14 Leopard tanks to Ukraine, but that it needs Germany's permission to re-export them, first. Germany Vice Chancellor, Robert Habeck indicated it would not stand in Poland's way.

The United States heard Zelensky's pleas for more of what he needs to beat back a major Russian ground offensive. On January 6, 2023, the U.S. announced a new $3 billion aid package including 50 Bradley infantry fighting vehicles, 100 M113 armored personnel carriers, 55 mine resistant ambush protected vehicles (MRAPs), and 138 Humvees. The package also included 500 TOW anti-tank missiles, air defense missiles, 4,000 aircraft rockets, and more ammunition for the HIMARs missiles.

The United States announced in February 2023 that it will send M-1 Abrams tanks to Ukraine later this year, after training Ukrainian troops in how to use and maintain them.

Frankly, I think this announcement is a publicity stunt by the United States or an effort to shut up Ukraine's constant pleas for tanks. The reality is it will take upwards of a year to complete the necessary training and then deploy both the tanks and supply/maintenance packages to Ukraine.

A major consideration facing Ukraine's western allies is what weapons are best suited to Ukraine's style of warfare and the skill and training level of its troops. Ukraine's army largely consists of recent conscripts who have been learning to be soldiers on the fly in combat. They've proven to be smart, motivated, and eager to learn, but they still have to learn to use sophisticated western weapon systems coming to them from dozens of nations, each system slightly different from the next.

To date, Ukraine has been most effective at hit-and-run tactics and guerilla style warfare and not at large-scale tank battles or infantry battles. A large tank force run by professional tank officers and crews would undoubtedly be incredibly effective at driving back the older, less advanced Russian tank forces. But the West cannot send professional NATO tank crews along with its tanks, and it may take more time than Ukraine has to turn its volunteer army into professional tank soldiers.

The injection of western tanks into the war should help change the balance of power in the war in favor of Ukraine. But, it will take time. Ukraine's military will need time to adjust their fighting doctrine and to figure out the logistics of supplying and maintaining their new tanks. It remains to be seen if Putin will see the tanks as crossing a red line and lash out in some way, up to and including the use of nuclear weapons.

THE RUSSIAN REFUGEE CRISIS

In response to the call-up of 300,000 troops in September, some 250,000 Russian men of military service age immediately fled Russia. Within a week of the call-up, the traffic jam at the Finnish border was some 200 miles long and it took vehicles two to three days to reach the border crossing.

Remember, the young men called up in the first round were those recently released from their obligatory service, and many men who were simply snatched off the streets of small cities and villages across rural Russia. Men from the large cities were not kidnapped in any quantity, undoubtedly because Putin feared the backlash it would cause if it got widespread media coverage.

There were already protests of mothers and wives happening across the country as women demanded to know what had happened to their sons and husbands. The government was not releasing the names of the dead, wounded, and kidnapped, and as men's cell phones went silent by the tens of thousands, families got fed up with the lack of information from the government.

Side note: Ukraine very early in the war instituted a policy of, whenever a Russian soldier was kidnapped, letting him call his mother by phone to let her know he was alive, safe, and being treated well. Additionally, Ukrainians commenced sending photos of the dead home to family members in Russia whenever they could identify a body, along with a short message of condolence for their loss. These notices from Ukraine infuriated Putin, and as it turned out, infuriated Russian mothers and wives that the enemy was their only source of information.

As rumors circulated in late 2022 that another, larger

call-up of men was coming, the Russian population realized the only way for Putin to scrape up another half-million able-bodied men would be to move into the larger cities and take men from there.

Another mass exodus of Russian men ensued. As of February 1, 2023 estimates place the number of Russian male refugees out of Russia at no less than 500,000. This number does not include female family members or children fleeing with their husbands and fathers.

Because so many Russians are fleeing illegally to avoid Russian authorities, it has proven difficult to accurately count the full number of men who have left Russia to avoid the draft, and most agree the number of male refugees is much closer to 1 million men than the half-million who have officially been counted. The number of Russian refugees fleeing the draft continues to climb steeply as of the writing of this book.

Men who are leaving Russia are those who have enough money to own a car or to pay for a train or plane ticket. Russian State Security has resorted to stopping every man of military age at every airport and train station to be interrogated, often arresting and conscripting men on the spot. Hence, the majority of Russians are leaving by car or boat.

One gaming company in Russia, whose male employees were not exempt from the call-up as they technically didn't work in an IT (Information Technology) company, chartered a private jet and flew all 100 of its employees and their families out of the country. They plan to reestablish their business abroad and not to return to Russia.

Most of this flood of refugees have enough education to seek jobs in the West, and many of them are educated enough to speak another language. Some work for international companies willing to sponsor them abroad, and some have relatives abroad willing to help them establish themselves abroad.

The men fleeing Russia are largely middle- or upper-class, younger than age forty, the majority have at least some college education, they have some financial resources they're taking with them, and most importantly of all, the vast majority do not ever plan to return to Russia.

Some 85% of male Russian refugees surveyed across the globe by a major international aid agency say they will never return to Russia, and almost 100% of those who plan to stay abroad and are married say their wives and children have joined them or they are making plans for their families to join them.

These are not Russia's dirt poor, uneducated, ethnic minority men who are fleeing. These are the Russia's best and brightest, fleeing from western, urban Russia. They're taking their educations, ambitions, future earnings, and future contributions to Russia's society and economy with them as they go.

Demographers and economists agree that the brain drain and population drain in Russia is already so severe that Russia will never fully recover from it. Russia already is struggling to fill out an army and keep all its factories operating for lack of able-bodied men. The war has not only cost Russia closing in on 200,000 casualties but roughly another million men. . .and counting.

In the face of massive draft dodging, the Russian parliament passed a series of laws widening benefits for soldiers who serve in

Ukraine and for their family members, including freezes on debt repayments for mortgages and consumer loans A law was passed forgiving all the debts of soldiers killed or severely wounded in combat, along with the debts of their close family members. Parliament also approved special monthly salaries of 135,000 to 200,000 rubles ($2,290 to $3,400) for all soldiers serving in Ukraine, which are two to three times the national average salary. Laws were passed guaranteeing the jobs of returning war veterans and their spouses, as well.

Laws also had to be passed to help owners of small and medium businesses defer loan payments and stay in business as their male employees fled or were siphoned off to fight in the war. There simply aren't enough men to go around in Russia, as it turns out.

However, all these new laws prompted many in Russia to ask, if the government has all this money for cash incentives, why don't they have the money to properly train, equip, and supply soldiers?

The Russian government is already offering financial incentives for Russian refugees abroad to return home—amnesty for fleeing and one-time payments of up to ~$15,000 dollars, along with guaranteed housing and jobs. However, Russia is not guaranteeing that any returning men will be spared from military service in Ukraine. To date, the program is going dismally with almost nobody taking up the government on its offer.

PART III:

UNHOLY

ALLIANCES

CHAPTER FIFTEEN:

CHINA'S LONG GAME

AT LAST, WE HAVE ARRIVED at the heart of this book. Why does it matter that Russia has invaded Ukraine? Why does it matter that Iran has a long history of extremist religious ideology revolving around the return of a long-gone imam? Why is it so problematic that Iran seems determined to build a nuclear weapon? Why is it a problem for everyone that Russia, Iran, and China have allied themselves so closely? And why does it all matter right now?

THE TIES BETWEEN CHINA AND IRAN

The ancient Persian and Chinese empires were connected for centuries by the Silk Road, across which they traded freely. Since the 1990's China has used Iran as a major oil supplier, and Iran has used China as one of its main sources of revenue that bypasses international sanctions against Iran. In 2012, when the Obama administration imposed strict oil sanctions against Iran, China acquired waivers for Iranian oil purchases. In 2019, The Trump administration ended all waivers on imports of Iranian Oil. China, however, has defied the United States and continues to purchase Iranian crude oil, albeit at a steep discount.

China has made major investments in Iranian oil fields and remains one of Iran's largest trade partners. China played a major role in Iran's reconstruction after the Iran-Iraq war and remains deeply involved with development of new Iranian infrastructure projects.

China has been one of the only countries willing to sell Iran weapons and military equipment since the 1980s. It is known that China has sold Iran ballistic missile components, anti-ship cruise missiles, and other defensive weapon technology. In the 2010s, China and Iran held multiple joint military exercises together.

CHINA'S ROLE IN IRAN'S NUCLEAR PROGRAM

China is known to have cooperated significantly with Iran on its nuclear program. China is believed to have helped build the Isfahan Nuclear Research Center that houses the bulk of Iran's uranium enrichment centrifuges. China has helped Iran with uranium exploration and mining, provided Iran with lasers necessary for uranium enrichment processes, and helped Iran redesign and modernize its Arak nuclear reactor.

Although the Chinese government agreed in 1997 to stop providing direct nuclear support to Iran, Chinese companies continued to sell Iran components and equipment with dual use in other industries and the nuclear industry. This is a standard Chinese tactic—the government agrees not to do a thing, but Chinese businesses, with a wink and a nudge from the government, do the thing anyway.

Much of North Korea's nuclear knowledge and capabilities come straight from China. It's likely China knows North Korea is sharing nuclear technology and equipment with Iran. In the same way China uses its private companies as proxies for itself, the Chinese government is probably using North Korea as its proxy to continue sharing nuclear development help with Iran.

IRAN-CHINA STRATEGIC AGREEMENT

In April 2012, Beijing and Tehran signed a 25-year strategic cooperation agreement. In it, China agreed to invest $400 billion in the energy, banking, telecommunications, and transport sectors of the Iranian economy. In return, Iran will sell oil and other energy products to China at a heavy discount from global market prices. In addition, Chinese companies will get priority over Iran's other trade partners when it comes to purchasing oil.

The agreement also reportedly says China will deploy 5,000 Chinese soldiers to Iran to protect China's various projects inside Iran. However, Iran denies this is true. The details of the agreement were never released to the public, so it's impossible to verify the claim that Chinese forces will deploy inside Iran in the near future.

If this happens, it could throw a serious wrench in Israel of the United States' abilities to launch any kind of military strike against Iran and avoid provoking Chinese retaliation. This, of course, is precisely why it would make sense for Iran to invite in some thousands of Chinese troops.

While the investments and deployments of this agreement have yet to occur, and may not ever occur, it nonetheless represents a formal deepening of Iran's ties with China. Reports of the agreement caused widespread criticism of Iran for becoming nothing more than a "vassal state" of China. It's likely the Iranian leadership sees the agreement as a way to increase foreign investment in Iran, to update and modernize its infrastructure, and to increase a friendly superpower's commitment to Iran as an ally.

CHINA AND RUSSIA DRAW CLOSER

In the meantime, China has not only strengthened its ties with Iran. It is also working to strengthen its ties with Russia. And these are of even more concern to the West.

Russia and China (and Iran, for that matter) share a deep antipathy for democracies and see them as a threat to their system of government. They would both like to see the United States weakened, and both nations see themselves rising to dominance as world powers in the next fifty years.

In Russia's—or more specifically Putin's—case, this notion is a delusion. Russia's population was collapsing before the Russia-Ukraine War began, and now its loss of young, working aged men has accelerated dramatically. We are witnessing the sunset of Russia as a superpower. Unfortunately, Russia and Putin have yet to acknowledge that reality.

In the aftermath of its disastrous war with Ukraine, Russia will be forced take a hard look at itself and accept that:

+ its military is no longer that of a superpower (with the lone exception of its nuclear arsenal)

+ its economy is going to be decades recovering from the war and reintegrating into the global economy.

It may be decades before it lures back investment and presence in Russia of major international brands and businesses

+ the world is rapidly moving beyond oil—and doing so more quickly because of the upheaval in oil markets caused by its own war

+ Russia's invasion has made it a global pariah. It will take decades or longer for Russia's reputation and standing in the world to recover from what it has done in Ukraine.

China, however, can realistically aim to become a dominant world power in the next fifty years. One way it's going about doing this is to ensure a long-term supply of cheap oil for its industrial and production economy to continue to grow on, both from Russia and from Iran. Russia is one of the most resource rich nations on earth, and China also aims to take advantage of that fact. But more about that in a minute.

TIMELINE OF NEW CHINESE-RUSSIAN CLOSENESS

From the very beginning of the Russia-Ukraine War in February of 2022, Putin has worked hard to strengthen his ties to China and Xi Xinping, China's long-time premier. But what was China up to while the world's attention was riveted on Russia and Ukraine? Let's take a quick look.

February 4, 2022: Xi Xinping and Vladimir Putin meet in Beijing. They declare in a joint statement that "friendship between their two states has no limits, there are no 'forbidden' areas of co-operation".

February 22, 2022: Chinese government gives Chinese media censorship instructions not to say anything unfavorable about Russia or favorable to the West regarding Ukraine. The People's Daily (a large state newspaper in China) accuses the U.S. of reviving the Cold War mentality and creating confrontation. The Chinese Foreign Ministry refuses to draw parallels between what's brewing in Ukraine and Chinese ambitions regarding reabsorbing Taiwan in China.

February 23,2022: China's UN ambassador says in the U.N. Security Council that it will promote peace "in its own ways." China's foreign ministry accuses the U.S. of sending weapons to Ukraine and blames the U.S. for tensions and panic. The spokesperson also noted that Taiwan has always been an inalienable part of China's territory. China Customs relaxes restrictions on imports of Russian wheat.

February 24, 2022: Russia invades Ukraine.

February 24, 2022: China advises its citizens to display Chinese flags on their cars and challenges western media's use of the word 'invasion". Xi calls for negotiations to resolve the Ukraine issue. China abstains on a U.N. Security Council Resolution to end the Ukraine Crisis. (Russia vetoed it, killing the measure.)

February 26, 2022: China advises its citizens in Ukraine to avoid revealing their nationality as they're facing hostility from Ukrainians.

February 27, 2022: The West imposes SWIFT ban on bank transactions with Russia.

February 28, 2022: China's U.N. ambassador saying China does not approve of any approach that may exacerbate tension. However, internally, China announces it will continue normal trade with Russia. China ignores the SWIFT ban and allows Russia to conduct business to the rest of the world through its banks, allowing Russia to bypass the banking sanctions.

March 2, 2022: China abstains in a vote by the full U.N. to condemn Russia for its invasion and demanding immediate withdrawal. China announces it will not participate in any sanctions against Russia.

March 6, 2022: Several Russian banks commence issuing credit cards through Chinese banks that will allow Russians to continue shopping and banking abroad.

March 8, 2022: Xi tells German Chancellor Shultz and French President Macron that he's willing to mediate the conflict. Inside China, China pursues new investments in Russian energy and mining companies, bypassing international sanctions against Russia. Chinese Foreign Ministry accuses the United States of conducting biological warfare experiments.

March 11, 2022: People's Bank of China approves a floating rate of the ruble to RMB (China's official currency). This helps Russia exchange rubles for other currencies at Chinese banks. The ruble is frozen in sanctions across the world, so Russia must exchange rubles for other currencies to continue trading abroad and to make debt payments abroad.

March 13, 2022: China swears it has no part in the Ukraine crisis and it's not supplying Russia with any military equipment. (Even though it sold $128 million worth of equipment to Russia in December of 2021.)

March 17, 2022: A major Chinese newspaper, the PLA Daily, accuses the United States of causing the Ukraine crisis.

March 18, 2022: Xi Xinping and President Biden have a two-hour video conference call in which Biden warns Xi of the consequences if it provides material support to Russia. It's described as polite but terse and unproductive.

March 28, 2022: China increases purchases of Russian oil. Propaganda inside China accusing the U.S. of starting the Ukraine war and of being a bully ratchets up.

April 1, 2022: The Times of London reports that China coordinated a large cyber attack on Ukrainian military and nuclear facilities on February 23, the day before the Russian invasion.

April 5, 2022: China agrees to supply microchips for bank cards in Russia, an item sanctioned by the West.

April 6, 2022: the EU's top diplomat accuses China of having an ambiguous position on the Ukraine War. Reuters reports that Russian oil is being sold to Chinese oil companies using alternative payment mechanisms such as cash transfer to avoid scrutiny and reporting.

April 7, 2022: China votes against a U.N. General Assembly resolution to suspend Russia from the UN Human Rights Council. The resolution passes anyway with 93 nations voting in favor, 24 against, and 58 abstaining.

April 12, 2022: PLA Daily calls the U.S. a war monger and profiteer in an article examining America's despicable role in the Ukraine crisis. (which is to say, the anti-American rhetoric is getting turned up hard inside China.) Meanwhile, the Chinese Foreign Ministry is saying abroad that it's making great efforts to deescalate the situation, resolve the crisis, and build peace.

By this point in the timeline, you've probably figured out that China is saying one thing to a foreign audience and a different thing entirely to its domestic audience. Likewise, it's talking a big line about trade with Russia being reduced while it actively helps Russia evade sanctions and continues normal trade, including purchasing lots of oil. . .which is Russia's main source of revenue as a nation. Let's continue. . .

April 22, 2022: The U.S. State Dept and European Union release a joint statement saying that China's support for the Kremlin's illegal war against Ukraine undermines the rules-based international order. The U.S. accuses China of parroting Russia's concept of "indivisible security" wherein Russia controls all its neighbors to advance its own security. China reacts angrily.

April 28, 2022: China accuses NATO of throwing its weight around and stirring up conflicts in the Asia-Pacific region.

April 29, 2022: China accuses the U.S. of dragging out the Ukraine war to weaken Russia.

Put a pin in this accusation. We'll talk about it more in a minute.

April 30, 2022: Local governments across China announce increasing trade with Russian companies.

May 3, 2022: The Financial Times reports that oil refiners in China are stealthily buying Russian oil at a discount.

May 5, 2022: The Chinese Ambassador to China praises deepening China-Russia strategic cooperation on energy project, military technology, and space issues.

May 16, 2022: China accuses the G7 of "grossly interfering in China's internal affairs, maliciously slandering and smearing China, and once again exerting pressure on China using such pretexts as the Russia-Ukraine conflict."

May 24, 2022: China and Russia hold a joint military exercise, conducting joint aerial patrols near Japan's airspace. Japan calls it provocative.

May 26, 2022: China votes against a World Health Organization proposal to condemn Russia for creating a health emergency in Ukraine.

May 27, 2022: China hires ten additional supertankers to transport Russian crude oil to it.

Sales of Russian oil to China are really cranking up, now.

Not only is China getting cheap oil at a discount from Russia, but Putin is getting the money he needs to continue funding the war and keeping his economy afloat. A think tank based in Finland estimates that China has imported $13.2 billion in oil from Russia since the start of the war. . .and paid for it mostly in western currencies Putin can use to circumvent sanctions on the ruble.

> **June 15, 2022:** Xi and Putin hold a phone call and agree to "expand cooperation in energy, finance, the manufacturing industry, transport, and other areas, taking into account the global economic situation that has become more complicated because of the illegitimate sanctions policy pursued by the West."

> **June 20, 2022:** Russia becomes China's largest oil supplier for the first time, replacing Saudi Arabia.

> **June 28, 2022:** The U.S. State Dept sanctions five more Chinese companies for supplying technology and equipment to the Russian military, even though the China government continues to insist it is providing no military support to Russia for the war.

> **July 13, 2022:** China stops publishing data showing monthly natural gas imports from Russia, indicating that these imports have probably increased substantially. Western estimates place the increase in natural gas sales to China at 40%.

July 15, 2022: The Wall Street Journal reports that China's exports of microchips, electronic components, and raw materials to Russia have more than doubled in the first half of 2022. Many of these exports have direct military applications. The WSJ also reports China may be backfilling orders of defense components after Western nations cut off exports of them to Russia.

Sure, China isn't supporting Russia's war effort or supplying it with any military assistance. Let us continue...

July 19, 2022: The U.S. accuses China of hoarding grain and fertilizer, worsening the global food crisis. China responds by accusing the U.S. of intentionally starting a food crisis by sanctioning Russia.

July 20, 2022: Bloomberg reports that China imported 72% more Russian oil and gas in June 2022 than a year earlier. They say China has imported $25.3 billion in Russian energy between March and June 2022.

That's a lot of cash for Putin to use to fund his war. China pays for it in a combination of RMB and rubles, helping greatly to stabilize Russia's currency.

July 27, 2022: The U.S. Senate designates Russia as a state sponsor of terrorism. China is critical of it and defends Russia.

October 20, 2022: The EU imposes sanctions on three Iranian generals and Shahed Aviation Industries for supplying drones to the Russian military for use in Ukraine. China's Foreign Ministry is critical of the sanctions.

October 27, 2022: China's foreign minister tells Putin that China firmly supports his government and is willing to deepen exchanges with Russia at all levels.

November 2, 2022: Chinese knock-off parts are found in the remains of Iranian Shahed 131 and Shahed 136 drones used to attack Ukrainian cities.

November 29, 2022: Newsweek reports that Russian An-124 transport (a very large cargo plane similar to the American C-5 cargo plane) aircraft visited China nine times within seven days in November. The article reports that for some flights the aircraft turned off their transponders, causing speculation that the cargo included military aid.

Dececember 9, 2022: Bloomberg and Reuters report that China's independent oil refiners may be purchasing oil above a price cap on Russian crude oil that the Group of Seven industrialized nations (G7) introduced on December 5. The price cap is intended to reduce the revenue Russia receives on oil without fully cutting off supply from Russia.

February 25, 2023: CIA Director, William Burns, states in a television interview that the CIA "strongly" believes China is considering giving military weapons to Russia to use in the Ukraine war. President Biden warns China again not to do it—the implication being that the U.S. and E.U. will sanction China, which would be a serious economic blow to it. China seems very surprised that the U.S. and Europe are reacting so forcefully and with such coordination to the war.

Whereas China bought massive quantities of Russian oil cheap in the first months of the war, it has reversed course and is now paying above oil's market price caps (imposed by the E.U. to keep oil flowing but leave no profit for Putin over production and transport costs). This is a blatant attempt to shore up Russia's economy and support the cost of its war.

CHINA'S BALANCING ACT

China has spent the entire war walking a tightrope, on the one hand appeasing the global diplomatic community and not outright supplying Russia with military equipment for the war, and on the other hand doing its level best to help Russia as much as it can without provoking retaliation from the West.

No matter how much the West wanted to keep China completely on the sidelines of the Ukraine War, China and Russia were having no part of that. China has talked a big line in the West about wanting peace and de-escalation, all the while lambasting the United States inside China and steadfastly providing critical financial support to Putin.

China has walked a tightrope regarding military support for Putin, as well. It has not provided tanks, weapons, or missiles outright. But, it has provided parts to repair Iranian drones, computer chips necessary to operate guided missile systems, tires, and other critical spare parts for various Russian weapon systems. It's not exactly the direct military assistance Putin has reportedly asked for and the United States has warned China against providing, but it's close.

China seems genuinely surprised that western democracies are not showing weakness, indecision, or lack of follow-through. Xi seemed to think the United States and European nations were not capable of long-term, expensive, economically painful support for Ukraine. Both Xi and Putin seemed convinced that no coalition made up of dissolute, self-centered, weak democracies could stay the course in this war. Perhaps that was one reason why China was so willing to enter into an alliance with Iran and Russia at the beginning of the conflict.

In late 2022 and early 2023, China has pivoted to what can only be termed a charm offensive with its major western export customers. It clearly does not want to lose access to lucrative western markets. This may be a huge boon to Ukraine. If, to preserve trade and avoid sanctions, China remains carefully balanced on its tightrope between the West and Russia, it will be unlikely to supply Russia directly with weapons, missiles, vehicles, and other key military equipment.

CHINA'S INTERESTS IN A RUSSIAN
WIN OR AT LEAST A LONG WAR

China has several key strategic interests in wanting Russia to win in Ukraine. Perhaps most important to China, it hopes to annex and re-absorb Taiwan in much the same way Putin is trying to annex and reabsorb Ukraine. You'd better believe China is taking notes on how Putin's invasion went and what went wrong. China will not make the same mistakes Russia did if and when it chooses to invade Taiwan.

Second, China isn't any more fond of a Ukraine that's a NATO member than Russia is. China has no interest in seeing NATO creep further east toward it by another thousand miles, nor in seeing NATO pose an even more serious threat of encirclement to Russia. China would rather not see NATO get stronger and bigger as a western geopolitical threat.

Ukraine is (or was until the war) a large, western-style democracy with a growing economy. It would bring significant economic and natural resources to NATO (and still would after it is rebuilt following the conclusion of the war.) The Ukrainian population is highly educated and tech savvy and will integrate easily into the European economy going forward.

Ukraine is also strategically located between China and Europe. Any land routes as part of China's enormous Silk Road initiative to connect its economy directly to the rest of the world via new overland rail and road routes will pass through Ukraine or have to go around it through Russia. Ukraine would be an ideal and cheap transit hub for China, particularly if it were to fall back under the control of its good friend, Russia.

China, like Russia, undoubtedly sees this crisis as an opportunity to expand its global economic influence. Countries that relied on Ukraine for grain imports have turned to China for food assistance, and China continues to expend its influence in Africa.

China believes that democracies are fundamentally flawed and unproductive. Worse, they pose a threat to the communist model. China would like to see democracy fail in Ukraine. If Ukraine, a big, young democracy were to fail, it would discourage other nations from choosing to that political path.

It's also an outstanding opportunity to drain NATO and the United States of their military resources. It is going to take the West years of production and increased military spending to replace the vast military resources that have been expended in Ukraine fending off the Russian invasion.

In the meantime, NATO and the United States are not going to be in ideal position to fight any more major wars with their greatly depleted stores of heavy equipment, missiles, weapons, and ammunition. If China is looking ahead to invade Taiwan in the near future, a weakened West is ideal for their purposes.

A WEAKENED RUSSIAN ARMY

Do you remember earlier when I told you we would circle back to China's accusations that the United States is keeping the Ukraine war dragging on to weaken Russia? It's no skin off China's nose, either, if the Russian military is greatly weakened. This is one of those cases where China is probably accusing the U.S. of doing something it is actually doing.

The Ukraine war has decimated the Russian military. While

it's true that corruption, outmoded thinking, technology shortfalls compared to the West, manpower shortages, and dreadful morale have taken their toll, the final nail in the Red Army's coffin has been the massive influx of money, Western military supplies, and military support that have kept a stubborn Ukrainian resistance on the battlefield.

Although it is far too sophisticated and nuanced diplomatically to admit it, China has to be having a two-fold reaction to the disintegration of the Russian armed forces.

One the one hand, China must be dismayed. They chose to partner with Russia in this war despite repeated warnings from the West not to be on the wrong side of history. On the other hand, Russia and China share a 2,000 mile border and have been raiding and invading each other for millennia. Old enmities and rivalries between the two nations run bone deep.

Many years ago, I had occasion to meet a Chinese scholar visiting the United States. Out of curiosity, I asked her, "Who does China consider to be its greatest enemy?" Without hesitation, she answered, "Russia. Of course, Russia." Some years later, on a visit to Russia, I was speaking with a Russian military officer. Interested to see how he would react, I made a casual comment about the United States being Russia's greatest enemy. He stared at me as if I had grown a second head, and blurted, "Oh, no. You are not our greatest enemy. China is."

While these points of view do not reflect the current diplomatic reality of Russia and China's very close alliance, we should not lose sight of the fact that these two nations traditionally, culturally, viscerally, do not like each other at all.

They are not good friends. They haven't been friends for 2,000 years. They are partners with common interests. They will remain partners only as long as their common interests align.

As annoyed as Xi must be that Putin has messed up this war as badly as he has, I cannot help but think that, deep down, Xi is pleased that a depleted and largely destroyed Russian army cannot possibly pose a threat to China of ground invasion in the foreseeable future.

Although these two countries are thick as thieves at the moment, this is not necessarily a permanent state of affairs. For example, should the relationship become wildly lopsided, favoring the interests of one a great deal more than those of the other—perhaps at the *expense* of the other—this partnership would dissolve rather rapidly, indeed. I'll talk more about how this may already be happening in a moment.

With Russia's global diplomatic reputation destroyed, China has an opportunity to step up as a global diplomatic power and fill the vacuum left by Russia's catastrophic decline in world standing.

Let us not forget that 82 countries in the United Nations were unwilling to vote against Russia in various votes condemning it for the Ukraine invasion. The vast majority of these nations are poor, third-world or developing nations who are, or were until recently, reliant on Russia for food, trade, and export of their natural resources.

In multiple countries, China is now stepping in for Russia to provide food, give economic aid, and assume trade roles with these nations. Particularly in Africa, China's influence and importance are surging as Russia remains distracted by the Ukraine war and without the financial resources to engage in (or blocked by sanctions from engaging in) much foreign trade.

THE SIBERIAN ANGLE

Russia and China have effectively tangled together their banking systems. Most international banking done by Russian citizens or the Russian government passes through Chinese banks, now. Russia has transitioned to using exclusively Chinese debit card and credit cards systems, and the ruble now floats alongside the renminbi (RMB), China's currency.

China has built multiple new, close, long-term business relationships with Russian companies over the past year. Because of Russia's desperate need for cash, in most of these deals, Russia has given China excellent terms and bargain basement prices on natural resources and raw materials for export to it. By obtaining advantageous terms in many trade and resource export agreements from Siberia, China has set itself up to have a significant production cost advantage against the rest of the manufacturing world for years to come.

More importantly and more alarmingly for the West, China is snapping up mineral resources in Siberia in mega-deal after mega-deal with Russia. China is buying everything from gold, iron ore, diamonds, timber, coal, oil, and natural gas to a slew of rare earth minerals.

Russia and China are busily building rail lines and bridges between their countries, and more oil and gas pipelines directly into China are under construction or on the drawing board. China is financing construction of infrastructure inside

Siberia in return for preferential trade relationships all across Siberia.

Huge Chinese manufacturing cities are springing up all along the Chinese side of the Amur River (called the Heilong Jiang in Chinese). For 1,100 miles, the Amur forms the border between far east Russia (Siberia) and northeast China. These Chinese industrial cities on the Amur use resources shipped directly out of Siberia to their factories and production facilities.

The Chinese city, Heihe, in the province of Heilongjiang, has a population of nearly 1.7 million, supported almost entirely by manufacturing dependent on Siberian natural resources. (The population of Heilongjiang province alone has swelled to more than the entire population of Siberia in recent years.)

Some analysts go so far as to suggest that, China may be positioning itself one day to take back a large swatch of Siberia that was ceded to Russia in 1860 in the Amur Annexation. This annexation included a series of wildly unequal treaties forced upon the Qing Dynasty by colonizers. All of Outer Mongolia, an area of 350,000 square miles (910,000 square km), was handed over to the Russian Empire by British and French councils intent on forcing an end to the devastating Opium Wars in China.

This area constitutes some of the most mineral rich territory on the planet. It's entirely possible that China's long game will include making an eventual move to regain that territory. But for now, China seems content to exploit the region to its exclusive benefit as much as possible. The Russia-Ukraine War has greatly assisted it in achieving this goal.

Without the war, Russia would not have had to agree to some

of the cut-rate prices and exclusivity terms China insisted on. It's possible Russia would have demanded more control over the oil pipelines, rail lines, bridges, and roads Chinese labor is constructing and, when finished, will be operated by Chinese workers.

The only obvious downside for China in this war is the expansion and strengthening of ties within NATO and the general unity within the European Union against Russia and in support of Ukraine. China understands NATO to be its only true military rival and is neither pleased to see the alliance reinvigorated nor to see NATO member nations greatly expanding their military spending budgets to enhance NATO's capabilities.

Although China has found itself in a difficult diplomatic position globally as it tries not to be too supportive of a clearly illegal Russian invasion of a sovereign nation, China is, at the end of the day, looking out for its own interests first and foremost. It has a great deal to gain from this war, and it has moved quietly to take advantage of the war.

China has purchased oil in vast quantities at steep discounts. It has locked down contracts in Siberia for cheap mineral resources for decades to come. It has advanced its global importance significantly in the economic, political, financial, and diplomatic arenas, and it has watched its main rivals on the world-stage—the United States and Russia—expend vast amounts of their wealth, resources, and military strength weakening themselves and their economies in the process.

Meanwhile, China has been vague and talked in general terms about de-escalation, peace being good for all, and offering to negotiate a settlement to the war. (which is an empty offer, given that neither Ukraine nor Russia shows the slightest interest in sitting down to peace talks.)

China looks measured, rational, and reasonable in how it's conducting itself. Nobody can point at any direct military help China has given Russia in the war, and for the most part, China has kept its hands clean of this war on the global stage.

All in all, this Russia-Ukraine War hasn't been a bad deal for China.

Any future U.S. policy toward Iran or Russia will have to take China into account. And this is exactly how China has maneuvered the global reality to be. It wants to be not only at the table, but sitting at the head of the table, in any important global situations going forward.

U.S. policymakers must keep in mind that both Russia and China have defied sanctions and trade embargoes with Iran and are likely to continue doing so. Likewise, both Russia and China have in the past and likely will in the future provide advanced military equipment and weapons systems to Iran, particularly if doing so causes heartburn to the United States.

And the United States must never forget that China takes care of itself, first and foremost. It is interested in its own best interests and not those of anyone else.

CHAPTER SIXTEEN:

RUSSIA AND IRAN UNITE

"Iranian deadly drones sent to Russia in hundreds—
in hundreds—became a threat to our critical infrastructure.
That is how one terrorist has found the other."

—President Volodymyr Zelensky
to U.S. Congress December 2022

"Three to four years ago, when US-Russia relations were bad,
but not catastrophic, I would be pretty skeptical that Russia
would provide Iran with help. But under today's conditions,
under which US-Russia relations are extremely bad
and Russian-Iranian relations are getting better,
I think the equation looks quite different for Russia."

—James Acton, co-director Nuclear Policy Program,
Carnegie Endowment for International Peace

A COMPLEX RELATIONSHIP

Moscow's relationship with Tehran has been a complicated one.
Russia and Iran have done business for decades and Russia has a
long history of selling military equipment to Iran. They really found
common ground in Syria, when Russian troops intervened in 2015
and fought beside Iranian-backed militias to prop up the regime of
Syrian President, Bashar al-Assad.

Both nations were interested in having a strong ally geographically close to Israel, which often shares a common interest with the United States in Middle East affairs. Both Russia and Iran are deeply interested in diminishing the power, prestige, and international role of the United States. In each other, they have found a partner who will stand with them against the West.

It wouldn't be fair to say that they've been close allies in the past. Russia was one of the few nations willing to ignore U.S. and United Nations sanctions against Iran and do business with it, anyway. The two countries engaged in a lot of talks, but in reality, they didn't actually do that much of substance with each other.

It would probably be more accurate to say they shared a partnership of convenience. However, in the past there was always an undertone of wariness and perhaps of distrust. Of course, that has all changed since Russia invaded Ukraine.

Since the invasion, the tables have turned. Russia's economy is struggling under the weight of international sanctions. Now Iran is one of the few nations willing to ignore the sanctions and do business with Russia.

Iran is willing to sell much-needed military supplies and weapons to Russia, and Iran is also willing to act as an outlet for Russian-made goods and products, helping to keep Russia's badly battered economy afloat.

In the late fall of 2022, Iranian and Russian officials quietly made a deal for Russia to buy the Iranian kamikaze drones that have been so destructive and deadly in Ukraine. In recent months, top Russian officials, including Russian Security Council Secretary

Nikolai Patrushev, have visited Iran—rumored to be there to finalize a deal to purchase Iranian ballistic missiles.

The two nations have never formed a full-fledged, formal alliance, but Russia has fully turned to China and Iran for friendship abroad. Military analysts agree that Iran's support to Russia is critical to the Kremlin. U.S. officials say that, as Iran continues to provide military resources and support to Russia, it is prolonging the bloody war and contributing to more deaths in Ukraine (both military and civilian).

U.S. officials and regional experts also warn that:

> "If the Russian government delivers new forms of military technology and high-end weapons systems to Iran in return for its friendship and support, this could greatly endanger U.S. allies in the Middle East."

Behind that bland diplomatic language lies a deadly threat. The only new military technology and high-end weapon systems that interest Iran are nuclear weapons and missiles to deliver those weapons over very long distances, say, to the United States. And let's be clear. The U.S.'s greatest ally in the Middle East is Israel.

The trade-off is beneficial to both Russia and Iran: Iran gives Russia weaponized drones to destroy Ukrainian infrastructure and cities, and Iran gets the technology it needs to become a nuclear power.

When Western experts warn of this possible trade for nuclear technology, both Russia and Iran are quick to deny the claim. Instead, they point at Su-35 fighter jets or Russia's S-400 advanced air defense system as the type of technology Russia is offering in return for Iranian drones and ballistic missiles.

A DEEPENING RELATIONSHIP

Not only does Iran want to increase its ties to nuclear-savvy Russia, but Russia wants to deepen its ties with nations like Iran, too.

> "Further from Europe, Russia wants to be a power broker in the Middle East and has in the last few years solidified relationships with Iran, Syria, and Saudi Arabia.
>
> Russian mercenaries unofficially under Kremlin control, such as the Wagner Group, have fanned out across poorly governed countries such as Libya, Sudan, Syria, and Mali. Hiring private contractors helps the Putin regime avoid official casualty counts and gives the Kremlin plausible deniability for abuses such as looting, torture, executions, and forced disappearances.
>
> Closer to the United States, Russia has successfully cultivated relationships with atrocious regimes in Cuba and Venezuela as part of a plan to gain military footholds in the Western hemisphere, close to America's borders."
>
> —Mike Pompeo, former U.S. Secretary of State
> excerpt from his book, *Never Give an Inch*

The deepening partnership between Russia and Iran extends well beyond arms deals. Iran is pushing for lucrative trade deals with Russian companies that have in the past refused to invest in Iran. The two countries are building extensive new trade networks aimed at circumventing Western sanctions. These include supply routes by river and rail as well as new shipping routes through the Caspian Sea.

The Caspian Sea (also known as the Dead Sea) is the world's largest inland body of water. It's a fully landlocked body of water about 750 miles long from north to south, with Russia bordering its northwest end and Iran bordering its south end.

Using cargo ships in the Caspian Sea, Russia and Iran can deliver goods and equipment directly to each other without having to cross through any other sovereign nations, a fact of great concern to western intelligence experts. There are no means of stopping the two countries from shipping anything they want to each other—be it drones, missiles, or in a worst case scenario, nuclear materials.

On the diplomatic front, Putin has stayed home in Russia for the most part since Russia's invasion of Ukraine. However, he made his first visit outside a former Soviet Bloc nation to Tehran in July of 2022 for a major summit with Iran's supreme leader, Ayatollah Ali Khamenei. The timing of this trip couldn't have been better for Iran. The Iranians were coming under intense pressure to restore the JCPOA, which they really didn't want to do. By hosting a visit from Putin, they signaled that they have other options and are not desperate for a deal with the West.

In August of 2022, Russia agreed to launch an Iranian satellite on behalf of Iran, whose own space program still hasn't successfully gotten off the ground. U.S. intelligence officials say the Iranian satellite is parked over Ukraine and actively gathering intelligence

MICHAEL EVANS

for Russia. Not surprisingly, Iran declares the claims to be false and insists the satellite is being used for scientific research. One wonders what "science" Iran is studying in Ukraine for many months on end that requires intelligence gathering technology aboard a satellite.

Since the invasion of Ukraine, Russia has been forced to withdraw troops from Syria to redeploy them in Ukraine and also to reposition large quantities of military equipment into the Ukraine theater. Because of this, Russia has had to depend on Iran to step into Syria and fill the gap left by its departing troops and equipment. This increased Iranian presence in Syria has been necessary for the al-Assad regime to maintain control of the portions of Syria it currently occupies.

The longer Russia remains bogged down in Ukraine and unable to help out much in Syria, the stronger Iran's influence will continue to grow there. This is a source of great concern to Syria's neighbors, none of whom are fans of Iran. Syria is bordered by Lebanon and Israel to the west and southwest, Jordan to the south, Iraq to the east, and Turkey to the north.

IRAN ISN'T UNANIMOUS IN LOVING RUSSIA

Most officials within the Iranian regime tend to be distrustful of both Russia and the West, in general. Iranian leaders have a long history of seeing themselves as a lone, strategic actor on the world stage. Even as they've raced full speed ahead with developing a nuclear arsenal, Iranian leaders have tended to take a fairly neutral stance on international matters. Which is to say, they've been staying out of trouble and keeping their heads down while they've pursued their secret ambition to build a nuclear weapon.

Most analysts agree that Iran's senior leadership is divided into two differing schools of thought regarding foreign policy. One is in favor of strengthening and extending ties with Russia. They want to deepen their alliance with Russia. This camp most importantly includes Supreme Leader Khamenei. It also includes various top foreign policy advisors and top generals in the Islamic Revolutionary Guard Corps.

The second camp is comprised of various former top Iranian officials who are not particularly powerful at the moment. They include former Iranian president Rouhani, the former Foreign Minister Zarif, and a small group of moderate IRGC commanders. They think it's a mistake to rely so heavily on Russia economically and militarily and want to maintain important relationships with the West. They point out that Iran and Russia, both as oil producing nations, actually compete against each other for a share in the global energy market.

U.S. foreign policy experts suggest that the second group could gain more traction in coming years, particularly if the Ukraine War continues to destroy Russia's economic and military strength or if the new economic ties between Iran and Russia don't provide the large economic gains Iran is desperate for. On its surface, this second group seems uninterested in gaining nuclear weapons and using them to blackmail Iran's neighbors or start a nuclear conflagration.

At the moment, the first, pro-Russia camp is firmly in charge. The debate is not permanently settled, however, particularly in light of serious social upheaval inside Iran.

THE HIJAB PROTESTS

On September 16, 2022, a 22-year-old woman named Mahsa Amini died in police custody in Tehran. It was revealed she died because of police brutality while in custody of the Guidance Patrol, more commonly known as the Morality Police. She had been arrested for wearing her hijab improperly and exposing too much hair outside of it.

A hijab is a head covering worn in public by some Muslim women. In Iran, wearing a hijab became compulsory for all women in 1979 when the Ayatollah Khomeini announced that all women should observe Islamic dress code. His announcement sparked widespread protests and demonstrations, largely by women, who were violently attacked by pro-Revolution supporters.

In 1983, hijab use became mandatory by law. Breaking this law is punishable by fines and two days to two weeks in prison. Iran is the only country in the world that requires non-Muslim women to wear a headscarf.

Across the world, wearing the hijab is a personal religious choice. However, in Iran it has become a symbol of marginalization and oppression of women. Rejection of the hijab by protestors reacting to Mahsa Amini's death doesn't necessarily mean Iranian women are rejecting Islam or Islamic values. Rather, it represents frustration and anger over being deprived of basic freedom of choice.

The death of Amini sparked widespread anti-hijab protests across Iran. On September 20, 2022, a 16-year-old Iranian girl named Nika Shakarami disappeared in Tehran during protests

THE **END TIMES** AND **ARMAGEDDON**

over Amini's death. Her family was informed of her death ten days later. She died under suspicious circumstances involving violence by security forces.

The protests only grew after the second young woman's death, increasing to an unprecedented scale in Iran, both in terms of how widely across the country protests have been occurring and the diverse social backgrounds of the demonstrators. Men and women of all ages and socioeconomic classes are participating in the protests.

Demonstrations have taken place not only in large cities but in small communities that are traditionally very conservative and pro-government. Protests have been especially strong in Kurdish areas as Amini was of Kurdish descent. The demonstrations have included millions of women burning their hijabs and cutting their hair in defiance of the law.

Of course, the protests are not just about hair length or head covering. They've served as a wider platform for protest against oppression of women. Prior to the Islamic Revolution, Iranian women enjoyed substantial freedoms, were educated alongside men, and participated fully in the workforce. The protests have evolved over the past six months to symbolize even wider demands for political and economic reform.

The Iranian government has responded to the Mahsa Amini protests with brute force and mass arrests. A number of Iranian sports figures and celebrities have joined in the demonstrations or made statements of their own by competing in sporting events without head covering or making public statements critical of the regime.

The current round of protests is unique in how many women are participating and, indeed, leading the protest movement. Also, the current protests are not limited to the middle class and university educated as they have been in the past several decades. Both working class citizens and members of the wealthy merchant class are participating. It's indicative of a society-wide backlash against the governance and ideology of the regime.

The regime's security forces are concentrated almost exclusively in a few large, urban centers. If these protests continue across the country in smaller cities where there is little or no security force presence, this could pose a serious problem for the Iranian government maintaining control of the nation.

It's worth noting that the Iranian economy has been largely destroyed by decades of western sanctions. Despite its new agreements with Russia, those may be too little, too late to appease the Iranian people. The unpopularity of the Islamic republic was on full display as Iranians poured out into the streets by the millions in the fall of 2022.

The Iranian regime has resorted to sentencing a number of celebrities and prominent Iranians to death for their criticism of the government and making very public examples of them. At the same time, the government has announced a round of mass pardons for protestors who were rounded up off the streets and thrown into Iranian jails that are now full to bursting.

Following an intense crackdown by the government, the major cities are quieter as 2023 rolls around. The government deployed snipers to kill protestors and scatter crowds, and the number of protestors is going down, but they're not going away entirely.

Public hangings are ongoing, a few at a time, in what appears to be a calculated display of cruelty and violence by the government to instill terror in its citizens. The government is counting on fear to silence the population. However, many in Iran say openly that they have nothing to lose anymore. They've had enough, and they're not afraid of dying at the hands of the government.

Up to 50 protestors remain on death row, some 500 protestors are believed to have been killed by security forces, and approximately 14,000 protestors have been jailed. Protestors across Iran report being tortured, beaten, and sexually abused in police custody. Prisoners also report their family members being threatened if they don't confess to heinous crimes they didn't commit. (In the bloodbath immediately after the Revolution, it was common practice to execute a dissident and then hunt down and execute their spouse.)

Iranians report the presence of spies everywhere and a dramatic uptick in surveillance measures by the government. Protestors are being arrested at hospitals if they go to seek medical treatment for injuries sustained during demonstrations. Security forces are confiscating medical supplies at checkpoints outside of large cities. University students report spies in their classrooms, repeating to the Security Forces anything negative about the government that anyone says.

Social media played a huge role publicizing Mahsa Amini's murder and was used to organize protests. Hence, the Iranian government has blocked Internet access to almost all of its 80 million citizens, censored activists and journalists, and runs a relentless, Russian-style propaganda campaign aimed at the population.

Only senior government officials have social media or Internet access these days.

Western news outlets reported in December 2022 that Iran asked Russia to send advisors to Tehran amid concerns of the regime lacking manpower and resources to quell the mass protests. Moscow is said to have sent senior Russian State Security officers to advise the government in more effective terror campaigns to control the population. Russia is thought to be providing intelligence assistance to Iran to help it spy on its population. Not only will this help Iran control its people but it will help the regime assess the strength of the uprising.

White House Press Secretary, Karine Jean-Pierre, put it succinctly:

> "The United States is concerned that Moscow may be advising Tehran on best practices to manage protests, drawing on Russia's extensive experience in suppressing open demonstrations. The evidence that Iran is helping Russia in the war in Ukraine is clear and public."

HOW WILL RUSSIA REPAY IRAN?

The looming question most Iran-Russia watchers are asking these days is, what will Iran ask for in return for its vital assistance in the Russia-Ukraine war, and what will a grateful Russia be willing to give Iran in return? Communications between Russian and Iranian leaders suggest that Putin and his generals very much appreciate Iran's timely and continuous flow of military aid.

While I was writing this, three separate Israeli generals told me it's entirely possible Russia will send Iran several non-strategic nuclear weapons in the very near future.

If this were to happen, Iran would not have to finish developing its own nuclear weapons before it begins engaging in nuclear-backed "diplomacy." Iran could use Russian tactical nuclear weapons to hold Israel and the entire Middle East hostage while Iran finishes building its own, homegrown nuclear arsenal.

We already know that Iran has sent hundreds of Shahed drones to Russia and has sent its own trainers to Crimea to help the Russian military make good use of the drones in Ukraine. Recent reports indicate that Iran is planning to provide Russia with advanced, short-range ballistic missiles and that Iran is finally helping Russia establish its own production facilities for building more Shahed-style drones.

We also know that Russia has sent to Iran various western weapons seized in the Ukraine war. The expectation is that Iran is using these captured weapons to reverse engineer them with two objectives in mind:

1) learning how to better defend itself against these weapons

2) learning how to design and build their own versions of similar weapons.

In January 2023, a massive shipment of Iranian weapons bound for Houthi rebels in Yemen was seized by the U.S. Navy. It included over 12,000 assault rifles, over a half million rounds of ammunition, dozens of antitank missiles, and anti-aircraft systems designed partially based on U.S. made surface-to-air missile systems. Additional proof of this technology theft has been found in recently downed Iranian drones in Ukraine which show new design elements lifted from captured U.S. drones.

JETS AND AIR DEFENSE SYSTEMS

Rumors persist that Russia has sold 24 advanced SU-35 fighter jets to Iran. The jets were supposed to be sold to Egypt, but when that deal was scuttled, Russia pivoted to selling the airplanes to Iran instead. Iranian pilots are believed to be in Russia already, receiving flight training in SU-35s. Construction and other preparations have been observed at Iranian air force bases for the arrival of advanced fighter aircraft along the lines of SU-35s.

The jets are likely to be delivered sometime in the summer or fall of 2023. They will pose a serious security threat to all of Iran's immediate neighbors. But perhaps more importantly, they will give Iran a fast-response, aggressive means of defending its own airspace from incursions by outside attacks.

In the past, Iran has asked for high-tech air defense systems, namely state of the art surface-to-air missile systems. Historically, Russia has turned down such requests, citing the problems it would create with other Middle East countries, including Israel, Saudi Arabia, the United Arab Emirates, and Turkey. All of these nations strongly object to Iran obtaining high-powered weapons of this kind.

Should Iran obtain advanced air-defense systems from Russia, it will be much better equipped to thwart any future possible attack on its nuclear infrastructure or other strategic facilities. Israel and other Middle East nations are convinced that the threat of an attack from outside Iran is one of the last remaining deterrents to Iran completing construction of a nuclear weapon.

Should Israel and others' ability to strike a nuclear development facility in Iran be thwarted by a strong Iranian air defense system, comprised of high-tech fighter jets and high-tech surface-to-air defense missiles, there would be nothing standing in the way of Iran going ahead and building a nuclear bomb.

OTHER POSSIBLE REPAYMENTS

If Russia were to share intelligence with Iran, this could quickly upset the fragile balance of power in the Middle East. Russia possesses advanced capabilities in both imagery and signals intelligence and could decide to share intelligence it has collected, or Russia might choose to share the technology for Iran to collect its own advanced intelligence going forward.

In the past, Russia has been hesitant to share intelligence information with Iran. While they were friendly nations, they were not actually close friends. But that may have changed since the invasion of Ukraine and the subsequent setbacks to Russia. Given the enemies Iran has made and the risks it has taken onto itself by helping arm Russia, Putin may be more disposed to be forthcoming with high-level intelligence for its new friend.

Cyber capabilities are another area in which Russia could share important technology and knowledge. Iran already has advanced cyber attack capabilities. Russia, however, is a cyber superpower. There is plenty Russia can teach Iranian hackers, and Russia might choose to share known vulnerabilities in critical enemy infrastructure, intelligence, government, and economic systems.

In the past, intelligence and foreign policy analysts were confident Russia would not try to disrupt the delicate balance of power between Israel and Iran. They pointed to Benjamin Netanyahu's positive working relationship with Vladimir Putin and the fact that Russia does a fair bit of trade and business with Israel.

These same analysts cited Russian fears that, if Putin got too cozy with Iran, such a friendship might push Israel to take sides in the Ukraine war and provide Ukraine with state-of-the art air defense systems.

Israel's Iron Dome air defense system is thought to be one the most effective air defense technologies in the world today. Giving Ukraine access to Iron Dome-style self-defense would cripple Russia's air forces and entirely stop the missile bombardment campaign that has been Russia's only effective weapon in the war overall.

As long as Russia and Iran remain global pariahs and deeply isolated by international sanctions, we should expect them to continue doing business with each other and strengthening their ties.

As Russia's prospects for winning a war against Ukraine diminish, and it's forced to turn more and more to its few allies willing to openly provide it with military equipment and weapons, we can expect Russia to buy more and more Iranian missiles, and in return, we can expect Iran to up the pressure on Russia to cough up nuclear technology to the Iranian regime.

CHAPTER SEVENTEEN

NORTH KOREA, RUSSIA, AND IRAN: THE AXIS OF PARIAHS

"[Regarding Russia, Iran, North Korea, and Belarus]
They're geographically spread out. They don't have things
that they want to buy and sell from each other.
And they don't like each other. It's a terrible club to be in."

—Peter Piatetsky,
former U.S. Treasury Department official, CEO Castellum A.I.

"A year or two ago, the relationship between Russia and Iran was that
Russia was a great power that people feared was going to provide
a lot of weapons to Iran. Now Russia has been so attrited in terms of
its conventional power in Ukraine that they're going to Tehran and
Pyongyang and elsewhere to try to make up for the fact that they have
spent down an enormous amount of their artillery and a huge amount
of their precision-guided weapons."

—Colin Kahl, Undersecretary of Defense for Policy

BEFORE WE LEAVE THE TOPIC of Russia's new strategic alliance with Iran, we would remiss if we didn't mention North Korea and how it plays into Russia and Iran's blossoming friendship.

As heavy and debilitating as the economic sanctions against Iran and Russia are, the sanctions imposed against North Korea are even more draconian and damaging. These sanctions were imposed by the United States and United Nations in response to

North Korea's development of a nuclear weapons program and a series of missile tests North Korea has conducted over most of the past decade.

Sound familiar? It should.

BACKGROUND

Communist North Korea was founded in 1948, with the support of the Soviet Union. North Korea later tried to take over South Korea and unify Korea under communist rule. The United States and United Nations, concerned about the spread of communism, rushed in to support South Korea in what turned into the first proxy war between the communist and democratic worlds.

North Korea, with extensive help from China and the Soviet Union, fought South Korea and its allies to a stalemate in the 1950-1953 Korean War.

For decades after that, North Korea relied heavily on the Soviet Union for economic assistance and trade. The collapse of the Soviet Union caused significant interruptions in Russian economic assistance to North Korea, including food aid.

This disruption, combined with economic mismanagement and a series of floods and droughts, caused a deadly famine in North Korea. Known as the Arduous March or the March of Suffering, it lasted from 1994 to 1998. Official figures report that out of a population of 22 million, 240,000 people starved, but western estimates place the death toll at closer to 3.5 million.

Wary of becoming solely dependent on a single benefactor nation again, North Korean leadership developed new relationships with both China and Russia in the aftermath of the famine.

Kim Jong Un, North Korea's premier, came to power after the death of his father in 2011. Both he and his father had relatively cool relationships with China and Russia, both of whom joined the United States and other nations in imposing heavy sanctions on North Korea in response to its nuclear tests.

However, in 2017, Kim changed course and set out to repair and strengthen the relationships with his two superpower neighbors. In 2019, Kim and Vladimir Putin met for the first time in Vladivostok for a summit that resulted in various new trade deals.

In the past few years, Russia has joined China in vetoing new United Nations sanctions against North Korea, and Kim has returned the favor with public support for Russia after it invaded Ukraine. North Korea recognized the independence of Luhansk and Donetsk immediately after Putin declared them sovereign nations. In October 2022, Kim sent a birthday greeting to Putin, congratulating him for "crushing the challenges and threats of the United States."

In November 2022, the United States said it had information indicating that North Korea is covertly supplying Russia with "significant" numbers of artillery shells.

As Russia's isolation has grown in the past year, it may see increasing value in a relationship with North Korea. For North Korea's part, it remains a heavily sanctioned pariah nation sorely in need of trading partners and revenue sources.

WHAT DOES NORTH KOREA HAVE TO GAIN?

On November 2, 2022, for the first time since rail service was stopped between the two countries because of the Covid pandemic, rail service was restored between Suzdal, Russia and Khasan, North Korea. As an aside, the first shipment on the train was 30 gray horses called Orlov Trotters, Russia's most famous horse breed. They are presumed to have been a gift for Kim Jong Un, who is an avid horseman.

This rail line reopening is not significant for horse trade, but rather for North Korean trade in general. The vast majority of North Korea's trade goes through China, but Russia is potentially an important future trading partner for North Korea. In particular, North Korea is an oil poor nation and desperately needs a steady supplier for oil.

The United Nations has accused Russia of evading oil trade sanctions by exporting oil to North Korea that the North Koreans keep some of to use and sell the rest on the open market. North Korea and Russia deny the claims, of course. But providing Russia with help it desperately needs now can only serve to make Putin grateful and willing to do more deals with North Korea going forward.

Meanwhile, North Korea and Russia have openly discussed a deal to send between 20,000 and 50,000 North Korean workers to manpower-strapped Russia. North Korea struggles to feed and employ its population, so a chance to send excess people abroad, reduce the number of mouths to feed at home, have them earn money, and bring some of it back home to spend must be appealing to Kim. United Nations Security Council resolutions ban such arrangements.

Russian leaders in Luhansk and Donetsk are reported to be discussing hiring North Korean workers to help rebuild those areas after hostilities cease, on the presumption that the two regions will be absorbed back into the Russian Federation. This is yet another reason it's in North Korea's best interest for Russia to win this war.

John Kirby, the National Security Council Coordinator for Strategic Communications at the White House, reiterated his team's analysis on January 20, 2023 that "North Korea delivered infantry rockets and missiles into Russia for use by Wagner toward the end of last year."

Both Russia and North Korea deny claims by the United States that Russia has tried to buy millions of rounds of ammunition and other weapons in short supply in the Russian army from North Korea.

While Kim may not be a major supplier of military equipment to Russia yet, North Korea's entry into the proxy war in Ukraine poses a problem for the West, which is hoping to starve Russia out of the war because of lack of military equipment and men.

Another major benefit to North Korea of supporting Russia is getting a chance to demonize the United States as an imperialist state weakening regional stability.

North Korea would love to convince the international community, particularly nations that already dislike the United States, that North Korea's nuclear program is an unwanted but necessary tool to defend it and countries like it from the United States and its allies.

Calling its nuclear program a means for self-defense, North Korea persistently paints the United States as the main state actor escalating tensions on the Korean Peninsula. Never mind that North Korea often serves as a mouthpiece for and proxy of China, which is the main actor causes tensions in an around Taiwan to escalate sharply in recent months. And never mind that it is North Korea firing missiles all over the South Pacific in provocative "scientific missile tests."

If the United States and its allies help Ukraine to win the war, NATO will be solidified and strengthened considerably. Not only will Sweden and Finland end up in NATO, but likely Ukraine will also apply for and get membership in NATO. A stronger United States means a stronger South Korea and a stronger Japan, neither of which are good news for North Korea.

If Russia loses this war, it could potentially send a message to the North Korean people that authoritarian regimes are defeatable. This is a message Kim emphatically needs to keep away from the deeply oppressed and suffering people of his nation. The Pyongyang regime works around the clock to brainwash and propagandize the North Korean population to remain loyal to their dear leader, but surely Kim knows how vulnerable he is if there were ever to be a serious uprising within his nation.

Lastly, a Russian victory in the Ukraine war could help North Korea pressure an embarrassed and internationally contracting United States to lift the economic sanctions against North Korea that have devastated its economy. And this is perhaps the biggest incentive of all for Kim Jong Un.

NORTH KOREA AND IRAN

North Korea and Iran had no ties to speak of until the Iran-Iraq War in the late 1970's, when North Korea provided military assistance to Iran. Iraq broke off diplomatic relations with North Korea over it in October of 1980. These weapons sales formed the basis of what grew into today's relationship between the two nations.

In 1982, Pyongyang secretly invited Iraqi diplomats to visit North Korea. The Iraqi sent an unofficial delegation, and the talks failed. This demonstrated that North Korea wasn't especially committed to Iraq as an ally.

North Korea and Iran came together again when both provided military assistance to Hezbollah in Israel, and both supported Bashar al-Assad in Syria. In July of 2009, when a cache of arms was discovered hidden on a cargo ship, Israel accused North Korea of secretly sending weapons to Hezbollah and Hamas. North Korea has also been accused of helping Hezbollah's build its Land of Tunnels, an extensive tunnel network in Lebanon that stretches all the way from Beirut to Hezbollah outposts in southern Lebanon.

North Korea is also believed to be clandestinely supplying weapons to Houthi rebels in Yemen. Missiles used against Saudi Arabian targets in 2015 are reported to have closely resembled Scud-C or Hwasong-6 missiles from North Korea. A United Nations reported from 2018 also reported that North Korea was still supplying small arms and ballistic missiles to the Houthis. The true scale of these transfers is unknown as they are taking place in secret. It is thought at least some of the transfers from North Korea to the Houthis are being arranged by a Syrian arms dealer, Hussein al-Ali.

It would be easy to explain North Korea and Iran's relationship as being driven by shared anti-American attitudes. But they also can be of great mutual benefit to each other as they both strive to develop a homegrown nuclear weapon. Regardless of various disagreements between the two nations in other areas of interest, they are very closely aligned in the sphere of military technology.

Since the 1980's North Korea has been willing to sell arms to pretty much any nation willing to buy weapons from it. They have consistently ignored international sanctions and have on multiple occasions sold weapons to known terrorist groups.

During the 1980's North Korea sold Soviet tanks, ammunition, and Chinese-made military equipment to Iran. While the USSR and China loudly proclaimed their innocence to the world, swearing they were not supporting Iran, North Korea did the dirty work for them. By 1990, North Korea was even supplying military advisors to the Iranian armed forces and selling Russian Scud missiles to Iran.

During the first Gulf War, North Korea sold Iran an array of weapons, including artillery, anti-aircraft weapons, mortars, ammunition, tanks, rifles and other small arms, naval mines, anti-tank missiles, and surface-to-air missiles.

In December 2009, a shipment of North Korean weapons enroute to Iran was intercepted in Thailand. It included rocket launchers and surface-to-air missile parts.

North Korea and Iran actively exchange military expertise, as well. North Korea is thought to have taught Iranian special operators in advanced infiltration techniques and other special operations, and it's thought that North Korea helped Iran develop technologies and techniques related to building underground facilities. These underground facilities have become the backbone of the Iranian nuclear development effort.

For its part, Iran is thought to have provided missile technology to North Korea. Experts cite the similarities between the second stage of North Korea's Hwasong-14 ICBM and the upper stages of

Iranian space launch vehicles.

A 2021 United Nations reported stated that North Korea and Iran are cooperating on several long-term missile development projects. This cooperation includes shipping missile parts back and forth and sharing technological discoveries and advances. Recent hypersonic missile tests by North Korea are raising concerns that this technology may be transferred to Iran, which has already developed a testing facility for hypersonic weapons.

BALLISTIC MISSILE COOPERATION

North Korea has been a major supplier to Iran of not only missiles but other technologies related to missiles. In 1995, North Korea shipped Scud transporter-erector-launchers to Iran. These are huge flatbed trucks that can move a Scud missile around, stop, point it upward, and act as a launch platform. The capacity to move and hide missiles as easily as climbing into a truck and driving off makes finding and destroying Scud missiles immeasurably more difficult for Iran's adversaries.

In November 1999, U.S. intelligence reported that North Korea had transferred 12 Nodong missile engines to Iran in defiance of strict United Nations sanctions against North Korea.

In 2006 and 2009, North Korea engaged in its first nuclear tests, and fears mounted that North Korea might be sharing nuclear technology and test results with Iran. A May 2011 United Nations report revealed that civilian airline flights between North Korea and Iran were being used to ship missile-related equipment.

In the 2000's, Iran bought Musudan missiles from North Korea, and new Iranian submarines unveiled in 2007 looked suspiciously similar to North Korean subs. In this time frame, North Korea also helped Iran develop an 80-ton rocket booster that would act as a "space launch vehicle" for Iran's "space program". North Korea was not so coy back home, declaring the identical rocket booster part of its ICBM development program.

KNOW-HOW FLOWS BOTH WAYS

Iranian scientists were present at North Korea's 2009 and 2012 Unha rocket launches and thought to have brought technological expertise with them to assist the North Koreans.

In 2010, North Korea unveiled a new Nodong missile warhead that strikingly resembled Iran's Shahab-3 warhead. Various Iranian defense contractors sent technicians to North Korea through the 2010's, undoubtedly to continue sharing information.

In response to this extensive cooperation on developing missiles, the United States sanctioned all Iranian entities that cooperated with North Korea. The sanctions had little effect. Both countries ignored them, continuing to trade technicians, information, parts, and actual weapons in secret.

The National Council of Resistance in Iran (NCRI) alleges that North Korean nuclear scientists visited Iran in 2015. Not long after that, Iran's nuclear enrichment program really picked up speed.

The collapse of the JCPOA and the failure to reinstate it means that Iran can continue to collaborate and cooperate with North Korea, largely unobserved. We can reasonably expect whatever North Korea learns that can advance its nuclear ambitions is going to be shared with Iran in short order and vice versa. The two nations will continue to progress together toward building their own nuclear arsenals.

In exactly the same way that Russia and Iran have been thrown together as unexpected allies, so have Iran and North Korea. The three nations share similar interests in finding trade partners to keep their devastated economies afloat. They all want to see the West defeated and humiliated, and they all show no compunction at the idea of using nuclear weapons.

Together, Russia, Iran, and North Korea form an alarming axis of unlikely allies. As long as these three remain global pariahs and deeply isolated by international sanctions, we can expect them to continue doing business with one another, strengthening their ties, and most alarmingly of all, sharing their missile and nuclear weapons technologies.

PART IV:

TO WIPE

ISRAEL

FROM

THE MAP

CHAPTER EIGHTEEN:

WHERE THINGS STAND NOW

DURING MY FIRST TRIP to Ukraine after the war began, my son and I were taking in truckloads of humanitarian supplies to feed and warm Ukrainian civilians. As we crossed the border into Ukraine, I saw miles and miles of military equipment lined up at the border, waiting to cross into Ukraine from all over the western world. I turned to my driver and said, "World War III is already being fought. . . with plausible deniability."

The ninth president of Israel, Shimon Peres, told me once that the new wars of the 21st century would be economic wars, ideological wars, media wars, and proxy wars. All four of those are being fought on the ground in Ukraine right now.

ON THE GROUND IN UKRAINE

The Kiel Institute for the World Economy estimates that the United States and Europe pledged roughly $100 billion in military and economic aid to Ukraine in the first year since the Russian invasion began. That includes increasingly sophisticated military equipment ranging from Patriot air defense systems to the Leopard 2 and M1A2 Abrams tanks.

Billions of additional dollars in mostly humanitarian aid have poured into Ukraine from private humanitarian organizations. Countless billions more have been spent by countries across Europe housing and assisting the millions of Ukrainian refugees (and fleeing Russian men) who have flooded their countries.

The living conditions in Ukraine after a year of war and protracted artillery and missile bombardment are, in a word, terrible. At any given time, half the electric power grid is down. Nobody has electricity all the time. Everyone is subject to daily rolling blackouts. The usual power schedule on a good day is four hours with power, four hours without power.

Running water, working toilets, heat for one's home, and lights are luxuries. Internet and phone service are intermittent at best, and many people go for days at a time without either.

Putin calculated that by plunging all of Ukraine into a long-term blackout in the middle of winter, he could force Ukraine to the negotiating table and get it to relinquish all the currently Russian-occupied territories in Ukraine. Russian forces have specifically targeted substations and power generation plants for maximum damage. Every single power generation plant in Ukraine has been hit by missiles or drones.

Much of Ukraine's power grid is built of old, Soviet era parts, including crucial equipment in the energy sector, from power-generating turbines to transformers and control-panel switches. It has been a scramble to bring in Russian parts from former Soviet republics. And there has been a steep learning curve in how to replace destroyed Soviet parts with newer western parts that must be adapted and installed into the existing grid one part at a time.

Ukrainian utility repair workers are an army of their own. They work around the clock to repair damage from attacks and cobble together a working power grid. The very systems they're working to repair often come under attack while they're working on them. The line workers and repairmen work as long as they can, sprint for cover when the air raid sirens go off, wait for the attack to finish, and then go right back out to work. Before the war, utility repairmen couldn't expect to die on the job. Now, that's a real risk.

Likewise, rail repair crews in Ukraine work around the clock repairing damaged rail lines and keeping the trains running. The rail system in Ukraine has become a vital lifeline for moving refugees out of harm's way and moving critical supplies forward to Ukrainian military units. Like power grid repair crews, these railway repair teams work heroically through combat conditions and risk dying on the job.

Over 80% of Ukrainians polled say they want Ukraine to continue the war—exactly the same percentage as before the attacks on the power grid and other infrastructure began. Which is to say that, although Putin succeeded in making Ukrainians miserable over the winter, he failed to move the needle even a tiny bit on their resolve to continue fighting.

Over time, Ukraine's air defenses have improved and less missiles are getting through to strike targets on the ground. Russia's stock of long-range missiles is running low, and missile attacks are less frequent and smaller than they were in October and November of 2022. Major barrages (as many as 70 or 80 missiles at a time) of incoming missiles and drones happen more like once per week instead of several times per day, now.

The arrival of spring will reduce electricity consumption in Ukraine, and the head of Ukrenergo (Ukraine's national electric company) says the Ukrainian power grid will stabilize when that happens. He adds,

> "Russia did not achieve its ultimate goal. Yes, they managed to create problems for nearly every Ukrainian family. But, instead of making us scared and unhappy, it made us angry, more resolved to win. They did not lower the morale of the nation: they mobilized the nation."

In a recent television interview, when asked if Russian attacks on the power grid amounted to terrorism against civilians, he answered unequivocally, "Yes."

According to the United Nations, some 2.5 million Ukrainians are internally displaced as refugees inside Ukraine as of February 2023. Over 8 million more Ukrainians have been recorded fleeing the country for other places in Europe. 90% of Ukrainian refugees are women and children.

Some 2,600 schools and 700 hospitals have been hit by missiles. Thousands of homes and businesses have been destroyed by missiles allegedly aimed at military targets. But it's hard to believe Russian missiles are so consistently and excessively off target every single time. International observers believe Russian missiles and drones have intentionally been aimed at civilian targets in a terror campaign aimed at breaking the spirit of the Ukrainian people.

Everything is scarce: food, clean water, heat, medical care, gasoline, you name it. Billions of dollars' worth of humanitarian aid continues to pour into Ukraine, and it's a desperate race for Ukrainians and aid workers to distribute it to those most in need.

But life goes on. Warming and power centers are open in the major cities. A rotating schedule of power outages is posted every day across the nation, typically four hours on then four hours off. Ukrainians cook and heat coffee and bathe when they can. Children go to school online and go outside to play in between air raid warnings.

People live by candlelight at night and collect scraps of wood for small, wood-burning stoves if they're lucky enough to have one to heat their homes. They haul water to their homes from wells and water trucks, and they store it in plastic bottles, buckets, or old milk bottles. They use rechargeable car batteries to run lights and small appliances during the power outages.

It has become a common joke in Ukraine to say that, if the temperature rises above freezing, Ukrainians open their windows to let the warm air in.

Ukrainians have apps on their phones that project the paths of incoming missiles in real time. They have other phone apps for reporting sightings of Russian military forces. When Russians started seizing the phones of civilians and shooting the phone owners if such a reporting app was found installed on the phone, Ukrainians encrypted the apps and made them self-erasing if a special code isn't entered into the phone upon activating it.

The Ukrainians have adapted to living in a war zone. Ukraine has 2 million men signed up for military service who have not yet been called up. It has millions of women it can call into combat if necessary and who will fight if called.

While most nations traditionally prefer to keep the bearers of their future children out of war, in a war for a country's survival, if the nation dies it doesn't matter if the women die, too. Given the brutal and genocidal tendencies Putin and his armed forces have demonstrated in the past decade, many Ukrainian women would undoubtedly choose to fight and die rather than live and suffer the wrath of the Russians if Ukraine loses the war.

WHY THEY'RE FIGHTING

Pretty much all the Ukrainians left in Ukraine viscerally loathe the Russian invaders at this point. This hatred makes even everyday Ukrainians not only willing but happy to risk their lives if it means one more Russian soldier will go home in a body bag.

For the Ukrainian people, this is total war. This is a battle for their very survival. They will throw every resource they have at surviving. They will put up with every privation and whatever suffering is necessary. They will sacrifice every bit of infrastructure they have in the knowledge that it will be rebuilt one day. Not just soldiers in the Ukrainian army are willing to die. Everyone in Ukraine understands that his or her future is on the line. Every last one of them accepts that he or she may die. But the alternative—subjugation by a vicious, genocidal Russian regime is worse than death. They are *all* in this together.

Should the Russian army prevail in the end, Putin and company will find themselves holding a tiger by the tail. Even in defeat, a united and defiant Ukrainian people will do everything in their power to sabotage a Russian regime in Ukraine. They will never stop working to make life miserable for any Russian overlords and to force the Russians out.

It is perhaps the most basic tenet of warfare that armies must believe in what they're fighting for. In war, young men are being asked to die, and for them to be willing to do so, they must understand why what they're fighting for is worth dying for.

It is crystal clear in the dismal morale the Russian forces have demonstrated in Ukraine for the past year that the vast majority of Russian soldiers either do not understand what they're supposed to be dying for or they do not believe in what they're being asked to die for.

Interviews with Russian prisoners of war bear this out. The majority of them readily admit to having no stomach for the war. They express confusion at going to war against Ukrainians many of whom have family members, friends, neighbors, and deep ties inside Russia and vice versa. The majority of captured Russian soldiers express thinking the war is wrong, and practically all of them express a desire to just go home.

PUTIN'S GREAT MISCALCULATION

The Russian army is not fighting for the survival of its homeland as it has in almost every other war in Russian history, a fact that Putin seems to have forgotten. He seems wildly enamored of the idea of a great, patriotic Russian army sweeping across the former Soviet republics in a glorious display of might, and furthermore of his armies being welcomed with parades, flowers, and kisses by the masses, overjoyed to come home to Mother Russia.

Putin appears to be the victim of his own propaganda. He believed the Russian army was invincible. He believed massive numbers of Russian tanks and infantry soldiers could overwhelm anything in their path. He believed that Ukrainians wanted to return to living under Russian rule. And he believed that he could impose his will on anyone he wanted to.

It's easy to see how his past invasions of tiny, poor Chechnya, tiny, isolated Georgia, war-ravaged Syria, and a few isolated provinces at the edges of Ukraine might have fueled his misconceptions. However, he failed to realize that invading wealthy, educated, westernized Ukraine in its entirety was something else altogether—a fact he clearly miscalculated terribly.

Even worse, he grossly underestimated international reaction to invading an entire sovereign nation, in a blatant and illegal land grab. Furthermore, he seemed not to grasp that he was attacking a nation full of Caucasians. When television coverage of the war was broadcast in the West, the Ukrainians would look, sound, and live just like most people in Europe and the United States.

To the entire Western world, Ukrainians are just like us. It's not hard for any westerner to place himself or herself in the shoes of the Ukrainians suffering or dead on our television sets and feel immediate sympathy for Ukraine's plight.

Volodymyr Zelensky is nothing if not a master of social media and of the television medium. He knows how to make a biting comment that's sound byte ready for social media platforms or a news broadcast. He delivers a stirring speech with the consummate skill of the trained actor he is. And, he knows how to get ahead of Putin's propaganda and disinformation and ridicule it or discredit it before Putin's state media can even deliver the lie.

While it's not in the scope of this book to dive deeply into Putin's propaganda machine, propaganda is a vital tool in the arsenal of any authoritarian dictator. Controlling what is said and perceived about the Russian regime and manipulating the Russian people to be slavishly loyal to him is arguably Putin's most important tool for staying in power.

No matter how large or powerful Putin's State Security Force is—it currently stands at 400,000+ armed thugs who report only to Putin personally—if millions of Russians were to take to the streets and rise up in revolt, no army could stand against them. Putin absolutely knows this. In fact, I expect this is the stuff of his worst nightmares.

Putin *must* keep his population docile and convinced he's in total control. Not only his job, but his life, depends on it.

Hence, when I tell you that Volodymyr Zelensky has, hands down, won the media war with Russia and rendered almost all of Putin's attempts at disinformation in the West and much of the propaganda inside Russia meaningless, that's a very big deal.

Putin still seems to believe in the legendary willingness of the Russian people and Russian soldiers to suffer unbelievable hardships on behalf of the motherland. He probably would not be wrong if an outside enemy were to invade Russia. But he has grossly misjudged the willingness of Russian soldiers to do the same horrendous suffering when they are, instead, invaders in another country.

Russian soldiers have no deep, vested interest in winning in Ukraine other than not dying, following orders, or perhaps a vague notion of reuniting the USSR like back in the good old days, a time most Russian soldiers aren't old enough to remember. If Russia loses this war, Russia will still exist. Russian people will go on with their lives, and things will remain fairly normal back home (the devastating damage of the economic sanctions notwithstanding).

Putin has failed to give his soldiers a believable, compelling justification for dying—for Russia, or for him.

In stark contrast, the Ukrainians know exactly what they're fighting for. Their lives. Their homes. Their futures. Their freedom. And most importantly, their children.

WHAT COMES NEXT IN THE WAR

Rumors persisted throughout January 2023 that Putin was planning to call up 500,000 more Russian men to fight in the war. Military experts inside Russia itself warned, however, that the Russian military had yet to properly train, equip, and utilize the 300,000 men it mobilized last September and that the Russian army is not ready to handle the additional influx of new soldiers.

However, it seems clear that Putin will, at some point, throw hundreds of thousands more Russian soldiers into the war.

After the initial call up of 300,000 men, as many as a million Russians left the country. When it was announced that the full 300,000 soldiers had been conscripted, the panic began to fade and some Russian men began to return to Russia. As of the end of January 2023, it was estimated that around 700,000 Russian men remained abroad.

One has to wonder if the Russian people will eventually have enough of the staggering losses Putin is accumulating in this war.

To date, it's estimated Russia has suffered 200,000 casualties. Combining those with the men who have fled, this war has already cost Russia upwards of a million healthy, working-age men.

Russia's ground forces still do not receive robust air support from the Russian Air Force. The number of tanks and armored personnel carriers Russia can send onto the battlefield to support infantry troops is significantly reduced, as well. Russia is reported still not to have enough rifles for every soldier to have one, yet. At one point last fall, it was reported there was only one rifle per every three Russian soldiers, and they might or might not have any ammunition for it.

Meanwhile, Ukraine continues to receive equipment, weapons, and ammunition from the West. Every Ukrainian soldier does have a weapon and ammunition for it. In fact, many civilians have rifles and ammunition, as well. In early 2023, Ukraine was burning through staggering amounts of ammunition, even more than it was receiving from its allies, but shipments of ammunition to Ukraine have been increased sharply from the West in recent days.

It's thought that, come spring, Putin will start over, invading Ukraine again from multiple directions much the same way he did in February 2022—Ukrainian Invasion 2.0, as it were. It's thought he'll pursue the same objectives he did the first time:

1) Race to Kyiv and seize the capitol

2) Capture or kill Zelensky and decapitate the Ukrainian government, throwing the country into chaos

3) Shock the Ukrainian people into submission and surrender with the speed and efficiency of the takeover by a massive and superior Russian army

4) Seize all of Ukraine and declare it part of Russia

This time he will have twice as many men, but something like half as much heavy equipment. He won't have the element of surprise on his side. Although in 2022, everyone expected him to invade, nobody knew precisely when he would do it. He held the initiative the first time around.

Now, the Ukrainians are ready and waiting for him. The Ukrainian military is much larger, much better equipped, and has had a year to learn battle tactics. A group of the smartest western military advisors on the planet has gathered in Kyiv to assist the Ukrainian military in planning its war strategy and has had a year to figure out how best to defend against a second major attack.

Most civilian Ukrainians are out of the way of the potential battle areas. There will not be the same humanitarian crisis to deal with that the Ukrainian government had to handle in February of 2022 as its population clogged roads and hastily fled the Russian advance.

Massive military aid flows into Ukraine every day. Those supply lines are fully established and in good working order. They do not have to be hastily built like they did in 2022.

And last, but not least, the Ukrainians are angry. In February of 2022, they were shocked, scared, and unsure of what to do. They know exactly what they have to do, this time around.

Western analysts believe it will be a bloodbath for the Russians.

The Russians may succeed in seizing some territory, or even a lot of territory. And Russian forces may even succeed in pushing waves of troops deep into Ukraine. But at some point, their logistics and supply chains, which haven't been fixed in any meaningful way, will collapse again, stranding hundreds of thousands of Russian troops in enemy territory without the means to continue fighting. Then they will be at the mercy of the Ukrainians.

Putin was able to get the first batch of 300,000 extra troops largely from small towns and rural areas. In major cities, there was serious pushback against random men being grabbed off the streets and conscripted, and the rules of who was and wasn't eligible to be called up were followed more closely in urban areas. The exemptions for college students, workers in critical jobs, tech workers, and various factory workers meant that most urban men were exempt from going to fight in Ukraine.

However, if Putin is going to mobilize a half million more men, this time he's going to have to get a lot of those warm bodies from big cities. There will have to be less exemptions from who's eligible to go, as well. He's going to have to force college students, older men, educated men working in white collar jobs, middle-class men, and factory workers to serve. All of a sudden, the war won't be some distant thing to urban Russians that's taking place far away and not really affecting them and their loved ones.

Even the rumor of a big, new call up has sent another wave of Russian men fleeing for the borders. If, in fact, Putin does order another 500,000 men into the war, the number of men fleeing Russia will swell even more. Current estimates are that, in the event of another mobilization of men, the number of men leaving Russia will surpass 1 million by spring.

Analysts also suggest that, given Russia's current model of conducting combat and given its continued lack of training, supplies, military equipment, and competent leadership, it's reasonable to expect Russia to lose another 250,000 men or more by the end of this summer.

WHO WINS IF THE WAR DRAGS ON?

This is one of the questions being hotly debated among analysts these days. The common wisdom among western analysts is that time is on Ukraine's side. They argue that the staggering casualties Russia is stacking up will surely catch up with Putin at some point, that the Russian people will throw up their hands and say enough as they lose an entire generation of young men.

But others point at previous Russian wars where casualties have run into the millions without Russia surrendering. This is a nation of people who know suffering. They've done it before, and Putin seems convinced they're prepared to do it again.

Given the total control of Russia that Putin currently commands, he may be correct in thinking that the Russian people will not revolt. Going into World War II, Stalin held the USSR in a firm grip of terror, and the people neither revolted against him or against the horrific losses in the "Great Patriotic War", which is how Russians refer to World War II.

Former Secretary of State Condoleeza Rice had this to say on the question on February 26, 2023, one year into the war:

"Vladimir Putin seems to believe that time is not on the Ukrainian side. He believes if he throws in the Russian way of war, mass at the problem, poor boys from Dagestan who are just kind of cannon fodder, if he engages in terrorist activities against the Ukrainian population, he'll wear the Ukrainians down, he'll wear us down, he'll wear the Europeans down. I don't think that's right. But we have to do everything that we can to convince him that it is indeed wrong."

Ukraine is completely dependent on continuing military and humanitarian support from the West to remain in this war. Cut off that flow of support, and Ukraine will lose the war nearly immediately.

The question then, is not whether Ukraine can stay in this war for the long term. Rather, it is will the West be able to stay in this war for the long term?

If Putin is, indeed, willing to throw Russian cannon fodder against the Ukrainians indefinitely, then the West must also be prepared to continue supplying Ukraine for just as long if Ukraine is to stand a chance of coming out of this war intact as a nation.

This is the true nature of proxy wars. Which side in the conflict has the backing of the superpower willing to stick with the war the longest?

As for who the loser is in this war? That would be the Ukrianian people. They have died by the tens of thousands, suffered incredible atrocities against them, seen their homes, the country, and their entire way of life reduced to rubble. It is they who are paying the ultimate price to stop Putin and his lust for power and glory.

THE UNKNOWNS

No matter how enthusiastic hardliners are for the war inside Russia, and no matter how much Russian State television tells the Russian people the war is going swimmingly well, at some point, the Russian people will figure out they've lost upwards of two million men from a combination of casualty and flight.

Surely, it will dawn on them at some point that something is terribly wrong with their army and their government if they couldn't win in a matter of days, way back in February 2022, against a tiny, weak neighbor like Ukraine.

To keep the Russian populace from figuring this out, Putin's propaganda machine is shouting at the top of its lungs that the United States caused this war and that the U.S. is giving Ukraine everything it needs to destroy Russia. . .and that this is America's intent. Putin is *desperate* to distract the Russian people from how dismally his army is performing in this war.

What happens if the Russian people figure out how bad their army is? Unknown.

It's worth pointing out that Russians may be willing to sustain massive casualties in the name of standing up to the United States, their hereditary enemy and greatest threat globally. They will continue to support Putin and his bloody war for a while, at least.

How long will the Russian people continue to support this war? Unknown.

For now, Putin is firmly in control inside the Kremlin and rules

Russia with an iron fist, using his State Security Forces to keep any dissent whatsoever completely suppressed. It's widely believed that he has surrounded himself with hardliners and pro-war extremists. Interestingly enough, this group could pose a threat to Putin if they decided he's not being brutal and forceful enough in how he's running the war.

Outside his inner circle but certainly inside the Kremlin halls of power, there are highly placed officials in the intelligence services and armed forces who have a clear picture of what has gone on for the past year and how bad the situation is for Russia in Ukraine. It's possible some of them could get fed up and try to overthrow Putin, or at least to reveal the truth about the war.

Will Putin's support inside the Kremlin fail at some point? Unknown.

This leads us to another one of the great unknowns of this war—who might emerge victorious in a coup d'état that deposes Putin. For the most part, Putin has fired or murdered all the moderates within his inner circle of power. If a coup were to come from within that close circle of advisors, it's reasonable to expect someone at least as hardline as Putin might take control of the country.

However, if a coup were to come from outside that inner circle, say from a group of military generals and/or FSB leadership, they might be considerably more interested in ending the war in Ukraine.

Which group is likely to emerge victorious if Putin is deposed? Unknown.

Can the superior western technology and much smaller Ukrainian army hold off a massive offensive by vast numbers of Russian soldiers? Unknown.

Will the Russian army fight with any kind of resolve when it is flung against the Ukrainians and sustains heavy casualties? Unknown.

Will Putin be able to retain his control of the Russian media narrative—and through it the hearts and minds of Russian people—if his great offensive of 2023 fizzles and stalls? Unknown.

If Putin's offensive does stall in the spring/summer of 2023 (which, let's face it, would constitute a failure for him and his army) will he really continue throwing men into the meat grinder of the war indefinitely? Unknown.

How many Russian men is Putin willing to kill in order to win? Unknown.

How much military aid in the form of military equipment, money, and other forms of support will Iran, China, and North Korea give to Putin to keep this war going, knowing that doing so will cause even more sanctions and more consequences to their nations? Unknown.

If the Russian offensive of 2023 fails, will Putin's military and manpower resources be so exhausted he cannot continue with the war in its current format? Unknown.

THE GREATEST UNKNOWN OF ALL

That leads us to the greatest unknown of all and takes us one step closer to the crux of this entire book—if it becomes clear to Vladimir Putin that he is going to lose the war in Ukraine, will he resort to using nuclear weapons?

Unknown.

CHAPTER NINETEEN:

THE LOOMING NUCLEAR CRISIS

"We pray to the Lord that he brings the madmen to reason
and helps them understand that any desire to destroy Russia
will mean the end of the world."

—Patriarch Kirill,
head of the Russian Orthodox Church

"From the very beginning, when we entered the nuclear activity,
our goal was to build a bomb and strengthen the deterrent forces,
but we could not maintain the secrecy of this issue,
and the secret reports were revealed by a group of hypocrites."

—Ali Motahari, former Iranian MP

IN PART I OF THIS BOOK, I laid out the history of Iran and how it became an extremist Islamic nation. I explained where the concept of a messianic Islamic figure called the Mahdi came from and how the supreme leadership of Iran, both religious and political, is controlled by a handful of religious zealots called Twelvers, who eagerly await the return of the Mahdi.

We looked at how Iran's ruling ayatollahs believe it is their holy duty to usher in the return of the Mahdi by creating an apocalypse in the Middle East. When this is accomplished, the Mahdi will return, bringing with him immediate conversion of the entire world to Shia Islam and a Muslim caliphate spanning the entire earth.

This is why Iran's government has been urgently pursuing building a nuclear weapon of its own. As soon as Iran has a nuclear bomb and a missile capable of delivering it, they make no secret of their intent to launch it at Israel.

We looked at how Iran has hidden its uranium enrichment program and worked frantically to develop short- and medium-range missiles, and how they're using a "space" program to develop ICBMs.

Lastly, in Part I, we discussed how Iran is only a few days away from having enough weapons grade uranium to fuel a nuclear weapon. As soon as it builds a working warhead, Iran will have everything it needs to launch its own version of Armageddon.

In Part II of this book, I traced Vladimir Putin's history and how he became the paranoid, brutal, expansionist leader of Russia that he is today. I discussed the lessons he learned from his invasions of Chechnya, Georgia, and Syria, and how the world demonstrated little or no interest in stopping him.

We took a look at the roots of the Russia-Ukraine conflict, extending back some 30 years. I then did a short recap of the war for you. It was not my intent to give you a blow-by-blow history of the war. Historians will write plenty of those in years to come, and I happily leave the task to them. I did, however, discuss why the war did not go as planned for Putin and how much trouble he's in now.

And last, we took a look at how the United States, NATO, and the western world have united behind a commitment that Ukraine must survive as a nation.

In Part III of this book, I traced how Putin's catastrophic

failures in Ukraine have forced him into a series of unholy alliances with other pariah nations.

We discussed Russia's new closeness with China and how China is blatantly taking advantage of Russia's weakness. We looked at how China is walking a tightrope, supporting Russia as much as it can without actually sending direct military weapons to Russia to use in Ukraine.

We looked at Russia and Iran's sudden friendship as a result of the Ukraine War. Iran has jumped to provide thousands of weapons for Russia to continue bombing Ukraine and terrorizing its civilian population, and how big Russia owes Iran.

We also looked at North Korea and how it has cozied up to both Russia and Iran. We talked about how North Korea and Iran are gleefully sharing nuclear technology, parts, and probably manufacturing equipment to help each other achieve their parallel nuclear ambitions.

We took a look at a few of Putin's many gross miscalculations as he made the decision to invade Ukraine, at where Ukraine stands now, and what might happen going forward in 2023.

We finished up Part III with a long list of questions whose answers are unknown at this time, ending with the most important question of all: if Putin is going to lose the Ukraine War, will he resort to using nuclear weapons?

Let's take a closer look at that question now.

IS PUTIN WILLING TO USE NUCLEAR WEAPONS?

The short answer to this question is yes.

Unequivocally, Putin is willing to use nuclear weapons. He's been saying so for months, and Putin has a long history of doing exactly what he says he's going to do.

I've quoted this elsewhere in this book, but it bears repeating. On the very first day of the invasion, February 24, 2022, Putin threatened:

> "To anyone who would consider interfering from outside: if you do, you will face consequences greater than any you have faced in history. All the relevant decisions have been taken. I hope you hear me."

The international diplomatic community unanimously interpreted this as a threat to use nuclear weapons, particularly since he alluded in the same speech to the substantial nuclear arsenal Russia possess, and he was at pains to point out that Russia "is today one of the most powerful nuclear powers."

A few days after the war began, Putin stated:

> "NATO countries are making aggressive statements about our country. As a result, Russia's nuclear forces will be moved to a special regime of combat duty."

Why put your nuclear forces on a higher alert status if you have no plans to use them? Putin's increased nuclear readiness posture forced the West to step up its monitoring of known nuclear sites, including storage facilities and missile silos to watch for signs of preparations by Russia to launch nuclear weapons. To date, none have been detected. But that could change at a moment's notice.

On September 21, 2022, in the same speech where Putin announced the mobilization of 300,000 additional troops, he falsely accused the West of "nuclear blackmail." He went on to accuse the West of threatening to use nuclear weapons.

> NOTE: A quick reminder that it's a standard disinformation tactic to falsely accuse someone of doing the thing you have done or are about to do. It puts that adversary on the defensive, forcing them to deny your claims, and it puts you in a position of being able to "retaliate" for this terrible thing you've accused your enemy of. After all, you're merely responding in kind. You didn't start the fight, you didn't escalate it to the bad thing you accused your enemy of, and you're justified in reacting by doing the same thing.

In his September 21st speech, Putin went on to say that officials in NATO countries had spoken "about the possibility and admissibility of using weapons of mass destruction against Russia—nuclear weapons." This, too, was a completely false accusation.

He then went on to threaten:

> "To those who allow themselves to make such statements about Russia, I would like to remind you that our country also has various means of destruction, and for some components more modern than those of the NATO countries. And if the territorial integrity of our country is threatened, we will certainly use all the means at our disposal to protect Russia and our people. This is not a bluff."

On September 30, 2022, in the speech where Putin declared that the regions of Luhansk, Donetsk, Zaporizhzhia, and Kherson had been annexed and were now officially Russian territory, he went on to declare:

> "If the territorial integrity of our country is threatened, we will without a doubt use all available means to protect Russia and our people—this is not a bluff. . .The United States and NATO are the ones engaging in nuclear blackmail. . .those who try to blackmail us with nuclear weapons should know that the weathervane can turn and point towards them."

In October 2022, Putin claimed Ukraine was planning to launch a nuclear strike on itself. He said Ukraine was going to detonate a warhead somewhere in Ukraine that would be filled with radioactive waste. Putin said that in this false-flag operation, Ukraine planned to blame Russia for the explosion.

Although Putin has for the most part threatened indirectly to use nuclear weapons, not coming right out and saying he was thinking about dropping a nuclear bomb on Ukraine, the propaganda outlets he controls haven't been subtle about it at all.

A number of Russian lawmakers and state media figures have openly threatened nuclear strikes in the past year. Keep in mind that a mosquito doesn't sneeze in the Kremlin without Putin's permission. If influential government and media figures are threatening nuclear war, they have Putin's blessing to do so.

Margarita Simonyan, editor in chief of Russia Today said in April, 2022:

> "I think World War III is more realistic, knowing
> us, knowing our leader. . .That all this will end with
> a nuclear strike seems more probable to me. . . death
> would be better than succumbing to the monstrous
> organism known as the collective Western world."

Andrey Gurulyov, a retired major-general and member of the Duma (the Russian Parliament) is often called Putin's mouthpiece because of how faithfully he parrots the party line. In September, 2022, on Russian state television, Gurulyov threatened nuclear strikes on Britain and Germany if they didn't immediately stop providing aid to Ukraine. He went on to declare that the United States did not have the fortitude to retaliate to a nuclear strike on a NATO ally:

> "If we turn the British Isles into a Martian desert
> in three minutes flat using tactical nuclear weap-
> ons, not strategic ones—they [the United States]
> could use Article 5, but for whom? A nonexistent
> country turned into a Martian desert? They won't
> respond."

Article 5 is the portion of the NATO treaty that declares if one NATO country has been attacked, they all have been attacked, and they will all come to the defense of the attacked nation.

I suspect Britain's nuclear submarines would also have something to say about a country-ending nuclear attack on their home.

Britain's nuclear arsenal includes around 225 warheads, 120 of which are operational at any given time. Russia might make a Martian desert of Britain but not without sustaining significant desertification of its own inside Russia.

Vladimir Solovyov, a popular television broadcaster said in December 2022:

> "We'll either win, or humanity will cease to exist because the Lord won't stand for the triumph of warriors of the Antichrist. We are Russian. God is with us."

On January 19, 2023, Dmitry Medvedev, deputy head of Russia's Security Council and a close ally of Vladimir Putin, warned:

> "The loss by a nuclear power in a conventional war can provoke the outbreak of a nuclear war. The nuclear powers do not lose major conflicts on which their fate depends."

Russia's doctrine regarding use of nuclear weapons does allow for the use of nuclear weapons after aggression against the Russian Federation with conventional weapons when the very existence of the state is threatened. This is known as a first strike doctrine. They are willing to strike first with nuclear weapons if they're going to lose a war that threatens Russia's existence.

It's interesting to note that Medvedev's remarks were also the first time that any Russian government official has actually admitted the possibility of defeat in Ukraine.

SPREADING REVERENCE FOR NUCLEAR WEAPONS

An alarming fascination with and approval for using nuclear weapons is popping up in Russian popular culture. At a November 2022 rally in central Moscow staged by the Kremlin, demonstrators marched through the streets behind a mock-up of an RS-28 Sarmat ICBM and sang the Queen song, "We Will Rock You" with new lyrics calling for the destruction of Washington, D.C.

Denis Maidenow, a popular Russian singer-songwriter who serves in the Duma released a music video in December 2022 with these lyrics:

> "It'll scatter our enemies into dust in an instant,
> It's ready to carry out the sentence,
> For the Sarmat there's only pleasure,
> To trouble NATO's dreams!"

Dimitry Adamsky is a professor at the Lauder School of Government, Diplomacy and Strategy at Reichman University, in Israel. In his book, Russian Nuclear Orthodoxy, published in 2019, Adamsky describes Putin's multiyear effort to spread the mystical teachings of the Russian Orthodox Church among the personnel who handle nuclear weapons as a means of fostering patriotism, discipline, and obedience:

> "Each leg of the nuclear triad has its patron saint,
> and their icons hang on the walls of the consecrated
> headquarters and command posts."

Russian military members are taught that God and the Russian Orthodox Church approve of them using nuclear weapons, and that Russia has been given nuclear weapons as part of its special, mystical role as the Russian Orthodox Church's representative and defender on earth.

PUTIN AS GOD'S CHOSEN ONE

I could write an entire book about Putin's belief that he is the chosen savior of the Russian Orthodox Church. He believes that he, personally, is destined to restore the Church in Russia to its former glory and then to spread its teachings to the world. He has been obsessed with this idea for many years. Indeed, his perception of himself as a savior to the Russian people has been building for a decade or more.

Perhaps with age, paranoia, and isolation, he's becoming delusional. Perhaps absolute power has corrupted him absolutely. Perhaps he has spent far too long surrounded by yes-men and sycophants who do nothing but boost his ego and tell him exactly what he wants to hear—that he is, indeed, the savior of Russia.

Note: not *a* savior of Russia. *The* savior of Russia.

Putin has aggressively used the Russian Orthodox Church to reinforce his popularity and power inside Russia. He has not hesitated to make the church part of his own personal propaganda machine.

Kirill of Moscow, the Patriarch of the Russian Orthodox Church, is firmly in Putin's pocket and the staunchest of Putin's supporters. Kirill personally preaches from the pulpit that Vladimir Putin is God's envoy on earth and the savior of the Russian Orthodox Church.

While not many Russians attend church regularly, the vast majority—close to 90% of Russians—say they are religious. About 80% call themselves Russian Orthodox. When the Church itself is saying that Putin is its savior, it's hard to argue against that.

Hence, when Vladimir Putin stands up and says something to the effect of, "God approves of my using nuclear weapons," the Russian people have been primed for years to take him at his word. Not only have they heard this over and over on the evening news, but they've also been taught this in church.

Adamsky goes on to quote Putin saying about a nuclear war with NATO:

> "We as martyrs would go to paradise, while they will simply perish because they won't even have time to repent their sins."

Putin has gone to great lengths to convince the Russian people that if they are the chosen of God, it is not only their right, but their duty, to use nuclear weapons to preserve themselves.

Take a moment to re-read that.

Vladimir Putin not only believes himself to be the leader of Russia, he also believes himself to be the savior of Russia's church and, furthermore, the savior of the entire nation.

He personally is going to restore the USSR, bring Russia back to its old glory days of being feared worldwide, and he is going to demonstrate to the world that Russia is the world's greatest military power once more. He also believes he is the *only* person who can do all of this for Russia. He has been chosen for the task. He is irreplaceable—Russia's only hope for a return to greatness.

He *is* Russia. In his mind, a threat to him is a threat to all of Russia. He does not distinguish between himself and the nation anymore. In his mind, a threat to his job or his life is a direct threat to the continued existence of Russia.

If it's acceptable to use nuclear weapons to defend the existence of Russia, then it's also perfectly acceptable to use nuclear weapons to defend his own existence. In fact, it is his sacred duty to use nuclear weapons to protect himself.

Putin knows he bears full responsibility for the Ukraine War. It was his idea. He planned it. He started it. He's made all the major decisions in how the war was fought. Win or lose, he will be hailed as a hero or bitterly blamed for losing by the Russian people. He knows he is in total control of what Russia does, and so does everyone else. Therefore, if Russia loses the war, it will be his fault.

If he loses the war in Ukraine, Putin knows full well he will be removed from power. He has bet his entire future on the outcome of this war. If Russia loses the war, at best, he'll lose his job. At worst, he'll lose his life.

He has made it clear he believes it is his right to protect himself by whatever means Russia has at its disposal, up to and including using nuclear weapons to prevent Russia—or more accurately, himself—from losing the war.

Is Putin willing to use nuclear weapons in Ukraine? Yes. Absolutely.

CHAPTER TWENTY:

ISRAEL'S DILEMMAS

"With regard to the Russia-Ukraine issue,
we will do one thing for certain—in public—we will talk less."

—Eli Cohen,
Israeli Foreign Minister, January 2023

YOU MAY HAVE NOTICED THAT, for the vast majority of this book, I have not talked much about Israel. That's about to change. Indeed, the whole purpose of this book so far has been to lay the groundwork for understanding the existential crisis currently facing Israel. It is a crisis the United States may soon face, as well.

First, we have Vladimir Putin engaged in a war that's not going well for him. He's made it clear to anyone who will listen that he *will* use nuclear weapons if that's what it takes to bring Ukraine to its knees so he can win the war.

On the other hand, we have Iran poised on the brink of completing its first nuclear weapon, a weapon which Iranian leaders have stated repeatedly they can't wait to use on Israel.

Second, we have Putin on the one hand, whose entire persona and position relies on him projecting aggressive, macho strength. His reputation is being badly tarnished by Russia's failures in Ukraine, and he's desperate to shore up his strongman image. Many analysts believe he's actually eager to use a nuclear weapon and looking for any excuse to do it.

Third, we have the unholy alliance formed between these two nuclear-eager powers as a result of the Ukraine War. Russia is desperate for the weapons Iran is providing it, and Iran is desperate for the final nuclear technology Russia can provide it.

If you were the prime minister of Israel today, how well would you be sleeping at night, right now? How worried would you be that Putin, in his gratitude for Iran's help may give in at last and give Iran the nuclear technology it persistently continues to ask for?

At what point will Vladimir Putin decide he's tired of getting a bloody nose from the United States, and America's proxy, Ukraine? At what point does he decide to give Iran the nuclear information it needs so it will be America's turn to get a bloody nose when one of its closest allies gets obliterated?

I've spoken with my friend, Benjamin Netanyahu, who is the prime minister of Israel recently and at length on this topic. And I can tell you, he's not sleeping well at all these days.

NUCLEAR DILEMMAS MOUNT

What if, when Iran finally does get nuclear weapons—which is not a question of if, but only of when—Iranian government and military officials choose not to use it immediately against Israel? Perhaps cooler heads will prevail and the most rabid of Twelvers

THE END TIMES AND ARMAGEDDON

will be outvoted on starting their own Armageddon. Or perhaps, the Supreme Leader will wait for a sign of some kind indicating that the Mahdi is ready to return and that the moment is right to launch Armageddon. How will that scenario play out?

Even if Iran doesn't immediately launch a nuclear strike once it obtains nuclear weapons, what will that do to the balance of power in the Middle East?

Saudi Foreign Minister, Prince Faisal bin Farhan Al-Saud, speaking at the World Policy Conference in Abu Dhabi, said in December of 2022 that the Iran's Gulf neighbors will not sit by if Tehran produces nuclear weapons:

> "If Iran gets an operational nuclear weapon, all bets are off. . .We are in a very dangerous space in the region. . . you can expect that regional states will certainly look towards how they can ensure their own security."

What would this arms race look like, and how quickly would it spread to other Gulf states?

Turkey's president, Tayyip Erdogan, has been complaining for years that it's unacceptable for nuclear-armed states to forbid Ankara from obtaining its own nuclear weapons:

> "Some countries have missiles with nuclear warheads, not one or two. But they tell us we can't have them. This, I cannot accept. There is no developed nation in the world that doesn't have them. We have Israel nearby, as almost neighbors. They scare other nations by possessing these."

If he's scared of Israel's nuclear arsenal, which Israel has had for decades without using and which Israel steadfastly declares will only be used for the defense of itself, how will Erdogan feel when a radical, messianic, violent, unstable regime like Iran's obtains them?

These are all questions of vital importance to the continued survival of Israel.

TO HAVE BUT NOT TO USE

It's one thing for a nation to obtain nuclear weapons, it's another thing altogether for that nation to exercise restraint—over decades—and refrain from using those nuclear weapons. In a nation with a stable government, a rational foreign policy, and an economy sufficient to provide for its people, the odds of its leaders turning to nuclear weapons are very, very low.

Every nation that is currently a member of the nuclear club has a clearly defined nuclear doctrine that spells out exactly when it will and won't use nuclear weapons. These nations have, for three quarters of a century, adhered to those doctrines.

If, however, a radical, extremist regime like the Islamic Republic in Iran gets a hold of nuclear weapons, what are the odds that the Supreme Leader and his followers in the government and military will refrain from using them?

If a nuclear arms race breaks out in the Middle East, what are the odds that nobody in that tense, religiously contentious part of the world will ever use a nuclear weapon?

There are not many things in this world that people are willing to die for, but religion is one of them. If we have a Russian Orthodox true believer just itching to use a nuclear weapon to prove how big a man he is, and we have a radical Islamic regime counting the days until it can annihilate its Jewish neighbor, and we have a bunch of nervous Sunni states eyeing their unstable Shiite neighbor, how long is it going to be before one of them launches a nuclear weapon?

Most military analysts suggest it will take around ten years for a Middle East arms race to result in most of the nations in the region to having at least a few nuclear weapons. The question, then, is how long can various Gulf states withstand the temptation to use their nuclear arsenals once they have them?

The officials at the very top levels of the Israeli government, whom I'm talking to often, estimate it will take no more than ten years after the arms race is complete for someone in the Middle East to use a nuclear weapon. These same officials are convinced that use of one weapon will set off a chain reaction of nuclear strikes that obliterates the entire Middle East.

ISRAEL DISRUPTS IRAN'S NUCLEAR PROGRAM

For years, Israel has watched Iran's secret uranium enrichment program, its secret underground bunkers holding centrifuges, and missile construction and testing facilities with deep alarm.

On September 6, 2007, the Israeli Air Force carried out an airstrike that destroyed a suspected nuclear reactor in Syria. Ten North Koreans were reportedly killed in the attack.

Throughout 2010, a wave of assassinations of Iranian nuclear scientists took place. Although Israel never claimed responsibility for the killings, it's widely believed the Mossad, Israel's foreign intelligence service, was behind them.

In June, 2010, Stuxnet, an advanced computer worm—a particularly damaging type of computer virus—was discovered. It's believed to have been developed by the United States and Israel to attack Iran's nuclear facilities. It's estimated that Stuxnet damaged as many as 1,000 centrifuges in Iran, which constituted about 10% of all their installed centrifuges at the time.

Iran says the Duqu and Flame computer viruses, both reportedly related to Stuxnet, were also engineered to destroy Iran's uranium enriching centrifuges. Iran also claims it is routinely sold faulty equipment and attacked by new computer viruses in an effort to sabotage its nuclear program.

In March, 2011, the Mossad was suspected of causing an explosion at Iran's nuclear facility at Isfahan. Iran denied that any explosion occurred, but based on satellite images and Israeli intelligence sources, the blast did, indeed, damage the nuclear site and was not an accident.

It's possible this attack was meant to damage the nuclear reactors at Isfahan. Some speculate the target might have been a research facility for designing hypersonic missiles with Russia's help.

Reports have also surfaced that the attack might have hit an Iranian manufacturing facility building drones to send to Russia. This rumor is possibly borne out by Russia's sharp reaction to the attack and the veiled threat Russia made to Israel in response to it, saying:

> "Such destructive actions could have unpredictable consequences for peace and stability in the Middle

East. . .That has to be understood by the organizers of the brazen raid, their backers and those who are gloating over the issue, holding on to the futile hope for the weakening of Iran."

In November, 2011, there was another explosion, this time at an Iranian Revolutionary Guard missile base, which many believe was the work of the Mossad. General Hassan Moqaddam, a key figure in Iran's missile development program was killed in the blast. It's believed several lower-ranked Iranian missile experts had already been killed in other, smaller explosions at various sites.

In February, 2012, documents came to light, stolen and released by the hacking group, Anonymous, claiming that Israeli commandos, in collaboration with Kurdish fighters, destroyed several underground Iranian facilities used for nuclear and defense research.

In October, 2012, Sudan claimed that Israel bombed a munitions factory south of Khartoum that allegedly belonged to Iran's Revolutionary Guard.

In May, 2013, citizens of Tehran reported hearing three explosions coming from an area where Iran conducts missile research and has a missile depot. Iran claimed the blasts came from a privately owned chemical factory.

In 2014, an explosion took place at a military explosives factory southeast of Tehran very near a suspected nuclear reactor. Iran seemed to order a retaliatory strike by Hezbollah against Israel, prompting observers to conclude Israel caused the explosion in Iran.

In January, 2018, Mossad agents drove to a secure warehouse in Tehran late at night in a semitrailer. Using high intensity torches, they cut into dozens of safes and carried out some 50,000 pages of documents, 163 compact discs of memos, videos, and plans, before making their escape. Israel shared the documents and files with the United States and European countries. The stolen information demonstrated that Iran was definitely working to develop a nuclear weapon and revealed two nuclear sites in Iran that had been completely hidden from inspectors.

On January 3, 2020, the United States joined Israel's efforts to sabotage the Iranian military by assassinating Iranian Major General Qasem Soleimani. He was the commander of the Quds Force, responsible for clandestine military operations and operations outside of Iran. He was considered by some to be Supreme Leader Khamenei's right-hand man and the second most powerful person in Iran.

In June and July of 2020, a series of explosions targeted Iran's nuclear and missile programs. Accidents and damages were reported in the Parchin military complex near a nuclear reactor, at the Natanz nuclear facility, and at various other sites. Intelligence officials estimated the damage at the Natanz centrifuge plant alone was significant enough to delay the Iranian nuclear program by one or two years.

On July 9, 2020, explosions were reported at a missile depot belonging to Iran's Revolutionary Guard Corps.

On November 27, 2020, Mohsen Fakhrizadeh, head of Iran's nuclear weapons program and often called the father of Iran's nuclear program, was assassinated.

On April 10, 2021, the Mossad caused an accident in the electricity distribution network for the Natanz centrifuges, one day after Iran began injecting the centrifuges with uranium hexafluoride gas.

On May 7, 2021, a massive fire broke out at the Bushehr nuclear power plant, Iran's only operating nuclear power plant, and the same one built for it by the Russians.

On June 23, 2021, major damage was caused by a fire to one of the buildings of Iran's Atomic Energy Organization.

On September 26, 2021, three people were injured in a fire at an IRGC research facility outside of Tehran.

In the summer of 2022, multiple scientists and engineers involved in Iran's aerospace program died in suspicious accidents or were killed outright.

On June 19, 2022, an explosion was reported at an IRGC missile base west of Tehran.

On January 28, 2023, a series of bomb-carrying Israeli drones attacked an Iranian defense factory at Isfahan, causing material damage to the plant. Isfahan is thought to be the main nuclear weapons facility in Iran. Although Israeli defense officials refuse to give any specifics, they expressed delight with the results of the attack.

The January, 28 attack was Israel's first direct air attack on Iranian soil and constitutes a significant escalation in hostilities between the two nations. Iran claims the damage at Isfahan was only minor. This may be true, but the psychological impact of the attack upon Iranian officials was not. Israel served them notice that it would not hesitate to attack at the very heart of Iran if necessary to prevent Iran from completing development of a nuclear weapon.

It cannot be said that Israel isn't trying to stop Iran from getting a nuclear weapon. By using shadow operations and indirect attacks, they've done their best to disrupt Iran's progress for two decades without provoking an outright war between their nations. However, the day is coming soon when Iran will come close enough to having a nuclear weapon that Israel may have to take much more direct action.

IRANIAN RESPONSE TO ISRAEL'S SABOTAGE

It's worth pointing out that, in the past, when Israel was suspected of bombing an Iranian military target or of assassinating an Iranian scientist, Iranian citizens poured out into the streets to demonstrate and chant death-to-Israel-style slogans.

However, after Israel's January 28 drone attack, there was no protest to speak of by the Iranian populace. They seem not to care if their military is attacked, or they may be much more occupied with internal political problems and simply not be interested in foreign affairs at this juncture.

This lack of public anger at the Israeli attack surely did not go unnoticed by Iranian leaders. Which raises the question of just how much has the Iranian government lost the support of the population? How much danger is the Iranian regime in of further civil unrest or outright uprising if conditions inside Iran get much worse?

Iran has retaliated for many of Israel's attacks over the years, some in the form of Iranian sabotage, assassinations, and covert attacks. Much of the Iranian retaliation took the form of Hezbollah attacks against Israel.

This low-intensity conflict has been ongoing between Iran and Israel for many years. Because of Iran's secrecy and habit of lying about the status of its nuclear program, we have no way of knowing just how much Israel has managed to disrupt it. But, given that Israel has continued its covert operations over the years, we must assume that it's having enough of an effect to make it worth the risk to Israel and to its operatives.

RECENT ISRAELI DIPLOMACY

Israel has maintained cordial relations with China, which include intelligence and military cooperation. Israel has also worked not to anger Russia to prevent Russia from denying it access to Syrian airspace. Israel needs access to overflights of Syria to bomb Iranian targets. Prime Minister Benjamin Netanyahu and Vladimir Putin are described as having a good working relationship, and scholars agree that Netanyahu seems to understand Putin very well.

Israel has offered its services as a mediator in the Russia-Ukraine conflict although neither side has taken it up on the offer at this point.

The growing Iran threat has played an important role in normalization of relations between Israel and several of its Arab neighbors recently, the United Arab Emirates and Bahrain in particular.

Saudi Arabia, Iran's other major rival, and Israel are undoubtedly going to put up a united anti-Iranian front going forward. The crown prince of Saudi Arabia, Muhammed bin Salman, is pragmatic about foreign policy and sees the need for closer, or at least less hostile, relations with Israel to deal with the Iran threat. We may not see this rapprochement until he becomes king in Saudi Arabia, but Iran could force Saudi Arabia's hand sooner than that if it insists on finishing development of a nuclear weapon.

Benjamin Netanyahu has vowed to do whatever is necessary to stop Iran from producing nuclear weapons. It is stated Israeli policy that it will fight back, and, in fact, engage in a preemptive first strike against any attempt to destroy the Jews. 'Never again' is the motto of Jews worldwide after the Holocaust.

The scene is set for a dangerous confrontation in the Middle East. Israel is certainly aware of the devastating costs such a confrontation could have. I would like to think the Iran's Khamenei is not so obsessed with ushering in the return of the Mahdi that he has lost sight of the human toll a nuclear exchange with Israel would have upon Iran.

For many years, Israel and Iran have managed to attack each other while avoiding all-out war. But will this shadow war come out into the open and grow into something larger as the tensions between the two nations continue to rise?

These, too, are serious dilemmas Israel faces today—when should it attack Iran, how aggressively should it attack Iran, what are the risks and costs of attacking Iran?

HOW FIGHTER JETS CHANGE ISRAEL'S CALCULATIONS

Iran is rumored to have bought 24 SU-35 fighter jets for air defense. As soon as those are in place over its skies, perhaps along with an upgraded and state-of -the-art air defense system provided by

Russia, Iran may feel confident in revealing that it has nuclear weapons. Iran may feel safe in the knowledge that Israel can't successfully bypass Iran's air defenses to attack its nuclear arsenal and destroy it.

Israel's air forces are among the best in the world. They fly state-of-the art equipment and their pilots are considered to be the best of the best. If the day comes when Iran's SU-35s go up against Israel's finest, it won't be much of a contest.

But, it may not have to be. It's entirely possible that Russia will send technical advisors and instructors to Iran along with the SU-35s. Those Russians on the ground could act as a human shield for Iran. Now closely allied with Russia, Iran may have some sort of deal with Russia that, if its people on the ground are attacked, Russia will come to Iran's defense. Indeed, Iran may have a deal with Russia that any major attack upon it will provoke a Russian response.

Surface-to-air defense systems have come a long way since the first Patriot missile knocked down a SCUD missile a quarter of a century ago. These could pose a serious problem for Israeli aircraft attempting to deliver precision bunker buster munitions to Iranian nuclear facilities. If reports on the construction of Iranian underground nuclear facilities are accurate—and we have no reason to believe they're not—it will take tactical nuclear munitions to "bust" Iran's bunkers.

It would likely take multiple waves of Israeli aircraft to penetrate Iran's defenses and destroy Iran's nuclear facilities. After a first surprise attack, the later waves of aircraft would find Iranian fighter jets and air defenses waiting for them.

While Israel may have no choice but to accept the losses the scenario presents, Israeli leaders also have to think about what would happen if their attack fails. What if Iran's defenses prevent Israel from crippling Iran's nuclear program? What will be the global fallout (literal and metaphorical) of having preemptively launched nuclear munitions against Iran?

IS IRAN RATIONAL OR NOT?

So far, Iran's big talk of wiping Israel off the face of the earth amounts to mostly empty threats, covert support of terrorist groups that bedevil Israel, and low-level, shadow operations against Israel...and of course, Iran's nuclear weapon development program.

Some western political analysts push back against Israel's concerns regarding Iran's nuclear threats. These analysts point out that, so far, Iran has talked irrationally but acted rationally.

Israel counters this argument by pointing out Iran's rational behavior may merely be its leaders biding their time while its scientists develop nuclear weapons. Once Iran has a nuclear arsenal, Israel says Iran may act as irrationally as it has been talking for all these years and may very well launch the nuclear attack against Israel that it has been threatening for decades.

In spite of all its uranium enrichment activity, Iran has never tested a nuclear device, let alone a deliverable weapon. Whether it has been technical problems or political decisions keeping the Iranians from actually finishing development of a working nuclear weapon, nobody knows.

But we do know they are close, very close, to succeeding now.

A slow-moving crisis has been unfolding for years around

Iran's nuclear ambitions, and until now, Israel's response has also been slow-moving and deliberate.

The Iranians have intentionally obfuscated and hidden just how far along their nuclear program really is. We do know they want to maintain the appearance of being on the verge of sudden success. The problem now is that Iran truly may be on the verge of that success. Nobody knows for sure. Does Israel dare wait for proof positive before attacking, or will it be too late by then?

Israel's dilemma of whether or not to attack Iran 's nuclear facilities is complicated by all the lengths Iran has gone to to disperse its nuclear program and to develop it entirely underground in deep, hardened bunkers. Can Israel even successfully destroy Iran's nuclear program were it to decide to try?

Throughout the past decade, Iran has used its nuclear program to great political effect. It has lifted its status on the world stage to nearly that of a global superpower. It has gained great respect within much of the Muslim world, and it has gained international political significance.

By developing weapons it has not yet built, Iran has not forced anyone to act against it. Yet.

But Israel's dilemma may be coming to a crisis point. It may be forced to act sooner rather than later.

WHAT IF ISRAEL ATTACKS IRAN'S ECONOMY?

Israel does have more than one option in this growing crisis.

Rather than attacking Iran's nuclear facilities directly, it could choose to launch a different attack at a very different Iranian target. Its economy.

Instead of attacking dispersed, underground nuclear facilities, Israel could choose another target, one right out in the open, which wouldn't even require breaching Iranian airspace.

Israel could launch a full-scale air attack at Iran's port cities and oil refineries that line its coasts. This would not require Israel to successfully get airplanes past Iran's air defenses or fighter jets. It would merely require Israel's fighter jets to get close enough to Iran to aim their missiles at the Iranian coastline.

Without delving into the technical details, SU-35s are not equipped with particularly good radar and targeting systems relative to other 4th generation fighter aircraft. The planes flown by the Israeli Air Force have significantly longer radar ranges and targeting systems. This means Israeli aircraft can stand off the Iranian coast and hit their targets inside Iran while the SU-35s would still not be in range to see or shoot at the Israeli planes.

Unlike its uranium enrichment facilities, Iran's oil fields, oil pipelines, and refineries are not widely dispersed. All of its major oil fields sit in the far southwest corner of Iran near Iraq and the Persian Gulf.

Ahvaz Oil Field is the 3rd largest oil field in the world with proven reserves of 65 billion barrels of oil. It's located just 100 miles from the Iraq border and 75 miles from the Persian Gulf.

It would be an easy matter for Israeli fighters in international airspace, well beyond the reach of Iran's air defenses to devastate Iran's oil production facilities. While they were at it, they could devastate Iran's ports, destroy a major oil pipeline or two, and hit a few major oil refineries.

Iran's economy is in shambles. Its population has experienced a massive decline in the standard of living under four decades of Islamic revolutionary rule. Inflation is high. Women in Iran are fed up at their lack of personal freedom and personal choice. Young people have few prospects for a decent future. Government mismanagement and corruption are rampant, and attempted reforms have been botched. The government is oppressive, violent, and subjects the civilian population to constant surveillance.

Last fall's gigantic demonstrations in the aftermath of Mahsa Amini's murder and the fact that the protests were widespread across all regions, all economic groups, and went on for months signals just how unhappy the Iranian population is with the current regime.

Iran's annual inflation rate is projected to be 47% at the end of the first quarter of 2023. That's not a typographical error—forty-seven. Global macroeconomic models suggest it will experience 25% inflation in 2024 and at least 20% inflation in 2025.

A little over 17% of Iran's GDP comes from oil revenue. If Iran's already terrible economy were to lose 17% of its GDP combined with a crisis in exports and imports because of destruction of its port cities, we could expect Iran to experience an existential economic crisis.

History suggests Iran would experience hyperinflation, a banking crisis, loss of access to credit, a spike in unemployment, destruction of personal wealth, shortages of basic supplies, inability to afford basic food items, and financial chaos. It's entirely possible Iran would experience complete economic collapse.

Given how unpopular the regime already is, it's entirely possible that such a financial calamity would result in a general uprising and possibly a revolt against the government. While Iran's Revolutionary Guard is violent, even brutal, it cannot stand against tens of millions of angry Iranian citizens. It would be overwhelmed fairly quickly if the Iranian populace united against it.

If the Islamic Revolutionary regime were to be overthrown, the odds are excellent it would be replaced by a more rational government. Which is to say no government the Iranian people put into power after the ayatollahs could be much more irrational.

In this scenario, Israel doesn't attack Iran's nuclear program. Instead, it provokes regime change in hopes of Iran emerging with a more rational regime, not fixated on Israel's destruction.

It's a risky gambit. Perhaps the Iranian people seize the moment to overthrow the ayatollahs. But perhaps they unite in patriotic hatred of Israel, instead, and get support the Iranian regime through whatever economic crisis ensues. Is it worth taking the risk? This is yet another dilemma facing Israel's leaders.

WHAT IF PUTIN DROPS A NUCELAR WEAPON?

Some intelligence analysts suggest that if Vladimir Putin is going to drop a nuclear bomb on (or more likely fire a nuclear missile at) Ukraine, he will probably target the city of Kryvyi Rih. It's a major city in south central Ukraine with a population of around 600,000 people.

Over one-third of the population of Hiroshima died and up to half the population of Nagasaki died in the nuclear attacks upon them. We can expect a similar death toll in an attack on a Ukrainian

THE END TIMES AND ARMAGEDDON

city. The idea of killing a quarter-million Ukrainians is undoubtedly satisfyingly high for Putin.

Although some of Kryvyi Rih's citizens have fled Ukraine, more have refugeed into the city from Russian-occupied territories, and the population remains steady at about 600,000. The prevailing winds are west-to-east, which would carry radiation and nuclear fallout largely across Ukrainian territory, rendering only Ukrainian farmland unusable for years to come.

And most importantly, Kryvyi Rih is Volodymyr Zelensky's hometown. Vladimr Putin is unquestionably vindictive enough to choose it as a target just to take a personal pot shot at the man who has so frustrated his ambitions.

The same analysts who believe this will be Putin's target of choice also believe he will probably use a single tactical nuclear weapon in the attack. He's not looking to start World War III, after all—he's looking to use a nuclear weapon and get away with it, not to provoke full-scale nuclear retaliation by Ukraine's allies.

A tactical nuclear weapon is smaller than a strategic nuclear weapon. Whereas strategic nuclear warheads are carried on inter-continental ballistic weapons and meant to take out huge areas, tactical nukes are designed to be used on the battlefield and against enemy cities, factories, and specific target areas.

Tactical nuclear weapons can vary from less than one kiloton in yield up to about 50 kilotons. Strategic weapons range from about 100 kilotons up to more than a megaton (1,000 kilotons). For comparison, the Hiroshima bomb was about 15 kilotons, and the Nagasaki bomb was about 25 kilotons. (One kiloton is the unit of measurement that described the damage done by 1,000 tons of TNT, also known as dynamite.)

Lastly, these analysts suggest that if Putin is going to use a tactical nuclear weapon of undetermined yield on Kryvyi Rih, he will probably do it late in the spring of 2023. The thinking goes that Putin's big spring invasion is going to stall out by then, and it will become clear that Putin is not going to win the war. As his losses in men and machines mount, he will—either in frustration or desperation—turn to a nuclear weapon.

The Ukrainian people have made it clear that even if Putin drops a nuclear weapon, they will not lay down their weapons and surrender. Putin's final gambit to terrorize the Ukrainian people into surrendering to him is doomed to fail.

However, if Putin does use a nuclear weapon, the consequences of it will ripple across the world.

POTENTIAL CONSEQUENCES OF A RUSSIAN NUCLEAR ATTACK

It goes without saying that the world will be shocked and horrified. Condemnation will be swift against Putin. The Russian people will probably be about equally divided in whether or not it was a good idea—in the same way they're about equally divided over whether the war is good or bad, over whether the United States started the war or not, and over whether Russia should stay in the war until it wins.

+ Every sanction the free world can think of will be put upon Russia with the intent to completely destroy its economy.

- Intense pressure will be put upon China to get its ally under control and stop propping up Russia. Economic sanctions will undoubtedly be imposed upon China if it does not condemn Russia's attack, stop buying Russian oil, and take severe action to punish Putin.

- It's possible (not probable, but possible) that in the shocked aftermath of such an event, China will seize the moment to invade Taiwan. The world's wrath will be largely aimed at Russia, and it would be an ideal distraction that lets China to get away with attacking and retaking Taiwan.

In all fairness, China is the most prosperous and experiences the most growth when the world is at peace. Booming trade and commerce are good for China, whose economy relies heavily on production of goods for export.

Whereas Russia's national temperament is oriented to using bullying and fear to gain international status, China would rather be seen as steady, calm, and rational. It is probably the topic of an entire other book to debate whether or not China will one day resort to using force to invade Taiwan or any other territory it wishes to absorb into itself.

Faced with a choice between devastating sanctions against its economy or falling in line with the rest of the world to punish Putin, my money is on China to protect its economy and look out for its own interests. If Putin drops a nuclear weapon, I believe China will not support him. (It may do its best not to stand against him, but it won't stand with him.)

- NATO and the United States will have to decide whether or not they are going to send in the offensive weapons and support Ukraine needs to defeat Russia once and for all.

- They will also have to decide if they're going to send NATO and U.S. troops into Ukraine to directly fight against Russian forces.

- They'll have to decide if and how they're going to retaliate directly against Russia militarily.

None of these will be easy or simple choices and consensus will be difficult, if not impossible, to achieve. We may see multiple NATO states choosing to take unilateral action against Russia, up to and including launching their own military attacks against it.

- In the Middle East, Iran may respond to the complete isolation of Russia in the aftermath of a nuclear attack by demanding that Russia give it nuclear technology in return for continued cooperation, trade, and military support.

- But more importantly, Iran may feel that if Russia can drop a tactical nuclear weapon and get away with it, so can it. That could be the moment when Iran sprints across the finish line of nuclear development.

All of the nuclear nations of the world are going to have to take a serious look at one another. Who else among them is willing to break the nuclear taboo? How far are they willing to go to punish another nuclear nation for breaking the taboo, and how will they prevent a runaway escalation of the crisis into an all-out nuclear exchange?

If you'll recall, I mentioned that a nuclear Iran is likely to lead to a Middle Eastern nuclear arms race. In turn, I suggested this will one day lead to someone using a nuclear weapon against its neighbor, which could set off a chain reaction of nuclear attacks that obliterates the Middle East. (We'll talk about this in much more detail in another chapter).

These are just a few of the more obvious possible outcomes of Putin using a nuclear weapon.

PUTIN'S RATIONALE

Would it be a rational decision for Vladimir Putin to preemptively strike Ukraine with a nuclear weapon? Not at all. My little list of possible responses to him doing so is far from complete, but it's certainly sufficient to make the point that it would be a truly insane decision for Putin to go nuclear.

If Putin uses a nuclear weapon, he has to know the world will do everything in its power to destroy him. Every rational nation in the world will turn against him.

But there's one nation in the world with a wholly irrational supreme leader. One nation whose leadership is obsessed with obtaining and using nuclear weapons, too.

Iran.

Iran is the one nation that not only will not turn its back on Putin but will likely reach out to offer Putin all the support it can.

NOTE: While North Korea also has a nuclear-obsessed and irrational leader, Pyongyang is firmly under the thumb of China. As goes China in this scenario, so will North Korea go.

We know the Iranians invented chess. We know they've been playing a secret chess game for twenty years in pursuit of obtaining a nuclear weapon. They're smart, and they're opportunistic. And Vladimir Putin going nuclear and getting himself ostracized by the entire world is just the opening the Iranian chess masters can and will capitalize on.

This is the moment when Iran will call in its favor owed for all the weapons and support it has given Russia throughout the Ukraine war. This is when Iran will ask for the final nuclear technology it needs to build its own nuclear weapons.

Putin will have nothing left to lose. He and his nation will be pariahs. Under his rule, Russia will wither and shrink into insignificance instead of regaining old glory and reconstituting the old USSR. He will have failed utterly. But, he might just have one last chance to snatch victory from the jaws of defeat.

If Putin were to give Iran what it needed to build nuclear weapons and the means to protect itself from attacks, a nuclear Iran would surely provoke a Middle East arms race. With or without a little Russian intervention and pot stirring, an eventual nuclear exchange could very well happen in the Middle East. And this would be a fantastic turn of events for Russia.

In the blink of an eye, a third of the world's oil production would be wiped off the map. Oil prices would skyrocket, and regardless of what sanctions might be in place to limit its oil sales, Russia would immediately have to be allowed to sell its oil to whomever it wanted at whatever price it wanted to charge. The alternative would be a global economic collapse of epic proportions.

Russia would be back in the driver's seat. Using massive oil profits, it could rebuild its economy and its military. It could engage in oil blackmail to force huge, oil poor nations like China and India to their knees. And it could position itself once more as a great superpower.

That's a chilling prospect, isn't it? Mind you, the scenario I just painted doesn't have to be rational. It doesn't even have to be workable. I'm just trying to make the point that if Vladimir Putin drops a nuclear weapon, we will know once and for all that we are dealing with an irrational monster, and all bets are off as to what he could do next.

I should point out that I didn't even discuss Putin going ahead and launching his entire nuclear arsenal in a fit of, "If Russia is destroyed, then I'll just destroy the whole world." That will have to wait for another book all its own.

THE BOTTOM LINE

Israel faces a series of terrible dilemmas as Iran draws close to building its first nuclear weapon.

Likewise, the entire world faces a series of terrible dilemmas if Vladimir Putin chooses to use a nuclear weapon.

Worse, if Putin chooses to go nuclear, that could be exactly the catalyst that causes Iran to go nuclear as well. We're going to spend the remainder of this book examining the possible outcomes if Iran does, in fact, achieve breakout and obtain nuclear weapons.

This is the looming crisis in the Middle East that might very well lead to a nuclear Armageddon and even to the End Times themselves.

COMMITTED TO ERADICATING ISRAEL

"Islam makes it incumbent on all adult males, provided they
are not disabled and incapacitated, to prepare themselves
for the conquest of other countries so that the writ of Islam
is obeyed in every country of the world."

—Ayatollah Ruhollah Khomeini,
published in Qom, 1948

A CORNERSTONE OF Ayatollah Khomeini's 1979 revolution in Iran was the religious conviction that Israel was an illegitimate state that Islam was destined to eliminate. Until now, Iran has lacked the military strength to make that threat a reality.

Should Iran achieve the capability to deliver even a crude atomic bomb of relatively low yield, the political equation in the Middle East would change immediately.

Americans would do well to remember that tiny Israel is the last firewall between a plague of suicide bombers and America, especially in light of the developments in Iran in the past two decades. In Iran, radical Islamic revolutionaries maintain their grip upon the nation and its people through a combination of religious fervor and brutal repression, in preparation for their planned final assault on Israel.

The radical religious extremists ruling Iran believe their destiny was pre-ordained by God, as written in the Koran and prophesied by Ayatollah Khomeini. Their mission is to establish their radical Islamic revolution worldwide.

The revolution begun by Khomeini in 1979 will not be accomplished successfully until Islam is victorious over all its enemies, most importantly triumphs over the dual archenemies of Israel and America. The radical clerics ruling Iran see world events playing right into their hands.

SHIITE BELIEFS IN CURENT TIMES

Shiites have a messianic belief that the way needs to be prepared for the return of the Twelfth Imam, much as many orthodox Jews await the appearance of the Messiah, and Evangelical Christians await the Second Coming of Jesus Christ.

Ayatollah Khomeini, as he and his followers saw it, was on a mission from God. As such, divine destiny preordained that Khomeini would return to Iran. Divine destiny preordained that the theocracy Khomeini would establish in Iran would sweep across the world.

Khomeini predicted that the Shah of Iran would be deposed, that the Soviet Union would dissolve, and that Saddam Hussein would lose control of Iraq and die. Since all of these prophecies came true, the Shiite faithful have no reason to question the inevitability of the ayatollah's final and most important prophecies—namely, that

Israel and America will be defeated and their destruction will usher in the second coming of the Mahdi.

The revolution Khomeini fomented was not just an Iranian revolution. The revolution was meant to be one in which all of Shiite Islam was destined by God to control all governments and all peoples wherever they might be. Nonbelievers did not fit into the mission. Nonbelievers were infidels, infidels were evil, and evil was destined to be destroyed.

Khomeini planned to establish the *velayat-e faqih,* the "rule of the jurisprudent." This utopian Islamic society would first be ruled by Khomeini, a theocratic philosopher-king with sufficient authority and wisdom to set the divine laws on earth and to exact just punishments.

But the Ayatollah died with his work unfinished. Before he died, Khomeini had succeeded only in establishing his theocracy in Iran. The Jews remained in Israel and America still held a strong military presence in the Middle East.

Two suicide attacks in 1983 drove the U.S. out of Lebanon. Those events have become the yardstick for all of Iran's more recent activities. They believe that if the heat is sufficient, America will retreat.

Ayatollah Khomeini's successor, Ayatollah Khamenei, and Iran's current president, Ebrahim Raisi carry on with the cause. These two leaders believe it is their divine mission to complete the radical Islamic revolution that Ayatollah Khomeini began.

Around 95% of Iran's 90 million citizens profess to believe in the Twelver teachings. It's impossible to know how accurate a number this, of course. Iran is a deeply authoritarian spy state with pervasive surveillance. No citizen of Iran would feel safe expressing anything but utter devotion to the state religion.

Worldwide, there are approximately 150 to 200 million Twelvers. They comprise the majority of the populations of Iran, Iraq, and Azerbaijan. Twelvers are a sizable minority in Bahrain, Lebanon, India, Pakistan, Afghanistan, Saudi Arabia. Bangladesh, Kuwait, Oman, UAE, Qatar, Nigeria, Chad, and Tanzania.

Twelvers are not just an Iranian phenomenon. They are a global presence, and as such are potentially a global threat. They are not a tiny, isolated group of zealots with an irrational desire to start a nuclear war in the Middle East. They span the globe, and they all share the goal of ushering in the return of the Mahdi.

THE SECOND COMING OF THE MAHDI

Shiite Muslims believe that the Twelfth Imam went into "occultation"—a form of being yet alive, but mystically hidden from view—when he disappeared down the well in 941 A.D. Devout Shiites believe the Mahdi will emerge from the well in his Second Coming. But first, they believe the world will go through great calamities and upheavals. This apocalypse will set the conditions for the Mahdi's return.

The sacred well devoted to the Twelfth Imam is today located within the Jamkaran Mosque in Qom, Iran. There, a green "post office" box over the well has been built to permit devout Shiites to write prayer requests on small pieces of paper and "mail" them to the Mahdi. The practice bears a resemblance to devout

Jews writing prayer requests to Yahweh on small pieces of paper that are placed in the cracks of the Western Temple Wall in Jerusalem.

The Jamkaran Mosque in Qom is also revered as the religious center from where Ayatollah Khomeini lived prior to being forced to leave Iran in exile. Here, Khomeini led his opposition to the Pahlavi dynasty.

The Iran Press Service operating out of Paris, France observed,

> "In private and public meetings, these [religious leaders inside Iran] insist that Government must stand firm to international pressures over the legitimate and natural right of Iran to have nuclear technology for the question is one of the ways to prepare for the re-apparition of the Mahdi."

Secular diplomats find it hard to believe that today the political leader of a nation would be driven by religious views. This short-sightedness blinds many to Iranian politicians' perception of their mission. They have committed their lives to preparing for the Second Coming of the Mahdi. They and the ayatollahs believe the moment is imminent for the Twelfth Imam to come out of occultation.

As the nuclear crisis with Iran deepens, millions of Christians worldwide are consulting the Bible and praying to sort out how current world events fit into "last days" prophecies. Similarly, millions of Iranians are listening to the teachings of the Ayatollah Khamenei, to prepare for the Second Coming of the Mahdi.

IRANIAN LEADERS REPEATEDLY
THREATEN ISRAEL

From the very beginning of the Islamic Revolution in Iran, its leadership has made no secret of its end goal to obtain nuclear weapons and to destroy Israel with them.

Before he became president of Iran, but after he was a prominent cleric in 2001, Akbar Hashemi Rafsanjani said of Israel:

> "If a day comes when the world of Islam is duly equipped with the arms Israel has in its possession (nuclear weapons), the strategy of colonialism would face a stalemate because application of an atomic bomb would not leave anything in Israel, but the same thing would just produce damages in the Muslim world."

His meaning was clear. Iran was willing to sustain whatever collateral damage came of a nuclear attack on tiny, crowded Israel, safe in the assumption that all of Israel would be destroyed, but only some of the Shiite chosen in more geographically spread out Iran would be similarly devastated.

Several years later in 2005, President Ahmadinajad, who succeeded Rafsanjani in the office said:

> "Our dear Imam (Khomeini) ordered that the occupying regime in Jerusalem must be wiped off the face of the earth. This was a very wise statement. . .Very soon, this stain of disgrace [Israel] will be purged from the center of the Islamic world—and this is attainable."

In 2015, President Raisi said:

"The Zionist regime [Israel], you should know that
. . . if you take the slightest move against our nation,
our armed forces will target the heart of the Zionist
regime."

In 2020, Ayatollah Khamenei's spokesman said in a fiery
sermon:

"The global arrogance led by America with com-
plicity of Israel seeks to delay the realization of an
important issue, which is the destruction of the
Zionist regime."

Esmail Ghaani, the commander of Iran's Quds Force, which
manages most of Iran's military, intelligence and political affairs in
Iraq, Syria, Lebanon and Yemen, said in August of 2022:

"Hezbollah's sons are making plans to bring down
the last blow against the Zionist regime. . .and to
realize the wish of Imam Khomeini to eradicate
Israel from the map and the face of the Earth. The
enemies of [Iran's] Islamic government, led by
America and the Zionist regime should know that
we will never stop self-sacrifice and will move forward on the path of resistance.

The honorable path of martyrs will be pursued
until the complete destruction of the enemies of the
Islamic system. These two traitor and murderous

regimes will receive a response in the shortest time for each crime they commit. The Islamic Republic makes plans to respond to all crimes that America and the usurper Zionist regime commit and will give its decisive answer at the appropriate time."

Iran's message has always been clear and unequivocal. Its end goal is the total destruction of Israel and the United States. This litany of pronouncements is virtually a declaration of war on Israel. Will the world community come to the defense of Israel when Iran finally attacks it? Or is Israel on its own to defend itself?

How will Israel endure the menace posed by Iran? This is a question we can no longer avoid asking, not in the face of a growing nuclear threat from an increasingly defiant Iran. A confrontation with Iran is building to the point where a crisis is inevitable. Rapidly, Israel is approaching the point where only one alternative is left to assure the survival of the Jewish state.

CHAPTER TWENTYTWO:

HOW WILL ISRAEL ENDURE?

"For Israel, no doubt, an Iranian nuclear bomb is a nightmare.
An Iranian nuclear bomb is a threat to our existence. No doubt about it.
This is the reason that I claim we should stop it. But we,
and when I say we, must stop Iran from getting a nuclear weapon.
I consider all the Western world must be involved in stopping Iran
because Iran considers Israel as part of the West.
Defeating Israel is a stage for Iran on the way to defeating the West.
So, we, the West, and of course, Israel, should do our best not to allow
this unconventional regime to acquire unconventional capabilities."

— **General Moshe Ya'alon,**
former Chief of Staff, Israeli Defense Force (IDF)

IS ISRAEL'S SURVIVAL ON THE LINE?

Israel remains a one-bomb state, in that one nuclear weapon, even one of relatively small size, detonated successfully over Tel Aviv would destroy the modern Jewish state as we know it.

Israel has only two major cities, Jerusalem and Tel Aviv. Jerusalem is approaching a population of a million people, and the Tel Aviv-Haifa metropolitan area has a population of 4.4 million people. Israel's total population is about 9.1 million people as of early 2023.

Tel Aviv is the business and finance center of Israel. Its destruction would plunge Israel into financial chaos, compounded by a telecommunications nightmare, to say nothing of the massive human suffering inflicted by such a strike.

Iran has 3,000+ ballistic missiles, most of which can reach Israel. Syria has several hundred military ballistic missiles and chemical warheads. Hezbollah has tens of thousands of smaller rockets, which are not devastating individually but would comprise a serious threat to Israel if launched simultaneously.

While Israel has very advanced air defense systems, they are not 100% impenetrable. If a massive barrage of missiles and rockets were launched at Israel simultaneously along with one or more nuclear weapons, in the chaos of thousands of incoming missiles, would Israeli's defense forces be able to pick out the handful of nuclear warheads and destroy them all before one of them destroyed Israel? More to the point, is Israel willing to take that risk?

DOES AMERICA HAVE THE RESOLVE THIS CRISIS WILL TAKE?

I have given much thought to a conversation I had in 1982. I was summoned to New York by Reuven Hecht, who was then-aide to Prime Minister Menachem Begin. Israel had just invaded Lebanon to root out Arafat's terrorist infrastructure.

Hecht had just come from Washington, where he had just met with then-secretary of state Alexander Haig. The conversation shook Hecht. Haig told him that, after the terrorist bombing of the Marine barracks in Beirut, the Reagan Administration had decided to pull out of Lebanon. America was no longer going to support Israel's war against terrorism in Lebanon. Hecht was in shock.

I did not know how to respond. I too was in shock. How were we going to defeat radical Islam, I wondered then, if we couldn't stay the course in much-less contentious Lebanon? Yes, the casualties in Lebanon were horrible, but the victims were Marines. My mind flashed to the staggering casualties our Marines took in the island warfare against Japan in World War II. Still, America continued, despite the fatalities, until we were victorious. Were we now going to abandon Israel in its fight against Hezbollah in Lebanon, and in its larger, existential fight against eradication as a nation? Unfortunately, that is exactly what we did.

Today we stand at yet another crossroads, much like 1982. How strong is America's resolve? What will the Middle East look like twenty years from now? Will Israel endure if Iran does succeed in developing nuclear weapons? Iran is at the center of the terror network today, attacking both Israel and America. Will we and Israel have the resolve to stand up to the mullahs, or will we lack the determination to protect ourselves once again?

RUSSIA'S MIDDLE EAST OBJECTIVES

Russia sees that Iran has real potential to advance Russian objectives in the Middle East.

The lines of alliance go from Russia to Iran to Syria. All three oppose a continued active presence of the United States in the Middle East. Without Israel, the United States would lose our major ally in the region. Without Israel, we would lose the oldest, most established, and *only* democracy in the Middle East.

David Kramer, Executive Director of the George W. Bush Institute, in 2022 described the Middle East like this:

"The region has experienced terrible violence, crackdowns, chaos, and a return to authoritarianism. . .Democracy in the Middle East, in other words, looks like a desert."

The Middle East is again at a pivotal point. If Israel is defeated as Iran intends, the democracy movement in the Middle East may die so completely that reviving it will be virtually impossible.

Russia clearly hopes to strengthen its position in the Middle East balance of power equation by supporting Syria and Iran as much as possible, particularly if and when those nations attack or weaken Israel.

Russia continues to maintain a military presence in Syria, although the demands of its war with Ukraine have greatly reduced that presence for the moment. Likewise, Russia's war against Ukraine is causing the current flow of military equipment and weapons to flow from Iran to Russia instead of from Russia to its Middle East allies. When the Russia-Ukraine War ends, however, we can expect to see a sharp reversal of that flow. . .assuming Russia's economy remains intact enough to produce weapons for foreign sale.

As long as the United States continues to maintain a strong military presence in the Middle East, Russia will remain nervous. Russia will see anything that damages the U.S. position in the region as an opportunity for Russian gain.

Should Iran be attacked by Israel, Iran can count on Russia's unconditional support. But can Israel count on the unqualified support of the United States? Today, I'm not so sure.

One thing I do know for sure. The threat to Israel is real and immediate. It is surrounded by enemies, many of whom have deep ties with Iran. Multiple terrorist organizations in the region receive weapons, training, and financial support from Iran, and in return, these terror networks take their orders from Iran.

Many years ago, then Prime Minister Benjamin Netanyahu made a prescient observation. Once again Prime Minister of Israel, his comments hold as true today as they did then:

> "One thing I can tell you for sure, is that this leopard will not change its spots. Hamas is a beast that will not be domesticated—it is like the Taliban. When the Taliban came to power, people said, 'Power will make them more responsible.' That did not happen.
>
> It is the same with the ayatollahs. When the ayatollahs came into power, people said, 'Power will make them more responsible.' Yet it did not happen. The Taliban destroyed Afghanistan. The Taliban invited al-Qaeda to establish terror camps inside Afghanistan. There Bin Laden trained the hijackers who flew into the World Trade Center.
>
> If Mohammad Atta had nuclear weapons on 9/11, don't you think he would have used them? This is the problem we have with Iran, and it is same with all who take their orders from Tehran—including both Hamas and Hezbollah."

I have known Benjamin Netanyahu for many years, and I have never heard him as serious as he was that day, contemplating the threat from Iran.

And that threat has moved considerably closer, now.

THE FIGHT OF CIVILIZATIONS

Many years ago, I had the honor of interviewing General Moshe Ya'alon, then the retired Chief of Staff of the Israeli Defense Forces. I quoted him from that interview to open this chapter, in fact. In our discussion, he cogently described the threat facing not only Israel, but the entire world. Unfortunately, his words have proven to be prophetic.

General Ya'alon believed that the fight against Islam was a fight of cultures, a fight of civilizations. Israel might today be in the lead position, but ultimately radical Islam is at war with America and with the West in general:

> "What we are facing today is not just the challenge of the Israeli-Palestinian conflict, or the challenge of the Israeli-Arab conflict. It has become, in the last decade, a clash between civilizations—a conflict between Islam and the infidels. This is the challenge today, not just for the State of Israel; this is the challenge for the Western world, and we should not ignore it.
>
> Listening to Khaled Mashaal, the Hamas leader, in his victory speech in the Damascus mosque, February 12, 2006, after the elections. He said, "The

nation of Islam will sit on the throne of the world, and the world will be full of remorse." He didn't speak just about the Palestinian people; he spoke about the nation of Islam.

He didn't speak just about Israel; he spoke about the West. This the way Khaled Mashaal feels, and I'm not surprised. This is the way that the Muslim Brotherhood in Egypt sees this, as a clash between the Western world and Islam.

They claim to impose what they call national Islam, a new caliphate to defeat the West, to defeat the Western culture, to defeat the Western values. Not to allow any Christianity or Judaism—no infidels. All the world would be Muslim. And they mean it.

Unfortunately, in the last couple of years, those elements are encouraged by the lack of determination on the behalf of Israel and the West. This is the case of Osama bin Laden. . . He planned to defeat the West. And this is the case with President Ahmadinejad. When he said in Teheran that Israel should be wiped off the map. . . he saw a world without Israel and without America.

You have to listen to what Ahmadinejad is saying. He is talking about a nation of Islam all over the world, defeating the West, and on the way to defeating the West, Israel should be annihilated. . . wiped off the map. He means it.

What they are doing now, all of them, Hamas, al-Qaeda, Iran is terrorism. . . terrorism against Israel, terrorism against Western targets. . . they are using terrorism, threatening the regimes with the assassination of their leaders, and this is the Hamas, al-Qaeda, Iranian way to deal with our culture, with our values.

This is the challenge, not just to the State of Israel. We need a wake-up call in Israel, but we need a wake-up call everywhere, in Europe and in the United States to understand the situation, not to ignore it, but to deal with it.

And we are strong enough in the West to deal with it, either to prevent the Iranian nuclear capabilities or at least, to demonstrate more determination by forcing Iran to pay the price.

Yet if we don't isolate Iran or impose sanctions, the Iranians do not pay the price. They are sure that the West is afraid of them; this is the case. So, this is a challenge, not just for the State of Israel; this is a challenge for the Western world today.

The only way to deal with it is moral clarity, strategic clarity, and strategic decisions."

A few of the names from that conversation have changed: President Ahmadinejad has been replaced by President Raisi; Ayman al-Zawahiri was killed by U.S. troops in Pakistan, and a new Al

Qaeda leader has yet to emerge; ISIS can be added to the general's list of terrorists.

But the core message of the general's comments remains as true today as it was the day he spoke with me:

> Radical Islamic terrorists are at war with the West. Whether we like it or not, this war will continue as long as countries like Iran have reason to believe they will not be stopped in their pursuit of terrorism to advance their religious cause worldwide. . .and as long as Iran believes it will one day build a nuclear weapon of its own that it can use to annihilate its enemies.

PART V:

THE

CHALLENGE

TO

AMERICA

CHAPTER TWENTYTHREE:

WE ARE AT A CROSSROADS

"The defeat of a nuclear power in a conventional war
may trigger a nuclear war. Nuclear powers have never lost
major conflicts on which their fate depends."

—Dmitry Medvedev,
former Russian President, September, 2022

"First of all, our main enemy is certainly the United States.
What does the U.S. react to? They react to two things:
the threat of physical annihilation and the liquidation of a certain
number of military personnel. What we know based on wars
in Vietnam and Korea is that several tens of thousands of annihilated
American servicemen will cause the public opinion in the U.S. to be
severely strained. . .this is one of the objectives if we want to influence
the American leadership. We have absolutely nothing to lose."

— Yevgeny Satanovsky,
President of the Institute of the Middle East in Russia

THIS IS A HISTORIC MOMENT

Those who saw the coming Nazi threat in the 1930s were likely to be written off as alarmists, at least until Hitler invaded Poland and turned his armies toward France.

Now, we're watching Vladimir Putin invade Ukraine. He makes no secret of his plan to continue on to taking Moldova, Georgia, and Armenia next. In February of 2023, a classified Russian document was leaked outlining Putin's plan to take over Belarus after he completes his conquest of Ukraine. Like Hitler, he will only stop invading and conquering when the rest of the world goes to war against him and makes him stop.

Stopping Hitler in the 1940s cost the world an estimated 60 million deaths in scores of countries across the globe. Will stopping Putin. . .and an atomic Iran. . .cost 600 million deaths in an international nuclear war? Only time will tell.

Today the international diplomatic resolve to bring Iran's nuclear program within genuinely transparent IAEA inspection seems lacking. The JCPOA has been collapsed for years, and Iran continues to make outrageous and unreasonable demands before reinstating the agreement. All that's transparent about Iran right now is its complete lack of interest in restoring any nuclear inspection protocol in Iran.

As clearly as world diplomats preferred appeasement in the 1930s, today world diplomats continue to believe that strong admonitions will have a deterrent effect upon the religious zealots who control Iran's radical Islamic regime.

Now is the moment for decisive leadership on Iran. Will the United States step up and support Israel as the showdown with Iran enters the endgame that will ultimately determine who wins and who loses? These questions remain to be answered.

ISRAEL'S "OCTOPUS DOCTRINE"

Mossad Director, David Barnea describes the Octopus Doctrine this way:

"If Iranian proxies come after us, we will hit Iran directly," he said. "We will convince the leader [Khamenei] that terror is not worth it and too costly. . . We will not close our eyes to the proven truth.

The Iranian regime will have no immunity. The Iranian leadership must understand that attacks against Israel or Israelis, directly or indirectly by proxies, will be met with a painful retaliation. . . We will not pursue the proxies, but the ones who armed them and gave the orders, and this will happen in Iran."

Meaning, if any Iranian proxies target Iran in the future, Iran will be held directly responsible by Israel. Furthermore, Israel is reserving the right to respond with military force directly against Iran instead of against the proxy attacker.

Israeli officials have revealed a name for this strategy: the "Octopus Doctrine." In a June interview, former Israel prime minister Naftali Bennett explained, "We no longer play with the tentacles, with Iran's proxies: we've created a new equation by going for the head."

IRAN'S RESPONSE

So far, Iran has responded with fury to Israel's direct attacks. In lieu of shutting down nuclear facilities, Iran is building bigger and more protected ones. Iran is building its newest underground facility deep into the mountains, where it can withstand the U.S.'

cyberattacks and Israeli bunker-penetrating bombs, mitigating against potential damage in future attacks.

Israel now faces a more protracted problem as it does not possess the necessary weapons to damage the new underground facilities effectively. This reality could embolden Iran to ramp up uranium production because it knows Israel alone is incapable of stopping it.

In addition to fortifying its nuclear facilities from attacks, Iran has also reduced the visibility of international monitoring organizations. In 2022, Iran switched off surveillance cameras used by the IAEA to monitor activity at the country's key nuclear facilities.

Israel's strategy also appears to have increased Iran's desire to retaliate. The recent removal of Hossein Taeb, the Iran Revolutionary Guard Corps (IRGC) intelligence chief, exemplifies this strengthened desire to respond aggressively. Taeb was removed from office following thirteen years of service after receiving internal criticism for his failed attempts to protect Iran against Israeli attacks. As an analyst close to Iran's government said, "He had failed to stop Israel's infiltration and wasn't very successful in retaliation operations outside the borders."

The removal of Taeb demonstrates Iran's push to become more aggressive in its attempts to punish Israel. Taeb will likely be replaced with someone more aggressive and willing to reciprocate, increasing tensions and making diplomatic solutions unlikely.

WHY ISRAEL IS IMPORTANT TO AMERICA

Is Israel's survival important to America's national security today? Are we right to defend Israel at all costs, even against an Iranian nuclear threat? In the context of a coming nuclear showdown between Israel and Iran, these questions take on added importance.

Israel is the only stable democracy in the Middle East. Without Israel, the United States would have no ally with which to counterbalance Russia's ambitions to dominate the region.

Iran's radical Islamic religion is anti-democratic by nature. The Islamic Republic of Iran is a theocracy. All political authority in the government derives from the unquestioned decision-making of the Supreme Leader, Ayatollah Khamenei, the nation's top cleric.

If America were to abandon Israel in the face of the threat from Iran, we would send a message the Middle East would be sure to hear: that our commitment to democracy was not strong enough for us to stand by Israel in a moment of challenge and need. If America abandons its longtime and close ally Israel, how can any democracy anywhere in the world rely upon America's offer of support? This is a message America cannot afford to send, not if we value our own freedom at home.

Russia, which has acted through surrogate states since the heyday of Stalin, would relish the defeat of Israel. America, on the other hand, would face a radical Middle East completely dominated by Islamic authoritarianism. As long as we remain dependent on the Middle East for oil, this would be nothing short of a catastrophe for the United States.

Israel is also vital to the United States because it stands in the breach between a nuclear Iran and us. Iran has returned to a policy of direct confrontation that we have not seen in the Middle East since Israel's founding in 1948, when Egypt tried to destroy it. In the 1950s, Egypt's ally was Russia. Egypt fought Israel primarily with the military arms provided for the purpose by the Soviet Union. Once again, Russia has sided against Israel, this time allying with Syria and Iran.

Iran is happy to give Russia military assistance in Ukraine now because it hopes to receive payment in the final nuclear technology it needs to build its own nuclear weapons. Iran's agenda is to expand its radical revolution through the region, and ultimately worldwide, whether or not that conforms with Russia's nationalistic interests in the Middle East.

AN ISRAELI PREEMPTIVE STRIKE AGAINST IRAN

For a relatively small country with limited economic resources, preemptive first strikes are best suited to take tactical advantage of Israel's superior technological military sophistication and training.

Israel can be expected to launch a preemptive strike on Iran the moment Israel is convinced it is the midnight hour. If America backs down, Israel will be forced to do this alone, no matter how great the cost to the Jewish people.

European diplomats have argued that Iran could be contained even after it has a nuclear weapon. They believe classic deterrence theories of preventing self-destruction would keep Iran from using nuclear weapons.

The first problem with pursuing a containment strategy is a single nuclear bomb will destroy Israel. Iran doesn't need to build an entire arsenal to destroy its enemy. The world would have to stop Iran from getting any bombs at all to "contain" it.

The second problem with a containment strategy is Iran can only be contained diplomatically if its leaders are rational enough to fear nuclear retaliation by Israel that will obliterate Iran and most of its population.

Military planners in the United States and Israel have gone over various war scenarios. They agree that the most likely pre-emptive attack seems to be a targeted Israeli air attack on selected Iranian nuclear facilities. Most military professionals expect the attack to be coordinated with U.S. military forces in the region and Saudi Arabia, if only to grant Israel air-rights over Saudi Arabia.

An attack led by a missile strike, including sea launched cruise missiles, would save Israel's fighter jets for later sorties. The distance problems inherent in an Israeli air strike on Iran make refueling a likely part of the operation. A cruise missile attack, however, could target major facilities, such as Isfahan and Natanz, as well as Iran's reactor at Bushehr and their heavy-water facility at Arak, inflicting major damage before any fighter plane had to enter Iranian air space.

A missile attack by Israel would have the added advantage of not engaging any new fighter jets Iran might obtain from Russia. It remains to be seen if Russia will provide Iran with some sort of advanced anti-missile defense system, and if so, whether it will be sufficient to stop Israel's missiles.

Win or lose in Ukraine, Russia is going to have to rebuild its economy and its own military resources before it can consider providing surface-to-air defense missiles or advanced anti-missile systems to Iran. Depending on the degree of destruction to the Russian economy, military stockpiles, and production capabilities, it may take some years before Russia is able to share much by way of weaponry with Iran.

Russia might agree to share technology for building its own advanced anti-missile systems to Iran, but that, too, will take years for Iran to understand and implement. Either way, Israel still has a small window of opportunity to make a preemptive missile strike on Iran.

It's probable that Israel would have no appetite for a prolonged ground war with Iran involving its ground forces. If war comes, we should expect Israel to hit first and to hit hard. The goal will be to destroy or severely damage Iran's nuclear program so as to postpone indefinitely the day when Iran might be expected to have deliverable nuclear weapons.

CAN A WAR WITH IRAN BE AVERTED?

Both Israel and the United States have stated repeatedly that Iran armed with nuclear weapons is unacceptable.

Clearly Iran has continued to pursue getting nuclear weapons, anyway. Using a combination of obfuscation, zigzag diplomatic maneuvering, and outright lies, Iran has successfully bought itself much needed time to work on developing its nuclear program. But the patience of the international diplomatic community has worn thin.

On key issues, like rejoining the JCPOA or resuming IAEA inspections of its nuclear facilities, Iran has become increasingly unwilling to negotiate. Iran openly insists that pursuing the "full nuclear fuel cycle" is within Iran's sovereign rights. Iran insists that uranium enrichment should and will be pursued on its own soil, regardless of what world diplomats say.

In the absence of any concessions by Iran, how is diplomacy

to succeed? Iran is acting as if the mullahs have concluded that eventually the Europeans and the IAEA will give in, abandoning the United States and Israel.

If Iran wanted to assure the world community that the regime's nuclear purposes were entirely peaceful, establishing transparency in the Iranian nuclear program should not be difficult. Russia has clearly indicated a willingness to provide Iran all the enriched uranium needed to run nuclear technology for peaceful purposes. The IAEA is more than willing to conduct the type of inspections that could put even the United States and Israel at ease. Yet, rather than complying, Iran is stonewalling the negotiations to resume inspections, refusing to make concessions.

For the United States and Israel to accept a nuclear armed Iran, both countries would need to see meaningful confirmation that Iran had accepted Israel's legitimate right to exist. Iran would have to drop demands that the Jewish state should disappear in the Middle East or relocate to Europe.

In addition, the United States and Israel would also require proof that Iran has stopped funding and supporting anti-Israel and anti-American terrorist groups including Hezbollah, Hamas, Islamic Jihad, and various other jihadist groups. Nothing in the current posture of the Islamic Republic of Iran gives any reason to believe Iran is ready to make this necessary concession.

What the United States and Israel are increasingly unwilling to do is to give Iran more latitude within which to conceal a covert nuclear weapons program. Thus, the United States and Israel have moved toward bright-line tests. If Iran continues uranium processing and enrichment at both Isfahan and Natanz, then the risk of a preemptive military strike escalates. The U.S. and Israel have asked Iran to resume their voluntary moratorium on uranium enrichment. Iran refused. At this point, negotiating with Iran is at an impasse.

CAN IRAN OUTMANEUVER EVERYONE?

In the past, Iran has been good at wiggling out of diplomatic tight moments. It appears to have calculated correctly that world diplomatic resolve will eventually crack and crumble. Iran is counting on Russia and China to oppose any Security Council vote to tighten sanctions on it or to take any direct UN action against its nuclear program.

Absent international resolve to stop Iran diplomatically, military action is the only recourse to change Iran's nuclear direction. Conceivably, this dance of double talk, global inaction, and occasional Israeli sabotage, could go on until Iran has a nuclear weapon ready to deliver. Then the game will shift to whether or not Iran can be deterred from using the weapon.

Iran appears resolutely headed in a confrontational direction.

Israel has survived since 1948 by being aware of the reality of politics in a hostile world. For 75 years since achieving statehood, Israel has lived constantly on the edge, always ready to face the ultimate existential threat—that a hostile Islamic neighbor might someday succeed in wiping the Jewish state off the map.

For the Iranians to outmaneuver the world's diplomats, they must also outmaneuver Israel diplomatically. And that is unlikely to happen. Israel is pragmatic, clear-headed, wary, and alert where Iran is concerned.

What is much more likely is that Israel's patience will run out. At that point, history predicts Israel will launch a preemptive attack against Iran, regardless of what the consequences may be. Israel knows that to strike first offers the best chance of victory.

In this game of nuclear chicken, Israel cannot afford to wait too long, not when the outcome may be that Iran secretly does develop nuclear weapons and decides this time to be the one who strikes first.

WHAT IF ISRAEL ATTACKS?

⸻

"Regarding Iran, Israel will take whatever action
is necessary to protect itself."

—Prime Minister Benjamin Netanyahu

THE SAMPSON OPTION

Israel's nuclear weapons have always been considered the core
of what has commonly been known as the *Sampson Option*. The
strategy is named after the biblical story of Sampson using his great
strength to bring down a temple, killing a great number of enemy
Philistines, as well as himself, in the process (Judges 16: 4-30).

Israel has sworn "never again" in relation to the possibility of
another Holocaust. Given this determination, the *Sampson Option*
postulates that Israel would be willing to use extreme measures if
the country's survival was at stake.

In the crisis with Iran, the *Sampson Option* means that Israel
would attack Iran in a preemptive war and would be willing to use
nuclear weapons. Iran's possession of nuclear weapons is seen as a

threat to Israel's continued existence. In other words, Israel might be willing to attack Iran even if the result of an Israeli preemptive strike ended up being retaliation by Iran that caused Israel's destruction.

The Israelis judge that destruction in a military conflict with an aggressor like Iran would still be better than doing nothing and waiting to be destroyed. Passivity in the face of aggression has always been judged to be a fatal mistake European Jews made against Hitler.

"Never again!" is the oath the Israelis swear to make clear to aggressors that they will never sit by idly again. In extreme situations, Israel can be expected to attack, rather than to delay too long. This is why Israel's patience for negotiations with the mullahs can be expected to run out at some point. Israel knows the mullahs are trying to buy time and that time in this crisis works against Israel.

ISRAEL'S NUCLEAR ARSENAL

Israel's current nuclear arsenal opens up many strategic possibilities short of the *Sampson Option*.

Israel has relatively low-yield tactical nuclear weapons that can be selectively fired to eliminate specific targets. They could be used to hit the type of hardened underground centrifuge farm which Iran has built at Natanz to enrich uranium.

Israel's strategic nuclear warheads can be fired at large urban areas. The Jericho III is truly an intercontinental ballistic missile with a range of around 3,000 miles, (4,800 kilometers).

Israel also has cruise missiles that can be adapted with nuclear warheads such as the Popeye Turbo that is designed to be air-launched from Israel's F-15 and F-16 fighter jets. The Popeye Turbo can also be launched from the three Dolphin-class submarines the Germans built for Israel.

Conceivably, Israel could mix tactical nuclear weapons delivered via fighter aircraft with cruise missiles fired from sea. Higher-yield nuclear warheads deliverable by Israel's Jericho missiles would most likely be held in reserve, waiting to see what retaliatory response Iran launches and how the war escalates from the initial attack.

IRAN OBJECTS TO ISRAEL'S NUCLEAR WEAPONS

Iran continually complains about the one-sided nature of U.S. foreign policy in the Middle East. America accepts Israel's nuclear weapons program, but U.S. government officials have repeatedly stated their clear determination that Iran will not be permitted to develop nuclear weapons capability.

Iran retorts that their developing nuclear weapons would be a counterforce to Israel's nuclear weapons, much as Pakistan's nuclear arsenal keeps India in check. Pursuing this logic, the Iranians have argued that their development of nuclear weapons capability would stabilize the region. The object would be to take away Israel's ability to act unilaterally. Clearly, Israel has a tactical advantage as the only nuclear-armed Middle Eastern state.

The United States counters that Iran's history of supporting terrorism and its openly belligerent posture against Jews remove Iran from the community of peace-minded states. We argue that Iran's goal is to destabilize the Middle East while Israel's goal is regional stability.

Iran has also suggested that their nuclear weapons capabilities might be developed, but not fully. In other words, Iran would pursue nuclear weapons development to "within the turn of a screw" of being completely functional but would stop there. This way Iran would never actually make an atomic bomb, even though it would be capable of making one relatively quickly.

Again, America is skeptical. Iran's well-documented attempts to repeatedly conceal material aspects of its nuclear program give us pause. Who knows if Iran would keep their word on this promise? What would happen if Iran lied and actually did make a few atomic weapons?

Besides, if Iran were permitted to develop nuclear weapons technology to an advanced point, internal political pressures would surely push Iran's scientists to go all the way. Zealots among the mullahs might insist that nuclear weapons be produced clandestinely, under the cover of being "ready to make" nuclear weapons.

IRAN'S ABILITY TO RETALIATE AGAINST ISRAEL

Iran's nuclear facilities were constructed in anticipation of Israel or the United States launching a preemptive strike at some point.

The mullahs learned from the Israeli attack in 1981 on Iraq's nuclear reactor at Osirak. Iraq's Osirak facility was geographically compact, hence relatively easy to hit with a targeted military strike. In contrast, Iran's nuclear facilities are now geographically dispersed, with several important research facilities embedded in heavily populated areas.

Still, Israel could target five or six major facilities, such as the uranium processing plant at Isfahan, the uranium enrichment plant at Natanz, the heavy water facility at Arak, and the Russian-built reactor at Bushehr.

In January, 2023, Israel launched a drone attack on the Iranian production facility at Isfahan. Several explosions appear to have damaged buildings above ground, but not to have damaged the underground centrifuges.

Iranians angrily decried the attack and announced that no damage was done. The Israelis, however, appear delighted at the results of their attack. As well they should be. Drones are slow, relatively easy targets to shoot down. If the Israelis can insert three drones into Iranian airspace and strike an important nuclear enrichment plant with impunity, it bodes very well, indeed, for a serious attack by Israel to destroy the entire centrifuge array.

Of course, military experience as far back as the massive allied strategic bombing campaign against the Nazis in World War II demonstrates how quickly bombed machinery can be recovered and operations restored. At best, an Israeli attack on Iranian enrichment and weapons development sites would slow down the progress of the Iranian nuclear weapons program. At worst, world reaction against Israel might go very badly.

In the face of an Israeli attack, Iran might easily win global agreement that now Iran has a clear case for pursuing of nuclear weapons for self-defense. European countries trying to contain Iran's nuclear efforts now might reverse their position. Some European nations would inevitably see opportunities to seize lucrative Iranian nuclear technology contracts. Iran might rebuild relatively quickly, ending up with better or newer versions of whatever nuclear facilities an Israeli preemptive military strike managed to destroy.

Israel needs to consider carefully before attacking Iran. Even should it succeed in scoring major damage on Iran's nuclear facilities by launching a surprise, preemptive air attack, Israel might ultimately lose.

In retaliation for a military strike on Iran, Hezbollah would undoubtedly launch rocket attacks on Israel from Lebanon. Hamas would probably launch rocket attacks from the Gaza. The Syrian government might decide to join in and launch its ballistic missiles at Israel. We might even see a resumption of the suicide bombings that marked the Palestinian *intifada*.

IRAN WOULD RETALIATE WITH MISSILE ATTACKS

Iran's military is no match for the United States or for Israel, not in any type of a conventional war. The U.S. military could easily defeat Iran's military on the battlefield, though a land invasion would be costly to the U.S. and probably extremely unpopular.

In response to a preemptive Israeli strike, the Iranians would most likely retaliate with missile attacks that could be quite harmful both to the United States and Israel. Shahab-3 missiles, even conventionally armed, could cause considerable casualties on U.S. military bases throughout the Gulf Region. All of Israel's cities, as well as Israel's nuclear facilities at Dimona in the Negev Desert are within range of Iran's Shahab-3.

Israel's Iron Dome Air Defense System is highly effective, and Israel is in the middle of designing the next generation anti-missile defense system, Iron Beam. But while these anti-missile defenses might be effective in stopping several missile attacks at once, the defense system would have trouble taking down many missiles at once.

Russia, as we have noted, may agree to supply Iran with updated surface-to-air, anti-missile defense systems. Once these are in place, an Israeli attack on Iran's nuclear facilities would be much harder.

Moreover, after an Israeli strike on Iran, Russia could very well decide to enter the conflict on the side of Iran. This would pit the United States and Russia head-to-head even more directly than in the current Russia-Ukraine war.

COULD IRAN RETALIATE AGAINST OIL TANKERS?

Iran could also retaliate against the United States by attacking oil tankers in the Persian Gulf. Iran maintains a key geographical position on the northern coast of the Strait of Hormuz, positioning Iran to easily attack oil shipments passing through the Gulf.

The U.S. Energy Information Agency (EIA) explains the strategic importance of the Strait of Hormuz flow of oil in the Gulf:

> "The vast majority (about 90%) of oil exported from the Persian Gulf transits by tanker through the Straits of Hormuz, located between Oman and Iran. The Strait consists of 2-mile-wide channels for inbound and outbound tanker traffic, as well as a 2-mile-wide buffer zone. Oil flowing through the Strait of Hormuz accounts for roughly two-fifths of all world traded oil, and closure of the Strait of

Hormuz would require use of longer alternative routes (if available) at increased transportation costs."

Iran attacking shipping in the Straits of Hormuz would be a perfect example of "asymmetric warfare," wherein disproportionate damage is inflicted by a weaker enemy using minimal force at a strategic point of attack.

HOW LIKELY IS ISRAEL TO ATTACK?

The key insight in evaluating *Sampson Option* thinking is that Israel remains a one-bomb state. As Iran advances to develop an atomic bomb covertly, Israel may have no recourse but to attack.

The point of the *Sampson Option* is that Israel must be willing to use desperate tactics if there is no other way to stop an enemy set on the destruction of the Jewish state.

Remember, Israel today is the strongest military power in the Middle East. It could destroy Iran's most important nuclear facilities by launching a massive missile attack/air strike designed to last a few days at most. If Iran retaliated aggressively, Israel could expand the attack on Iran with tactical nuclear weapons, suggesting Israel's willingness to escalate the conflict if necessary.

A ground invasion of Iran by Israel is out of the question. Such a scenario would mobilize the entire Islamic world. It would produce a tactical dilemma for Israel even to get into the country.

If Israel did decide to launch a preemptive air strike on Iran, the *Sampson Option* would be exercised, and Israel would go on high nuclear alert. Iran would most certainly retaliate with missiles and call for terrorist attacks on Jews worldwide. And then Israel would, itself, face a dilemma of whether or not to escalate to using nuclear weapons.

This would not have posed a huge problem for Israel prior to the outbreak of the Russia-Ukraine war. But now that Russia and Iran have become so closely allied, an escalation to tactical nuclear weapons in Iran might very well draw a retaliatory response from Russia that complicates the matter greatly.

CHAPTER TWENTYFIVE:

WHAT IF AMERICA ATTACKS?

"I made it clear, and I'll make it clear again,
that we will use military might to protect our ally Israel."

—President George W. Bush

THE UNITED STATES could take some preparatory steps to move military resources into the region in case a preemptive strike against Iran became necessary. Moving more military forces to the region would signal to Iran the seriousness of the United States to stand by its declaration that Iran will not be permitted to have nuclear weapons.

At the same time, the U.S. government's goal will surely be to use every diplomatic measure possible to make clear that the goal is to get Iran to abandon its nuclear ambitions, allow complete IAEA inspections, and rejoin the JCPOA.

Currently, regime change is not the policy of the U.S. government toward Iran. The United States State Department could announce that U.S. foreign policy toward Iran has been changed such that regime change is now our goal. This would be a strong message to dissidents inside Iran as well as to the ex-patriot Iranian freedom-fighting community worldwide.

The State Department could back up the announcement by making financial resources available to support non-governmental organizations in the United States with the capabilities of support-ing dissidents in Iran. Congress could advance new legislation with the aim of providing even more funding for the State Department to disperse to responsible organizations capable of affecting regime change in Iran.

All these efforts could be put in place short of going to war. If Iran sees the U.S. government moving toward a regime change policy, perhaps the additional pressure would warn Iran not to continue in a defiant path.

However, the United States will encounter the same dilemma Israel already has. What if the government of Iran is not rational? Whereas a rational regime might be alarmed if the United States announced its intent to facilitate regime change, an irrational regime might respond even more defiantly and aggressive.

U.S. MILITARY PREPARATIONS FOR WAR

What military preparedness steps could be taken in advance of an attack?

Here are the types of military preparedness steps we and other observers will be carefully watching for to detect any moves the U.S. makes toward going to war against Iran:

- additional aircraft carriers in the region

- submarine mobilization

- deployment of additional cruise missiles in the Persian Gulf

- U.S. ground forces train for Middle East operations

- U.S. ground forces are deployed to or near the Middle East

- CIA and/or State Department officials confer with NATO about Iran

The point is that prior to actually launching an attack, the ramp-up to an attack could be used as an additional, final opportunity to increase pressure on the regime in Iran to reconsider the nuclear option.

JUNIPER OAK

In January 2023, The United States and Israel Defense Forces engaged in a large-scale joint military exercise called Juniper Oak 2023. It involved 140 aircraft, 12 naval vessels, and artillery systems from both nations. Some 6,400 American soldiers participated and about 1,100 Israeli personnel participated. Infantry and Special Forces from both countries were involved as well.

Juniper Oak was aimed at showing our adversaries—namely Iran—that the United States is not too distracted by Russia's invasion of Ukraine and threats from China to mobilize a large military force.

It's the largest joint exercise between Israel and the United States in history, and there's no question the United States and Israel were flexing their military muscle for Iran's benefit.

Regarding whether or not it was meant for Iran's consumption, an unnamed U.S. military official commented:

> "It's really meant mostly to kick the tires on our ability to do things at this scale with the Israelis against a whole range of different threats. But, you know, it would not surprise me if Iran sees the scale and the nature of these activities and understands what the two of us are capable of doing."

THE U.S. ATTACKS IRAN: THE FINAL MANEUVERING

Our assumption for the remainder of this chapter is that all diplomatic efforts to avert war fail. What then?

We can expect a reasonably short period will precede the attack upon Iran. During this time, a final ultimatum to Iran will be issued. This pause will be used to prepare the American public for a preemptive attack in the Middle East. Even in this final stage, when the U.S. military is positioning for attack, Iran still will have a last opportunity to see the seriousness of the situation and recant.

The probability of Iran reversing course is small. If anything, Iran may become even more defiant. The Supreme Leader can be expected to argue that now Iran has no choice but to develop nuclear weapons as fast as possible since the United States has taken military steps to prepare for an attack against it.

As we have repeatedly noted, the religious zealots ruling Iran believe war and destruction are a necessary precondition for the second coming of the Mahdi. Moreover, the hard-liners in the Iranian regime believe that the United States will overextend by attacking Iran. They believe Iran is *destined* to defeat the United States in a Middle East war.

The religious zealots ruling Iran will undoubtedly see a war with the United States as the beginning of the fulfillment of Ayatollah Khomeini's prediction that Israel and the United States will fall just as he predicted the Shah, the Soviet Union, and Saddam Hussein would fall.

THE U.S. ATTACKS: A BATTLE PLAN

A U.S. strike on Iran would probably consist primarily of an air attack combined with Special Forces operations on the ground. A move to a full-scale invasion would only follow an official U.S. determination that regime change has become official U.S. foreign policy with regard to Iran.

The goal in a more limited military attack would be to knock out Iran's major nuclear facilities, causing a major setback in Iran's ability to make nuclear weapons.

The decision to attack Iran would involve applying the "Bush Doctrine," which says a preemptive attack can be launched to protect U.S. national security interests.

The U.S. could argue that Iran's ability to produce a nuclear weapon constitutes a threat to our national security, in that Iran might supply an Improvised Nuclear Device (IND) to a terrorist group planning to use it against the United States. The U.S. would also argue that protecting our ally Israel against a preemptive nuclear attack from Iran is a U.S. national security interest.

If the U.S. decided to lead the attack, Israel could easily play a supportive role. But that would not change the overall tactics of the attack. Israel would be assigned certain military objectives as part of a coalition effort and the U.S. would attack others.

The following Iranian nuclear facilities are likely primary targets:

+ Arak, Iran's heavy water plant, about 154 miles southwest of Tehran

+ Bushehr, Iran's nuclear reactor, located along the Persian Gulf, approximately 250 miles south of Tehran

+ Isfahan, Iran's nuclear processing plant

+ Natanz, Iran's nuclear enrichment plant

+ Saghand, Iran's uranium mine

About a dozen smaller facilities devoted to Iran's nuclear efforts would also be targeted, some of which are located within cities and will require precision bombs.

In February 2023, Iran revealed the existence of an entirely underground air force base called Eagle 44. It's large enough to hold fighter jets. Supposedly the base can launch and support both fighter jets and drones. A day after the announcement of the new air base, the Tasnim News Agency showed images of a large, hangar-sized space with what seems to be a surface-to-surface ballistic missile in a launcher. The words, "Death to Israel" were written in Hebrew down its side. This type of facility could also expect to be targeted.

While several hundred facilities may play some role contributing to Iran's nuclear technologies, the goal would be to target the major facilities that would need to be destroyed to stop Iran's progress toward enriching uranium and pursuing nuclear weapons technology.

Iran's missile facilities have been systematically catalogued and studied by U.S. military intelligence. Likewise, Iran's military bases are also well known to the U.S. Iran's Shahab missiles, however, are launched from mobile carriers; a satellite intelligence effort will have to be made in the days immediately prior to an attack to identify their current locations.

Secondary targets would include government buildings, including military buildings; Iran's media and telecommunications infrastructure, including radio and television stations; telephone switching facilities; government buildings; conventional power plants; bridges and highways; rail lines; port facilities.

Unlike Russia, the United States possesses an extensive arsenal of highly precise guided, cruise, and ballistic missiles that are capable of hitting a target within only a few feet. If the U.S. targets Iran's infrastructure, it's likely to succeed in destroying it.

Hardened facilities, such as the underground centrifuge plants at Natanz, might be attacked with tactical nuclear weapons, either on ship-launched Tomahawk cruise missiles, or launched via air strike. Otherwise, the munitions utilized would be conventional, precision-guided bombs and bunker buster bombs.

The goal will be to apply massive air power to destroy key targets as rapidly as possible; catching the enemy unprepared, even surprised. The air attack could occur over the span of a few days, with no plan to launch a ground invasion, unless Iranian counterattack measures required an expanded war effort.

While the air attack most likely would not eliminate Iran's ability to produce nuclear weapons permanently, its program could be significantly set back, perhaps to a point where recovery would be extremely costly, requiring several years to reach a pre-attack status. Our goal would be to gain more time to deal with the government in Tehran.

IRAN RETALIATES TO A U.S. AIRSTRIKE

Inflicting major damage on Iran's nuclear facilities could be accomplished by the U.S. military launching a "shock and awe" air attack. Unless Iran's military capabilities were destroyed in the first few hours, however, a military and political counterattack could be costly.

Many, if not the majority of the mobile Shahab missile launchers may survive air strikes, ready to hit selected targets, including the many U.S. military bases we have in surrounding nations. Thousands of U.S. military personnel could be killed in the days and weeks after a U.S. air attack.

Additionally, Hezbollah terrorists in Lebanon as well as Hamas and the Islamic Jihad in Gaza would most likely launch retaliatory strikes on Israel. Iran could launch conventionally armed missiles against Israel's major cities, with a likelihood of inflicting thousands of human casualties and causing substantial infrastructure damage.

Even if Iron Dome were to stop most of the incoming missiles, there would still be significant damage inside Israel.

If any Iranian military fighter planes survived, a missile war could be supplemented by Iranian fighter sorties against U.S. bases in the area and against Israel. A missile war, even a conventional missile war, would cost thousands of lives on all sides and would draw both Iran and Israel into the conflict, even if the United States tried to position the attack as a solely U.S. preemptive strike.

COULD IRAN'S DISSIDENTS REVOLT?

Within Iran today, there is a considerable base of opposition to the current regime. However, a preemptive military strike launched by the United States against Iran risks stirring up Iranian nationalism, even among the nation's dissidents. An entire generation of Iranians has been raised and conditioned to hate America.

We should not underestimate the power of that early teaching to the children of Iran nor should we blindly assume that the civilian population would inevitably rise up against the regime. Iranians could oppose what would be portrayed as U.S. aggression against Iran, with the regime certainly arguing that the attack was completely unjustified.

The Shiite majority in Iraq cannot ordinarily be considered supporters of the Shiites in Iran. During the 1980s Iran-Iraq war, Iraqi Shiites fought bitterly against Iranian Shiites. Even after the fall of Saddam Hussein, the Shiites in Iraq maintained their primary allegiance to Iraq, working to maintain their position in the newly formed Iraqi government, not allying with their religious brethren in Iran. Still, a U.S. preemptive attack on Iran might be the trigger to move Iraq's Shiites closer to Shiite Iran.

If America were seen as opposing Islam, not simply going after Iran's nuclear facilities, a region-wide Islamic uprising might unify in support of Iran, regardless of whether the Muslims involved were Shiite or Sunni.

Right now, many of Iran's Muslim neighbors, including Turkey, are concerned about their own national security as Iran pursues nuclear technology aggressively. Even Saudi Arabia has taken a position opposing Iran's defiant pursuit of nuclear technology. But, by launching a preemptive attack against Iran, the U.S. could well reverse that trend and intensify anti-American sentiment throughout the Islamic world.

TERRORIST RETALIATION TO A
U.S. STRIKE ON IRAN

Wherever terrorist sleeper cells have operational capabilities, a U.S. military attack against Iran would provide an occasion for renewed attacks. Even if the attacks were only limited to the type of rail transportation and subway bombs we've seen before, terrorists could cause havoc by launching attacks in various Western countries simultaneously. The United States would be blamed for these terrorist attacks and cast in the role of international aggressor.

Even if we characterize our war against Iran as a war of self-defense for ourselves and Israel, worldwide public opinion will most likely be against the United States. A preemptive attack on Iran would bear heavy political consequences for the United States, not only in the Islamic world, but among many traditional allies as well.

The aftermath of a preemptive military strike against Iran would be risky for the United States, even if the attack achieved the objective of knocking out Iran's nuclear capabilities. A long war in Iran could be disastrous, given the potential to stir up anti-American terrorism and Islamic insurgencies in the aftermath. As the United States learned in Iraq and Afghanistan, a rapid military victory may only be the first chapter to managing a successful peace.

THE REGIME CHANGE OPTION

In a previous chapter, we discussed an indirect attempt at regime change inside Iran. In this chapter, we'll discuss a direct attempt to seek regime change inside Iran, namely a land invasion specifically targeting the Iranian government.

Thinking through the scenarios of a preemptive strike, the U.S. government may conclude that military action should aim at regime change in Iran, even if that option necessitates a land invasion. Reasons in favor of the regime-change solution include:

+ If Ayatollah Khamenei and President Raisi remain in power after a U.S. preemptive military strike, the current regime structure can be expected to move toward declaring war on the United States.

+ The current regime will move to reconstitute its nuclear program immediately. Moreover, those countries who feel the U.S. attack was unjustified

(Russia, North Korea, and China) may provide even more technical and financial support to Iran than before.

+ A U.S. military attack on Iran undoubtedly will cause world oil prices to spike violently, with the resulting increases reflected in U.S. gasoline and heating oil costs.

+ If the Iranian regime withstands a U.S. military pre-emptive attack, we can expect retaliation to involve an oil war. At a minimum, Iran will urge OPEC to restrict supplies. The tanker war that ensued in the 1980s Iran-Iraq war may only be a small prelude to the chaos Iran could cause with oil transportation through the Persian Gulf region. Approximately 40 percent of the world's oil supply passes through the Straits of Hormuz, a narrow area Iran might seek to close down to all oil traffic, regardless of nationality of ship transport.

+ The decision to depose the current Iranian government would avoid leaving in place a regime who would declare the United States an enemy to be destroyed at all costs.

+ Once rebuilt, Iran's nuclear program would be harder to control a second time. Withdrawing from the Nuclear Nonproliferation Treaty (NPT), Iran could immediately begin rebuilding their nuclear facilities, this time with the resolve to develop weapons.

+ Having once defied the world community, Iran's current regime would not hesitate the second time to present the world with the choice of deposing the regime or facing the prospect of an atomic Iran armed with nuclear weapons.

+ Having survived one attack, the Iranian regime would harden its relationships with Russia, North Korea, and China into a tight alliance with what could amount to a mutual security pact in which the allies declare that any further attacks will be considered an attack on them as well.

+ Terrorist organizations would use the U.S. preemptive attack as the justification for their open declaration of wishing to obtain nuclear weapons. The current regime might oblige them.

+ Intensified terrorism in support of Iran would be aimed at further destabilizing the Middle East, Europe, and America. The current regime would be disposed to help them as much as possible.

The Iranian regime would have to rebuild the physical facilities destroyed in the attack. The human talent, however, of Iran's nuclear scientists and engineers would remain in place, unless a large percentage of Iran's nuclear experts were killed at facilities that the attack damaged or destroyed.

The second time such facilities are constructed will be easier than the first. Conceivably the second time, better facilities might be reconstructed faster, cheaper, and more secure from further attack. Ironically, Iran's nuclear infrastructure might emerge superior to that which was destroyed.

In rebuilding its nuclear infrastructure, Iran could go immediately to advanced-generation nuclear technologies. In the long run, we might have done Iran a favor to eliminate their old and experimental nuclear facilities so the regime can rebuild their nuclear program with new, state-of-the-art technologies. Within a short time, Iran's nuclear program could be back, fully functioning, possibly even more advanced than it was before the attack.

SHOULD A MILITARY ATTACK AIM AT REGIME CHANGE?

The Israelis and Americans clearly realize that a preemptive strike aimed at taking out Iran's nuclear facilities attacks the symptoms and doesn't solve the problem. If this can be communicated to the American people, an attack aimed at creating regime change in Iran offers a more realistic chance that the nuclear threat presented by Iran can be removed altogether, not just postponed.

Ironically, the political repercussions to the United States from a full-scale invasion of Iran might be less than if we launch a more limited preemptive attack. With the Iranian regime left in place, the mullahs and their supporters would have a continuing podium from which to project their anti-American grievances.

In the aftermath of removing the current Iranian regime, dissidents within Iran and expatriate opponents of the regime abroad, will have to come forward to reorganize what would hopefully emerge as a more democratic Iran.

The United States would need to demonstrate a desire to withdraw from Iran once a new Iranian government is installed. This is the same model the United States followed at the end of World War II in which our goal was to establish democratic governments in Germany and Japan as a pre-condition for the U.S. withdrawing.

IRANIAN REGIME CHANGE AND THE WAR ON TERRORISM

The current regime in Iran is a central instigator of terrorism worldwide. As we have noted repeatedly, Hezbollah, Hamas, and the Islamic Jihad virtually owe their financial survival to the mullahs in Iran. Al Qaeda operatives work actively with the Iranian government to further mutually held aims.

By eliminating the Iranian regime, a central part of the war on terrorism would be won. Without support from the mullahs in Tehran, Bashar al-Assad would have a much more difficult time staying in control of Syria. Without the constant encouragement from Tehran that Israel might one day be eliminated from the Middle East, the Palestinian Authority might come to a compromise on the status of Jerusalem that would be acceptable to both the Israelis and the Palestinians.

The ayatollahs have been a roadblock to Middle East peace since the 1979 revolution. As long as they remain in power, we cannot expect the war on terrorism to end. Conversely, with interference from Tehran removed, the war on terrorism might take important strides to a successful conclusion.

America has taken great strides since the 1980s in reconciling with a wide range of Middle Eastern countries, including Egypt, Jordan, and Lebanon as well as Saudi Arabia. If Iran's current regime fell, Syria would have to re-evaluate its anti-American policies.

Eliminating the regime of the mullahs would represent an important movement toward freedom and democracy in the Middle East, as well as the potential for a more complete reconciliation of Islamic peoples worldwide with America and the West.

Looked at from this perspective, the United States might well calculate that rather than launching a limited strike on Iran's nuclear facilities, we might suffer less by going after the regime itself. We could make the decision not to postpone dealing with the radical regime in Tehran until it obtains nuclear weapons.

HOW WOULD A REGIME-CHANGE WAR BE LAUNCHED AGAINST IRAN?

A ground war most likely would be started by virtually the same "shock and awe" air strike described above. The first objectives would be to destroy key Iranian nuclear facilities while simultaneously destroying Iran's military capabilities and decapitating the Iranian government.

The objectives of a "shock and awe" air strike would be expanded to include additional government targets since our goal now would be to topple the government of the mullahs.

Iran would undoubtedly retaliate, as we described above, but the Iranian military forces would most likely be ineffective against a technologically superior American force. The Russia-Ukraine War has demonstrated just how lopsided the technology gap is between the U.S-NATO alliance and the rest of the world.

Winning a military invasion of Iran will be easier than establishing peace in Iran. Yet, ironically, removing the oppressive regime of Iran might set in motion positive forces throughout the Middle East.

Russia, while opposed to any U.S. invasion of Iran, might stand aside in light of how completely it has been humiliated and depleted in Ukraine in a conventional ground war. Not only is the Russian military running very low on weapons and soldiers, but it never came up against a full-blown U.S.-NATO force. (Or at least it hasn't as of the writing of this book.) Had the U.S. and NATO intervened directly in Ukraine, Russia's defeat would have been disastrous, indeed.

Skeptics will argue that an invasion of Iran would overstretch the U.S. military and prove too costly to undertake. Clearly, a military invasion of Iran will not be the option first considered by the U.S. government. Yet, after a serious attempt is made to deal with the Iranian regime on a more limited basis of engagement, the government may arrive at the regime-change decision because it's the only option that makes sense.

Of course, all other options should be explored first. Still, after months of pursuing more limited objectives and tactical methodologies, America may face a fundamental choice: remove the ayatollahs once and for all or accept the reality that sooner or later they will end up with nuclear weapons.

In the final analysis, we may end up invading simply because we can identify no other solution that has any real hope of long-term success. The problem is that with Iran's determined push to develop nuclear weapons, we may not have a decade to explore alternatives.

IRAN COULD END THE NUCLEAR CRISIS EASILY

We should remember that Iran has an easy solution to the entire crisis. If Iran's only intent with their nuclear program is peaceful, then all Iran has to do is to comply with the IAEA's request for verifiable inspections in conducting a transparent nuclear power program aimed 100% at civilian purposes.

Iran could have to accept Russia's invitation to form a joint venture company under which uranium for Iran could be enriched on Russian soil. If Iran's intentions are entirely peaceful, what is wrong with this compromise?

If Iran wanted to be sure no one country could deny it access to the enriched uranium it needs to run a peaceful program, the IAEA can create a multi-nation "uranium bank" from which Iran can draw the enriched uranium it needs on the basis of an internationally guaranteed, continuous supply.

The Iranian nuclear crisis can be solved fairly easily and quickly by mature and experienced international diplomats, provided that Iran's intentions are truly peaceful and that Iran stops being defiant.

While such a solution is being negotiated, Iran should also agree to stop verbally threatening to annihilate Israel and stop supporting terrorist organizations such as Hezbollah.

The last option the United States or Israel wants is a military attack of any kind. The military option, if used by the United States, reflects a failure of diplomacy, not a victory of the policy pursued by the international community to resolve the nuclear crisis with Iran.

PART VI:

A

NUCLEAR

IRAN

WHAT IF IRAN GETS THE BOMB?

"There is common agreement that the Iranians should not
have a nuclear weapon, the capacity to make a nuclear weapon,
or the knowledge how to make a nuclear weapon.
The reason there's common agreement is because the Iranian
government with such a weapon as is now constituted
would pose a serious threat to world security."

—President George W. Bush

PERHAPS THE IRANIAN REGIME has already reached the conclusion that there are no measures short of war that the West could take to block their nuclear progress. The Iranian regime may doubt that either Israel or the United States wants to launch a full-scale, preemptive attack. The mullahs may believe that only the United States can inflict serious military damage and they judge that the United States lacks the will to do so.

Given these calculations, the mullahs ruling Iran may feel certain that, one way or another, their nuclear weapons program will precede virtually unimpeded. We are going to assume in this chapter that Iran succeeds in developing nuclear weapons.

THE PROSPECT OF NUCLEAR BLACKMAIL

Iran may never need to attack Israel with nuclear weapons. A more effective approach may simply be to threaten Israel with specific demands, especially if the world knows that Tehran is capable of launching a nuclear attack on Israel at any moment.

The simple reality is that the world of international diplomacy and the balance of power in the Middle East will change the moment Iran succeeds in developing a nuclear weapon that can be delivered on a missile they possess.

Tehran might well launch a series of demands on Israel, with the prospect of a nuclear attack on Israel if demands such as these are not met:

- That Jerusalem be divided, with the Palestinians controlling half the city

- That Jerusalem be handed over to the Palestinians in its entirety, with the Israelis forced to relocate the capital of Israel to Tel Aviv

- That Israel withdraw from the West Bank immediately

- That Israel return the Golan Heights immediately

- That Israel allow free passage from Gaza to the West Bank

- That Israel take down the wall built to keep suicide bombers out

Iran's leaders openly doubt the Holocaust ever occurred and the creation of a Jewish state was not warranted. Various Iranian leaders have demanded that Israel relocate to Europe because any guilt for killing Jews during World War II had nothing to do with the Palestinians.

Tehran could demand that Israel be moved somewhere else, so Palestine could be given to the Palestinians. If this demand were not met, Tehran could threaten to obliterate Israel.

All these scenarios include a period of threat and possible negotiations before simply dropping an atomic bomb on Tel Aviv. The advantage to Tehran is that Israel might be forced by international pressure to concede to Tehran's demands, at least in part, so as to avoid a nuclear war in the Middle East.

The strategy would be for Tehran to engage in a series of demands and concessions. The end result would be to seriously reduce or completely undermine Israel's international position while repeatedly bringing into question the legitimacy of its sovereignty. The goal would be to isolate Israel and make demands that are considered ridiculous or extreme today seem more reasonable, such as Iran's demand that Israel be relocated.

WHY MAD DOES NOT APPLY TO IRAN

The term mutually assured destruction (MAD) explains the mutual deterrence strategies of major superpowers in the nuclear era. You kill us, we kill you—we all die. Conventional deterrence theory is predicated on the assumption that no state would launch a nuclear attack on another state if a nuclear retaliation were certain to make the initial decision suicidal. The logic of MAD, however, may not apply to Iran.

Dr. Mark Clark, professor of political science and director of the National Security Studies Program at California State University, San Bernardino, explains the MAD assumption of "rational actor" as follows:

> "Theories of deterrence hold axiomatically to the Rational Actor assumption about state behavior and choices with respect to nuclear weapons. Rationality assumes a pure "cost/benefit" analysis with perfect information that ignores or downplays individual differences among states. According to "rationality" in deterrence theory, the costs of nuclear use will always outweigh any conceivable gains.
>
> While not disparaging of the utility of such an assumption, by definition it ignores how individual state leaders, bureaucracies, beliefs, and ideologies shape nuclear strategies. Indeed, it imposes a uniform calculus on very different actors with very different strategic "personalities."
>
> Further, an assumption of rationality is, by definition, not necessarily true. The criterion for employing such theoretical assumptions is whether they are useful. The usefulness of the assumption of rationality has been challenged."

Iran clearly challenges the "rational actor" assumption. If the Supreme Leader believes apocalyptic death and destruction are necessary pre-conditions for the Second Coming of the Mahdi, then causing a nuclear exchange with Israel may be seen as fulfillment of a divine mission.

It's worth remembering that the political culture of the Islamic Shiites gave birth to the modern concept of suicide bombers. This glorification of martyrdom has been absorbed by terrorist organizations such as Hezbollah and Hamas with the tactic aggressively used against Israel.

The former chief of staff of Iran's Army, Major General Ali Shahbazi, has commented on Iran's radical view of religious martyrdom, raising a disturbing point:

> ". . . . the United States or some country incited by it may be able to begin a military conflict . . . it will not be strong enough to end it. This is because only Muslims believe that whether we kill or are killed, we are the victors. Others do not think this way."

Rather than being deterred by the logic of MAD, an extremist such as Khamenei may be attracted by nuclear suicide as long as Israel is destroyed in the process.

We are reminded that even Rafsanjani argued that Iran and the Islamic world could absorb millions of casualties in a nuclear exchange, but Israel would be destroyed. With over one billion Muslims worldwide, his numbers calculation is not irrational except that it is predicated upon suicide with possibly millions, maybe even hundreds of millions, killed in a multi-national thermonuclear exchange.

An international nuclear war triggered by an Iran atomic attack on Israel would be justified then, according to the messianic logic of the Mahdi believers. Even if hundreds of millions of Muslims were killed, the war would be justified as long as millions of Jews were also killed and Israel was destroyed in the process. A thermonuclear war of this nature would, by their calculus, occasion the return of the Mahdi and the ultimate triumph of Islam worldwide.

This vision is madness, but only if we calculate that life here on Earth has an intrinsic value. And that is where the rest of the world differs from the ayatollahs.

NUCLEAR WEAPONS AND OIL EXTORTION

Iran's 132 billion barrels of estimated oil reserves mean that Iran controls roughly 10 percent of the world's oil. Iran is the world's fifth largest oil exporter, ranked only behind Saudi Arabia, Russia, the United States, and Canada.

Even though the United States imports no oil from Iran, the worldwide price of oil is still impacted by the volume of oil that Iran exports. If Iran were to restrict supply, world oil prices would be expected to increase, at least in the short run, until other exporters increased their production to make up the shortfall.

With oil exports constituting 80-90% of Iran's total export earnings and some 40-50% of the government budget, we might think Iran would do nothing to disrupt its ability to sell oil. But, if Iran can cause world oil prices to go up by restricting supply, Iran might increase oil revenue by selling less. The mullahs view oil as a weapon they can use.

A second strategic point for Iranian oil extortion is the Strait of Hormuz.

Iran is well aware of its ability to cause havoc simply by closing the Strait of Hormuz to oil tanker traffic. As Douglas Streusand, the founder and coordinator of the Global Strategy Seminar of the Center for Security Studies, points out:

> "The Strait draws special attention because more petroleum is more vulnerable there than anywhere else. Although the Iranian military lacks the ability to sustain a blockade of the Strait against a sustained U.S. effort to open it, it certainly has the ability to close the Strait temporarily."

Armed with nuclear weapons, Iran could decide which energy contracts to honor after demanding additional political concessions from oil trading partners. Every oil dispute with Iran would run the risk of escalating into a nuclear confrontation.

THE AGE OF ISLAMIC NUCLEAR TERRORISM

"Why do you use an ax when you can use a bulldozer?"

—Question of Osama bin Laden

to Kahlid Sheik Mohammad, the chief planner of the 9/11 attack.

IRAN HAS USED conventionally armed terrorist groups as surrogates to carry out Iran's aggressive international intents without Iran having to take the blame directly. Terrorists armed with atomic weapons or protected by Iran's nuclear arsenal open up whole new dimensions of nuclear terrorism that the world has yet to fully contemplate.

NUCLEAR TERRORISM

Terrorist organizations lack the formal structures needed to produce even simple nuclear devices. Hunted by intelligence agents and military units in the war on terror, groups like Hezbollah, Hamas, Islamic Jihad, and Al Qaeda are typically on the move. Stealing nuclear material or warheads is extraordinarily difficult, suitcase nuclear weapons, while spectacular in concept, require sophisticated maintenance to remain operational.

Many of these practical barriers are solved when a rogue state such as Iran has nuclear weapons. Iran already has expended billions of dollars, employed thousands of nuclear scientists and engineers, and constructed facilities for enriching uranium. Once it has the ability to build nuclear weapons, Iran's nuclear program could easily be assigned the mission of developing portable nuclear devices that could be delivered to terrorist organizations for use around the world.

The devices could take the form of Improvised Nuclear Devices (INDs), broken down so they could be assembled relatively easily after they were smuggled across borders.

Lest you think this is too farfetched to be real, on January 10, 2023, reports surfaced in British newspapers of a shipment of uranium that was intercepted at Heathrow International Airport outside of London. The package originated in Pakistan and arrived in the cargo hold of an Oman Air passenger jet. It is thought to have been bound for UK-based Iranians. Scanners detected potentially lethal uranium, triggering alarms. It was isolated and seized.

Suitcase or backpack nuclear devices would place at risk buildings, subways, and passenger trains that are rarely protected by the type of security systems that reliably checks all passers-by or the packages and cases they carry.

Atomic devices of less than 1 kiloton yield could destroy skyscrapers, bridges, or tunnels, causing chaos and thousands of casualties as well as widespread contamination.

A 10 to 20 kiloton atomic device could fit into the back of a commercial truck. A bomb of this size would devastate the heart of any major U.S. city with resulting radiation and fire damage that would extend the death and destruction over a larger radius.

Does anyone doubt that human suicide-bombers willing to die carrying conventional bombs into urban areas would hesitate at the chance to carry an atomic device in a suitcase or a backpack?

Even before Iran was capable of supplying small nuclear devices to terrorists, Tehran would be able to extend the protection of its nuclear umbrella over terrorist groups that Iran wanted to support. Then the consequences of Israel retaliating against missiles from Hezbollah in Lebanon or from Hamas in the Gaza might risk nuclear retaliation from Iran.

Would the United States be willing to place bounties on terrorists and hunt them down worldwide if Iran announced their lives were protected by its nuclear arsenal?

A nuclear Iran can provide a completely safe home base for terrorists to operate out of. In fact, Iran already shelters the leadership of Al Qaeda within its borders. According to former Secretary of State, Mike Pompeo:

> "As I exposed definitively in January 2021, Tehran is today the home base of top al-Qaeda leadership. That's right. Al-Qaeda's operational headquarters is not in Tora Bora, Afghanistan or in Pakistan. It's not in Syria or Iraq. It's in the capital of Iran.
>
> The ayatollahs are harboring the leaders of a group that murdered nearly three thousand

Americans on 9/11. Years before his death at the hands of Navy SEALS in 2011, Osama bin Laden himself wrote: "Iran is our main artery for funds, personnel, and communication . . . There is no need to fight with Iran unless you are forced to."

IS IRAN ALREADY AT WAR WITH THE UNITED STATES?

Frank Gaffney, Director of the Washington-based Center for Security Policy, has pointed out the need to take seriously Iran's support of terrorism when contemplating the risk of an atomic Iran:

> "The United States can never win the War for the Free World as long as the most active state sponsor of terrorism is allowed to continue unchecked in its support of violence against freedom-loving nations. . .We have for too long allowed Iran's nearly three-decade war against the United States to go unanswered.
>
> And, unless we deal with it effectively in the immediate future, we will be faced with a nuclear-armed terrorist regime that has shown no reluctance to attack American citizens and American interests throughout the world."

Iran continues to promote its stated goal of expanding its radical revolution throughout the Middle East as a prelude to expanding the revolution worldwide.

AN IRANIAN NUCLEAR ATTACK
ON AMERICAN SOIL

Nor is the United States going to be safe from an Iranian nuclear missile attack, even given the relatively limited range of Iran's current missiles. Iran is working at top speed to develop rocket technology that will fuel intercontinental ballistic missiles, and they'll figure it out sooner or later. . .particularly if Russia, with its mature space program, decides to share rocket technology with Iran.

Iran has submarines or even plain old freighters it could use to bring a short-range nuclear weapon close to American shores. A nuclear weapon exploded at high altitude over the United States would send out an electro-magnetic pulse (EMP) of high-energy electrons that could knock out electricity and telecommunications throughout large swaths of the continental United States.

Power grids, unprotected computers and microchips, all systems, equipment, and devices that depend on electricity and electronics—from medical instruments to military communications to your toaster—would be disabled or permanently destroyed. At risk are cell phones, cars and trucks, airplanes and trains, banking and finance, virtually everything that uses or generates electricity. All of it could be hit in what amounts to an electromagnetic tsunami.

This is not science fiction; the EMP threat was assessed in 2000 by a commission created by Congress to evaluate the risk. The EMP Threat Commission reported in the summer of 2004 that terrorists could execute an EMP attack by launching a small nuclear-armed missile from a freighter off the coast of the United States.

Iran has tested missiles fired at sea and exploded at high altitudes. Initially, western media described the test as a failure because the missile exploded. Intelligence experts disagreed, arguing that Iran's intent was to test an EMP attack that would require a missile to detonate at high altitudes. (Electromagnetic pulse devices are line-of-sight weapons. The higher you explode one, the further the damage travels before contact with the Earth stops the pulse.)

If Iran launched a successful EMP attack, the United States might have a very difficult time retaliating against it. Not only would government and military communications be impaired, we might even have difficulty determining who was responsible for launching the attack.

An EMP attack would turn one of our major strategic advantages, our technological superiority, into a major disadvantage because our technology is almost entirely dependent upon electronics.

THE NUCLEAR THREAT TO IRAN'S NEIGHBORS

Historically, the Islamic countries of the Middle East have waged war against each other many more times than they have united to wage war against Israel. If Iran should ever succeed in eliminating Israel from the Middle East, we should have no confidence that peace would come to the Middle East as an immediate consequence.

We could very well see the Arab states and non-Arab Islamic states of the Middle East resume fighting amongst themselves. We could see regional ethnic rivalries erupt into violence or fighting might break out based on religious differences.

Iran's neighbors could be faced with nuclear threats for no other reason than because Iran might decide they're too supportive of Israel and the United States. Put simply, an atomic Iran might declare any nation that did not affirm its commitment to wiping Israel from the map or who continued to supply oil or trade to the United States, an enemy of Iran. These enemies could be subject to nuclear attack unless their objectionable policies were changed immediately.

We should not assume Iran will be peaceful with Middle Eastern neighbors simply because the countries are all Islamic. Iran and Iraq fought bitterly against each other in an 8-year war in the 1980s with Shiite Iraqis facing off in battle against Shiite Iranians. Moreover, Iran's roots are Persian, not Arabian.

Fights among Middle Eastern countries have been going on for centuries, with the disputes complicated by language, religion, ethnicity, culture, and nationality. Even understanding disputes among Middle Eastern nations and ethnic groups requires an expertise not common among most Westerners.

Iran has been saber-rattling at Saudi Arabia recently, accusing its neighbor of fomenting the unrest that has plagued the Iranian regime since September, 2022. (Never mind that the unrest was caused by Mahsa Amini's murder and widespread discontent with living conditions in Iran.)

In November of 2022, Iran's intelligence minister, Esmail Khatib, told its regional rival Saudi Arabia that there is no guarantee of Tehran continuing its "strategic patience," adding:

> "Until now, Iran has adopted strategic patience with firm rationality, but it cannot guarantee that it will not run out if hostilities continue. If Iran decides to retaliate and punish, glass palaces will crumble

and these countries will not experience stability anymore."

Iran's Revolutionary Guard Chief weighed in as well, saying:

"I am warning the Saudi ruling family. . . . Watch your behavior and control these media . . . otherwise you will pay the price. This is our last warning because you are interfering in our state matters through these media. We told you, be careful."

Without nuclear weapons, Iran lacks the military power to concern a larger and stronger Saudi Arabia. With nuclear weapons, however, Iran would have the tools to threaten a conventionally armed Saudi Arabia. All Iran would have to do is to aim a few missiles at Riyadh. What would be Tehran's motivations?

+ The Iranians might demand that Saudi Arabia stop exporting oil to the United States, knowing that the U.S. is partly dependent upon importing Saudi oil.

+ Iran could demand that the Saudis cut all ties to America and the West, including diplomatic ties, not just trade relations or oil exports.

+ The Iranians could object to the Saudis strictly on a religious basis, demanding that the Saudis abandon their Sunni faith, especially now, in the "last days" when radical messianic Shiites are preparing for the Second Coming of the Mahdi.

✦ Iran might launch an atomic attack on the Saudi oil fields. Not only would this destroy the Saudi economy, but the resulting skyrocketing of oil prices would benefit the Iranians tremendously and send Western economies into severe recession or even depression.

A NUCLEAR IRAN COULD SEEK REGIONAL SUPREMACY

An atomic Iran could seek to reorganize alliances among the Islamic nations of the Middle East. Aligned with Syria, a nuclear Iran could demand that Lebanon submit to Syrian occupation.

Iran could reach out to radical Islamic politicians all across North Africa, from Egypt to Libya to Morocco, seeking to destabilize any regime that maintained ties to the United States or Europe.

An atomic Iran could demand the immediate withdrawal of all American military forces and diplomats from the Middle East.

An atomic Iran could ally even more closely with Russia and the two could prop up each other's economies and manipulate world oil prices together.

Iran could demand that Turkey (and other nations) withdraw from NATO.

Iran could demand to be admitted to the World Trade Organization ahead of any other Middle Eastern country.

A NUCLEAR IRAN COULD ATTACK THE U.S. DOLLAR

An atomic Iran could demand that the world move off the dollar as the preferred currency with which to settle oil transactions.

The goal would be to replace the dollar with the Islamic Gold Dinar, a currency Iran could seek to control.

The United States currently depends on the petro-dollar holdings of foreign nations to sell the Treasury debt we use to finance our continuing budget deficits. Without massive amounts of petro-dollars being held in foreign exchange currencies, the United States would face an immediate crisis financing a host of transfer payment systems, ranging from Social Security to all its welfare programs.

Cutbacks in government entitlement payments could be catastrophic to the U.S. economy as everyone from seniors to farmers to the nation's urban poor could face the immediate risk of losing their government checks.

If Iran were to demand that all nations begin settling oil transactions in the Gold Dinar, it would send the U.S. government into technical bankruptcy overnight.

AN IRRATIONAL WORLD ORDER

The world has always assumed that nuclear powers would be restrained by "rational calculations." Even the definition of "rationality" has to change when we take into consideration the thinking of radical theocrats whose political calculations stem from an extremist messianic religious view that is intolerant of any other religion and hates Jews.

If we want to see how Iran would seek to impose its will on the world, all we have to do is look at how the Iranian regime rules Iran:

- repression of religious freedom

- mullah-chosen political candidates

- oppression of women

- removal of women from the work force

- denial of education to women

- strict adherence to an Islamic moral code

- Sharia law (Islamic religious laws founded in the 8th and 9th centuries)

- criminal processes controlled by clerics

- violent punishments for crimes

- summary executions

- imprisonment without legal rights

- repression of all political dissent

- criticism of mullahs or the government forbidden

- government-controlled media

- a surveillance state

- spies planted in the population

WHY DIPLOMACY WILL FAIL

An Iranian nuclear first-strike is an especially serious threat when the mullahs might just be religiously motivated to follow through with the actual attack, regardless of the attack's self-destructive consequences.

How does a nation used to secular calculations of political power reason with or anticipate the actions of a head of state who believes he is on a messianic mission to fulfill a personal destiny pre-ordained by Allah?

This is especially difficult when we realize that Iran's definition of its divine mission may be to bring about apocalyptic death and destruction so the new age of the Mahdi can dawn upon Earth.

On all sides of Iran are military powers armed with nuclear arsenals. Russia, Pakistan, and India all are nuclear powers. The United States has bases all around Iran, and naval assets near Iranian shores. Never has the U.S. been more positioned for a land invasion of Iran.

The mullahs are also well aware of the internal dissent that is threatening again to depose the mullahs and their rigid theocracy. For the mullahs, obtaining nuclear weapons is the best insurance policy they could ever buy.

While Iran is fighting against the tide of international opinion to get nuclear weapons, the world will have a much harder time taking Iran's nuclear weapons away once it has them.

The mullahs are acting as if only a military strike can stop their progress toward nuclear weapons. For years, the mullahs were able to conduct a secret nuclear program. Yet today, the program has advanced to the point where secrecy will no longer work. Nuclear test explosions are impossible to hide no matter how far underground you conduct them. Seismometers will detect such explosions. Test firing long-range missiles will be observed by satellites from multiple nations.

For Iran to finish its nuclear development program, it will have to do so publicly. However, there is no reason to expect Iran to moderate its decades of defiance. Nor is there any reason to believe it will suddenly start engaging in rational diplomacy when it hasn't done so since the Islamic Revolution in 1979. Iran may not be wrong in assessing that the only way to stop it will be a military attack of some kind.

IRAN TAKES A STEP CLOSER TO A WEAPON

Iran will have a hard time enriching uranium to 90% pure weapons grade without the world's intelligence community finding out. Even harder will be developing and testing nuclear warheads. Every test-firing of an Iranian missile is monitored closely by satellite worldwide.

Concealment no longer works when a country's nuclear technologies have advanced as far as Iran's have. Iran may only be weeks away from having enough enriched uranium to make a few low-yield atomic bombs.

Bloomberg News reported on February 19, 2023 that atomic monitors put in place by the IAEA in Iran detected particles of uranium enriched to 84% purity, which is just below weapons-grade.

No surprise, Iran denied the report, calling it, "part of a conspiracy against Tehran". Iran's spokesman went on to say that in its efforts to enrich uranium to 60%, it may occasionally create a particle of higher enrichment. He declared what the monitor detected to be, "a particle of an atom that cannot be seen even under a microscope."

Daryl G. Kimball, executive director of the Washington-based Arms Control Association, responded to Iran's claim, saying:

> "There are variances in enrichment levels but usually not to the degree Iran is claiming. Until the IAEA provides more information, including on the sampling and the methods of their analysis, we cannot be sure.
>
> It may also be possible that Iran is testing the political response to enrichment of very small amounts of uranium at higher levels, and closer to bomb grade, or, less likely, they got caught experimenting with new centrifuge cascade configurations and how quickly they could enrich uranium to higher levels."

With uranium enriched to weapons grade, Iran's nuclear scientists should be able to take the remaining steps to produce a working warhead in a relatively short time, measured in months or a few years at most.

It they're that close to having nuclear weapons, the Iranian regime is going to be willing to sustain any harsh criticisms or new sanctions the world seeks to impose on it. Not to mention, with support from Russia, North Korea, and China, Iran has all the economic help it needs to withstand any more sanctions the United

States or the United Nations may seek to impose.

This close to the end game, Iran already sees the moves that will result in checkmate, regardless of what moves the United States, Israel, or the Security Council make. Iran has most likely won the game already. . .unless we activate military options and throw the chess board to the floor.

Much of the world is already preparing to deal with a nuclear Iran. Many countries quietly welcome the counterbalance to American power.

In reality, Iran is a relatively weak country, even with its nation's abundant oil and natural gas reserves. Its economy is unstable, ranked 14th out of 14 Middle Eastern countries in size. Its military has outdated technology and lacks world-class training. Nuclear weapons are the perfect asymmetric warfare option to level the playing field between the mullahs and the world.

By a willingness to go to the nuclear brink once they have nuclear weapons, the mullahs win the game. Their formula has always been that with nuclear weapons in hand, Iran will be able to assert its power and will upon the world. This is a dream that no amount of international diplomacy will reverse, no matter how skillfully or painfully the diplomacy is applied.

Iran has listened to the world and its answer is, "No." Iran has no intention of stopping now, especially when having nuclear weapons is so immediately at hand.

IRAN IS DEADLY SERIOUS

Much of what I have been proposing might happen reads like fiction. Yet the risks are real and the story is true. The world is dealing with a leader who doubts the Holocaust and wants to wipe Israel off the map.

Right until the end, Hitler dreamed that his scientists would hand him a miracle weapon that would produce victory out of the ashes of defeat. How could Hitler ever have imagined that his dream of a miracle weapon would be realized? Decades later, his Islamic counterparts are on the verge of creating a nuclear miracle for themselves.

Iran's push for nuclear weapons and the world's attempt to stop its progress will be a permanent part of each day's news cycle until the drama finally resolves. What happens when Iran gets nuclear weapons? What steps will the world have to take if Iran is to be stopped at all costs, as America and Israel have resolved? The prospects either way are bone-chilling and soul-frightening.

The problem is the moment Iran has nuclear weapons, all bets are off. We will enter a world of nuclear terrorism that we have never before experienced. That moment is imminent. Will the global community be able to stop Iran's nuclear program with diplomacy? Will war be the only alternative for Israel and the United States? If Iran's nuclear program is not stopped, how will the world live with an Iran armed with deliverable nuclear weapons?

We are living on the edge of an era of nuclear apocalypse, whether we realize it or not.

IRAN REPEATS MUHAMMED'S WARNING

On May 8, 2006, President George W. Bush received an 18-page letter from Iran's President Mahmoud Ahmadinejad.

The missive lectured Mr. Bush on the virtues of Islam and rebuked him for not applying the teachings of Jesus Christ to his foreign policy. It appears that someone forgot to tell Mr. Ahmadinejad that the war on terror is not a war against religion.

While the letter received much attention from the secular media, the majority of those who reported on it missed one of the most serious paragraphs in the letter, the Islamic statement at the end:

> "Vasalam Ala Man Ataba'al hod," that means "Peace only unto those who follow the true path."

This is a phrase with great historical significance in Islam. According to Islamic tradition, in year six of the Hejira—in the late 620s—the prophet Muhammed sent letters to the Byzantine emperor and the Sassanid emperor telling them to convert to the true faith of Islam or be conquered.

For Muhammed, the letters were a prelude to a Muslim offensive, a war launched for the purpose of imposing Islamic rule over infidels.

We can only assume Iran's Supreme Leader was doing the same thing through Ahmadinejad's letter. In it, Iran delivered a warning to the United States in the same way Muhammed did thousands of years ago, saying in the letter to President Bush:

> "Those with insight can already hear the sounds of the shattering and fall of the ideology and thoughts of the liberal democratic systems."

Iran was announcing to us and to the world its intention of duplicating—and finishing this time—Muhammed's quest. Iran has the exact same thing in mind that Mohammad did, to wit, the establishment of an Islamic caliphate that will encompass not just Iran, but indeed, the entire world.

EPILOGUE:

THE BIBLE SHOWS US A WAY FORWARD

"Arise, shine, for your light has come, and the glory
of the LORD rises upon you. See, darkness covers the earth
and thick darkness is over the peoples, but the LORD rises
upon you and his glory appears over you."

—(Isaiah 60:1-2, NIV)

AS WE END THIS BOOK, I reflect again on the prophecy of Isaiah 43:2. America is, indeed, passing through the waters and flames.

> *When thou passest through the waters I will be with thee; and through the rivers, they shall not overflow thee: when thou walkest through the fire, thou shalt not be burned; neither shall the flame kindle upon thee.* (Isaiah 43:2)

The driving force behind this book has been to illuminate how Russia's war in Ukraine has caused a cascade of global events that is bringing us perilously close to Armageddon and the End Times by way of Iran and its nuclear ambitions. It is my prayer that America will wake up and unite so that an apocalyptic catastrophe may be avoided.

THE DAYS AHEAD

I keep returning to the two 189-ton bombs—fully-fueled Boeing 767s—that crashed into the World Trade Center. If those terrorists had had a nuclear weapon, I have no doubt they would have used it.

While I have no special insight, it's plain to see that the cult of the Mahdi is firmly positioned at the center of the political philosophy of the theocracy ruling Iran. I fear that nothing short of war will dislodge Iran from the path of nuclear weapons.

After writing this book, I am more convinced than ever that the chess masters who are Iran's leaders are subtle and fully capable of manipulating international diplomacy in their favor. They have leveraged Russia's desperate need for military assistance in its invasion of Ukraine to their own benefit. They know Russia owes them a huge favor, and they know exactly what favor they're going to call in.

We in America are as vulnerable to Iranian-backed terrorism as the citizens of Israel. What the theocrats of radical Islam hate most is freedom and democracy. We are condemned because we are tolerant of religious differences and open to the advancement of the human spirit.

A PRAYER FOR THE FUTURE

In the final analysis, I believe we must protect Israel if we are to be serious about protecting our own nation. Israel is the last firewall between Islamic fundamentalists and the West.

Iran does not hate America because of Israel; it hates Israel because of America. Israel, its closest pro-West neighbor and only democratic nation in the Middle East, is an image of America and its values. This is the reason Israel is called "The Little Satan," and America, "The Great Satan."

Until the right of Israel to survive is assured, there can never be true peace in the Middle East. The moment Iran gets nuclear weapons, we will be much closer to Armageddon than we ever imagined possible.

For my entire adult life, I have studied the Bible and prayed these days would never come upon us. Now that we have no choice, I pray we will have the wisdom and the courage to reach the next day.

We must never permit Iran to have nuclear weapons. If we fail, a nuclear Iran will shape a world in which few of us will be secure. While we as Christians are prepared to be accepting of Islam, we can have no confidence that the radical Islamic zealots controlling Iran will be any more tolerant of us than they are toward the Jews and Israel, a nation Iran proclaims has no right to exist.

A showdown with a nuclear Iran is imminent. Though we all wish for this crisis to pass, I fear the moment is at hand where the reality a nuclear armed Iran is inevitably upon us all.

I pray that we get through the coming test with distinction. I pray that the crisis passes, and that Israel continues to thrive and the United States of America continues to be strong. Freedom can yet ring throughout the world, but only if we first get through the coming showdown with Iran, and freedom emerges the victor.

The information I've shared with you in this book is disturbing. But the good news is the Bible verse inscribed on a wall in the lobby of the CIA headquarters building is truer today than ever:

> *"And ye shall know the Truth and the Truth shall make you free."* (John 8:32)

Do not think for a moment that it's hopeless. It is not! Communism fell without a shot having been fired. The United States, Israel, and the world can avoid nuclear Armageddon, but only if good people stand up and speak out. The Truth will set us free.

Not only have I attempted to communicate the facts concerning this urgent crisis, but I appeal to you, the reader, to influence the course of human history and the destiny of America, Israel and the world through the power of prayer. I hope that we may prevent the greatest terrorist attack in American history from happening. In so doing, we will protect our children and grandchildren from an unspeakable holocaust.

THE BIBLE GIVES US HOPE

We began this book by talking about Biblical prophesy, and I would like to end with several messages of assurance from the Bible.

The Prophet Daniel, exiled to Babylon, was faced with a grave dilemma. He was in the region of the world that America now finds itself embroiled. Yet, Daniel was well-versed in prayer and intercession. Daniel prayed earnestly, and in response to his prayers, God heard and answered with glorious deliverance for his people in captivity.

In Daniel 2:21-22, we read:

> *"And He changes the times and the seasons; He removes kings and raises up kings; He gives wisdom to the wise and knowledge to those who have understanding. He reveals deep and secret things; He knows what is in the darkness, and light dwells with Him."*

America is facing a prolonged season of war and terrorism. Ultimately, that season can only be changed by God Almighty through the power of prayer. This is the reason I appeal to you to "know the truth" and stand up for the truth, and to commit yourself to prayer.

GOD LISTENS TO OUR PRAYERS

> *"For God has not given us the spirit of fear. . ."*
> (2 Timothy 1:7)

Prayer is to the believer what the umbilical cord is to an unborn child; it is the means of spiritual nourishment. It is prayer that touches the heart of God, turns the head of God, and moves the hand of God. Alfred Lord Tennyson said, "More things are wrought by prayer than this world dreams of." It is, however, the responsibility of dedicated prayer warriors to, "stand in the gap and make up the hedge" of protection over our individual homelands, and over Israel.

Earlier in this book, I told you the story of Esther, a Jewish orphan girl, who knew the power of prayer and intercession. Taken as a captive to Persia she was given to the Emperor Xerxes (spelled Ahasuerus in Hebrew), a tyrannical ruler who chose her to replace his recently banished queen. The emperor's cousin, Haman, hoped to eliminate the Jews from Persia.

Esther's cousin, Mordecai, challenges her to approach the king (a move that could be punishable by death) and ask for the salvation of her people. Esther's courageous response is worth repeating here:

> "Go, gather all the Jews to be found in Susa, and hold a fast on my behalf, and neither eat nor drink for three days, night or day. I and my maids will also fast as you do. Then I will go to the king, though it is against the law; and if I perish, I perish." (Esther 4:16 RSV)

With great trepidation, Esther approaches Ahasuerus and is granted an audience with the king. Esther obtains favor in the king's sight when the king extends his golden scepter. She prepares to bless the king, and in so doing, is supernaturally blessed.

Esther was used as an instrument of God. The plan for destruction of the Jews was thwarted and Esther's people were allowed to live in peace in Shushan.

Just ask Esther if prayer changes things. She came to the king in fear for her life but left with supernatural favor. She came in poverty but left with prosperity. She came in despair but left highly favored. She came representing a people who were marked for destruction and left the king's presence with a pardon.

Esther had fulfilled all the requirements of 2 Chronicles 7:14:

> "...if my people who are called by my name humble themselves, and pray and seek my face, and turn from their wicked ways, then I will hear from heaven, and will forgive their sin and heal their land."

All of the conditions set forth in this verse must be met for God to bring revival and bless our nation.

WE MUST NOT GIVE UP

Again, we see Daniel engaged in intercession in Daniel Chapter 10. For twenty-one days, the prophet immersed himself in prayer on the banks of a river, possibly the Tigris. As he seeks the face of God, Daniel has a vision of an angel.

The angel has startling news for Daniel, and for those of us who have prayed earnestly and diligently for answers to prayers: "The Prince of Persia"—apparently one of Lucifer's fallen angels—hindered the answer to Daniel's prayer.

Why is it important to know this? Persistence in prayer pays dividends! Had Daniel not continued to intercede for the twenty-one days necessary for the battle in the heavenlies to be fought and won, his prayers would not have been answered.

WE MUST HAVE COURAGE

King Hezekiah was faced, as are we today, with the threat of annihilation. The king of Assyria had threatened the Israelites with destruction. He made the unfortunate mistake of thinking that Hezekiah trusted in horses and chariots, and in his alliance with Egypt. Using the "town crier" method of communication, the commander-in-chief of the Assyrian army stood in the midst of the city square and taunted Hezekiah. He proclaimed that Yahweh himself had sent the Assyrians to defeat Judah.

When the king's threats were delivered to Hezekiah in the form of a written dispatch, he did the one most important thing he could have done. . .he went to the Temple, spread the letter on the altar, and prostrated himself before God. And Hezekiah prayed:

> *"Now therefore, O LORD our God, I beseech thee, save thou us out of his hand, that all the kingdoms of the earth may know that thou [art] the LORD God, [even] thou only."* (2 Kings 19:19)

God spoke the answer to Hezekiah's prayer to the Prophet Isaiah:

> *"For I will defend this city, to save it, for mine own sake, and for my servant David's sake."* (2 Kings 19:34)

The King could have heard no sweeter words than the promise that God would defend the City of David.

The epilogue to Hezekiah's prayer and God's answer did not bode well for the Assyrians:

"And it came to pass that night, that the angel of the LORD went out, and smote in the camp of the Assyrians an hundred fourscore and five thousand [185,000]: and when they arose early in the morning, behold, they [were] all dead corpses." (2 Kings 19:35)

GOD ANSWERS OUR PRAYERS

Nehemiah, too, knew the power of prayer and intercession. He had been exiled to Babylon and elevated to the position of cupbearer to the King. Nehemiah received a delegation of visitors from Jerusalem and was given the devastating news of the poverty and destruction in Jerusalem.

Nehemiah *"sat down and wept, and mourned [certain] days, and fasted, and prayed before the God of heaven. . ."* (Nehemiah 1:4) His heart was broken with the plight of his countrymen and of his beloved city.

God miraculously answered Nehemiah's prayer. He moved the heart of the king and gave Nehemiah great favor. Nehemiah was allowed to return to his homeland and rebuild the walls of Jerusalem.

The New Testament is rife with instances of prayer petitions answered and people delivered. . .Peter from prison, John the Revelator from death on the Isle of Patmos, Paul from drowning at sea.

Paul's ringing declaration while being tossed to and fro on the ship resonates: *"For there stood by me this night the angel of God, whose I am, and whom I serve. . ."* (Acts 27:23)

It is never too late for God to come to the aid of his children; and prayer is the means by which we touch Him.

WE NEED TO BE MODERN PRAYER WARRIORS

God raised up modern-day prayer warriors such as John "Praying" Hyde, Evan Roberts, Jonathan Goforth, Frank Bartleman, and of course, Corrie ten Boom's family. The ten Boom family were devoted Christians who dedicated their lives in service to their fellow man. Their home was always open for anyone in need. During the Second World War, the ten Boom home became a refuge, a hiding place, for fugitives and those hunted by the Nazis.

The family ten Boom began to pray for the Jewish people in 1844, after a moving worship service in the Dutch Reformed Church of Rev. Witteveen. Willem ten Boom felt the need to pray for the Jewish people so he started the weekly prayer meeting where the family and others who stopped by, specifically prayed for the peace of Jerusalem (Psalm 122:6).

These meetings took place every week for one hundred years, until February 28, 1944, when Nazi soldiers came to the house to take them away for helping local Jews and hiding them in a secret room. On that day, the family had gathered together for a Bible study and prayer meeting.

Like the famed Oscar Schindler, the ten Booms were instrumental in saving nearly 800 Jews from the Nazi death camps and were imprisoned themselves for their efforts. Life in the camp was almost unbearable, but Corrie and her sister, Betsie, spent their time sharing Jesus' love with their fellow prisoners.

Many women became Christians in that terrible place because of Corrie and Betsie's witness to them. Four members of the ten Boom family gave their lives for the family's commitment, but Corrie came home from the death camp. She realized her life was a gift from God, and she needed to share what she and Betsie had learned in Ravensbruck.

In 2002, I was inspired to take up the mantle and continue the tradition of the ten Boom family; the Jerusalem Prayer Team was born, and the 100-year prayer meeting begun by the ten Booms was revived. In 1986, I purchased and restored the ten Boom home and clock shop and am Chairman of the Board of the work.

The inaugural Jerusalem Prayer Summit drew people from around the world. Then-Mayor of Jerusalem, Ehud Olmert, flew to Dallas, Texas to help launch the Jerusalem Prayer Team. We now have prayer partners worldwide. You may join the Jerusalem Prayer Team at no cost by visiting our website at www.jpteam.org for more information. When you join, you will receive rapid-response Middle East News alerts.

> In Jeremiah 33:3 the Lord says, *"Call unto me and I will answer thee. . ."*

The time for apathy and indifference has passed. It is time for prayer warriors worldwide to put on the armor for intercessory battle and face the enemy head-on. Ephesians 6 admonishes the prayer warrior to:

> *". . .take unto you the whole armor of God. . . having your loins girt about with truth, and having on the breastplate of righteousness; And your feet shod with the preparation of the gospel of peace; Above all, taking the shield of faith, wherewith ye shall be able to quench*

all the fiery darts of the wicked. And take the helmet of salvation, and the sword of the Spirit, which is the word of God: Praying always with all prayer and supplication in the Spirit."

Jeremiah understood that God was eagerly waiting to answer his prayers and petitions, but first Jeremiah had to call!

As Paul wrote in his letter to the Philippians (4:6):

"Be anxious for nothing, but in everything by prayer and supplication, with thanksgiving, let your requests be made known to God. . ."

It is past time to turn to God with prayer and supplication and seek His divine intervention and deliverance.

In 1539, Martin Luther wrote "Our Father, Thou in Heaven Above" based on the Lord's Prayer. The first verse of stanza eight is an ideal prayer for our time:

"From evil, Lord, deliver us;
The times and days are perilous."

We do live in perilous times, but we do not have to live in fear. David cried out in Psalm 31:24:

"So be strong and take courage, all you who put your hope in the LORD!"

Theologians differ on the time that David wrote this verse, but all agree that he was in the midst of great distress. Was it when he was fleeing for his life from Saul? Perhaps it was during the time of betrayal by his son, Absalom? Whatever the cause of his distress, David knew where to go for the answer; David knew that his hope lay in the Lord and not in his own strength or wisdom.

In Psalm 22:3 (NLT), David again sang praises to God for deliverance:

> ". . .my God is my rock, in whom I find protection. He is my shield, the strength of my salvation, and my stronghold, my high tower, my savior, the one who saves me from violence."

On December 8, 1944, General George Patton requested that Third Army Chaplain, Msgr. James H. O'Neill, send a directive to the troops, a "Training Letter on this subject of Prayer to all the chaplains; write about nothing else, just the importance of prayer."

The Chaplain complied with the General's request in what has become known as "The Patton Prayer." It reads, in part:

> "Those who pray do more for the world than those who fight; and if the world goes from bad to worse, it is because there are more battles than prayers. Hands lifted up smash more battalions than hands that strike.
>
> Gideon of Bible fame was least in his father's house. He came from Israel's smallest tribe. But he was a mighty man of valor. His strength lay not in his military might, but in his recognition of God's proper claims upon his life. He reduced his Army from thirty-two thousand to three hundred men lest

the people of Israel would think that their valor had saved them.

We have no intention to reduce our vast striking force. But we must urge, instruct, and indoctrinate every fighting man to pray as well as fight. In Gideon's day, and in our own, spiritually alert minorities carry the burdens and bring the victories.

Urge all of your men to pray, not alone in church, but everywhere. Pray when driving. Pray when fighting. Pray alone. Pray with others. Pray by night and pray by day. . .Pray for the defeat of our wicked enemy whose banner is injustice and whose good is oppression. Pray for victory. Pray for our Army and Pray for Peace."

As the world tries desperately to find a resolution to the terrible war in Ukraine, to the ongoing threats from Iran, and the constant danger of terrorist attacks, the answer lies in our hands. . .we simply have to fold them together in prayer, for the sake of our children and grandchildren.

Together in prayer, we can influence the course of human history and the destiny of nations. Together in prayer, we can prevent the greatest terror attack ever planned from happening. I leave you with the words of three giants of the faith who faced similar crises:

Daniel: *"The people that do know their God shall be strong and do exploits."*

Esther: *"Do not flatter yourself that you shall escape in the king's palace any more than all the other Jews. For if you keep silent at this time, relief and deliverance shall arise for the Jews from elsewhere, but you and your father's house will perish. And who knows but that you have come to the kingdom for such a time as this and for this very occasion."* (Esther 4:13-14)

Isaiah: *"When the enemy comes in like a flood, The Spirit of the Lord will lift up a standard against him."* (Isaiah 59:19b)

The U. S. cannot appease Iran. The stakes are far too high for that, now. The Iranian Islamic regime believes it is on a mission from God. Iran's leaders value death, not life.

The purpose for my writing this book is, by now, obvious to you. In my heart, I know a nuclear confrontation with Iran is coming, but I, alone, cannot stop it. I believe this next decade will be the most critical in America's history.

Our mission is to unify millions of God-fearing and praying Americans who believe in moral clarity to stand up and to speak up while there is yet time. No matter what Iran does or does not do, millions of Ayatollah Khomeini's followers, whose only mission in life is to usher in the Twelfth Imam, will keep moving towards their goal.

Hopefully, millions of God-fearing Americans united in prayer can overcome the threat before us. This nation and the peace of the world depend on it to:

- influence the course of human history and the destiny of our nation

- prevent the greatest terrorist attack in American history from happening

- protect and bless our children and grandchildren

- mobilize and unify people nationwide to prayer and action

- deeply and personally influence world leaders—favor opens doors but influence changes nations

To receive notifications on intelligence reports and upcoming books and events contact Mike Evans at ***events@drmichaeldevans.com.***

BOOKS BY: MIKE EVANS

Israel: America's Key to Survival

Save Jerusalem

The Return

Jerusalem D.C.

Purity and Peace of Mind

Who Cries for the Hurting?

Living Fear Free

I Shall Not Want

Let My People Go

Jerusalem Betrayed

Seven Years of Shaking: A Vision

The Nuclear Bomb of Islam

Jerusalem Prophecies

Pray For Peace of Jerusalem

America's War:The Beginning of
    the End

The Jerusalem Scroll

The Prayer of David

The Unanswered Prayers of Jesus

God Wrestling

The American Prophecies

Beyond Iraq: The Next Move

The Final Move beyond Iraq

Showdown with Nuclear Iran

Jimmy Carter: The Liberal Leftand
    World Chaos

Atomic Iran

Cursed

Betrayed

The Light

Corrie's Reflections & Meditations

The Revolution

The Final Generation

Seven Days

The Locket

Persia: The Final Jihad

GAMECHANGER SERIES:

GameChanger

Samson Option

The Four Horsemen

THE PROTOCOLS SERIES:

The Protocols

The Candidate

Jerusalem

The History of Christian Zionism

Countdown

Ten Boom: Betsie, Promise of God

Commanded Blessing

BORN AGAIN SERIES:

Born Again: 1948

Born Again: 1967

TO PURCHASE, CONTACT: orders@TimeWorthyBooks.com
P. O. BOX 30000, PHOENIX, AZ 85046

MICHAEL DAVID EVANS is the #1 *New York Times* bestselling author of 112 published books. He is also a Nobel Peace Prize nominee. Evans is the founder of the Friends of Zion Heritage Center and Museum in Jerusalem, the Ten Boom Museum in Haarlem, Holland, and Jerusalem World News. Evans is also the founder of the Jerusalem Prayer Team, with more than 30 million followers just on Facebook. Evans has appeared on hundreds of network television and radio shows, including *Good Morning America*, *Crossfire* and *Nightline*, and *The Rush Limbaugh Show*, and on Fox Network, *CNN World News*, NBC, ABC, and CBS. His articles have been published in the *Wall Street Journal*, *USA Today*, *Washington Times*, *Jerusalem Post* and newspapers worldwide. More than twenty-five million copies of his books are in print, and he is the award-winning producer of nine documentaries based on his books. Evans is considered one of the world's leading experts on Israel and the Middle East, and is one of the most sought-after speakers on that subject. Evans' books include *The End Times and Armageddon*, *What I Learned as a Moron*, the novel *Gabriel*, *Showdown with Nuclear Iran*, *Atomic Iran*, *The Next Move Beyond Iraq*, *The Final Move Beyond Iraq*, and *Countdown*. Evans is available to speak or for interviews. Contact: EVENTS@drmichaeldevans.com

HIS BOOKS ARE AVAILABLE AT:
TimeWorthyBooks.com

JERUSALEM PRAYER TEAM
INTERNATIONAL

THE JERUSALEM PRAYER TEAM'S

mission is to build Friends of Zion to guard, defend, and protect the Jewish people and to pray for the peace of Jerusalem. Our goal is to enlist, inform, and encourage 100 million people worldwide to pray for the peace of Jerusalem as directed in Psalm 122:6. The Jerusalem Prayer Team also raises funds to meet the humanitarian needs of the Jewish people in Israel, providing coats, blankets, and shelter for those in need. The ministry has a website at JerusalemPrayerTeam.com and more than 30 million followers on Facebook at Facebook.com/JerusalemPrayerTeam

JerusalemPrayerTeam.org

foz

ידידי ישראל
FRIENDS OF ZION

The Friends of Zion Museum opened in 2015 in the heart of Jerusalem with the help of thousands of supporters of Israel worldwide. It presents a technologically advanced and interactive experience that tells the stories of the dream to restore the Jewish people to their historic homeland and the brave non-Jews who assisted them in realizing this dream. The Friends of Zion Museum serves as a platform for fighting BDS and anti-Semitism internationally. The Museum is a nonprofit organization operating in Jerusalem and supported by friends from all over the world. This is the first Christian museum in Israel, and here we are sharing the true stories of Christian love for God's Chosen People. Tours of the museum are available in more than a dozen languages, allowing guests to experience the full benefit of their visit. The thousands of visitors who fill the museum each month hail from across Israel and all around the world.

The Friends of Zion Award has been given to more than 26 world leaders. It was commissioned by the ninth president of Israel, the late Shimon Peres, who served as the international chairman of Friends of Zion. It has been given to us two U.S. presidents, Donald J. Trump in the Oval Office, and to George W. Bush.

FOZmuseum.com

TO KEEP UP
WITH THE VERY LATEST

on the work of the Jerusalem Prayer Team, and on events that impact the nation of the Israel and the Jewish people, you need to be reading Friends of Zion each month. This magazine is available to anyone who requests it at no charge.

In-depth articles on current and historical events and trends, Bible study and prophetic teaching, and the latest news on the ministry will come to your home each month. It will bring you the truth that goes beyond the often-slanted news our media gives us, and help you know both what is going on and how to pray more effectively for the peace of Jerusalem and the protection of God's Chosen People. Receive your complimentary copy of the FRIENDS OF ZION magazine by visiting:

JerusalemPrayerTeam.org/members

THE ONGOING WAR IN UKRAINE is perhaps the worst humanitarian crisis of our lifetimes. More than 10 million people—almost 1/4 of the entire population—have been forced to flee their homes, with just the few possessions they can carry. Those most impacted are the very elderly—precious Holocaust survivors—and the very young, including Jewish orphans. Tens of thousands are hungry because there is no food. They urgently need our help.

Friends of Zion has been in Ukraine for more than a decade, feeding impoverished Holocaust survivors. When Russia invaded Ukraine, Michael David Evans, the President of Friends of Zion Museum and the Director of UkraineHope.com, began ramping up the mission to bring food, blankets, medicine, and generators to impoverished refugees and Holocaust survivors. Since the war began, UkraineHope.com has brought more than 8 million pounds of food into the war zone.

Your generous gift today will provide food and other vital supplies to these precious people. We are already a vital lifeline for thousands of people, but there is so much more that needs to be done. **For just $40, we can provide a package of essential food that will feed one person for an entire week. For just $200, we can provide food for a week to a family of four.** Your gift today will help these struggling people. **THANK YOU!**

UkraineHope.com

THE CORRIE TEN BOOM MUSEUM

is located in the house where three generations of the Ten Boom family lived between 1837 and 1945 in Haarlem, Holland. During the Second World War, the Ten Boom home became a hiding place for fugitives and those hunted by the Nazis. By protecting these people, Casper and his daughters, Betsie and Corrie, risked their lives. This non-violent resistance against the Nazi oppressors was the Ten Boom's way of living out their Christian faith. During 1943 and into 1944, there were usually 5-6 people illegally living in the Ten Boom home. The Ten Boom Family and their many friends and co-workers of 'the BeJe group' saved the lives of an estimated 800 Jews and other refugees. You can contribute to this special work by supporting the activities of the Corrie ten Boom House Foundation with your prayer. Prayer is the mainstay of the work. In addition, you can also give financial support. The Foundation is entirely dependent on donations and revenues from the sale of books, DVDs, and other items, and rent from the shop space.

DISCOVER MORE ONLINE AT:

CorrieTenBoom.com